THE ETHNIC CHINESE
in East and Southeast Asia

Business, Culture and Politics

Yen Ching-hwang

TIMES ACADEMIC PRESS

© 2002 Times Media Private Limited

First published 2002 by Times International Publishing
under the imprint **Times Academic Press**
Times Media Academic Publishing
Times Centre, 1 New Industrial Road, Singapore 536196
Fax: (65) 6 2889 254   E-mail: tap@tpl.com.sg
Online Book Store: http://www.timesone.com.sg/tap

Printed by CMO Image Printing Enterprise, Singapore

National Library Board (Singapore) Cataloguing in Publication Data

Yan, Qinghuang
The Ethnic Chinese in East and Southeast Asia : Business, Culture and Politics
/ Yen Ching-hwang. – Singapore : Times Academic Press, c2002.
    p. cm.
    ISBN : 981-210-187-X

1. Chinese – East Asia. 2. Chinese – Asia, Southeastern. 3. Chinese – Singapore.
4. Corporations, Chinese – East Asia. 5. Corporations, Chinese – Asia,
Southeastern.   I. Title.

DS509.5.C5
305.895105 — dc21   SLS2002023165

Contents

About the Author   iv

Introduction   v

Part I: Business in Ethnic Chinese Society
1. The Rise of Ethnic Chinese Business in   1
    East and Southeast Asia
2. Ethnic Chinese Business Networks in   23
    East and Southeast Asia
3. Traditional Ethnic Chinese Business   51
    Organisations in Singapore and Malaysia
4. The Wing On Company in Hong Kong and   79
    Shanghai, 1907–1949: A Case Study of a
    Modern Overseas Chinese Business Enterprise
5. Tan Kah Kee and Overseas Chinese Entrepreneurship   123

Part II: Culture, Education and Politics in Ethnic Chinese Society
6. Ethnic Chinese Culture in Southeast   145
    Asia: Continuity and Change
7. Hokkien Immigrant Society and Modern   177
    Chinese Education in British Malaya, 1904–1941
8. Economic, Political and Social Change in the Chinese   217
    Communities in Malaysia and Singapore before
    the Second World War: A Historical Survey
9. Power Structure and Power Relations in   273
    the Teochew Community in Singapore, 1819–1930
10. Ch'ing China and the Singapore Chinese   307
    Chamber of Commerce, 1906–1911
11. Sun Yat-sen and the Chinese in Singapore   339
    and Malaya, 1900–1911
12. The Overseas Chinese and the Second   369
    Sino-Japanese War, 1937–1945

Index   389

About the Author

Yen Ching-hwang, formerly Chair Professor of History at the University of Hong Kong, is now Reader/Associate Professor in History at the University of Adelaide in Australia. He was born in Fujian, China, and brought up in Malaysia. A graduate of Nanyang University, Singapore, he obtained his PhD from the Australian National University, Canberra in 1970.

Fluent in both English and Chinese, he has many publications in both languages to his credit. His major publications in English are *The Overseas Chinese and the 1911 Revolution* (Oxford University Press, 1976), *Coolies and Mandarins* (Singapore University Press, 1985) and *A Social History of the Chinese in Singapore and Malaya* (Oxford University Press, 1986). All three books were subsequently translated by scholars in Taiwan and China, and published in 1982, 1990 and 1991, respectively.

In 1995, 23 of Professor Yen's academic articles were published by Times Academic Press into two separate books entitled *Studies in Modern Overseas Chinese History* and *Community and Politics: The Chinese in Colonial Singapore and Malaysia*.

In August 2000, he was named the inaugural Tan Lark Sye Visiting Professor of the Nanyang Technological University, Singapore.

Introduction

This book deals with some important aspects of the Ethnic Chinese in East and Southeast Asia. Since the rise of economic power of the Four Little Dragons — Taiwan, South Korea, Hong Kong and Singapore — in the 1970s, much attention has been drawn to the Ethnic Chinese, who constitute the majority population in Taiwan, Hong Kong and Singapore. How far have the Ethnic Chinese contributed to the rapid economic growth in the region? What accounts for the dynamics of the Ethnic Chinese business? What would be the future role of the Ethnic Chinese in the economic growth of the region, especially with China? These are the major questions asked by many interested observers, journalists, scholars and bureaucrats. This book aims to shed some light on these topics.

The term Ethnic Chinese has gained growing popularity among scholars. In the past, scholars used the term Overseas Chinese to describe those Chinese living and working outside Mainland China. There was no attempt to differentiate the political allegiance of various Overseas Chinese groups, due to the vague assumption that all of them were Chinese subjects, and one day they might go back to China to live. The use of this term was legitimate, since the region was controlled by Western colonial powers who talked in terms of empires rather than states. However, the rise of the new states after the Second World War in East and Southeast Asia, where the majority of Overseas Chinese resided, called for clearer political allegiance, and the concept of citizenship and its entitlements compelled the Overseas Chinese to make a painful choice. Since the majority of them had settled overseas for many years and their future rested more in the new lands than in China, they opted for the citizenship of newly emerged states in the region. As a result, a new term to describe their changed status was needed. The term Ethnic Chinese emphasised the ethnicity of the Chinese — their common cultural roots, their social customs and their physical appearance — and is applied to Chinese descendants outside mainland China who are not citizens of the People's Republic of China.

This includes broadly those Chinese in Taiwan, Hong Kong (before July 1997), Macao (before December 1999), Southeast Asia, North America, Europe and Australasia. A few years ago, a group of scholars under the leadership of Leo Suryadinata of the National University of Singapore discussed in great detail the concept and definition of the Ethnic Chinese in Southeast Asia. Their findings are useful, and should be adopted by other scholars working in this field.[1]

There have been many analyses of the dynamics of the Ethnic Chinese business in East and Southeast Asia. Historical, cultural, social, structural and strategic perspectives are useful for our understanding of this important phenomenon,[2] and can help us both to gauge the importance of Ethnic Chinese business and to predict its future role in the region.

This book is a collection of 12 articles, published and unpublished, written between 1993 and 2000. Although not centred on one particular theme, they all involve analyses of the main aspects of the Ethnic Chinese society in East and Southeast Asia: business, culture and politics. As a result, Part I of the book deals with the various aspects of Ethnic Chinese business, while Part II deals with culture (including education) and politics.

To retain the original form of the published articles, this book has adopted both Wade-Giles and Pinyin systems for the romanization of Chinese names and terms. It has also kept the original term 'Overseas Chinese' in several chapters.

Chapter 1 begins with a general discussion of the historical, cultural, economic and geo-political factors accounting for the rise of the Ethnic Chinese business in 1970s and 1980s in East and Southeast Asia. It concludes that the rise of Chinese business was not an accidental phenomenon, but the result of history, Confucian tradition and the internal dynamics of Ethnic Chinese business combining with a set of external factors at that time.

Chapter 2 deals with an important aspect of the Ethnic Chinese business — business networks. The role of business networks in

---

1.   See Leo Suryadinata (ed), *Ethnic Chinese as Southeast Asians* (Sydney, Allen & Unwin, 1997).
2.   See Ch. 3, fn. 1.

the success of Ethnic Chinese business has drawn the increasing attention of scholars. Many theories have been advanced to explain the origins, operation and the composition of the networks. This chapter takes a historical and cultural perspective to explain the rise of the Ethnic Chinese business networks in East and Southeast Asia, and argues that their origins were rooted in the history, culture and the special circumstances under which the Ethnic Chinese operated in the region. The transient nature of the early Chinese traders required them to establish business outposts in key ports in the region, and these outposts were then organised into strong networks over time. Although European political and economic control of East and Southeast Asia placed early Chinese traders in a subordinate position, the growth of the Ethnic Chinese communities in the region enabled Ethnic Chinese to entrench themselves in business. This chapter also distinguishes the differences between Ethnic Chinese business networks and the Japanese and Korean networks, showing how Ethnic Chinese networks are weaker in inter-firm relations and receive less government support than their Japanese and Korean counterparts. Chapter 2 also confirms the findings of other studies, that Ethnic Chinese business networks are built on traditional *guanxi* (personal connections) and *xinyong* (trust). It concludes that these business networks played an important role in the rise of Ethnic Chinese business in 1970s, and have been one of the many factors contributing to the success of Ethnic Chinese business.

Chapter 3 examines the traditional Ethnic Chinese business organisations, principally craft guilds and business guilds, in Singapore and Malaysia. This field of study has escaped the attention of scholars, partly due to scanty materials or linguistic barriers. However, this narrow but important topic does deserve special and in-depth study. Based primarily on rare Chinese sources, this chapter shows how traditional Ethnic Chinese business organisations provided important institutional support for Ethnic Chinese business by monopolising certain lines of trade and by offering training grounds for prospective entrepreneurs. They served as a mechanism through which *Bang* (dialect- and geographically-based entities) perpetuated its control over certain lines of business. These business organisations contained the seeds of progress which enabled the Ethnic Chinese to cope with changing environments, and also accounted partly for the dynamics of the Ethnic Chinese business in the region. This study also sheds light on the internal dynamics of the Ethnic Chinese business, and helps to explain the dominance of the Ethnic Chinese in business in Southeast Asia.

The importance of Ethnic Chinese entrepreneurship in the rise of the Ethnic Chinese business has received some attention before. Panglaykim and Palmer (1970) drew attention to the entrepreneurship of Oei Tiong Ham, which contributed significantly in the rise of Ethnic Chinese business in the Dutch East Indies.[3] Later followed Michael Godley's detailed study of Zhang Bishi (Chang Pi-shih), another famous Ethnic Chinese entrepreneur in Southeast Asia and South China in the late nineteenth and early twentieth century.[4] A decade ago, Wong Siu-lun's study of the Shanghaiese entrepreneurs in Hong Kong also shed light on this topic.[5] In Chapters 4 and 5, I have chosen the Kwok brothers (Kwok Lock and Kwok Chin) of Wing On Company in Hong Kong, and Tan Kah Kee in Singapore, as case studies of Ethnic Chinese entrepreneurship. Both chapters argue emphatically that Confucian values have strong input in the formation of Ethnic Chinese entrepreneurship, and establish the salient features of Ethnic Chinese entrepreneurship. A capitalist attitude; the ability to bring capital, labour and management together to found an enterprise; the courage to take initiatives and risks; the determination to implement ideas and the will to succeed; the ability to lead, to communicate and manage a successful enterprise — all of these qualities were reflected in the Kwok brothers' and Tan Kah Kee's entreprenerial activities. Both chapters also identify the Kwok

3. See J. Panglaykim and I. Palmer, 'Study of Entrepreneurship in Developing Countries: The Development of One Chinese Concern in Indonesia', in *Journal of Southeast Asian Studies*, vol. 1, no.1 (Singapore, March 1970), pp. 85–95.
4. See Michael R. Godley, *The Mandarin-capitalists from Nanyang: Overseas Chinese Enterprise in the Modernization of China, 1893–1911* (Cambridge, Cambridge University Press, 1981).
5. See Wong Siu-Lun, *Emigrant Entrepreneurs: Shanghai Industrialists in Hong Kong* (Hong Kong, Oxford University Press, 1988).

brothers and Tan Kah Kee not just as intermediaries between capital and labour, as traditionally defined entrepreneurs, but also as creators and perpetuators of modern business enterprises, possessing the schumpeterian qualitites of acquisitiveness, innovativeness and a willingness to take risks.

Part II of this book deals with the culture (including education) and politics of the Ethnic Chinese. Like business, Ethnic Chinese culture in Southeast Asia has drawn increasing interest from Western observers and scholars. The present conditions and future direction of Ethnic Chinese culture have had a significant impact in the region. In the past, assimilationist scholars saw the presence of a distinct Ethnic Chinese culture as a stumbling block for Ethnic Chinese assimilation into indigenous societies in Southeast Asia. On the contrary, nowadays multiculturalist scholars hail the flourishing of Ethnic Chinese culture as a blessing for the creation of multi-ethnic and multicultural societies in the region. In taking latter view, Chapter 6 investigates the formation of Ethnic Chinese culture in Southeast Asia: its historical origins and characteristics, its stages of development and the forces shaping its character. The chapter discusses the current position of Ethnic Chinese culture in Southeast Asia and its future direction. It argues that there is close link between Ethnic Chinese culture and Ethnic Chinese identity in the region. Ethnic Chinese culture has modified itself to adapt to new political and economic environments, and has transformed itself into an integral part of Southeast Asian culture. Although this Ethnic culture is still essentially Chinese, it has gained local flavour and is now very different from Chinese culture in Mainland China. It also argues that the so-called problem of Ethnic Chinese identity in Southeast Asia hinges upon the Chinese-indigenous inter-racial relationship. To resolve this problem, the Ethnic Chinese have to identify themselves as Southeast Asians (either Thai, Vietnamese, Malaysians, Singaporeans, Indonesians or Filipinos) first and Ethnic Chinese second, and they should try to help indigenous Southeast Asians wherever and whenever they can. On the other hand, indigenous Southeast Asians need to acknowledge the Ethnic Chinese as legitimate members of these new nations, while accepting the fact that the Ethnic Chinese are physically different from them and have the right to preserve their own beliefs, values, customs, language and education.

Ethnic Chinese education constitutes a main part of Ethnic Chinese culture in Southeast Asia. Ethnic Chinese culture would have been very different if Ethnic Chinese education had not been preserved and developed. With this perspective in mind, Chapter 7 investigates the rise of modern Chinese education in British Malaya in a period between 1904 and 1941. This period was significant because the modern Chinese education was introduced into British Malaya and other parts of Southeast Asia and achieved phenomenal growth, laying a solid foundation for its future development. Using Hokkien immigrant society and its promotion of modern Chinese education as a case study, this chapter looks at the introduction of modern Chinese schools into British Malaya during the last decade of Manchu rule in China. The first modern Chinese school in British Malaya, the Zhong Hua School, was established in Penang in 1904. Modern Chinese schools spread widely in British Malaya and other parts of Southeast Asia. During the Republican period between 1912 and 1941, modern Ethnic Chinese education achieved remarkable growth — from primary school to junior high school and then to senior high school — offering a genuine alternative to Western colonial education for Chinese children. The result of this development was the retention of many Confucian and modern Chinese cultural values, as well as shaping the character of the present Ethnic Chinese communities.

The last five chapters deal with the politics of the Ethnic Chinese before the Second World War. In contrast with current Chinese politics in Southeast Asia, which is characterised by direct participation in political parties, political involvement in the pre-war period was indirect and was more China-oriented. Chapter 8 surveys the political, economic, and social change in the Chinese communities in Singapore and Malaya before the Second World War, and the salient features of Chinese politics, particularly in relation to China, is discussed. In Chapter 9, politics within Ethnic Chinese communities is exemplified by a case study of the power structure and power relations in a Teochew community in Singapore. The Teochews, a major Chinese dialect group in Southeast Asia, were the pioneer planters in Singapore, and their community politics was played with skill and sophistication. Their economic influence is widely felt in parts of East and Southeast Asia such as Hong Kong, Thailand, Singapore and Malaysia.

The last three chapters are concerned with the politics of the Ethnic Chinese relating to China. During the period of Western colonial rule, the Ethnic Chinese in East and Southeast Asia, with the exception of a privileged few, had little involvement with politics. This was partly due to language barriers, which drew a clear line between the ruler and the ruled. The Ethnic Chinese were therefore principally involved only in Chinese communal politics and the politics relating to their homeland — China. Chapter 10 sets the scene for the power play between the Qing government, the revolutionaries and the reformists who had been competing for support among the Ethnic Chinese. The stage for the play was the Singapore Chinese Chamber of Commerce which was founded in 1905 by a leading Qing bureaucrat, Zhang Bishi, who was also an eminent Ethnic Chinese leader from British Malaya and the Dutch East Indies. The Chamber was originally founded as the umbrella social organisation for overseeing the Chinese community interests on the island. However, during the twilight years of the Manchu rule (1905-1911) it served as a pro-Qing organisation in Singapore, acting as a staunch supporter for the Qing government in helping to muster political support for the regime. It also developed close economic ties with China and helped to mobilise Ethnic Chinese capital in the service of Qing economic modernisation.

The political games of the Ethnic Chinese were played with skill and sophistication when Dr Sun Yat-sen, the renowned Chinese revolutionary leader, arrived in East and Southeast Asia. Of course, Sun did not just confine his activities to this region, but East and Southeast Asia were the main base for launching his armed revolts, and also served as a reservoir for his financial sources. Using Singapore and Malaya as case study, Chapter 11 examines Sun's revolutionary activities in the region and his appeals to the Ethnic Chinese for support. It shows how Sun established firm support among the Ethnic Chinese in Singapore and Malaya, with many loyal followers. Using organisational networks and propaganda agencies, Sun was able to mobilise substantial support, both financial and in terms of manpower, for his revolutionary ventures in China. With this first wave of Ethnic Chinese nationalism, Sun was able to overcome competition from the reformists led by Kang Youwei, and to combat his own adversaries within revolutionary ranks.

A second wave of Ethnic Chinese nationalism surged in the 1930s when China encountered the grave threat of Japanese invasion. China was fighting for its survival, and in response Ethnic Chinese around the world rose to fight against the invaders. This response took many forms: anti-Japanese propaganda, a boycott of Japanese goods and economic sanctions, as well as financial and material support for the war against the Japanese. Focusing on the Southeast Asian region, Chapter 12 examines these various forms of anti-Japanese activities, showing once again the effect of Ethnic Chinese involvement in Mainland Chinese politics.

PART I

BUSINESS IN ETHNIC CHINESE SOCIETY

CHAPTER 1

The Rise of Ethnic Chinese Business in East and Southeast Asia*

In this chapter, a general term, 'Ethnic Chinese',[1] is adopted to include the Chinese in Southeast Asia, Hong Kong, Macao and Taiwan. This term is stretched to its maximum limits. There is no political implication intended regarding China's claim on the sovereignty of Taiwan, nor would it deny the fact that the sovereignty of both Hong Kong and Macao reverted back to China in 1997 and 1999, respectively. 'Ethnic Chinese' is an ambiguous term which can mean different things to different people. Literally, the term means 'the ethnic Chinese who live overseas'. It does not convey whether they are

---

*   This chapter is based on a Public lecture delivered at the Nanyang Technological University Singapore, on 4 August 2000.

1.   For a discussion of the terms 'Overseas Chinese', 'Chinese Overseas' and 'Ethnic Chinese' and their cultural and political implications, see Leo Suryadinata, 'Ethnic Chinese in Southeast Asia: Overseas Chinese, Chinese Overseas or Southeast Asians', and Tan Chee Beng's comments in Leo Suryadinata (ed), *Ethnic Chinese as Southeast Asians* (Singapore, Institute of Southeast Asian Studies, 1997), pp.1–32.

Chinese nationals or not. They could be the citizens of many of the Southeast Asian countries, or citizens of Australia, New Zealand, The United States, Canada or European countries. 'Ethnic Chinese' is a general term used only to imply the ethnicity of a person. He or she must be of Chinese descent, which is distinguishable from other ethnic groups, and possess some Chinese cultural traits and customs. The Chinese term *haiwai huaren* is the closest in meaning to the English term 'Ethnic Chinese'.

Generally speaking, there are approximately 55 million Ethnic Chinese people throughout the world. An estimate taken in 1991 showed that about 50.3 million lived in Asia, which accounted for 91.3 percent; 3.4 million in the Americas, accounting for 6.3 percent; while 600,000 in Europe, 600,000 in Oceania and 100,000 in Africa combined to account for the remaining 2.4 percent.[2]

In Asia, the majority of the Ethnic Chinese are concentrated in East and Southeast Asia. They constitute the majority of the total population of three out of the Four Little Dragons: Taiwan, Hong Kong and Singapore. In Taiwan, the population is almost entirely Ethnic Chinese; in Hong Kong, the Ethnic Chinese comprise 92 percent of the population, while about 78 percent of Singaporeans are of Chinese descent. In other parts of the Southeast Asia, the Chinese account for about 32 percent of the Malaysian population, 18 percent in Brunei, 10 percent in Thailand, 4 percent in Indonesia, 1.5 percent in the Philippines and 1.2 percent in Vietnam.[3]

The economic strength of the Ethnic Chinese in East and Southeast Asia can be assessed in terms of Gross Domestic Product (GDP) or Gross National Product (GNP), and their influence in the in which countries they reside. If 51 million of the Ethnic Chinese in East and Southeast Asia are grouped together as a single economy, their annual GDP can match that of any medium-sized Western economic power such as Australia. According to Professor Gordon Redding of the University of Hong Kong, the Chinese in East and

---

2. See David C.L. Ch'ng, *The Overseas Chinese Entrepreneurs in East Asia: Background, Business Practices and International Networks* (Melbourne, Committee for Economic Development of Australia, 1993), p. 26, table 3.
3. Ibid., p. 27, table 4.

Southeast Asia produced an aggregate GDP of US$200 billion in 1988, which was almost equivalent to the Australia's GDP of US$239 billion in the same year.[4] Another estimate was offered by *The Economist* in England, which put the GNP of 51 million of the Ethnic Chinese in East and Southeast Asia in the year 1990 at US(?)$450 billion, a quarter bigger than China's GNP in the same year.[5] China at that time had a population of more than twenty times of the Ethnic Chinese population.

The economic strength of the Ethnic Chinese can also be understood in terms of their relative importance to the economies in East and Southeast Asia. In Taiwan, the economy is almost entirely in the hands of the Ethnic Chinese, while in Hong Kong and Singapore Ethnic Chinese control substantial portions of the economy, ranging from manufacturing and the service industries to real estate, wholesaling and retailing. In Southeast Asia, the Ethnic Chinese also control much of the wholesaling and retailing industries, and have played an important part in the manufacturing, banking and insurance industries. For instance, at the end of 1993 the Ethnic Chinese in Indonesia, who accounted only 3.5 percent of the population, controlled 68 percent of the top three hundred conglomerates and nine of the top ten business groups.[6]

4.   See S. Gordon Redding, *The Spirit of Chinese Capitalism* (Berlin & New York, Walter de Gruyter, 1990), p. 3; David C.L. Ch'ng, *op.cit.*, p. 27.

5.   See 'The Overseas Chinese: A Driving Force', in *The Economist*, vol. 324, no. 7768 (July 18 1992), p. 21.

6.   The top nine out of ten business conglomerates owned by Ethnic Chinese in 1993 were Salim (30,403.4 billion rp), Sinar Mas (14,623.7 billion rp), Bank Danamon (8,682.2 billion rp), Gadjah Tunggal (7,500 billion rp), Astra (7,492 billion rp), Lippo (7,076.6 billion rp), Dharmala (6,000 billion rp), Barito Pacific (5,887 billion rp) and Ongko (4,200 billion rp). See East Asia Analytical Unit, Overseas Chinese Business Networks in Asia (Canberra, Department of Foreign Affairs and Trade, 1995) p. 41, table 3.1.

The Historical Roots of Ethnic Chinese Business

Understanding the phenomenal growth of Ethnic Chinese business would be difficult without examining its historical roots. The Chinese had been trading actively with Southeast Asian countries since 12 AD.[7] They carried China's famous products — silk, porcelain and later tea — to Southeast Asia in exchange for Southeast Asian produce, which fetched high prices in Chinese markets at home. Permanent Chinese settlements were founded in various spots in Southeast Asia in the late fouteenth and early fifteenthth centuries, including trading posts in Vietnam, Thailand, the Malay Peninsula, Java and the Philippines.[8] These early Chinese communities depended a great deal on trade, and the Chinese as a whole had the lion's share of Southeast Asian trade before the coming of the Europeans in the sixteenth century. The pace of growth of Ethnic Chinese business was accelerated after the opening of China in the 1840s, following China's defeat by Britain in the famous

7. The Chinese began to trade with Southeast Asia as early as the second century BC, but did not trade actively with Southeast Asian countries until the twelfth century AD, during the Song dynasty. For the early trade, see Hsu Yun-ts'iao, 'Hua Qiao', in Yu Shukun, *Nanyang Nianjian* (The Nanyang Annals) (Singapore, Nanyang baoshe youxian gongsi, 1951), kui, p. 5; and Wang Gungwu, 'The Nanhai Trade: A Study of the Early History of Chinese Trade in the South China Sea' (independent issue), in *Journal of the Malayan Branch of the Royal Asiatic Society*, vol. 31, pt. 2 (June 1958). For trade with Southeast Asia during the Song and Yuan dynasties (960–1368 AD), see Chen Gaohua and Wu Tai, *Song, Yuan shiqi de haiwai maoyi* (China's Overseas Trade During the Song and Yuan Dynasties) (Tienjin, Tienjin renmin chubanshe, 1981); Li Donghua, 'Song Yuan shidai Quanzhou hai wai jiaotong de shengkuang' (Quanzhou's Overseas Communication and Trade during the Song and Yuan Periods), in *Zhongguo haiyang fazhanshi lunwenji* (Essays in the Maritime History of China) (Taipei, Zhongyang yanjiuyuan sanmin zhuyi yanjiuso, 1984) pp. 1–40.

8. See records of Ma Huan and Fei Xin, two officials who accompanied Admiral Zheng He in his expeditions to Southeast Asia and beyond during the early fifteenth century. Ma Huan (annotated by Feng Chengjun), *Yingya shenglan jiaozhu* (Beijing, Zhonghua shuju, 1955), pp. 1–17; Fei Xin (annotated by Feng Chengjun), *Xingcha shenglan jiaozhu* (Beijing, Zhonghua shuju, 1954), pp. 1–43.

Opium War. The war ended with the opening of the five Treaty ports (Guangzhou, Xiamen, Fuzhou, Ningbo and Shanghai) and the ceding of Hong Kong as a British colony, which provided British and, later, European businessmen with a permanent base from which they could gain access to the vast markets in China.[9] The war not only opened up coastal China for active foreign trade, but also stimulated business activities in the Southeast Asian region, and attracted a large number of Chinese immigrants to trade and settle.[10] Further opening up of China in the 1860s (into central and northeastern China and Taiwan), the introduction of modern transport systems such as steamers,[11] the adoption of Western business institutions and the birth of the Chinese comprador system,[12] joined China with the Ethnic Chinese communities in Hong Kong, Macao and Southeast Asia in creating an emerging capitalist system in East and Southeast Asia.[13]

9. For the study of opening of five Treaty ports and Western business activities in mid-nineteenth century China, see John K. Fairbank, *Trade and Diplomacy on the China Coast: The Opening of the Treaty Ports, 1842–1854* (Cambridge, Massachusetts, Harvard University Press, 1964); W.C. Costin, *Great Britain and China, 1833–1860* (Oxford, The Clarendon Press, 1968).

10. For the study of the impact of opening of the Chinese Treaty ports on Southeast Asian trade, especially for Singapore, see Wong Lin Ken, 'The Trade of Singapore, 1819–69' (independent issue), in *Journal of the Malayan Branch of the Royal Asiatic Society*, vol. 33, pt.4 (December 1960) pp. 125–33.

11. For the introduction of Western steamships to China's waters, and their rivalry for business in the region, see Kwang-ching Liu, *Anglo-American Steamship Rivalry in China, 1862–1874* (Cambridge, Massachusetts, Harvard University Press, 1962); Kwang-ching Liu, 'British-Chinese Steamship Rivalry in China, 1873–85', in C.D. Cowan (ed), *The Economic Development of China and Japan: Studies in Economic History and Political Economy* (London, George Allen & Unwin, 1964), pp. 49–78.

12. For the birth of the comprador system and its impact on nineteenth century China, see Yen-ping Hao, *The Comprador in Nineteenth Century China: Bridge between East and West* (Cambridge, Massachusetts, Harvard University Press, 1970).

13. For the integration of Hong Kong into the emerging world capitalist system after the opening of China, see *Jung-Fang Tsai, Hong Kong in Chinese History:*

The rapid economic changes in coastal China and Southeast Asia opened up a new world, and provided excellent business opportunities for those Chinese who possessed foresight, business acumen, courage and determination. Ironically, it was neither the scholar–gentry nor the Hong merchants — who traditionally served as intermediaries between Sino-Western trade — who made the best of these new opportunities. Rather it was the Ethnic Chinese, along with some Chinese from the coastal provinces of Guangdong and Fujian, who grasped these opportunities and benefited greatly from these changes. This was because the Ethnic Chinese were marginal people who had little or no chance to climb the social ladder in the traditional Chinese social system, and were therefore highly motivated to gain rapid economic advancement. Further, having had direct experience of living under Western colonial rule, they were in a better position than their compatriots in China to observe how Western business was organised and operated.

Modern Ethnic Chinese entrepreneurs, such as Ma Yingbiao and the Guo brothers of Australia and Hong Kong,[14] Gao Manhua and

---

Community and Social Unrest in the British Colony, 1842–1913 (New York, Columbia University Press, 1993), pp. 21–31.

14. Ma Yingbiao was the founder of the Sincere Company (Xianshi Gongsi), the first modern Chinese department store in Hong Kong and China. Ma was a native of Xiangshan (later Zhongshan district), Guangdong province, and an immigrant to Sydney, Australia. Having learnt how a modern Western department store worked in Sydney, he founded the Sincere Company in Hong Kong in 1900. Later, branches of Sincere Company were established in Shanghai, Guangzhou and other major cities in China and Overseas Chinese communities. For a study of Ma Yingbiao and the founding of the Sincere Company, see Wellington K.K. Chan, 'The Organizational Structure of the Traditional Chinese Firm and its Modern Reform', in *East Asian Business History* (A Special Issue of the Business History Review), vol. 56 (Summer 1982), especially pp. 229–32; 'Xianshi gongsi ershiwu nian jingguo shi' (A History of the Founding of the Sincere Company), in Zheng Tianjian (ed), *Xianshi gongsi ershiwu zhou jiniance* (The Sincere Company Limited: Twenty Fifth Anniversary, 1900–1924 (Hong Kong, Shangwu, 1924), *Jizai* column, pp. 1–5.

The Guo brothers were Guo Le (Kwok Lock or known as James Gocklock) and Guo Quan (Kwok Chin or known as Philip Gockchin) who,

Chen Huanyong of Hong Kong and Thailand,[15] Huang Zhixin (Oei Tjie Sien) and his son Huang Zhonghan (Oei Tiong Ham) of the Dutch East Indies[16] and Zhang Bishi of the Dutch East Indies

like Ma Yingbiao, were the natives of Xiangshan. The Guo brothers also took the same career path as Ma, first as immigrants to Australia and later founding the Wing On Company (Yong An gongsi), the second modern Chinese department store, in Hong Kong in 1907. Later, the company established many branches in China and Overseas Chinese communities and successfully diversified into a modern business conglomerate. For a study of the Guo brothers and the founding of the Wing On Company in Hong Kong and Shanghai, see Yen Ching-hwang, 'The Wing On Company in Hong Kong and Shanghai: A Case Study of Modern Overseas Chinese Enterprise, 1907–1949', in Yen Ching-hwang, *Studies in Modern Overseas Chinese History* (Singapore, Times Academic Press, 1995), pp. 196–236; for a revised version of the same article, see Yen Ching-hwang, 'Wing On and the Kwok Brothers: A Case Study of Pre-War Overseas Chinese entrepreneurs', in Kerrie L. MacPherson (ed.), Asian Department Stores (Richmond, Surrey, Curzon Press, 1998), pp. 47–65.

15.   Gao Manhua (also known as Gao Chuxiang or Gao Tingkai) and Chen Huanyong (also kwown as Chen Xuanyi), were Teochews from Cheng Hai district, Guangdong province. Both were dissatisfied with the rural poverty in their villages, and ventured into the new world to make their millions in Hong Kong and Thailand. Both became the founders of business empires based in these two regions. See Zhang Yingqiu, 'Taiguo zhi Chenghai yimin: Gao Huishi yu Chen Hongli jiazu de yeji' (The Immigrants of Cheng Hai in Thailand: The Records of Family Enterprises of Gao Huishi and Chen Hongli), in Lin Tianwei (ed), *Ya-Tai difang wenxian yanjiu lunwenji* (Collected Essays on Local History: The Asian-Pacific Region) (Hong Kong, Centre of Asian Studies, University of Hong Kong, 1991) p. 241. The same article is also published in 'Haiwai Chaoren shiliao chuanji', in *Shantou wenshi* (Collections of Historical Materials on Teochew Chinese Overseas) no. 8 (Swatow, n.d.), pp. 28–9; Chen Chinhuai, 'Shilun Xianggang Chaoshang jingji fazhan de lishi guocheng' (A Preliminary Study of the Historical Development of Teochew Business in Hong Kong), in Tay Lian Soo & Chang Chak-yan (eds), *Chaozhouxue guoji yantaohui lunwenji* (Collections of Essays from the First International Conference on Teochew Studies) (Guangzhou, Jinan daxue chubanshe, 1994), vol. 2, pp. 608–09.

16.   Oei Tjie Sien, a native of Tong An district of Fujian province, was born in 1835. He fled China to Java in 1858 because of his involvement in the Taiping movement. He worked first as a shop assistant and then became involved in trading. He became the founder of Kian Guan Trading Concern, which was

and British Malaya[17] took advantage of these new opportunities to build their transnational business empires in East and Southeast Asia. Their core business was trade, but they diversified into other businesses such as shipping, banking, manufacturing, mining, plantations and real estate. They had widely established business networks in the ports of East and Southeast Asia, and integrated their business activities in the region. The First World War saw the temporary retreat of European economic power, and provided excellent opportunities for Chinese business to grow. These entrepreneurs further consolidated their positions in banking, manufacturing and inter-regional trade up until the Second World War.

These historical roots have several important implications for the rise of Ethnic Chinese business in the 1970s and 1980s. Firstly, centuries of active business activity in the region enabled the Ethnic Chinese to accumulate an enormous amount of capital which could be mobilised and reinvested into any new business initiatives. Secondly, centuries of business activity in East and Southeast Asia created a business culture which emphasised money-making and the accumulation of wealth. This business culture helped nurture

later expanded by his son, Oei Tiong Ham, into a great trading empire in Southeast Asia with many branches throughout the region and South China. For a short biography of Oei Tjie Sien, see Zheng Guojin, 'Huang Zhonghan ji qi jiazu de xingcui' (The Rise and Fall of the Oei Tiong Ham Family Enterprise), in Zheng Min & Liang Cuming (eds), *Huaqiao Huaren shi yanjiuji* (Collections of Essays on the Study of Ethnic Chinese History) (Beijing, Haiyang chubanshe, 1989), vol. 1, pp. 433–35. The history of Oei Tjie Sien was also told by his grand daughter, Oei Hui Lan in her 'Reminiscences', reprinted in Yoshihara Kunio (ed), *Oei Tiong Ham Concern: The First Business Empire of Southeast Asia* (Kyoto, The Center for Southeast Asian Studies, Kyoto University, 1989), pp. 22–32. For studies of Kian Guan, see J. Panglaykim & I. Palmer, 'Study on Entrepreneurship in Developing Countries: The Development of One Chinese Concern in Indonesia', in *Journal of Southeast Asian Studies*, vol. 1, no. 1 (Singapore, March 1970) pp. 85–95; Yoshihara Kunio, 'Introduction', in Yoshihara Kunio (ed), op. cit., pp. 1–21.

17. Zhang Bishi (Chang Pi-shih or Zhang Chenxun, also known as Thio Tiauw Siat) was a Hakka who was born in Da Pu district of Guangdong

Ethnic Chinese entrepreneurs, who played an important role in the rise of Ethnic Chinese business. Thirdly, the restrictions on Ethnic Chinese holding land and on their entry into bureaucracies forced many young Ethnic Chinese to pursue business for social mobility. Fourthly, the pre-Second World War growth of Ethnic Chinese business laid solid foundations for its rise later. It placed Ethnic Chinese communities in an advantageous position *vis-à-vis* other ethnic communities in Southeast Asia in trade and business, and prepared them to take advantage of the new political and economic situations in the post-war period. Fifthly, the business networks established in East and Southeast Asia provided Ethnic Chinese businessmen with a competitive edge over other ethnic groups in the region.

External Factors Contributing to the Rise of Ethnic Chinese Business

At least three important external factors contributed directly and indirectly to the rise of Ethnic Chinese business in the 1970s and 1980s.

province in 1840. At the age of 17, he followed his relatives to the Dutch East Indies to seek his fortune. He started as an apprentice but ended up as a prominent Ethnic Chinese tycoon of his time. He had extensive businesses in Dutch East Indies, British Malaya and South China. He later entered the Qing bureaucracy, and was appointed the Imperial Commissioner for the Inspection of Commerce in Southeast Asia. For a short biography of Zhang Bishi, see Kuang Guoxiang, ' Zhang Bishi Qiren' (Mr Zhang Bishi), in *Kuang Guoxiang, Pingcheng sanji* (Anecdotal History of Penang) (Hong Kong, Shijie Book Store, 1958), pp. 97–107; Zheng Guanying, *Zhang Bishi jun shengping shilue* (A Brief Biography of Mr Zhang Bishi), in *Jindai Zhongguo shiliao congkan* (Collections of Historical Materials of Modern History of China), series 75 (Taipei, n. d.). For an excellent study of Zhang Bishi and his contribution to China's economic modernization during the late Qing period, see Michael Godley, *The Mandarin-capitalist from Nanyang: Overseas Chinese Enterprise in the Modernization of Chian 1893–1911* (Cambridge, Cambridge University Press, 1981).

Political Factors

Both international and regional political factors played a part in the rise of Ethnic Chinese business in the 1970s and 1980s. After the Second World War, the world entered into the era of the so-called Cold War (1946–1991). The world was divided into the capitalist camp, headed by the United States, and the socialist camp, headed by the Soviet Union. Both camps were engaged in ideological and military expansion. The victory of communism in North Vietnam and China in the second half of the 1940s speeded up the process of confrontation between world capitalism and communism.[18] In the early 1950s, the United States launched a containment policy to check the spread of communism in Southeast Asia. It formed the Southeast Asian Treaty Organisation and placed many East and Southeast Capitalist countries under its defense umbrella. At the same time, it also provided military and economic aid to these client nations. Apart from these defense and security arrangements, the United States also encouraged the newly independent Asian countries to adopt capitalist development strategies in an effort to compete with the so-called socialist industrialisation strategy adopted by China and other Asian socialist countries like North Vietnam and North Korea.[19] The savings from defense expenditure, American aid and the focus on economic development both directly and indirectly benefited the Ethnic Chinese in East and Southeast Asia, who were ready to take advantage of these new political change.

Regional political change in East and Southeast Asia saw the independence of many new states. The political retreat of Western

18.   For a comprehensive explanation of the build-up of confrontation between the United States and the Soviet Union during the post-war period, see William R. Keylor, *The Twentieth-Century World: An International History* (New York, Oxford University Press, 1996), Ch. 8, 'The Formation of the Bipolar World in the Truman-Stalin Era (1945–1953)'.

19.   For the United States' foreign policy during the post-war period, see Joyce and Gabriel Kolko, *The Limits of Power: The World and United States Foreign Policy, 1945–1954* (New York, Harper & Row Publishers, 1972). For the impact of the Cold War on Southeast Asia, see C.M. Turnbull's chapter entitled 'Regionalism and Nationalism', in Nicholas Tarling (ed), *The Cambridge History of Southeast Asia, volume 2* (Cambridge, Cambridge University Press, 1992), especially pp. 596–611.

colonial powers in Southeast Asia saw the gradual withdrawal of Western economic interests in the region. Many Western companies which had grown rapidly under the protective wing of colonialism felt insecure under the new regimes, and were prepared to pull out their investment and curtail their business activities.[20] Many of these companies sold their assets cheaply to the local population. Being dominant in business and having enormous capital reserves, the Ethnic Chinese were in the best position to take advantage of the European economic retreat.

Global Economic Growth

Ethnic Chinese business would not have achieved such a high growth rate had the global economy been depressed. In this sense, the argument that the East Asian 'economic miracle' was partly due to rapid global economic growth is a valid point. The world economy had recovered quickly during the post-war period, and development policies pursued by major Western capitalist states in North America and Europe propelled the world economy ahead. Consumer-driven strategies resulted in a market boom in the West in the 1960s and 1970s. Consumer demands and high labour costs in Western countries created excellent opportunities for East and Southeast Asian goods, which were cheap but of reasonable quality, and this opened up Western markets for manufactured goods from East and Southeast Asia. At the same time, Western multinational companies, especially textiles and the electronics industry, relocated their production to East and Southeast Asian countries to take advantage of cheap labour costs.[21] Being a dynamic business group in the region, the Ethnic Chinese were able to grasp this golden opportunity to increase and expand their business activities.

20. For economic and social changes in Southeast Asia during the post-war period, see Norman Owen's chapter entitled 'Economic and Social Change', in Nicholas Tarling (ed), *The Cambridge History of Southeast Asia, volume 2*, especially pp. 470–81.
21. Regarding Southeast Asian countries, see Ian Brown, *Economic Change in Southeast Asia, c.1830-1980* (Kuala Lumpur, Oxford University Press, 1997), pp. 261–62.

Government Economic Policies and Strategies

The governments in East and Southeast Asian countries played an important role in the rise of Ethnic Chinese business.[22] This is not to say that these governments favoured Ethnic Chinese at the expense of other groups. Rather, the successful economic policies and strategies pursued by these governments facilitated the rise of Ethnic Chinese business. On the contrary, had these governments adopted inappropriate economic policies or strategies it would have been more difficult for Ethnic Chinese business to achieve such phenomenal growth. Since many of these countries had acquired their independence during the post-war period, they were extremely anxious to shake off their colonial past and to restructure their economies. Invariably they all adopted development policies and pursued the path of rapid industrialisation. In the initial stages they adopted the 'Import substitution industrialisation' (ISI) strategy, which aimed to substitute foreign imported goods with local industrial products. Usually they started with light industry, which required less capital and technology input. This strategy effectively laid the foundations for faster economic growth. After a short period they adopted the strategy of 'Export-oriented industrialisation' (EOI),[23] because the domestic market was saturated and light industry had to find external markets for sustainable growth. Taking advantage of consumer demand in the United States and Europe, many East and Southeast Asian countries scored great success in the implementation of this strategy.

22. Government roles were expressed in the policies adopted and their intervention in the economic process. See World Bank, *The East Asian Miracle: Economic Growth and Public Policy* (New York, Oxford University Press, 1995), pp. 5–7. For the government's role in Japan's economic success, see Chalmers Johnson, *MITI and the Japanese Miracle: The Growth of Industrial Policy, 1925–1975* (Stanford, Stanford University Press, 1988, paperback). For the government's role in Indonesian economic development, see Hal Hill, *Indonesia's Industrial Transformation* (Allen and Unwin, Sydney, 1998), pp. 301–23.
23. For a comprehensive explanation of the ISI and EOI strategies of these countries, see Gerald Tan, *The Newly Industrializing Countries of Asia* (Singapore, Times Academic Press, 1995, second edition), pp. 61–71.

The implementation of these new economic policies and strategies provided equal opportunities for all ethnic groups in East and Southeast Asian societies. However the Ethnic Chinese, who had accumulated enormous capital in the region over the centuries and had built intricate but effective business networks, were in a better position than other ethnic groups to take advantage of this new situation. In addition, some of the Ethnic Chinese entrepreneurs who had cultivated political connections and won over the indigenous elite to their side had a competitive advantage over their compatriots in the building of their business empires.

Confucianism and the Business Ideology of the Ethnic Chinese

Most of the Ethnic Chinese in East and Southeast Asia are the descendants of the Chinese immigrants who arrived in the nineteenthth and early twentiethth centuries. Despite changes in the political and economic environment and the adjustments they have to make to adapt to new situations, the Ethnic Chinese in the region have invariably retained many Confucian values and Chinese traditions. Obviously the Ethnic Chinese in Taiwan, Hong Kong and Macao tend to preserve more of these values than the Chinese in Southeast Asia. Confucian values were transmitted to the Ethnic Chinese communities through education, customs and social practices. The China-born Ethnic Chinese invariably picked up some Confucian values either through family or village schools in their communities in South China;[24] while the local-born Ethnic Chinese were exposed to the influence of Confucianism through Chinese schools, Chinese customs or social practices.[25] Confucian values of

---

24.   For a study of the spread of Confucian values through the family system in imperial China, see Patricia Ebrey, 'The Chinese Family and the Spread of Confucian Values', in Gilbert Rozman (ed), *East Asian Region: Confucian Heritage and Its Modern Adaptation* (Princeton, New Jersey, Princeton University Press, 1991), pp. 45–83.

25.   In 1885, there were an estimated 115 Chinese schools in the Straits Settlements (Singapore, Penang and Malacca), and most of them were small private schools (*sishu*). Texts used in these *sishus* were closely connected

filial piety, loyalty, the importance of family, reciprocity, and respect for age and authority filtered down to all sections of the Ethnic Chinese communities through family teachings, ancestral worship, functions of the clan and dialect organisations, and traditional festivities such as Qing Ming (laying sacrifices to deceased ancestors).[26] These Confucian values set frameworks for the Ethnic Chinese, providing them with guidance in their behaviour and laying the foundations for business ideology in the Ethnic Chinese communities.

Important concepts in modern Ethnic Chinese business ideology are 'harmony', 'reciprocity', 'hierarchy and paternalism', 'innovation' and 'progress'. The concept of harmony (*he*) is perhaps the most important, and it is derived from Confucian concepts of benevolence (*ren*) and propriety (*li*). Most modern Ethnic Chinese entrepreneurs regard their enterprises as an extended family, and they and their employees only assume different status and role within that large family. It is on the basis of this harmony that members of the company co-operate and the company prospers. However, to achieve greater success for the company members of this large family should understand their positions and roles in the enterprise, and develop their own potentials within the organisation. Ethnic Chinese entrepreneurs are not unaware of the potential conflict of interest between employers and employees. Gains for the employees could mean losses for the employers. Unlike the Marxists, who see industrial relations strictly in class terms and tend to regard the class relationship as antagonistic and irreconcilable, Ethnic Chinese entrepreneurs

with Confucianism. See 'Annual Education Report for the Straits Settlements for the Year 1885', in *Straits Settlements Legislative Council* Proceedings, 1886, appendix 17, table E; Yen Ching-hwang, *A Social History of the Chinese in Singapore and Malaya, 1800–1911* (Singapore, Oxford University Press, 1986), p. 298.

26. For the influence of Confucian values on the Chinese in Singapore and Malaysia in the nineteenth and early twentieth centuries, see Yen Ching-hwang, ibid., pp. 84–8. For the influence of Confucian values on the Chinese in contemporary Singapore, see Eddie C.Y. Kuo, 'Confucianism and the Chinese Family in Singapore: Continuities and Changes' (Singapore, Department of Sociology, National University of Singapore, 1987, Working Papers, no. 83), pp. 10–25.

perceive the employer–employee relationship as a senior–junior partnership in a common endeavour, and their relationship to be harmonious, co-operative and complementary.[27]

Another major concept in the business ideology of the Ethnic Chinese is reciprocity. Again, this concept seems to have grown out of the Confucian concepts of benevolence and loyalty (*zhong*) which govern the bonds between superior and subordinate. A subordinate, who has the right to be treated benevolently by his superior, also has the moral duty to give his superior absolute loyalty. Similarly, a superior is morally obliged to behave with benevolence towards his subordinate but at the same time has the right to demand absolute loyalty. Chinese tradition seems to have made it the duty of the superior to initiate this reciprocal relationship. In applying this concept of reciprocity to a business enterprise, modern Ethnic Chinese entrepreneurs aptly use it to cultivate good relationships with their employees, and appear to seal a strong bond with them, thus helping to smooth industrial relations.[28]

27. See Yen Ching-hwang, 'Modern Overseas Chinese Business Enterprise: A Preliminary Study', in Yen Ching-hwang, *Studies in Modern Overseas Chinese History* (Singapore, Times Academic Press, 1995), p. 241.

28. For instance, the Guo (Kwok) brothers, Guo Le (Kwok Lock) and Guo Quan (Kwok Chin) felt obligated to look after the interests of their employees in the Wing On Company in Hong Kong. They improved their employees' education, looked after their health and offered them lifetime employment. In return, they expected employees to be absolutely loyal to the company. See Guo Quan (Kwok Chin), *Yongan jingshen zhi fazhan ji qi zhangcheng shilue* (The Origins of Wing On Spirit and Its Development) (Hong Kong, Wing On Company Ltd. ? 1961), pp. 27–8; Liu Tianren, 'Pen gongsi — ershiwu zhounian zhi jingguo' (Twenty Five Year's History of the Wing On Company), in *Xianggang Yongan youxian gongsi nianwu zhounian jinianlu* (Souvenir Magazine of the Silver Jubilee Celebration of the Wing On Company of Hong Kong) (Hong Kong, Tian Xing Press, 1932), *Shi lueh* (history) column, pp. 5–8. See also Yen Ching-hwang, 'The Wing On Company in Hong Kong and Shanghai: A Case Study of Modern Ethnic Chinese Enterprise, 1907–1949', in *Proceedings of Conference on Eighty Years History of the Republic of China, 1912–1991* (Taipei, Jindai Zhongguo chubanshe, 1991) vol.4, pp. 91–2.

Concepts of hierarchy and paternalism also form important elements of modern Ethnic Chinese business ideology. Confucian society was structured hierarchically by class and status, and was further organised into hierarchies of age, gender and generation within family and clan.[29] The Confucian concept of social hierarchy, in contrast to the Western concept of equality, is based on the assumption that individuals are inherently unequal in ability and morality, and they should therefore be given different status and roles in society. Inequality is therefore considered to be natural and justified. Brought up in Chinese families and communities which are hierarchically stratified, modern Ethnic Chinese businessmen tend to perceive others from that perspective, seeing the business world in two separate hierarchies: external and internal. In the external hierarchy, business enterprises large and small are competing among themselves, and they are far from equal. Large and financially powerful enterprises are at the top, followed by medium-sized enterprises, with small and financially weak ones at the bottom of the hierarchy. Competition in the business world is fierce, so successful enterprises expand and move up to the top while less successful ones move downwards and even disappear all together. In the internal hierarchy, all members of the enterprise are also structured hierarchically according to position and role and in order to be able to contribute their utmost to the enterprise. Within this internal structure, those who occupy leadership positions are expected to lead and to show a good example for their subordinates to follow, while at the same time treating their subordinates with benevolence. This internal hierarchy and its relations give rise to the concept of paternalism.[30] The leaders feel morally obligated to lead and to discipline

29. For the structure of clan or lineage, see Hugh D.R. Baker, *Chinese Family and Kinship* (London, The MacMillan Press Ltd, 1979), pp. 49–70; Hsien Chin Hu, *The Common Descent Group in China and Its Fuctions* (New York, Johnson Reprint Corporation, 1968), pp. 18–20.
30. For a discussion of the origins of Chinese paternalism and its relation to Ethnic Chinese entrepreneurs, see S. Gordon Redding, *The Spirit of Chinese Capitalism* (Berlin and New York, Walter de Gruyter, 1990), pp. 127–35. For the paternalistic management style of Chinese entrepreneurs like Tan Kah Kee, see Yen Ching-hwang, 'Tan Kah Kee and the Overseas Chinese

their subordinates for the common good of the enterprise.[31] Undoubtedly, these concepts of hierarchy and paternalism generate a strong sense of competitiveness and self-motivation which helps to motivate and discipline the work force, and serve as a driving force behind modern Ethnic Chinese business enterprises.

The Nature of Ethnic Chinese Business

Ethnic Chinese businesses in East and Southeast Asia are characterised by family ownership, strong business networking, strong cultural input (Confucianism) in business organisation and management. The majority of the Ethnic Chinese business in East and Southeast Asia are small and medium-sized companies owned by families. Family becomes the focus of business activity. It provides capital, labour and management. With the expansion of business activities, the family remains in control of management and recruitment policies, and reaps the profits and or bears the loss of the business. The strength of the family business lies in its flexibility of decision-making and operation, and the devotion and loyalty of its labour force, but its family origins also tend to restrict its expansion and diversification.[32] When a family business has developed to become a public company, the family or group of related families still maintain control of the majority of the stock and management.[33]

Entrepreneurship', in *Asian Culture*, no. 22 (Singapore, Singapore Society of Asian Studies, June 1998), p. 5; Lim How Seng, 'Chen Jiageng de jingying linian yu qiye guanli' (The Entrepreneurial Ideas and Management of Tan Kah Kee), in Lim How Seng, *Xinjiapo huashe yu huashang* (The Chinese Society and Chinese Merchants in Singapore) (Singapore, Singapore Society of Asian Studies, 1995), pp. 153–66.

31. See Yen Ching-hwang, 'The Wing On Company of Hong Kong and Shanghai', in Yen Ching-hwang, *Studies in Modern Ethnic Chinese History*, p. 210.

32. For discussions of the advantages and disadvantages of family businesses, see Siu-lun Wong, 'The Chinese Family Firm: A Model', in *British Journal of Sociology*, vol. 36, pp. 58–72; S. Gordon Redding, *The Spirit of Chinese Capitalism*, pp. 143–81.

33. For a general study of ownership and control of some large Ethnic Chinese business conglomerates in Malaysia, see Lim Mah Hui, *Ownership and*

Strong business networking is an important characteristic of Ethnic Chinese business.[34] As Ethnic Chinese communities grew and developed in Southeast Asia under the Western colonial rule, Chinese traders had to develop elaborate networks for survival and growth. These networks provide facilities for capital accumulation, marketing information and distribution of goods and services. Underpinning Ethnic Chinese business networks are the ideas of *guanxi* (*kuan-hsi*, personal connections) and xinyong (*hsin-yung*, personal trust). The former is based on traditional dialect and kinship ties, and is reinforced by marriage and other social ties such as school-mates;[35] while the latter is based on honesty and reliability

Control of the One Hundred Largest Corporations in Malaysia (Kuala Lumpur, Oxford University Press, 1981), especially pp. 82–112. For a case study of Ethnic Chinese business conglomerates in Southeast Asia, the Hong Leong Group of companies in Singapore and Malaysia, see Tong Chee Kiong, 'Centripetal Authority, Differentiated Networks: The Social Organization of Chinese Firms in Singapore', in Gary Hamilton (ed), *Business Networks and Economic Development in East and Southeast Asia* (Hong Kong, Centre of Asian Studies, University of Hong Kong, 1991), especially pp. 190–97. For another case study of Ethnic Chinese business conglomerates in Southeast Asia, the CP (Charoen Pokphand) Group in Thailand, see Akira Suehiro, 'Modern Family Business and Corporation Capability in Thailand: A Case Study of the CP Group' (paper presented to the Workshop on Asian Business Networks, held in Singapore, 31 March to 2 April 1998).

34. Studies of Ethnic Chinese business networks are many. A more recent publication in this field is Chan Kwok Bun's edited book entitled *Chinese Business Networks: State, Economy and Culture* (Singapore, Prentice Hall, 2000, 336pp.).

35. One of the earliest scholars using the concept of *guanxi* (*kuan-hsi*) to study Ethnic Chinese politics was J. Bruce Jacobs. He used this concept to study the local politics in Taiwan in the late 1970s. See J. Bruce Jacobs, *Local Politics in a Rural Chinese Cultural Setting: A Field Study of Mazu Township, Taiwan* (Canberra, Contemporary China Centre, Research School of Pacific Studies, Australian National University, 1980). Since then, the concept of *guanxi* has gained currency in the studies of Ethnic Chinese and Chinese economies. For an excellent analysis of concept of *guanxi* and its social meaning, see Ambrose Yeo-chi King, 'Kuan-hsi

between two concerned parties. It is to certain extent like modern-day credit-rating, the mechanism through which the lender or creditor assesses the reliability of the borrower; but it is more than credit-rating, as it applies to both parties and involves two individuals, then two companies and later two groups of companies. Although *xinyong* has no legal basis, it has serious social and economic implications. A Chinese who has lost *xinyong* in business would lose his social status and ruin his business.[36]

Strong cultural input (Confucianism) in organisation and management is another important feature of Ethnic Chinese business. The Confucian values of hierarchy, harmony, loyalty and reciprocity are reflected in the hierarchical structure and paternalistic management of the Ethnic Chinese businesses. Most Ethnic Chinese business are organised in a pyramid structure with top-down command, where power and authority are concentrated at the top. At the same time, management and ownership are intertwined and the owner–manager possesses a greater power than a salaried manager

and Network Building: A Sociological Interpretation', in Tu Wei-ming (ed), *The Living Tree: The Changing Meaning of Being Chinese Today* (Stanford, Stanford University Press, 1994), pp. 109–26. For studies of *guanxi* in Taiwan's business enterprises, see Ichiro Numazaki, 'The Role of Personal Networks in the Making of Taiwan's Guanxiqiye', in Gary Hamilton (ed), *Business Networks and Economic Development in East and Southeast Asia*, pp. 77–93. For an excellent study of Taiwan's *guanxiqiye*, Tainanbang, see Xie Guoxing (Hsieh Kuo-hsing), *Qiye fazhan yu Taiwan jingyan: Tainanbang de ge an yanjiu* (Corporation Development and Taiwan Experience: A Case Study of Tainan Group) (Nankang, Taipei, Institute of Modern History, Academia Sinica, 1994). For a systematic study of *guanxi* and its socio-economic and political meanings in China, see Mayfair Mei-hui Yang, *Gifts, Favors and Banquets: The Art of Social Relations in China* (Ithaca and London, Cornell University Press, 1994).

36.   For a study of *xinyong*'s role in Ethnic Chinese business by using the Chinese in South Vietnam as example, see Clifton Barton, 'Trust and Credit: Some Observations Regarding Business Strategies of Overseas Chinese Traders in South Vietnam', in Linda Y.C. Lim & L.A.Peter Gosling (eds), *The Chinese in Southeast Asia*, vol. 1 (Singapore, Maruzen Asia, 1983), pp. 46–64.

in Anglo-American companies,[37] although his power is constrained by the Confucian concepts of paternalism and reciprocity. The owner-manager has the welfare of his employees at heart and will mete out justice to them; in return he and his company receive loyalty and dedication from his employees. Thus, harmony and co-operation between employers and employees prevails.[38] Of course, there are cases where Chinese employers exploit their employees, but they are the exception rather than the rule.

Summary

Over 90 percent of the Ethnic Chinese worldwide are concentrated in East and Southeast Asia. Their economic strength has grown phenomenally since 1970s and formed a formidable force in the region.

What contributed to the rise of the economic power of the Ethnic Chinese is the combination and interaction of several important factors: historical, global economic and geo-political, governmental and cultural. Historical factors set the framework for the birth and growth of Ethnic Chinese business, and moulded the attitude of Ethnic Chinese businessmen and their future direction in business. Global economic and geo-political factors created a favourable economic environment for rapid economic growth in the region, while the economic policies and strategies of some countries made fast economic growth in the region possible. Last but not least, Confucian values enhanced the chance of success for Ethnic Chinese businesses.

37.   See S. Gordon Redding, *The Spirit of Chinese Capitalism*, pp. 158–59; Yen Ching-hwang, 'Modern Overseas Chinese Business Enterprise: A Preliminary Study', in Yen Ching-hwang, *Studies in Modern Overseas Chinese History*, pp. 245–46.

38.   For instance, the head of the Salim Group of companies, Liem Soe Liong, believed in harmony and co-operation between employer and employees. See Sung Chek Mei (Song Zhemei), *Lin Shaoliang zhuan* (A Biography of Liem Soe Liong) (Hong Kong, Southeast Asia Research Institute, 1988), pp. 69–70. For another example, the head of the Golden Lion Group of companies in Hong Kong, Zeng Xianzi, also believes in harmony and co-operation between management and workers. See Xia Ping, *Zeng Xianzi zhuan* (A Biography of Zeng Xianzi) (Beijing, Zuojia chubanshe, 1995), pp. 284–97.

CHAPTER 2

Ethnic Chinese Business Networks in East and Southeast Asia*

The origins of the Ethnic Chinese business networks are rooted in the history, culture and special circumstances in which the Chinese operated in Southeast Asia. Early Chinese came to Southeast Asia not to settle but to trade. Unlike European colonisers, Chinese traders stayed in Southeast Asia for a short period of time to conduct business, and returned to China with enormous profits. The transient nature of early Chinese traders required them to set up various outposts in key ports in Southeast Asia.[1] Starting from the Tang dynasty in the seventh century, Chinese traders had already begun

---

*   This chapter is based on a paper delivered at the Chinese Business History Seminar, University of Queensland in May 1998.

1.   For discussion of early Chinese trading activities in Southeast Asia, see Anthony Reid, 'The Unthreatening Alternatives: Chinese Shipping in Southeast Asia, 1567–1842' (an unpublished paper presented to the Conference on Island Southeast Asia and the World Economy, 1790s–1990s, held at the Australian National University, Canberra, 24–26 November 1992); Anthony Reid, *Southeast Asia in the Age of Commerce 1450–1680*,

to construct such a trading network, and it was improved and consolidated through the Song and Yuan dynasties. By the end of the Ming and early Qing dynasties in the mid-seventeenth century, Chinese trading networks were well-established.[2] However, during this period European economic penetration into Southeast Asia posed great challenge to Chinese traders and threatened their economic well-being. The subordination and integration of the Chinese traders into the European economic system in the eighteenth and nineteenth centuries did not destroy existing Chinese business networks, but rather they were left to grow as far as they posed no direct threat to European interests.

Large-scale migration and settlement of the Chinese in Southeast Asia since the mid-nineteenth century changed the nature of Chinese business networks in the region. The enlargement of Chinese communities in various parts of Southeast Asia and the demands for Chinese foodstuffs and other consumer items expanded trade between Southeast Asia and China, and made Chinese business activities viable in the region.[3] At the same time, the emergence of Hong Kong and the opening of several treaty ports on the China coast following the defeat

Volume 2: Expansion and Crisis (New Haven and London, Yale University Press, 1993), pp. 1–61.

2. See Li Jinming, *Mingdai haiwai maoyishi* (A History of Foreign Trade of the Ming Dynasty) (Beijing, Zhongguo shehui kexie chubanshe, 1990), pp. 114–21; Chang Pin-ch'un (Zhang Pinchun), 'Shiliu zhi shiba shiji Huaren zai Tongnanya shuiyu de maoyi youshi' (The Advantageous Position of the Chinese in East Asian Waters between the 16th and 18th Centuries), in Chang Yen-hsien (Zhang Yanxian) (ed), *Zhongguo Haiyang Fazhanshi Lunwenji*, disanji (Essays on the China's Maritime History, volume 3) (Nangang, Taiwan, Zhongyang Yanjiuyuan Zhongshan Renwen Shehui Kexie Yanjiuso, 1988), pp. 345–68.

3. See for instance, the trade between Singapore and China in the year 1829–30 was estimated to have 72,357 tons. This figure increased to 181,834 tons in the year 1844–45, three years after the opening of the Treaty ports in China. It increased phenomenally to 444,740 tons in the year 1865–66. See Wong Lin Ken, 'The Trade of Singapore, 1819–69', an independent issue of the *Journal of the Malayan Branch, Royal Asiatic Society* , vol. 33, pt. 4 (December 1960), p. 123.

of China in the Opium War in 1842 provided a new framework for regional trade between East and Southeast Asia. Chinese traders and merchants were able to take advantage of the new situation to strengthen their existing business networks in Southeast Asia,[4] thus making trading activities between East and Southeast Asia more integrated and profitable.

Apart from a small number of prominent Chinese business families who had succeeded in constructing business networks in Southeast Asia and beyond, many descendants of early Chinese settlers in Southeast Asia were banned from holding land, which was reserved for indigenous people, and were also denied the opportunity of employment in colonial or indigenous government services. What *was* open for ambitious Chinese immigrants was business. Not only did it offer them a promising opportunity to obtain wealth, but it also opened a path leading to a bright future for their descendants. Once a business was established, it would bring material comfort as well as social prestige and political status.[5] Thus, the pursuit of wealth almost became a common aspiration for many young Southeast Asian Chinese. The retreat of the European powers and the rise of new indigenous states in Southeast Asia after the Second World War did not shift the focus of the Ethnic Chinese in business, for many of them were still discriminated against or barred from working in the civil service. To pursue a career in business was regarded not only as respectable, but also as necessary as far as many young Southeast

4.   For the linkage between Hong Kong and Southeast Asian trade after the opening of Hong Kong, see Jung-Fang Tsai, *Hong Kong in Chinese History: Community and Social Unrest in the British Colony, 1842–1913* (New York, Columbia University Press, 1993), pp. 26–31.

5. .   For a discussion of the relationship between wealth and social prestige and status in the Chinese communities in Singapore and Malaya in the late nineteenth and early twentieth centuries, see Yen Ching-hwang, 'Ch'ing's Sale of Honours and the Chinese Leadership in Singapore and Malaya, 1877–1912', in *Journal of Southeast Asian Studies*, vol. 1, no. 2 (Singapore, McGraw-Hill Far Eastern Publishers, 1970), pp. 20–32; see also the same article reprinted in Yen Ching-hwang, *Community and Politics: The Chinese in Colonial Singapore and Malaysia* (Singapore, Times Academic Press, 1995), pp. 177–98.

Asian Chinese were concerned, and to preserve and expand existing Chinese business networks for survival is still a common concern for many Ethnic Chinese in the region.

There are many explanations for the fast economic growth of East and Southeast Asian economies in the last three decades. They range from economic and political to social and cultural factors. Among the economic factors, the most frequently cited are successful economic policies and strategies such as import-substitution, export-oriented industrialisation, induced foreign investment and cheap labour costs.[6] Increasingly, however, scholars have been interested in exploring the role of business organisations in the success of East and Southeast Asian economies.[7] What is clearly discernible in these Asian capitalist economies is the domination of clusters of business networks or groups. The top six business groups in Japan, the top ten in South Korea and the top five in Hong Kong have achieved control over a large portion of key sectors in their economies. In contrast with Western companies, which operate more or less autonomously in competition with one another, business firms in East and Southeast Asia are organised into corporate networks or groups. Such groups are not based on a headquarters-and-branches relationship, nor are they organised hierarchically on the basis of superior–subordinate relations. Instead, they are quite independent and free from frequent managerial interference. They share some common names, logos and membership

6. See The World Bank, *The East Asian Miracle: Economic Growth and Public Policy* (New York, Oxford University Press, 1993); Gerald Tan, *The Newly Industrializing Countries of Asia* (Singapore, Times Academic Press, 1995, second edition), pp. 93–131.

7. For instance, a group of scholars interested in the role of business organisations in the economic development in East and Southeast Asia met in 1986 at the University of California, Davis, and laid the groundwork for the formation of research teams at the University of Hong Kong, National University of Singapore, Tunghai University in Taichung, Taiwan and the University of California, Davis. The group held its first conference at Hong Kong University, 20–22 1989, which resulted in the publication of the papers in a book entitled *Business Networks and Economic Development in East and Southeast Asia*, edited by Gary Hamilton.

of some exclusive clubs.[8] In this sense, they are like an industrial octopus, swallowing large chunks of the market and reaching long arms into other parts of the world.

This network structure of Asian capitalist economies and its immense economic power makes the patterns of Asian economies different from those of competitive economies in the West. However, what should be noted here is that Asian economic networks or groups are not uniform. Japanese business networks differ from the South Korean networks, and they are different from Ethnic Chinese business networks found in Taiwan, Hong Kong and Singapore.

Ethnic Chinese business networks differ from the Japanese and South Korean networks at least in two areas: the inter–firm relationship and the government-firm relationship. Firstly, as family loyalty overrides all other loyalties in Ethnic Chinese communities, business relationships are also primarily dictated by family interests. This means that the ties between firms owned by the same family are stronger than those between firms owned by different families. In contrast, because of their feudalistic history, the Japanese and South Koreans have developed a stronger commitment to broader institutions than to their families or extended families. Therefore, the inter-firm relationships in Japanese *zaibutsu* groups and South Korean *chaebol* groups are built firmly on mutual obligations to the group per se. This allows Japanese and South Korean business groups to grow more quickly and easily. Further, inter-firm relationships within Ethnic Chinese business networks are also affected by the different basis of personal trust. In Ethnic Chinese communities, personal relationships (*guanxi*) are based on familial, kinship, geographical and dialect ties, thus affecting business relationships in accordance with the distance or closeness of the personal relationships; while Japanese and South Korean obligation networks are able to cut across these kinship and geographical ties, and have the ability to form strong bonds with people of different backgrounds.[9]

---

8. See Marco Orru, 'Practical and Theoretical Aspects of Japanese Business Networks', in Gary Hamilton (ed), *Business Networks and Economic Development in East and Southeast Asia*, p. 248.
9. See Gilbert Wong, 'Business Groups in Hong Kong ', ibid., p. 130.

Secondly, Ethnic Chinese businessmen enjoy less government patronage than their counterparts in Japan and South Korea. Most Ethnic Chinese in Southeast Asia live under a different ethnic government, and their businesses are not seen as identical to the national interests of the country, nor given strong government support. Thus, Ethnic Chinese businessmen have to strive to cultivate cordial relationships with the government and establish some kind of *ad hoc* or permanent relationship with the local ruling elite.[10] Their capacity to build political connections has become an important element in the success of their businesses.[11] In contrast, Japanese *zaibatsus* and South Korean *chaebols* have been well-integrated into the main stream of their national economies, and have enjoyed a high degree of patronage by their governments. In fact, many large *chaebols* were the creation of the South Korean government under President Park Chung Hee in 1960s.[12]

The Foundation of the Ethnic Chinese Business Networks

Many qualities of the Ethnic Chinese that allow the business networks to function efficiently stem from Chinese cultural tradition. From this legacy have emerged traits central to the operation of the

10. For instance, Chinese businessmen cultivated good relationships with the politically influential Malay elite by offering them board directorship. See James V. Jesudason, *Ethnicity and the Economy: The State, Chinese Business, and Multinationals in Malaysia* (Singapore, Oxford University Press, 1990), p. 129.
11. See Robert Cribb, 'Political Structures and Chinese Business Connections in the Malay World', in Chan Kwok Bun (ed), *Chinese Business Networks: State, Economy and Culture* (Singapore, Prentice Hall, 2000), p. 187; Edmund Terence Gomez, *Chinese Business in Malaysia: Accumulation, Ascendance, Accommodation* (Richmond, Surrey, Curzon Press, 1999), pp. 64, 128, 180–81, 186–88.
12. For the relationship between the state and *chaebols*, see Kim Eu Mee, 'From Dominance to Symbiosis: State and Chaebol in the Korean Economy, 1960–1985' (Ann Arbor, UMI Dissertation Service, Xerox reproduction, 1994); Karl J. Fields, 'Chaebol and the State in Korea', in Karl J. Fields, *Enterprise and the State in Korea and Taiwan* (Ithaca and London, Cornell University Press, 1995), pp. 28–62.

networks: hierarchy and paternalism, reliability and trust, reciprocity and 'face'.

The relationship between business and social organisations in Ethnic Chinese communities is a relatively under-explored area. Much of the scholarly work on Ethnic Chinese social organisations tends to focus on their internal structure and functions, leadership and the use of power, (includes some of my own works on the Chinese in Singapore and Malaya).[13] However, in the next chapter I will discuss the significance of the Kwok brothers in using dialect and regional organisations for mobilising Ethnic Chinese capital.[14] Clifton Barton and other scholars have also drawn our attention to the intimate relationship between business and social organisations.[15]

Ethnic Chinese social organisations provide an useful mechanism for businessmen to build business networks and to display their wealth. There are a variety of social organisations in which businessmen can participate. These include kinship associations, dialect or regional associations, Chinese school management boards, religious organisations, cultural societies, alumni associations, sports organisations and international business associations such as Lions and Rotary clubs.[16] As has been conceded by some businessmen, their

13. See, for instance, my work entitled *A Social History of the Chinese in Singapore and Malaya* (Singapore, Oxford University Press, 1986).

14. See Yen Ching–hwang, 'The Wing On Company in Hong Kong and Shanghai: A Case Study of Modern Overseas Chinese Enterprise, 1907–1949', in *Proceedings of Conference on Eighty Years' History of the Republic of China 1912–1991*, vol. IV (Taipei, 1991), English section, pp. 100–01; see also the same article in Yen Ching–hwang, *Studies in Modern Overseas Chinese History* (Singapore, Times Academic Press, 1995), pp. 218–19.

15. See G. William Skinner, *Leadership and Power in the Chinese Community in Thailand* (New York, 1958); Clifton Barton, 'Trust and Credit: Some Observations Regarding Business Strategies of Overseas Chinese Traders in South Vietnam', in Linda Y.C. Lim & L.A. Peter Gosling (eds), *The Chinese in Southeast Asia, Vol. 1: Ethnicity and Economic Activity*, pp. 57–8.

16. For merchants' involvement in Chinese social organisations in Singapore in the nineteenth and twentieth centuries, see Yong Ching Fatt, 'Chinese Leadership in Nineteenth Century Singapore', in *Xinshe xuebao* (Journal of Island Society) vol.1 (Singapore), English section, pp. 6–12; C.F. Yong, 'A

involvement in these organisations is motivated mainly by the gain of prestige and social standing which indirectly benefits their business.[17] However, involvement in the activities of these social organisations requires time and money. Devotion of time will not make a businessman the leader of an organisation, but rather the amount of money he can offer. This is because a lot of the work of the associations requires money, and it is a common practice that the leader of the association has to set a good example by donating a large sum. Monetary requirements attached to the leadership position rule out many candidates who do not possess sufficient wealth. Thus, the leadership position in social organisations is effectively used as a way for businessmen to display their wealth, and is taken as a symbol of prestige and social standing[18] — although leadership positions vary in prestige and social standing, in line with the amount they cost to acquire. A more prestigious and coveted position would entail more money, but the return of benefits could also be greater. The donations made by leaders are usually displayed conspicuously, either published in local Chinese newspapers, in acknowledgment booklets (*zhengxin lu*) [19], in souvenir magazines of particular associations, or displayed prominently

Preliminary Study of Chinese Leadership in Singapore, 1900–1941', in *Journal of Southeast Asian History*, vol. 9, no. 2 (Singapore, September 1968), pp. 258–85. For Chinese merchants' involvement in social organisations in Thailand, see G. William Skinner, *Leadership and Power in the Chinese Community in Thailand*, ibid.

17. Several years ago when I was deeply involved in the Chinese Association of South Australia (being the President of that Association for eight years), I was told by a former Chinese businessman from South Vietnam how Chinese businessmen benefited from their involvement in *huiquan* activities.

18. In the Chinese communities in Southeast Asia, Hong Kong and Taiwan, it is still a common practice to list one's name card with positions held in social organisations, as an indication of social standing and prestige.

19. For instance, the Kheng Jai Wee Kuan (Qiongya huiguan, the Hainanese Association) of Muar, Malaysia, published in 1971 a 90-page acknowledgment booklet (*zhengxin lu*) acknowledging donations made by members or supporters for the extension of Association's club house. See *Mabo Qiongya huiguan kuangjian xinxia zhengxin* lu (Acknowledgments of Donations for the Extension of the Club House of the Hainanese Association of Muar) (Muar, 1971).

in plaques hung in schools, temples and association halls.[20] The acquisition of such prestige and social standing indirectly enhances one's credentials and credibility, attracting attention and trust in the Ethnic Chinese community. As a result, the individual's *xinyong* (trust) in business circles has also been greatly increased.

Guanxi

The foundation of the Ethnic Chinese business networks is personal connections(*guanxi*) and personal trust (*xinyong*). 'Guanxi' is not an analytical concept; rather, it indicates a personal relationship loaded with affection and mutual obligations. It has been defined as 'personalistic, particularistic and non-ideological ties between persons — based on a commonality of shared identification'.[21] In the context of Ethnic Chinese society, this shared identity may be based on kinship, geographical ties, dialect ties, year of birth (*tongnian*) and education. The pattern of immigration and the nature of the Ethnic Chinese communities strengthened these kinship and geographical-dialect ties. A lack of home government protection further convinced Ethnic Chinese businessmen that they had to rely on these traditional Chinese social ties if they wanted to survive and prosper. Right from very beginning of

---

20. This practice is still common in the Chinese communities in Singapore and Malaysia.

21. See J. Bruce Jacobs, 'The Cultural Bases of Factional Alignment and Division in a Rural Taiwanese Township', in *The Journal of Asian Studies*, vol.36, no.1 (November 1976) pp. 80–1. For further explanation of the concept of *guanxi*, see J. Bruce Jacobs, *Local Politics in a Rural Chinese Cultural Setting: A Field Study of Mazu Township, Taiwan* (Canberra, Contemporary China Centre, Research School of Pacific Studies, Australian National University, 1980), pp. 40–60. For a sociological analysis of the relationship between *guanxi* and Chinese networking, see Ambrose Yeo-chi King, 'Kuan-hsi(Guanxi) and Network Building: A Sociological Interpretation', in Tu Wei-ming (ed), *The Living Tree: The Changing Meaning of Being Chinese Today* (Stanford, Stanford University Press, 1994), pp. 109–26; Chinese version of this article entitled 'Guanxi yu wanglo de jiangou: yige shehuixue de quanxu', in Jin Yaoji (Ambrose Yeo-chi King), *Zhongguo shehui yu wenhua* (Chinese Society and Culture) (Hong Kong, Oxford University, 1992), pp. 64–85.

the existence of the Ethnic Chinese communities in Taiwan, Hong Kong and those in Southeast Asia, the founding of clan organisations (based on kinship ties) and *huiguan* (based on geographical and dialect ties) demonstrated the importance of kinship and geographical bonds among the early Chinese immigrants.[22] These kinship and dialect-based organisations had tight grips on their members, including on their jobs and social and cultural lives as well as on their business activities.[23]

The modernisation of the Ethnic Chinese communities has weakened these traditional ties, but they nevertheless survived and still form an important basis for business grouping. In Taiwan, the formation and development of the famous *Tainanbang* (the Tainan business clique) is a case in point. This business group consists of twenty-seven companies in 1987, and was dominated by three core companies, the Tainan Spinning Company Limited, Universal Cements Limited and the President Enterprise Corporation.[24] The group has been controlled by three families, Wu Kedu and sons, Hou Yuli and family, and Wu Sanlian and family, which all came from the same village of Bei Men of the Tainan district of Taiwan. Not only did they come from the same village, they also spoke the same dialect, the southern Hokkien dialect. Geographical and dialect ties laid the foundation of their business alliance. Moreover, Wu Kedu and Wu Sanlian also shared

22. For a study of kinship, geographical ties and dialect ties in the Chinese communities in Singapore and Malaysia between 1800 and 1911, see Yen Ching-hwang, *A Social History of the Chinese in Singapore and Malaya, 1800–1911* (Singapore, Oxford University Press, 1986), pp. 35–109.

23. For a study of relations between dialect groups and occupation in the early Chinese communities in Singapore and Malaysia, See Mak Lau Fong, 'Occupation and Chinese Dialect Group in British Malaya', in Leo Suryadinata (ed), *Chinese Adaptation and Diversity: Essays on Society and Literature in Indonesia, Malaysia & Singapore* (Singapore, Centre for Advanced Studies, National University of Singapore & Singapore University Press, 1993), pp. 8–27; Mak Lau Fong, 'The Structure of Occupation, Trade and Industry', in Mak Lau Fong, *The Dynamics of Chinese Dialect Groups in Early Malaya* (Singapore, Singapore Society of Asian Studies, 1995), pp. 58–79.

24. See Ichiro Numazaki, 'The Role of Personal Networks in the Making of Taiwan's Guanxiqiye (Related Enterprises)', in Gary Hamilton (ed), *Business Networks and Economic Development in East and Southeast Asia* , pp. 81–3.

the same surname, Wu. Although the two Wu families were not directly connected through kinship, they nevertheless believed that they had a common remote ancestor sometime in history. This common surname relationship, called *tongzong* in Chinese, further strengthened the alliance. On the other hand, the relationship between Wu Kedu's family and Hou Yuli's family was also consolidated through history and a former employer–employee relationship. This relationship can be traced back as early as the 1920s when Taiwan was still under the Japanese rule. Wu Kedu worked as an account keeper in a clothes store owned by Hou Yuli. Later, Wu Kedu's elder son was also accepted as an apprentice in the same shop. Although Wu Kedu and sons later became established in their own business, they invariably felt indebted to the Hou family because of this past relationship.[25]

The real foundation of the *Tainanbang* was laid with the founding of the Tainan Spinning Company Limited in 1955. In 1953, the Nationalist government in Taiwan announced the first four-year economic plan for the development of the island economy. Light industry was given top priority, and the development of a modern large textile industry was targeted. Two new 10,000 spindle spinning factories were planned, and private companies were encouraged to apply for licenses. Taking this opportunity, the Wu and Hou families joined forces and succeeded in bidding for one of the two coveted permits out of more than ten competitors. Their success was mainly due to the lobbying efforts of Wu San-lian, who had been mayor of Taipei and had commanded enormous political influence within the Nationalist party. Wu was subsequently made a minor partner and the first managing director of the Tainan Spinning Company Limited when it was founded. The Wu Kedu and Hou Yuli families were the largest shareholders of Tainan Spinning (Hou's family had contributed $6.66

---

25.   For an excellent study on the origins and development of the *Tainanbang*, see Hsueh Kuo-hsing (Xie Guoxing), 'Zai chuantong yu xiandai zhi jian: Tai-nan-pang de chuancheng, 1926–1955' (Between Tradition and Modernity: The Formation of the Tainanbang, 1926–1955), in *Zhonghua minguo jianguo bashinian xueshu taolunji* (Proceedings of the Conference on Eighty Years History of the Republic of China, 1912–1991), Vol.4: Social and Economic History (Taipei, 1991), pp. 500–27.

million out of the $15 million paid for the company, over 44 percent, while Wu Kedu's family had contributed $5 million, over 33 percent of the total capital) and controlled the company.[26] After the successful operation of the Tainan Spinning, Wu and Hou families further established a string of companies which formed important part of the *Tainanbang*, including the famous President Enterprise Corporation.[27] In the process of expanding the *Tainanbang*, the Wu and Hou families frequently used their geographical, kinship, marriage and other ties to recruit more companies into the group.

The history and growth of the Oversea-Chinese Banking Corporation (OCBC) in Singapore and Malaysia offers another example of how personal networks (*guanxi*) worked in the formation and development of the Ethnic Chinese business groups. The Malaysian scholar Lim Mah Hui, in his 1978 study of ownership and control of one hundred largest corporations in Malaysia, identified eight business cliques. The OCBC–Sime Darby clique was considered the largest and most powerful of these, and was dubbed the 'queen' of the business cliques in Malaysia.[28] It was composed of two interest groups, the OCBC and the Sime Darby groups. The critical link between the two groups was OCBC which, together with its subsidiaries, owned about ten percent of Sime Darby Holdings capital — the largest block of shares held in Sime Darby in 1976. The OCBC-Sime Darby clique embraced 38 of the top 100 corporations in Malaysia, and 13 out of the 38 were core companies.

26. Ibid., pp. 516–21.
27. For a detailed study of the rise of the President Enterprise Corporation and its globalisation, see Hsueh Kuo-hsing (Xie Guoxing), 'Tongyi qiye: Yige Taiwan xiangtu qiye de guojihua' (The President Enterprise Corporation: The Globalisation of an Indigenous Taiwanese Enterprise), in *Guofu jiandang geming yibai zhounian xueshu taolunji, Disice –Taiwan guangfu yu jianshe shi* (Proceedings of the Centennial Symposium on Sun Yat-sen's Founding of the Kuomintang for Revolution) Vol.4: Republic of China on Taiwan, 1950–1993 (Taipei, Jindai Zhongguo chubanshe, 1995), pp. 461–504.
28. See Lim Mah Hui, *Ownership and Control of the One Hundred Largest Corporations in Malaysia* (Kuala Lumpur, Oxford University Press, 1981), pp. 87–91.

In the OCBC–Sime Darby clique, OCBC was most important. Its status in the business world in Singapore and Malaysia could be equated with that of the house of Morgan or Rockefeller in the United States. In 1976, the total assets of OCBC were estimated to be in the vicinity of $4.3 billion, while its net worth was estimated at $929 million. OCBC business activities were wide-ranging: banking, insurance, tin-mining and smelting, rubber plantations, trading, hotels, properties, investment, manufacturing and management services. The OCBC group in the late 1970s was controlled by a few Chinese families. At the forefront was the family of Lee Seng Wee (son of Lee Kong Chian, the world-renowned rubber king), which was the largest shareholder, owning about twenty percent of OCBC stocks. Lee Rubber Company Pte Ltd and Lee Rubber (Selangor) Sdn Berhad, as satellites of the clique, were in fact Lee's family companies, but Lee preferred to keep a low profile.

Other big shareholders of the OCBC included the Lee Choon Seng, Lee Wee Nam, Tan Siak Kew, Tan Hoon Siang and Tan Tock San families. However, although the OCBC was owned by a few wealthy Chinese families, most of them preferred to keep a low profile, electing directors such as Tan Chin Tuan, Yong Pang How and S.Q. Wong to represent their interests.[29]

The Oversea-Chinese Banking Corporation came into being on 31 October 1932 as a result of the merger of three existing Chinese banks in Singapore: the Ho Hong Bank Ltd, the Oversea-Chinese Bank Ltd and the Chinese Commercial Bank Ltd. In response to the impact of the world depression in the early 1930s on business in the Singapore–Malaysian region, these three Chinese banks were amalgamated to strengthen their financial base and avoid competition.[30] Apart from

29. Ibid., pp. 91–96.; Lim Mah Hui, 'The Ownership and Control of Large Corporations in Malaysia: The Role of Chinese Businessmen', in Linda Y.C. Lim & L.A. Peter Gosling (eds), *The Chinese in Southeast Asia, Vol. 1: Ethnicity and Economic Activity* (Singapore, Maruzen Asia, 1983), pp. 285–89.

30. See Tan Ee-leong, 'The Chinese Banks Incorporated in Singapore and Malaya', in *Journal of the Malayan Branch of Royal Asiatic Society*, vol. 26, pt. 1 (July 1953), pp. 117–27; Dick Wilson, *Solid As A Rock: The First Forty Years of the Oversea–Chinese Banking Corporation* (Singapore, Oversea-Chinese Banking Corporation Ltd, 1972), pp. 3–6.

financial considerations, what made the amalgamation possible was personal networks based on geographical and dialect ties. They either shared some common founders, or their founders or major shareholders had shared common geographical and dialect backgrounds. For instance, Dr Lim Boon Keng was a founder of all the three banks, while Lim Peng Siang was a founder of both the Chinese Commercial Bank and the Ho Hong Bank. In addition, all of the founders and major shareholders of the three banks came from the southern part of Fujian province and spoke a common southern Hokkien dialect.[31] These men not only spoke the same dialect, but also knew each other well from frequenting the same associations and clubs. Thus, business interests intertwined with the *bang* (geographical and dialect entity) interests. It has been claimed that Chee Swee Cheng (chairman of the Ho Hong Bank), Lee Kong Chian (vice chairman of the Chinese Commercial Bank) and Tan Ean Kiam (managing director of the Oversea-Chinese Bank), who were all southern Hokkiens, were the men who initiated the lengthy discussions which led to the founding of the OCBC.[32]

After the depression of the 1930s, OCBC grew rapidly during the post-Second World War period. Taking advantage of the new political situation in the region and the retreat of British capital from Southeast Asia, it acquired control of important British companies such as Straits

---

31. Dr. Lim Boon Keng was a Zhangzhou Hokkien from Haicheng district, Fujian province, though he was born in Singapore. Lim Peng Siang was another Zhangzhou Hokkien from Longqi district. See Su Xiaoxian (ed), *Zhangzhou shishu lu Xing tongxianglu* (Records of the Zhangzhou People in Singapore) (Singapore, 1948), pp.62, 70; Lee Guan Ken, *Lin Wenqing de suxiang: Zhong Xi wenhua de huiliu yu maotun* (The Thoughts of Dr Lim Boon Keng: Convergency and Contradiction between Chinese and Western Cultures) (Singapore, Singapore Society of Asian Studies, 1990), p. 22; Yong Ching Fatt, 'Minzu zibenjia Lin Bingxiang yu He Feng gongsi'(Indigenous Chinese Capitalist — Lim Peng Siang and the Ho Hong Company), in Yong Ching Fatt, *Zhanqian Xinghua shehui jiegou yu lingdaoceng chutan* (Chinese Community Structure and Leadership in Pre-War Singapore) (Singapore, South Seas Society, 1977), pp. 103–16.
32. See Grace Loh, Goh Chor Boon & Tan Teng Lang, *Building Bridges, Carving Niches: An Enduring Legacy* (Singapore, Oxford University Press, 2000, pp. 21–2.

Trading, Sime Darby and Petaling Tin, also diversifying into other businesses. Like the *Tainanbang*, OCBC used geographical and dialect ties to expand and recruit companies into its group. In addition to the existing links, the families which control the OCBC group also used kinship ties to consolidate their business relationship, and many of their family members intermarried. For instance, Lee Kong Chian, the founder of the prominent Lee family within the OCBC–Sime Darby group, married the daughter of Tan Kah Kee, the famous industrialist, business tycoon and philanthropist and a director of OCBC. Similarly, Tan Chin Tuan, director of many OCBC member companies, married the daughter of Wee Theam Seng, a former general manager of OCBC.[33]

Xinyong

It would not be an overstatement to claim that personal trust (*xinyong*) is the backbone of Ethnic Chinese business networks, and the basis for a particular type of business strategy which emphasises personal relations and long-term connections. The term *xinyong* (alternatively romanised as *hsin-yung* in accordance with the Wade-Giles system, or *sun yung* in accordance with Cantonese dialect) literally means the function of trust. The word *xin* can be translated into English as trust, trustworthiness, confidence or credibility, while the word *yong* can be translated as use or function. The concept of trust is vague and ill-defined. Based on sociological concepts, Professor Wong Siu-lun of Hong Kong University, pinpoints two types of trust in the Chinese business community in Hong Kong: system trust and personal trust. The former is based on legal institutions, the political system and opportunity structure; while the latter is based on a wide range of personal connections, principally on family and regional ties. Although Wong has not clearly defined the concept of trust, he nevertheless has helped to crystallise the scope and typology of trust in Ethnic Chinese business.[34]

33. See Lim Mah Hui, *Ownership and Control of the One Hundred Largest Corporations in Malaysia*, pp. 94–6.
34. See Wong Siu-lun, 'Chinese Entrepreneurs and Business Trust', in Gary Hamilton (ed), *Business Networks and Economic Development in East and Southeast Asia*, pp. 16–25.

The importance of the concept of *xinyong* in Ethnic Chinese business is beyond doubt. One can probably postulate that Ethnic Chinese business cannot operate without it, and indeed various empirical studies have testified to its importance. In a study of the Chinese in a small trading town in Java, Indonesia, Edward Ryan in 1961 found that the Chinese businessmen placed a high value on personal trust, *kepertjajaan*, in their business operation. They considered the possession of *kepertjajaan* was more important than the possession of capital.[35] In another study on a vegetable wholesale market in Hong Kong, Robert H. Silin in 1972 found that *xinyong* was the crucial factor in upholding the complex network of trading relations.[36] This was further attested by Clifton A. Barton's extensive study of Chinese businessmen and their business behaviour in South Vietnam prior to the Communist takeover in 1975. Barton discovered that *sun yung* (*xinyong*) was more than a Western concept of 'credit-rating', as it carried connotations of a businessman's total reputation for trustworthiness. He also noted that Chinese merchants in South Vietnam were successful in direct proportion to the amount of *sun yung* they possessed.[37] In his study of Shanghainese textile industrialists in Hong Kong, Professor Wong Siu-lun in 1988 found that the reputation of trustworthiness was one of the six most important factors for the success of Shanghainese industrialists.

---

35. See Edward J. Ryan, 'The Value System of a Chinese Community in Java' (unpublished PhD dissertation, Harvard University, 1961), p. 25, quoted in Wong Siu-lun, 'Chinese Entrepreneurs and Business Trust', in Gary Hamilton (ed), *Business Networks and Economic Development in East and Southeast Asia*, p.13.
36. See Robert H. Silin, 'Marketing and Credit in a Hong Kong Wholesale Market', in W.E. Willmott (ed), *Economic Organisation in Chinese Society* (Stanford, Stanford University Press, 1972), p. 337.
37. See Clifton A. Barton, 'Credit and Commercial Control: The Strategies and Methods of Chinese Businessmen in South Vietnam' (unpublished PhD dissertation, Cornell University, May 1977), p. 152; Clifton A. Barton, 'Trust and Credit: Some Observations Regarding Business Strategies of Overseas Chinese Traders in South Vietnam', in Linda Y.C. Lim & L.A. Peter Gosling, (eds), *The Chinese in Southeast Asia, Vol. 1: Ethnicity and Economic Activity* (Singapore, Maruzen Asia, 1983), pp. 49–50.

It was seen as an industrialist's most precious asset, and he had to be meticulous in honouring contracts and to be punctual with deliveries in order to preserve it.[38]

What can be established from these empirical studies is that *xinyong* exists and plays an important role in the operation of the Ethnic Chinese business. Its importance naturally leads us to probe further the questions of how it works and why it plays such a crucial role. Barton's relation of *xinyong* to credit-rating is illuminating. Credit-rating is based on an assessment of a borrower's income, assets and the ability to repay, and it is focused more on the borrower of a loan or receiver of goods and services; while *xinyong* applies to both borrower and creditor, receiver and supplier. Not only does a borrower have to keep his promise to repay a loan or a credit for goods and services on time; a promise made by a creditor or supplier has to be honoured as well, otherwise the person would loose his *xinyong*.[39]

In this sense, *xinyong* is a double-edged sword, cutting both parties. It is highly personal, accumulative and sometimes transferable. It is personal because it primarily involves two businessmen, and then two companies and lastly two groups of companies. It is accumulative because the business relationship between two men and between two companies has to go through the process of testing, and only through a long period of business transactions can a firm *xinyong* grow. Once a person's *xinyong* is established and grown, his reputation as a trustworthy businessman becomes known within business circles and then travels far and wide. He thus possesses a gold card which facilitates his business operations within the web of the Ethnic Chinese business world.

38. Wong Siu-lun, *Emigrant Entrepreneurs: Shanghai Industrialists in Hong Kong* (Hong Kong, Oxford University Press, 1988), p. 167.

39. Clifton A. Barton, 'Credit and Commercial Control: The Strategies and Methods of Chinese Businessmen in South Vietnam', pp. 172–80; also Clifton A. Barton, 'Trust and Credit: Some Observations Regarding Business Strategies of Overseas Chinese Traders in South Vietnam', in Linda Y.C. Lim & L.A. Peter Gosling (eds), *The Chinese in Southeast Asia, Vol.1: Ethnicity and Economic Activity*, pp. 53–7.

Once a person has acquired a good reputation of *xinyong*, he still has to maintain and consolidate it. It is still subject to constant scrutiny by his business partners or creditors. If a person has acquired good reputation for *xinyong* but does not bother to maintain it, it will be gradually weakened and diminish. If a person's *xinyong* is ruined, he will be ostracised in Chinese business circles and his business will decline and collapse. This is tantamount to a death sentence passed on his business. However, a well-maintained and well-consolidated reputation for *xinyong* will not only be of great benefit to the individual, his companies or even his groups of companies; it will also extend to his sons, relatives and even his business associates.[40] Indeed, this transferability of *xinyong* is one of the features of the Ethnic Chinese business.

Although *xinyong* has to be acquired through personal efforts, it tends to favour those businessmen who have the strong financial backing of their families, and to be harsher to those without such backing. This is because those with strong family financial backing inherit part of the *xinyong* from their fathers or companies, and it is relatively easier for them to get credit and loans than for those without strong family financial backing.

As Barton pointed out, *xinyong* operates in Ethnic Chinese business at two different levels: a specific interpersonal relationship and a general reputation for trustworthiness.[41] As most Ethnic Chinese businesses are conducted on the basis of personal relationships, businessmen initiate relationships through introduction by mutual friends or relatives. A personal relationship is thus established, and an informal credit standing begins to develop. In the ensuing transactions, which involve no official contracts or agreements, each party tests the *xinyong* of the other over a period of time. They thus proceed from

---

40. See Tong Chee Kiong, 'Centripetal Authority, Differentiated Networks: The Social Organisation of Chinese Firms in Singapore', in Gary Hamilton (ed), *Business Networks and Economic Development in East And Southeast Asia*, p. 182.
41. Clifton A. Barton, 'Credit and Commercial Control', p. 172; also Clifton A Barton, 'Trust and Credit: Some Observations Regarding Business Strategies of Overseas Chinese Traders in South Vietnam', p. 53.

small to large transactions, constantly testing and evaluating their *xinyong*. Once *xinyong* is firmly established between them, they try to consolidate their relationship on multiple dimensions. They are encouraged to share tips about new business opportunities, to exchange market information and to cooperate in new business ventures. The businessmen would further consolidate these ties by social and cultural activities such as inviting each other's family to dinner and to social and cultural functions, and giving each other assistance and support.[42] Thus interpersonal relationships develop from business to social and cultural arenas.

At the second level of operation, *xinyong* serves as a general measure of one's trustworthiness in society. Apart from personal qualities such as good character and integrity, possession of wealth is important to back up and sustain the individual's reputation. This demands demonstration of the possession of wealth, such as living in luxurious house, owning an expensive car, first-class overseas travel and staying in five-star hotels. This will invariably project an image of the individual as a successful man who possesses sufficient wealth to back up his *xinyong* in business dealings.[43] However, Ethnic Chinese businessmen are sometimes caught in a dilemma between the desire to display their wealth and concerns for their personal and family safety. The negative result of displaying wealth is to attract the attention of criminal elements, who may resort to blackmail or kidnapping of the businessman or his family members. Clifton Barton's suggestion that the excessive display of wealth among South Vietnamese Chinese businessmen would attract the attention of both the government and the taxman implies that most Ethnic Chinese businessmen were dishonest and trying to defraud taxes,[44] which can hardly be substantiated as a generalisation. Some wealthy Ethnic Chinese businessmen, particularly those of the older generation, are reluctant to display wealth partly because of their

---

42. Ibid., p. 174; also Clifton A Barton, pp. 54–5.
43. Clifton A Barton, 'Trust and Credit: Some Observations Regarding Business Strategies of Overseas Chinese Traders in South Vietnam', pp. 55–6.
44. Ibid., p. 56.

thrifty habits and partly because of their traditional belief that the excessive display of wealth would invite jealousy and end up with the loss of that wealth.[45]

Three major functions of *xinyong* can be discerned. Firstly, it functions as a lubricant for Ethnic Chinese business; secondly, it functions as a sanction against any improper business behaviour; and thirdly, it short-cuts financial transactions. Since Ethnic Chinese business is highly personalised and Ethnic Chinese businessmen have to depend on connections to do business, they need *xinyong* to sort out who can be trusted and who cannot. Sorting out the trustworthy clients from unworthy ones enables Ethnic Chinese businessmen to do business easier and to facilitate their business transactions. Most of the modern Chinese communities in Southeast Asia trace their roots back to the nineteenth century under Western colonial rule. A lack of protection from the Chinese government and the unfamiliarity with Western legal practices led Ethnic Chinese businessmen to develop their own mechanisms to deter undue business behaviour. *Xinyong* has been one of the most effective mechanisms that Ethnic Chinese have developed in their conduct of business. Any breach of promises and any fraudulent behaviour would diminish a person's *xinyong* and would result in the collapse of his business. Furthermore, *xinyong* also functions like a modern credit card, helping to simplify and short-cut the procedures of financial transactions between concerned parties.

The Role of Business Networking

It would not be an overstatement to say that that business networking played a major role in the rise of Ethnic Chinese business in East and Southeast Asia in the 1970s. Before this, however, networking was even more important because information technology and financial institutions were relatively underdeveloped, so traditional kinship and

---

45. This practice was common among the older generation of rich Chinese businessmen in Singapore and Malaysia. Some years ago, one of the richest Chinese businessmen, Dai Jishan, was run over by a car in Kuala Lumpur. Dai was reported to have been cycling on his old bicycle when the accident occurred.

dialect ties played a significant role in acquiring information about new business opportunities, raising capital, marketing and distribution. Before the 1970s, souvenir magazines distributed by the Chinese clan and dialect organisations were very useful for this purpose. The practice of soliciting advertisements from clansmen and people of the same dialect group provided a useful guide for those intending to enter the same line of business, and provided initial contacts with prospective customers. For instance, the souvenir magazine published by the Gugangzhou Six Districts Association of Malaya in 1964 consisted of 360 advertisements, the majority of which appear to have been contributed by members of the same dialect group. The advertisements covered a wide range of businesses, from manufacturing, banking, transport, restaurants, sawmills, furniture-making, Chinese sauce and candle manufacturing, and oil-milling, to electrical goods, photo studios, tyre-retreading, engineering and building contractors, wine and spirits, hotels, cinemas and goldsmiths.[46] Contributors of these advertisements were widely drawn from major cities in Singapore and Malaysia.[47] Most advertisements provided names of the companies in Chinese and English, with addresses and telephone numbers for contacts.[48]

The six districts of the Gugang Zhou (literally meaning 'Ancient Gang Prefecture') include Xinhui, Taishan, Kaiping, Enping, Heshan and Chixi. The first four districts are popularly known as the 'Four Districts' (See Yap). The people of the six districts speak a distinctive sub-dialect of Cantonese, and they are spread widely across Hong Kong, Southeast Asia, the United States, Canada and Australia.[49] The souvenir magazine produced by the Gugang Zhou Six Districts

---

46. See *Malaiya Gugang Zhou liuyi zonghui tekan* (Souvenir Magazine of Pan-Malayan Gugang Zhou Six Districts Association) (Penang, 1964), section on Commercial Advertisements.

47. Major cities included were Singapore, Kuala Lumpur, Malacca, Ipoh, Penang and Seremban, while minor cities such as Kampar, Taiping, Bidor and Batu Gajah were also included. Ibid.

48. Ibid.

49. See C.F. Yong, *The New Gold Mountain: The Chinese in Australia, 1901–1921* (Adelaide, Raphael Arts Pty. Ltd, 1977), pp. 1–8; Gunther Barth, *Bitter Strength: A History of the Chinese in the United States, 1850–1870* (Cambridge,

Association of Malaya was circulated widely among its members and the fraternal organisations overseas. Thus, the magazine effectively linked the members of this dialect group worldwide, and provided a useful mechanism for business networking. When a businessman from this dialect group in Penang wished to start a new business in electrical retailing, he could find out from the magazine who was in the electrical wholesale business in Singapore or Kuala Lumpur among his fellow district speakers. He would then make initial contacts using the information provided in the magazine. Having gathered the necessary information about the business, he could then purchase supplies either from that wholesaler or, through him, from other sources. A manufacturer of this dialect group could also find out potential agents or customers from the magazine. Certainly this was not the only way he could do business, but he would probably prefer to do business with someone who spoke the same dialect and was bound by common linguistic and cultural ties. Further, he would probably feel confident that his business was unlikely to be cheated because a social sanction against dishonesty existed within the dialect group.

In a broad historical perspective, the rise of the Ethnic Chinese business in East and Southeast Asia in 1970s was the result of the interaction of multiple factors. No single factor, regardless how important, can account for the emergence of this historical phenomenon. In this context, business networking is one of several important factors such as government policies and economic strategies, global economic environment, geo-political factors and cultural strength. It would be difficult to judge whether the rise of Ethnic Chinese business could have occurred without such networking, but it would be safe to suggest that the existence of these networks facilitated and speeded up the rise of Ethnic Chinese business in the region.

Some scholars tend to discount the importance of networking for the operation of Ethnic Chinese businesses, and even believe that networking will become irrelevant once Ethnic Chinese businesses

Massachusetts, Harvard University Press, 1964), pp. 1–31; Edgar Wickberg (ed), *From China to Canada: A History of the Chinese Communities in Canada* (Toronto, McClelland and Stewart Ltd, 1982), p. 7.

become corporations.[50] The argument for this view is based on the assumption that Chinese businesses will eventually shift towards Western practices and abandon traditional Chinese networking once they grow.[51] Undoubtedly, Ethnic Chinese businesses have to expand by adopting more Western approaches to accounting, planning and management. But they cannot change over completely to Western ways of doing business because they are dealing with mostly Asian customers. Asian values that underpinned business operations in the past still work to some extent today. A complete reversal of business practice from Chinese to Western could end disastrously. Businesses need to adopt good Western practices, and then combine them with the best of the Chinese values in order to produce a hybrid system which will suit the societies in which they operate.

There were signs that traditional Chinese dialect and kinship organisations were losing ground in East and Southeast Asia in the 1970s, when many of the Ethnic Chinese business became corporations. But this trend was arrested and reversed in 1980s. The single most important factor was the emergence of China as potentially the largest market in the world. China's shift of its focus from an ideology-driven to a market-driven economy after 1978 altered the perception of China by many Southeast Asian countries, and changed their policies towards the Ethnic Chinese in their midst. China's strategy of attracting Ethnic Chinese investment and technical expertise further stimulated the Ethnic Chinese communities in East and Southeast Asia to take advantage of that change.[52] Many Ethnic

50. Edmund Terence Gomez, a Malaysian economist, even called Chinese business networking a myth. See Edmund Terence Gomez, *Chinese Business in Malaysia: Accumulation, Ascendance, Accommodation* (Richmond, Surrey, Curzon Press, 1999), p. 183.
51. See Linda Y.C. Lim, 'Chinese Business, Multinationals and the State: Manufacturing for Export in Malaysia and Singapore', in Linda Y.C. Lim & L.A. Peter Gosling (eds), *The Chinese in Southeast Asia, Vol. 1: Ethnicity and Economic Activity* (Singapore, Maruzen Asia, 1983), pp. 245–74.
52. For a study of Ethnic Chinese response to the opportunities in China after its opening, see Constance Lever-Tracy, David Ip & Noel Tracy, *The Chinese Diasporas and Mainland China: An Emerging Economic Synergy* (London, McMillan Press Ltd., 1996), pp. 99–176.

Chinese businessmen in Southeast Asia regarded China not just as the birthplace of their ancestors, but also potentially the largest and most profitable market for investment and business. The Hong Kong Chinese, who had no political problems with investing in China, took the lead, and were followed by many Southeast Asian Chinese businessmen, and later by the Chinese from Taiwan. After the withdraw of Western and Japanese capital after the Tiananmen Incident in 1989, the Ethnic Chinese in East and Southeast Asia increased their investment to fill the gap left by the Western and Japanese investors.[53]

In the escalation of investment in China, and as globalisation gradually set in, those far-sighted Ethnic Chinese in the region believed that traditional kinship and dialect ties could be utilised for the service of their business. The idea was to extend the existing regional kinship and dialect ties, and to globalise them for the benefit of those who wanted to use them. The formation of several loose trans-continental dialect and kinship organisations — the Teochew International Convention (*Guoji Chaotuan Lianyi Nianhui*), the Hakka International Convention, and the Hainanese International Convention — in the 1980s crystallised that idea. This informal international dialect linkage provides regular contacts for the businessmen of the same dialect group worldwide through regular conventions held annually or biennially. An information centre or secretariat was set up to publish newsletters or bulletins, and to help facilitate the organisation of convention. The venue for conventions shifted from one place to another, partly designed not to impose heavy burdens on a particular regional organisation, and partly to attract

53.   See Chen Qiaozhi, 'Guangdong jingji tengfei yu Gang Ao he Dongnanya huaren ziben de zuoyong'(The Role of the Chinese Capital of Hong Kong, Macao and Southeast Asia and the Rise of the Guangdong Economy), in Lin Xiaosheng (Lim How Seng) (ed), *Dongnanya Huaren yu Zhongguo Jingji yu Shehui* (The Chinese in Southeast Asia and China's Economy and Society) (Singapore, Singapore Society of Asian Studies, 1995), pp. 61–6; Chen Chunlai, 'Foreign Direct Investment in China: Determinants, Origins and Impacts' (unpublished PhD thesis, Department of Economics, University of Adelaide, December 1997) pp. 13–4.

more participants to those conventions.[54] This globalisation also occurred in sub-dialect groups, such as at the An Xi International Convention and the Gan Clan International Convention in the 1980s and early 1990s.[55] All these loose international organisations published newsletters and bulletins to provide market information and business contacts,[56] and consolidated these business contacts at the regular biennial conventions.

All of these conventions provided opportunities for direct business contact and for business negotiations completed in pleasurable cultural and feasting environments. An example of this

54. For instance, the first Teochew International Convention, which was called in November 1981 in Hong Kong , resulted in the establishment of an information centre in Hong Kong with the responsibility of publishing a bulletin entitled *Guoji Chaoxun* (Teochew International Convention Bulletin). The convention was to be held biennially. After the first convention in Hong Kong, Teochew International conventions were successfully held in Thailand, Malaysia and Singapore respectively in 1983,1985 and 1987. The fifth convention was held in Macau, with nearly 2,000 delegates from 26 countries. See the 'Opening Speech delivered by the Chairman of the 5th Teochew International Convention, Xu Shiyuan in November 1989, Macau', in Guo Weichuan (ed), *Guoji Chaoxun*, no.11 (*Teochew International Convention Bulletin*, No.11) (Hong Kong, Internal Information Centre of the Teochew International Convention, March 1990), pp.2 & 6.

55. For details of the First International Gan Clan Convention held on 6 April 1991 in Singapore, and the second Convention held in Malacca, 26–28 October 1993, see *Xinjiapo Yanshi gonghui sanshi zhounian jinian ji disanjie shijie Yanshi zhongqin lianyihui tekan* (Souvenir Magazine of Singapore Gan Clan Association 30th Anniversary and 3rd World Gan Clan Conference, 11 May 1996) (Singapore, Gan Clan Association, 1996), pp. 130–44.

56. For instance, Teochew International Convention bulletins cover culture, history and reports of the activities of different regional organisations in the world. They also provide the addresses of regional organisations, and serve to bring together Teochews worldwide. They also help to facilitate businessmen to gather market information and establish contacts. See Guo Weichuan (ed), *Guoji Chaoxun*, no.10 (Teochew International Convention Bulletin no. 10) (Hong Kong, International Information Centre of the Teochew International Convention, September, 1989).

was the Thirteenth World Hakka Convention held in Singapore in November 1996. The convention was hosted by the Nanyang Khek (Hakka) Community Guild of Singapore, and it was attended by 1,485 delegates from various Hakka associations throughout the world.[57] To coincide with this, the Nanyang Khek (Hakka) Community Guild of Singapore, in conjunction with eight academic associations in Singapore, Hong Kong and France, hosted the Third International Conference on Hakkaology (Hakka Studies) in Singapore from 9–12 November 1996. I was privileged to be invited as the key-note speaker for the conference, which was attended by over 150 scholars from allover the world.[58] Being treated as part of the convention, the scholars were invited to attend important functions, and had the opportunity to talk with some of the delegates and to observe how the convention was utilised as a means of advancing both the business and cultural interests of the Hakka people. Each participating Hakka association prepared a booklet comprising a list of delegates with brief description of their business and interests, addresses, telephone and fax numbers; sometimes photographs were also printed for the convenience of identifying the delegates.[59] The convention was one

57. This is the number of delegates from Hakka associations all over the world except Singapore. They included China, Taiwan, Hong Kong, Macau, Japan, Malaysia, Indonesia, Thailand, India, Brunei, United States, Canada, Central America, South America, Europe, Britain, Australia and Africa. The bulk of the delegates came from China and Taiwan. Taiwan, for instance, sent 306 delegates. An estimated 3,000 people attended the convention, including local delegates and residents and the scholars who attended the 3rd International Conference on Hakkaology. See Liang Chunqing & Zhang Kelun (eds), *Di Shisan jie Shijie Keshu kenqin dahui* (Souvenir Magazine of the 13th World Hakka Convention, November 1996, Singapore) (Singapore, the Nanyang Khek Community Guild of Singapore, 1998), pp. 144–46.

58. See Ibid., p. 132. My keynote speech was entitled 'Hakka Chinese in Southeast Asian History', both in Chinese and English. See *Di Sanjie Kejiaxue Guoji Yentaohui: Lunwen Zhaiyaoji* (Outlines of Papers for the 3rd International Conference on Hakkaology) (Singapore, Nanyang Khek Community Guild of Singapore, 1996), pp. 1–20.

59. In one of the breakfasts at the Allson Hotel, Victoria Street, Singapore, I met some of the Hakka delegates from a town in Thailand, and was given a booklet

of the largest ever held in the world, and attracted much support from the government of Singapore and the general public. The Finance Minister, Mr Richard Hu, and the First Deputy Prime Minister, Mr Lee Hsien Lung, both of Hakka origin, were invited to address the convention. The convention was celebrated with a big exhibition of Hakka cultural heritage organised by the History Museum of Singapore, a grand opening, a feast for 3000 people and conducted tours for the delegates, and it was completed with a grand concert of Hakka ballads. The financial benefit for the hosting country was substantial. Apart from money spent on hotels, food and sightseeing, the delegates, through word of mouth, would bring in more tourists to Singapore in the future.[60] The convention also provided an excellent opportunity for Chinese businessmen to establish business contacts and to build bridges leading to future business transactions.

Perhaps the most serious attempt to institutionalise the existing business networks in the service of emerging Ethnic Chinese business worldwide is the convention of the world Chinese entrepreneurs. The first convention was hosted by the Singapore Chinese Chamber of Commerce and Industry at the Mandarin Hotel, Singapore from 10–12 August 1991. It was attended by 800 delegates from 75 cities in 30 countries.[61] It was addressed by prominent Chinese scholars and personalities such as Mr Lee Kuan Yew, the former Prime Minister and a senior cabinet minister of Singapore.[62] For the first time, the convention brought Ethnic Chinese business leaders worldwide together to discuss problems and prospects for their businesses as well as opportunities

with business information, addresses, telephone and fax numbers, and photographs of the delegates.

60. I was told that although many delegates had not been to Singapore before, the hospitality and good impressions they obtained from the Convention would encourage their relatives and friends to visit Singapore in the future.

61. See the Foreword by Tan Eng Joo, Chairman of Organising Committee and President of Singapore Chinese Chamber of Commerce and Industry, in *First World Chinese Entrepreneurs Convention: A Global Network* (Singapore, Singapore Chinese Chamber of Commerce and Industry, 1992), p. 7.

62. For the full text of Lee Kuan Yew's keynote address to the convention on 10 August in both English and Chinese, see ibid., pp. 23–9.

for business contacts.[63] The convention was made a regular one, to be held once every two years in the major cities in which the Ethnic Chinese reside, with the hosting institution, usually the Chinese Chamber of Commerce of different countries, organising the next convention. It was subsequently followed by conventions held in Hong Kong, Bangkok, Vancouver and Melbourne in 1993, 1995, 1997 and 1999 respectively.[64]

It could be asked whether the convention only serves the interests of a small group of people instead of all Ethnic Chinese entrepreneurs. Will it lose steam as time passes by? Will it still be useful in the rapidly changing economic and political environments of the world? Will it still be relevant when the world economy is more integrated? The value of this new transnational business network for Ethnic Chinese businessmen will face the test of time as the globalisation process is being speeded up.

63. The proceedings of the first convention in Singapore, which were published in 1992, contain information on 800 delegates worldwide, including names in Chinese and English, line of business, business addresses, telephone and fax numbers. This would form into a worldwide network for business contacts. The publication must have been sent to the participating organisations, and the information made available to those Chinese entrepreneurs. These fifty-four pages of names are attached as an appendix to the proceedings.

64. The Second World Chinese Entrepreneurs Convention was hosted by the Chinese General Chamber of Commerce, Hong Kong, at the Hong Kong Convention and Exhibition Centre from 22–24 November 1993, and was attended by 981 delegates from 94 cities in 21 countries or regions. See *The 2nd World Chinese Entrepreneurs Convention, 22–24 November 1993: Commemorative Album* (Hong Kong, The Chinese General Chamber of Commerce of Hong Kong, 1994), pp.5, 32. The fourth World Chinese Entrepreneurs Convention was held in Vancouver, Canada, for the first time outside Asia. It was hosted by the Chinese Entrepreneur Society of Canada from 25 to 28 August 1997, and was attended by more than 1,300 delegates from 20 different countries and regions. See *The 4th World Chinese Entrepreneurs Convention: Souvenir Album* (Vancouver, Chinese Entrepreneurs Society of Canada, April 1998), pp. 12–3.

CHAPTER

Traditional Ethnic Chinese Business Organisations in Singapore and Malaysia*

In search of an explanation for the rise of Ethnic Chinese business in East and Southeast Asia in recent decades, scholars have offered a range of different theories. Historical, cultural, social, structural and strategic explanations are certainly important to the understanding of this phenomenon,[1] but there is still room for other explanations. A new way of analysing the dynamics of Ethnic

---

*   This chapter is based on a paper presented at the International Conference on the Ethnic Chinese in Singapore and Malaysia: Dialogue between Tradition and Modernity, held at the Mandarin Hotel, Singapore, 30 June – 1 July 2001.

1   For a historical interpretation, see Wang Gungwu, 'Merchants without Empires: the Hokkien Sojourning Communities', and 'Little Dragons on the Confucian Periphery', in *China and the Chinese Overseas*, Wang Gungwu (Singapore, Times Academic Press, 1997), pp. 79-101, 258-721; Robert Cribb, 'Political Structures and Chinese Business Connections in the Malay World: A Historical Perspective', in *Chinese Business Networks: State, Economy and Culture*, Chan Kwok Bun (ed) (Singapore, Prentice-Hall, 2000), pp. 176-92; Chin Kong, 'Merchants and Other Sojourners: The Hokkiens

Chinese business is to look at it from an institutional perspective. The main focus of this study is examine whether traditional Ethnic Chinese business organisations had any role to play in this process, and to look at what contributed to the dominance of the Ethnic Chinese in business in Southeast Asia. The relationship between occupational monopolisation and *Bang* (dialect- and geographically-based entities) in the Ethnic Chinese communities in Southeast Asia is also discussed.[2]

This study is concerned mainly with the traditional Ethnic Chinese craft guilds and business guilds which constituted the main stream of the traditional business organisations. In addition, it will

Overseas, 1570-1760' (unpublished PhD thesis, History Department, University of Hong Kong, 1998). For a cultural intepretation, see S.G. Redding, *The Spirit of Chinese Capitalism* (Berlin and New York, Walter de Gruyter, 1990); Yen Ching-hwang, 'Modern Overseas Chinese Business Enterprise: A Preliminary Study', in *Studies in Modern Overseas Chinese History*, Yen Ching-hwang (Singapore, Times Academic Press, 1995), pp. 237-54; Yen Ching-hwang, 'Tan Kah Kee and the Overseas Chinese Entrepreneurship', in *Asian Culture*, vol. 22 (Singapore, Singapore Society of Asian Studies, June 1998), pp. 1-13. For a social interpretation, see John T. Omohundro, *The Chinese in Iloilo: Kin and Commerce in a Central Philippine City* (Athens, Ohio, Ohio University Press, 1981). For a structural interpretation, see various articles contributed by Wong Siu-lun, Kao Cheng-shu, Ichiro Numazaki, Tu I-ching, Eddie C.Y. Kuo and Tong Chee Kiong, in *Business Networks and Economic Development in East and Southeast Asia*, ed Gary Hamilton, (Hong Kong, Centre of Asian Studies, University of Hong Kong, 1991); various articles contributed by Chan Kwok Bun, David Schak, Qiu Liben, Edmund Terence Gomez and Peter S. Li, in *Chinese Business Networks*, Chan Kwok Mun (ed) (Singapore, Prentice-Hall, 2000). For a strategic interpretation, see Victor S. Limlingan, *The Overseas Chinese in ASEAN: Business Strategies and Management Practices* (Manila, De La Salle University Press, 1994).

2.   See Mak Lau Fong, 'Occupation and Chinese Dialect Group in British Malaya', in Leo Suryadinata (ed), *Chinese Adaptation and Diversity: Essays on Society and Literature in Indonesia, Malaysia & Singapore* (Singapore, Singapore University Press, 1993, pp. 8–27; Yen Ching-hwang, *A Social History of the Chinese in Singapore and Malaya, 1800–1911* (Singapore, Oxford University Press, 1986), pp.116–23.

deal with informal business organisations such as mutual-aid societies and businessmen's clubs. These subsidiary organisations, though peripheral, lend support to Ethnic Chinese businessmen and facilitate their activities.

Ethnic Chinese guilds originated in China. They were not the outgrowth of China's guilds, but rather they derived ideas and experience from China. The term 'guild' has its origins in European history. In the Germanic languages, the *gild* (guild) originally meant 'fraternities of young warriors practising the cult of heroes', and then came to refer to any group bound together by ties of rite and friendship with mutual support among its members.[3] From the fifth to the tenth century, the guilds were predominantly social organisations not dependent on blood ties. They did not assume a commercial character until around 1100 AD when craft guilds appeared in Italy.[4]

The earliest Chinese guilds can be traced back to the Song Dynasty (960–1279 AD). Robust domestic and foreign trade resulted in the rise of large cities during the Song, especially the Southern Song Dynasty. To facilitate imperial control over the urban population, people of the same trade were grouped together with recognised headmen in a section of the city, and given a designated term, *hang* (literally meaning 'line'), with their leader referred to as *hangtou* (head of a line) or *hanglao* (elder of a line). This Chinese term *hang* has been translated as 'guild'.[5] During the sixteenth and seventeenth centuries (late Ming and early Qing periods) the guilds took over the functions of the officially licensed brokers in some trades. The officially sanctioned brokerage that existed in Ming and early Qing times prevailed in every city and rural market. Licensed brokers were responsible to the government for the behaviour of roving merchants and for taxes to be collected on goods.[6] In the eighteenth century

---

3.　See Anthony Black, *Guilds and Civil Society in European Political Thought from the Twelfth Century to the Present* (London, Methuen & Co Ltd, 1984), p.3.

4.　Ibid., pp. 4–6.

5.　See Kwang-ching Liu, 'Chinese Merchant Guilds: A Historical Inquiry', in R. Ampalavanar Brown (ed), *Chinese Business Enterprise*, vol. 2 (London, Routledge, 1996), pp. 210–11.

6.　Ibid., pp. 212–13.

(mid Qing), Chinese guilds were predominantly merchant (business) guilds. They were identified as *huiguan*, literally meaning 'club house', and were formed by merchants who were away from their native places, giving the guilds a strong regional character. They enjoyed cordial relations with the government, protected their members by setting prices for their merchandise, and worshipped special deities. In the early nineteenth century a new kind of guild, the craft or service guild, became important in the cities. Both business and craft guilds grew rapidly after China was forced to open its doors in the wake of the Opium War (1839–42).[7] It was in this historical context that the traditional Ethnic Chinese business organisations were born and grew in an overseas environment.

Traditional Ethnic Chinese Craft Guilds

Traditional Ethnic Chinese business organisations carried the hallmark of their counterparts in China — strong regional and kinship affiliations — and were named *hang, gongsuo, gonghui, huiguan, ju* and *tang*.[8] Whatever name they assumed, they were better known as guilds. They existed in the major ports and cities in East and Southeast Asia. There is no evidence to suggest a direct link between these early Ethnic Chinese guilds and their counterparts in China. They were neither the overseas branches nor had they forged strong links with China's guilds. The force of overseas environment appeared to be paramount in their birth. They were mainly responding to both religious and economic needs in their new lands.

Two types of early Ethnic Chinese guilds can be discerned: craft guilds and business guilds. The former was the business organisation for craftsmen: carpenters, tailors, blacksmith, goldsmith, and building

---

7.   Ibid., pp.213–18.
8.   See Wu Hua, 'List of Chinese Guilds in Singapore', in Wu Hua, *Xinjiapo huazu huiguan zhi* (Records of the Singapore Chinese Associations), volume 3 (Singapore, South Seas Society,1977), front page; Sei'ichi Imahori (transl. Liu Guoyin), *Malaiya huaqiao shehui* (Overseas Chinese Society in Malaya), (Penang, Jiaying Association of Penang, 1972), p.3; Kwang-ching Liu, op.cit., p. 213.

tradesmen. The latter was the business organisation for a variety of businesses, including import-export trade, grocery, the cloth trade, the tea trade and restaurant businesses.

The existence of several craft guilds in early Penang and Singapore are beyond doubt. In Penang, the Hujing Goldsmith Guild (*Hujing tajin hang*) came into being in 1832.[9] It was followed by the North City Guild (*Beicheng hang*) for carpenters in 1856, the Nu City Guild (*Nucheng hang*) for concrete and brick layers in 1858, and the North Nu Guild (*Nubei hang*) for employee carpenters in 1886.[10] In Singapore, the carpenters' guild, the North City Guild (*Beicheng hang*), also led the way in 1868. It was followed by the tailors' guild, the Hean Yuen Guild (*Xian Yan guan*) in 1880, and the employee carpenters' guild, the North Nu Guild (*Nubei hang*) in 1890.[11]

Among the craftsmen, the carpenters were most active in founding their guilds in the protection of common interests. They founded four of the earliest Chinese craft guilds in the Singapore and Malaysia region (see above). The North City Guild of Penang, which came into being in 1856,[12] deserves special attention. North City (*Beicheng*), was the posthumous name of Nu Ban, the legendary craftsman of Chinese history who was worshipped as the patron deity of carpenters.[13] Scanty records do not allow us to reconstruct actual circumstances under which the North City Guild was established, but the worship of the legendary Nu Ban appears to

---

9.   Sei'ichi, ibid., pp.119–20.
10. Ibid., pp. 99,107,116.
11. See Wu Hua, op.cit., pp.1, 8,12.
12. Sei'ichi Imahori, op.cit., p. 99.
13. Nu Ban's surname was Gongshu while his name was Ban. He was born in the Nu state (in modern Shandong province, East China) during the Spring and Autumn period of Chinese history. He was an expert craftsman, setting standards for construction and the building of boats and carts. He was deified after his death, and was worshipped as the patron deity for all carpenters. Because he was born in the state of Nu, he was popularly known as Nu Ban rather than Gongshu Ban. During the Ming dynasty, he was posthumously conferred the title *Beicheng hou* (Lord of North City) by imperial decree.

have been the motivating force that brought Ethnic Chinese carpenters together to found this guild.[14]

What can be established from other evidence is that the majority of the carpenters in early Penang were the Chinese from Taishan (or Toishan) district, Guongdong.[15] Writing about the Chinese in Penang in 1854, J. D. Vaughan, a British observer, noted that all the carpenters, blacksmiths, shoemakers and others engaged in laborious work were natives of Quang-tung (Guangdong). His description of the 'natives of Quang-tung' most likely referred to a Cantonese-speaking or sub-Cantonese-speaking group,[16] probably the people of Taishan, one of the famous four districts in southern Guangdong that had sent many immigrants to North America and Australia. Although the Taishanese had already established their dialect association, the Ning Yang Association, in Penang in 1833,[17] the special religious need of Taishan carpenters led to the founding of the guild in 1856. Like their counterparts in China, religion played a significant role in the life of the Ethnic Chinese craft guilds.[18] It served as the rallying point for members of the North City Guild who were required to participate in the ceremonies in honour of the patron deity, Nu Ban, on the thirteenth day of the sixth moon every year.[19] Perceived to have possessed enormous power, the patron deity was not only to protect the guild members against any imminent danger and to ensure job security; he was also to serve as the symbol of unity and solidarity among members, and to resolve their potential conflicts. As the followers of Nu Ban, the members regarded each other as brothers and took the guild as their

---

14. Sei'ichi Imahori, op.cit., p. 99.
15. Ibid.
16. See J.D. Vaughan, 'Notes on Chinese of Pinang', in *Journal of Indian Archipelago and Eastern Asia*, vol. 8, 1854, p. 3.
17. See 'Taishan Ning Yang huiguan shiji' (A Short History of the Taishan Ning Yang Association of Penang), in *Xing Bin ribao* (The Xing Bin Daily), 2 October 1951.
18. See Peter J. Golas, 'Early Ch'ing Guilds', in G. William Skinner (ed), *The City in Late Imperial China* (Stanford, Stanford University Press, 1977, reprint, Taipei, Rainbow Bridge Book Co Ltd, 1983), p. 577.
19. See 'Pi-neng Nu Ban hang zhangcheng' (The Rules and Regulations of the Penang Nu Ban Guild (the successor to the North City Guild of Penang),

extended family. With the blessing of the patron deity and the protection of the guild, the members were able to cooperate and unite for a common goal — the protection of jobs and businesses — and to defuse any possible conflicts arising from the practice of the same trade.

The membership of the North City Guild of Penang was not just confined to carpenters, but also included other building workers such as brick and concrete layers. The rules and regulations of the North City Guild in the 1880s stipulated that the carpenters, brick and concrete layers were eligible to apply for membership.[20] Applicants had to be recommended by a member and supported by another. The applications then had to be approved by all of the members who congregated to celebrate the birthday of the patron deity (the thirteenth day of the sixth moon in the Chinese calendar). Membership of the guild in 1886 is estimated to have numbered 120.[21] The inclusion of the brick and concrete workers into the North City Guild revealed its desire to broaden its trade base, perhaps because the number of the carpenters was still small, though it was growing. Or their inclusion may have been due to the consideration that most large construction jobs in Penang at that time were obtained by tender, and grouping carpenters, brick and concrete layers together would have improved their chance of getting work.

Like any other guilds throughout the world, the most significant function of the Ethnic Chinese craft guilds was an economic one, particularly in preserving monopolies and preventing competition within a trade. Preserving a monopoly of a trade served not just to prevent the participation of outsiders in the business, but more importantly to exclude them from the guild. For example, since the majority of the carpenters were from the district of Taishan in Guangdong province, their distinctive sub-Cantonese dialect naturally barred carpenters speaking other dialects from joining the North City Guild. It was natural

revised and reprinted in November 1966). I have had this document in my possession since 1971. See also Sei'ichi Imahori, op.cit., p. 105.

20.   Item 4 of the Rules and Regulations stipulated that those involved in *shui ni* (water and soil work) and *mu* (carpentry work) could apply for membership. I translate those involved in 'water and soil work' as brick and concrete layers. See Sei'ichi Imahori, ibid.

21.   Ibid.

for early Chinese craftsmen speaking the same dialect to congregate for social gatherings and mutual aid, but dialect could also function as an agent excluding people from a particular organisation. However the dialect barrier alone could not ensure the monopoly of the trade by the Tai Shan people in future when circumstances changed: there was also a need to exclude carpenters or concrete workers of other dialect groups from joining the guild. In the 'Rules and Regulations of the Penang Nu Ban Guild' (the successor to the North City Guild)', revised in 1966, item 4 stipulated that applicants for membership must be 'persons from the province of Guangdong'.[22] This phrase should be interpreted more precisely as persons who spoke Cantonese or a sub-Cantonese dialect. Although the Teochews and Hakkas, who spoke distinctly different dialects from Cantonese, were also from the province of Guangdong, they appeared to have been excluded from joining the ranks of the guild.

The prevention of competition among members for jobs or business was in fact a useful function of the Ethnic Chinese guilds, as it acted not as a prohibition but rather as a promotion of co-operation and help. Neither the 1880s nor 1966 revised Rules and Regulations of the North City Guild prohibited poaching jobs, business or apprentices. Instead, they stipulated the need for co-operation and mutual assistance between members of the guild, including requirements to donate money for funerals and weddings and to help each other to find jobs.[23]

From a broader historical perspective, Ethnic Chinese guilds served as an institution which helped perpetuate the monopolisation of occupation by different dialect groups. I have argued elsewhere that the domination of certain occupations and businesses by different dialect groups in the Ethnic Chinese communities was mainly the result of the functions of dialect and clan organisations, and of the dialect-based secret societies being used as effective control mechanisms.[24]

22. See 'Pi-neng Nu Ban hang zhangcheng', item 4, 'Qualifications required for Membership'.
23. See Sei'ichi Imahori, op.cit., pp. 105–06; 'Pi-neng Nu Ban hang zhangcheng', item 15.
24. See Yen Ching-hwang, *A Social History of the Chinese in Singapore and Malaya, 1800–1911* (Singapore, Oxford University Press, 1986), pp.116–23.

Like the secret societies, guilds were instrumental in the control of certain lines of jobs and businesses.[25] In this sense, the guild and the secret society were the two sides of the same coin, serving the interests of Ethnic Chinese dialect groups in the monopolisation of occupation and business. The difference was that the former was an open and legal institution, while the latter was an informal and illegal one.

Underpinning these monopolistic craft guilds was the restrictive labour recruitment system — apprenticeship. Like their counterparts in Qing and early Republican China, a arbitrary three-year period of apprenticeship was adopted.[26] As Peter J. Golas has pointed out, this period was not so much to give the training required for a particular trade, but rather primarily a custom-sanctioned initiation before one could enter a trade.[27] In the case of a carpenters' training, the apprentice was required to reside in the shop learning the skill as well as manning the shop, cleaning and running errands. He received no salary, but was provided with food, clothing and pocket money.[28] Given the fact that many of the Chinese craftsmen were trained in China before coming overseas, they had invariably transmitted their experience to the overseas guilds. They expected the apprentices to go through a training process similar to the one they had gone through.

The relationship between master and apprentice was complex and contradictory one. On the one hand, the master was expected to treat the apprentice as his son and teach him the required skills. In return, the apprentice was required to give total submission to the master and respect him as his father, and this master–apprentice

25.   For the role of secret societies in the monopolisation of occupations in early Singapore and Malaysia, see Mak Lau Fong, *The Sociology of Secret Societies: A Study of Chinese Secret Societies in Singapore and Peninsular Malaysia* (Kuala Lumpur, Oxford University Press, 1981), pp. 45–6.

26.   See Peter J. Golas, 'Early Ch'ing Guilds', op.cit., p.566; Sei'ichi Imahori, *Overseas Chinese Society in Malaya*, p.102.

27.   Peter J. Golas, ibid.

28.   See Lin Yuqi, 'Malaiya jianzhu ye de poushi' (The Analysis of the Construction Business in Malaya), in *Malaiya huaqiao jianzao hang lianhe zonghui kaimu tekan* (Souvenir Magazine of the Federation of the Malayan Chinese Building Guilds), cited in Sei'ichi Imahori, *Overseas Chinese Society in Malaya*, p.102.

relationship, like father–son relationship, was to be harmonious. The old records of the North City Guild of Penang during the Xianfeng reign (1851–1861) emphasised the so-called 'law of nature' in human society, that required a father to be benevolent and a son to be filial. This law was to be applied to the teacher–student (master–apprentice) relationship which required the apprentice to be grateful and obedient.[29] This fictitious family relationship obliged the apprentice to respect his master as a son towards his father. On the other hand, the master was mindful that his apprentice could be his future competitor for jobs and business, which potentially could have led him to keep back some secrets of the trade and to exploit him for his own benefit. However, since the majority of the Chinese carpenters in early Penang were from Taisan of Guangdong,[30] geographical and dialect affinity strengthened the master–apprentice relationship, and prevented any such exploitation.

Traditional Ethnic Chinese Business Guilds

Like the craft guilds, Ethnic Chinese business guilds operated on the principles of monopoly and self-protection. The nature of urban life and the predominance of small business in the Ethnic Chinese communities meant that a wide variety of businesses existed in the port cities in East and Southeast Asia. Trading was the focus of Ethnic Chinese business life, and business guilds were born out of the need for trade and the special overseas environment. Those who were involved in the grocery trade, the cloth trade, the restaurant business and Chinese medicine were most active in organising their guilds for the promotion of common interests. In Singapore, the Restaurateurs' Guild of Singapore (*Xingzhou Gushu shenjing tang*, founded in 1876), the Singapore Piece Goods Traders' Guild (*Buhang shangwu ju*, founded in 1908)

---

29.   See the North City Guild of Penang old records, cited in Sei'ichi Imahori, ibid., p.114, note 18.
30.   Ibid., p.101.

and The Grocers' Guild of Singapore (*Xingzhou zahuo hang*) were among the earliest business guilds on the island.[31] In Kuala Lumpur, the Restaurateurs' Guild of Selangor (*Xue Shenzhong tang*, founded in 1892), the Builders' Guild of Selangor (*Xuelane Jianzhao hang*, also known as *Selangor Kin Cho Hong*, founded in 1917), the Selangor Wine and Spirit Dealers' Association (*Xuelane Jiushang gonghui*, founded in 1917) and the Selangor Grocers' Guild (*Xuelane Zahuo hang*, founded in 1924) were among the earliest Chinese business guilds in Malaysia.[32]

Like the early craft guilds, the early business guilds were characterised by strong dialect affiliation: they were mostly founded by businessmen from the same dialect origins, and their membership was dominated by a single dialect group. For instance, the Singapore Piece Goods Traders' Guild was founded on February 25, 1908 by a small group of Teochew cloth businessmen headed by Chen Delun (Tan Teck Lun) and Wang Bangjie (Heng Pang Kiat), two known leaders of Teochew

31. See Wu Hua, *Xinjiapo huazhu huiguan zhi* (The Chinese Associations in Singapore), vol. 3, pp. 6, 18–19; Yuan Xikang, 'Xinjiapo Gushu shenjing tang yian zeyao' (Outlines of the Minutes of the Restaurateurs' Guild of Singapore), in Huang Guoquan, et al (eds), *Xing Ma Gushu lianhe zonghui tekan* (Souvenir Magazine of the Federation of the Restaurateurs' Guild of Singapore and Malaya (Singapore, the Federation of the Restaurateurs' Guild of Singapore and Malaya, 1958), p. 27; Liu Zhanliang, 'Ben hang shilue' (A Short History of the Grocers' Guild of Singapore'), in *Xingzhou zahuo hang wushi zhounian jinxi jinian tekan* (Souvenir Magazine of the Golden Jubilee Celebration of the Grocers' Guild of Singapore) (Singapore, Xingzhou zahuo hang, 1957), p. 8.

32. See Li Jingpo, 'Xue Shenzhong tang shilue' (A Short History of the Restaurateurs' Guild of Selangor), in Huang Guoquan, et al (eds), *Xing Ma Gushu lianhe zonghui tekan*, p.162; Zhu Wen-shui, 'Xuelane Jianzhao hang jianshi' (A Short History of the Builders' Guild of Selangor) and Zhou Jisun, 'Xuelane Zahuo hang shilue' (A Short History of the Selangor Grocers' Guild), in *Xuelane hangtuan zonghui tekan* (Souvenir Magazine of the Federation of Chinese Guilds of Selangor) (Kuala Lumpur, Xuehua hangtuan zonghui, 1962), no page number; *Xuelane Jiushang gonghui jinxi jinian tekan* (Goldern Jubilee Publication of the Selangor Wine and Spirit Deaders' Association), (Kuala Lumpur, Xuelane Jiushang gonghui, 1967), p. 33.

community in Singapore.[33] The Guild, located at 75-B Circular Road, Singapore in the early 1970s, had twenty-three founding members, all of whom were Teochews dealing in cloth and piece goods primarily from Europe and America.[34] This trend appeared to have continued in the post-war period. In 1950, the membership of the Singapore Grocers' Guild consisted of 106 shop members and 242 individual members. Only ten shop members (mostly represented by the sole owner or the main partner) were non-Cantonese speakers (six Hokkiens, three Hakkas and one Teochew), while the remaining 96 were Cantonese or sub-Cantonese speakers from Xinhui, Nanhai and Shunde. Among the individual members, only six out of 242 members were Hokkien (four) and Hakka and Teochew (one each), and the remaining 236 were Cantonese and sub-Cantonese from Xinhui, Heshan, Shunde and Taishan.[35] This statistical evidence confirms beyond doubt that there was a strong link between the business guilds and dialect groups, clearly showing how the dialect monopolisation of occupation and business was still alive and kicking in the post-war period.

Similarly to the craft guilds, the business guilds also served as a mechanism through which dialect groups (*bang*) could exercise their control over certain occupations or businesses to which they perceived themselves to have rights and privileges. However, the *bangs'* monopoly could be undermined by changing political and economic circumstances and their inability to cope with change. For example, Teochew control over the planting of cash crops in Singapore and Johor (such as pepper and gambier) in the second half of the nineteenth century is well-

33.　See Wu Hua, *Xinjiapo huazhu huiguan zhi*, vol. 3, p.18; Pan Xingnong, *Malaiya Chaoqiao tongjian* (The Teochews in Malaya) (Singapore, Nandao chubanshe, 1950), pp.72, 137.

34.　See '*Xinjiapo Huaren bupiye* (The Chinese Piece Goods Trade in Singapore): A Report on the Singapore Chinese Piece Goods Business', conducted by the students of the History Department of Nanyang University, Singapore, 1971, p. 5.

35.　See 'Hanghao tongxinlu' (Addresses of the Shop Membership of the Guild) and 'Hangyan tongxinlu' (Addresses of the Individual Membership of the Guild), in *Xinjiapo Zahuo hang sishisan zhounian jinian tekan* (Souvenir Magazine of the Celebration of the 43rd Anniversary of the Singapore Grocers' Guild) (Singapore, Xinjiapo Zahuo hang, 1950), pp. 105–21.

documented.[36] However the rise of a new cash crop, rubber, at the beginning of the twentieth century and Hokkien control over it saw the subsequent decline of the Teochew monopoly of plantations and their associated industries in Singapore and Malaya.[37] On the other hand, a change of political and economic circumstances could also add new sources to the same trade, providing the opportunity for other dialect groups to participate; the newcomers would then form their own guilds to protect their interests. Thus the rise of Japan as a new provider of textile goods in post-war Singapore gave the Hokkiens and Hakkas the opportunity to participate in the piece-goods business, which had hitherto been monopolised by the Teochews. The Hokkien piece-good traders formed the Singapore Textile Dealers Friendly Association, while membership of the Singapore–Malaya Chinese Textile Merchants Association was predominantly made up of Hakkas.[38] The sharing of the same business by different dialect groups would not have necessarily led to constant rivalry and conflict. The expanding market resulting from a growing population could absorb more competitors who received supplies from different sources — Europe, North America, Japan and China — and enabled them to compete and co-exist in the same trade.

Economic interests and mutual aid were the principal functions of the Ethnic Chinese business guilds. These were usually stated in the aims or rules of the guilds, based on a common desire to minimise

---

36.   See Siah U Chin, 'General Sketch of the Numbers, Tribes, and Avocations of the Chinese in Singapore', in *Journal of the Indian Archipelago and Eastern Asia*, vol.2, 1848, p. 290; James C. Jackson, *Planters and Speculators: Chinese European Agricultural Enterprise in Malaya, 1786–1921* (Kuala Lumpur, University of Malaya Press, 1968), pp. 7–30; Carl A. Trocki, *Prince of Pirates: The Temenggongs and the Development of Johor and Singapore, 1784–1885* (Singapore, Singapore University Press, 1979), pp. 88–91, 145–52.

37.   For the rise of rubber and Hokkien participation in this new cash crop, see Wu Tiren, *Redai jingji zuowu — xiangjiao shu* (Rubber — the Tropical Cash Crop) (Singapore, Guanghua, 1951), pp. 6–8; James C. Jackson, ibid., pp. 211–18; J.H. Drabble, *Rubber in Malaya, 1876–1922: The Genesis of the Industry* (Kuala Lumpur, Oxford University Press, 1973), pp.14–9; Tan Kah Kee (Chen Jiageng), *Nanqiao huiyi lu* (Autobiography) (Singapore, Chen Jiageng guoji xuehui, 1993), vol. 2, pp. 489, 492.

38.   See 'Xinjiapo Huaren bupiye', op.cit., p. 17.

competition and maximise profits. For example, in 1908, the desire to reduce keen competition among Teochew piece-goods traders in Singapore brought into being the Singapore Piece Goods Traders' Guild. These traders had hitherto been hostile to each other because of business rivalry, and had even forbidden their apprentices to contact each other for the fear of leaking any business secrets.[39] The statement 'to cultivate good relationship among people of the same trade, and to advance common interests' (*lianlo tongye ganqing, gongmou tongye fuli*), commonly found among the rules and regulations of the guilds,[40] reveals a desire to co-operate for the common good. But co-operation and the common good were predicated on the ability of the guild to enforce the rules. Unlike their counterparts in China which enjoyed considerable judicial authority,[41] the Ethnic Chinese business guilds did not wield any legal power nor obtain any government support, so they had to negotiate with members for the implementation of the rules. Sometimes, a deterring clause was incorporated into the rules and regulations as part of the members' obligation to obey the rules and the decisions made by the guild.[42]

This lack of judicial power undermined the authority of the guilds, reducing their ability to enforce rules and sometimes resulting in their failure. The Guild of Chinese Medicines of Singapore (*Xinjiapo Zhong Yao gonghui*) is a case in point. The guild was founded in 1930 with the aim of protecting the common interests of the Chinese medicinal merchants.[43] With this long-term objective in mind, the guild

39. Ibid., p. 5.
40. See 'Bincheng Lianshang gonghui zhangcheng' (The Rules and Regulations of the Penang General Merchants Association), in *Bincheng Lianshang gonghui kaimu jinian ji zhounian huiqing hebian tekan* (Penang Lean Seong Kong Hoay [General Merchants Association] Inaugural Ceremony and First Anniversary Combined Souvenir) (Penang, 1960), p. 103.
41. See Joseph Fewsmith, 'From Guild to Interest Group: The Transformation of Public and Private in Late Qing China', in R. Ampalavanar Brown (ed), *Chinese Business Enterprise*, vol. 2 (London, Routledge, 1996), p. 231.
42. See rule number 11 of the 'Rules and Regulations of the Penang General Merchants Association', op. cit., p.103.
43. See '*Xinjiapo huaren zhongyao hangye shi* (A History of the Singapore Chinese Medicinal Trade): A Report on a Survey of Singapore Chinese Medicinal

introduced the so-called 'genuine medicine and fair price' (*zheng yao zheng jia*) measure which obliged members to sell genuine goods for a fair price. To ensure the quality, medicine sold by members had to be authenticated with a stamp from the guild, and the price set for the medicine had to be approved by the guild with a special code.[44] The authentication would weed out sub-standard and fake medicine, while the regulation of prices would prevent unhealthy competition and over-charging. This measure was designed to lift the image of the Chinese medicine and give the public more confidence. On a long-term basis, it aimed to ensure contining business for Chinese medicinal businessmen in competition with Western medicine in the Ethnic Chinese communities. The 'genuine medicine and fair price' was approved by the executive committee of the guild in January 1946, and was rigorously enforced. Members were required to sign a commitment letter kept by the guild, and Singapore was divided into six districts with two elected leaders to oversee the operation of the new scheme. Any disputes arising from the new measure would be resolved by the district leaders with the support of their members. A wooden plate with 'genuine medicine and fair price' was to be hung on the front of the members' shops, and investigators would be employed to check out the implementation of the measure.[45] The new scheme was put into practice in March 1947, but failed to achieve its desirable results after one and a half years' trial. Business competition, especially from non-members, the lack of judicial power of the guild, and the indifference of the colonial government in Singapore were the main factors contributing to the failure of the new scheme.[46]

Whatever rivalry and competition they might have experienced between them, business guilds could not deny the fact that they shared some common needs, such as mutual aid (including welfare). This was particularly true in a foreign environment such as Southeast Asia, ruled by Western colonial powers or by indigenous rulers who spoke different

Trade', conducted by the students of the History Department of Nanyang University, Singapore, 1971, p. 55.
44.   Ibid., p. 56.
45.   Ibid., pp. 56–57.
46.   Ibid., p. 58.

languages to the Ethnic Chinese. Linguistic barriers were not the only problem, government legislation and external competition (foreign and indigenous) also had a direct bearing on everyone in the business. With the spirit of mutual aid, the guild was able to mobilise talents within the trade and deal with such common problems. The collective power of the guild could change the legislation or the external environment in favour of the trade. In 1954, when the colonial government of the Federation of Malaya imposed a twenty-five percent tax on all imported Chinese medicines, the Selangor Chinese Medicinal Merchants' Guild (*Xuelane Huaqiao yaoye gonghui*), which was founded before the First World War, took the lead in organising a petition against the new import duty. The petition gained strong support from other Chinese medicinal guilds in other states in Malaya and Singapore. The result of this concerted effort was the lifting of the tax on imported raw Chinese medicine.[47]

The Ethnic Chinese business guilds also settled internal disputes among members, established contacts with foreign import–exporters,[48] assisted and promoted business, and strengthened the co-operation between employers and employees.[49] Sometimes, large business guilds were also involved in running Chinese schools and other community charity functions in an attempt to improve the image of the guild in the wider Chinese community. The Federation of the Selangor Chinese Guilds (*Xuelane Hangtuan zonghui*), founded in 1955 in Kuala Lumpur with forty one guilds in the state

47. See Lo Bojin, 'Xuelane Huaqiao yaoye gonghui shilue' (A Short History of the Selangor Chinese Medicinal Merchants' Guild), in *Xuelane hangtuan zonghui tekan* (Souvenir Magazine of the Federation of Chinese Guilds of Selangor), no page number.

48. See Hong Majin, 'Luetan benhui zhuzhi zhi dongji' (The Motives for the Founding of the Penang General Merchants Association), in *Bincheng lianshang gonghui kaimu jinian ji zhounian huiqing hebian tekan* (Penang Lean Seong Kong Hoay [General Merchants Association] Inaugural Ceremony and First Anniversary Combined Souvenir), p. 93.

49. See Liu Zhanliang, 'Ben Hang shilue' (A Short History of the Singapore Grocers' Guild), in *Xingzhou zahuo hang wushi zhounian jinxi jinian tekan* (Souvenir Magazine of the Jubilee Celebration of the Singapore Grocers' Guild), p.10.

of Selangor, ran a Chinese primary school (the Huaqiao School), acted as a pressure group to press the government for the use of Chinese language in public places, and was involved in educational matters such as education policy and the support given to the founding of Nanyang University (a Chinese language university) in Singapore.[50]

The foundation of the business guild was the apprentice system, without which the particular line of business would have declined and disappeared. Like the crafts trades, business recruited its labour force through kinship, marriage and dialect connections.[51] These kin and dialect ties became especially important in the immigrant societies because recruitment of labour usually started in China rather than overseas. Many successful Chinese entrepreneurs in Southeast Asia started with an apprenticeship in a relative's or kinsman's business in which they learnt the business fundamentals. The life stories of Zhang Bishi (Chang Pi-shih, also known as Thio Thiau Siat), a prominent businessman in Southeast Asia in the late nineteenth and early twentieth centuries, Yap Ah Loy (Ye Yalai or Ye Delai), the founder of Kuala Lumpur and a prominent tin miner, Wang Bangjie (Heng Pang Kiat), a prominent Teochew merchant in Singapore, and Foo Chee Choon (Hu Zichun), an eminent tin-mining tycoon in Perak, testify to this process.[52] The relationship between apprentice and employer (shop-owner or business partner, or owner–manager) was similar to that of the apprentice and

50. See Selection of newspaper reports on the activities of the Federation of Selangor Chinese Guilds, in *Xuelane Hangtuan zonghui tekan*, op. cit., no page number.
51. See *Xinjiapo Huaren zhongyao hangye shi*, p. 24; *Xinjiapo Huaren bupiye*, p. 7.
52. Zhang Bishi arrived in Batavia from China at the age of eighteen, and first worked as an apprentice in a rice shop. Yap Ah Loy worked as an apprentice in a shop of a kinsman, Yap Ng (Ye Wu), in Kesang, Malacca. Wang Bangjie worked as an apprentice in a cloth shop in Singapore after he arrived from China. Foo Chee Choon worked as an apprentice in a shop before he learnt the mining business from his uncle. See Kuang Guoxiang, 'Zhang Bishi qiren' (The Story of Zhang Bishi), and 'Xikuang dawang Hu Zichun' (Tin-mining King — Foo Chee Choon), in *Kuang Guoxiang, Bincheng sanji* (Anecdotal History of Penang) (Singapore, Shijie shuji, 1958), pp. 99, 114; Wang Zhiyuan,

master-craftsman — paternalistic and sometimes oppressive. The apprentice was to be obedient, respectful and faithful towards the employer, while the employer was expected to be paternal and caring, as in a father–son relationship.[53] The apprentice was to start learning from cleaning, moving and packaging goods, cooking and running errands — the so-called mundane jobs — in either a Chinese medicinal shop, a grocery shop or a trading company.[54] He usually worked long hours for a token salary. There was no fixed period of apprenticeship; it varied from business to business. Unlike a craft apprentice who had to learn a specific skill in order to qualify as a craftsman, the business apprentice could pick up essential business skills by observation, but his promotion to a proper paid job (a formal employee status) in the shop depended very much on his relationship with the employer — such as how close his relationship with the employer in terms of kinship or dialect ties — and his performance. The former seemed to have played a bigger role in determining his promotion.[55] After he had learnt how to run the business and had accumulated some savings, the apprentice could start a similar business on his own or in partnership with others. When his business expanded and needed more helping hands, he would then recruit apprentices from among the children of relatives, kinsmen and friends, either locally or from China.

Whether this low pay, long hours and paternalistic apprentice system should be regarded as a system of exploitation of cheap labour, or as a

---

Ye Delai zhuan (A Biography of Yap Ah Loy) (Kuala Lumpur, Yihua Publishing Company, 1958), pp. 19–20; S.M. Middlebrook, Yap Ah Loy (an independent issue), in *Journal of the Malayan Branch of Royal Asiatic Society* (Singapore, Malaya Publishing House Ltd., 1951), p. 13; 'Wang Bangjie xiansheng' (Mr Heng Pang Kiat), in Pan Xingnong (ed), *Malaiya Chaoqiao tongjian* (The Teochews in Malaya) , p. 72.

53.   See *Xinjiapo Huaren bupiye*: A Report on the Chinese Piece Goods Business, p. 6.

54.   Ibid.; 'Xinjiapo Huaren zhongyao hangye shi', p. 28; Tan Jingsheng, 'Zahuo shengyai ershi nian' (Twenty Years of My Life in a Grocery Shop), in *Xingzhou Zahuo hang wushi zhounian jingxi jinian tekan* (Souvenir Magazine of the Jubilee Celebration of the Singapore Grocers' Guild) (Singapore, Singapore Grocers' Guild, 1957), p. 15.

55.   See 'Xinjiapo Huaren zhongyao hangye shi', p. 29.

necessary training process to shape prospective businessmen's characters, is a matter for debate. In the absence of modern trade schools or business colleges, the apprentice system was the only means of training available for future businessmen. Long hours and low pay, doing petty and mundane works of apprenticeship, are sometimes claimed to be the Chinese way of character-building; being hard-working, thrifty and able to endure hardship are perhaps qualities which contribute to the success of a businessman. Of course, the system also worked to the advantage of the employer, who benefited from the low labour costs and indirectly increased his profit margins. Indeed, the mutual obligations and benefits between apprentice and employer were in line with the Confucian concept of mutual responsibility. And despite the rigours of the system, an apprenticeship was still coveted by many Ethnic Chinese immigrants and local-born Chinese. From a broader perspective, the Chinese apprentice system has contributed to the growth of the numbers of Chinese businessmen, and helped to perpetuate the dominant business position of Ethnic Chinese in Southeast Asia.

It would be a mistake to assume that traditional Ethnic Chinese business organisations are incapable of changing with time, and that they therefore tend to disappear or be replaced by new organisations. Traditional Ethnic Chinese business organisations, like their counterparts in China, are capable of coping with change and of making themselves relevant in the modern world. Of course, the ability to cope with change varies between individual organisations, and some are more capable than others, but on the whole traditional Ethnic Chinese business organisations do contain the seeds of change, partly derived from traditional Chinese culture itself. The core concept of change in *The Book of Change* (*Yi Jing*, romanised as *I Ching*), one of the five Confucian classics, was familiar to most of the Chinese. Concepts of change then led to ideas of progress, adaptation and reform. Kang Yuwei, the renowned Late Qing Confucian reformer, exalted Confucius as a great reformer who lived ahead of his time, and considered the idea of change and progress to be inherent in Confucian teachings.[56]

---

56.   See Kung-chuan Hsiao, 'K'ang Yu-wei and Confucianism', in *Monumenta Serica*, vol.18 (Nagoya, 1959), p. 165; Jung-pang Lo, *K'ang Yu-wei: A Biography and a Symposium* (Tucson, The University of Arizona Press, 1967), p. 6.

This idea of change and progress has filtered into the minds of ordinary Chinese, including the Ethnic Chinese in East and Southeast Asia. The dictums of '*qiong ze bian, bian ze tong*' (difficulty leads to change, and change leads to adaptation) and '*riri xin*' (to renew everyday), popularly found among the Chinese educated in Singapore and Malaysia, shows how much the Ethnic Chinese businessmen have been influenced by this traditional value.[57] This idea of change was also acquired due to geographical position of the Ethnic Chinese communities. Since most of the Ethnic Chinese were urban folks residing in major ports in East and Southeast Asia, they were exposed more readily to outside influences, both Western and Chinese, through media or business contacts. Many of the Ethnic Chinese businessmen who had contacts with foreign businessmen were at the forefront of change, because they were more aware of what was going on outside the Ethnic Chinese communities. There were also businessmen who were influenced by newspaper reports or socio-political change occurred in China. These outside influences would have impacted on their thinking and their attitude towards reform of the business organisations. The idea of change also grew out of the internal problems of the Ethnic Chinese communities. Dialect and kinship differences led to competition and rivalry in business, and to attempts to monopolise certain branches of business.

This awareness of change and progress was reflected in the public speeches of guild leaders or guilds' publications. For instance, the souvenir magazine for the celebration of anniversary of the Singapore Grocers' Guild published in October 1950 contains many articles with progressive themes. They included articles on 'Chinese business to survive in the international business competition', 'backwardness of Ethnic Chinese business and industry', 'the future of Ethnic Chinese business', 'economic status of the Ethnic Chinese in Southeast Asia' 'employer–employee co-

---

57. The author recalls that some Chinese shops carried names such as *ri xin* or *riri xin* in the small town of Mentakab, in the state of Pahang, Malaysia in 1960s and 1970s.

58. See Liang Bin, 'Lun zhengqu qiaohui zhi guoji shichang' (On the Chinese Remittance and International Market), Huang Shufen, 'Huaqiao shangye hougu yu qianzhan' (Retrospect and Prospect of the Ethnic Chinese Business), Feng Fuqi, 'Lueshu laozi hezuo yu wo huaqiao shangye zhi guanxi' (On

operation' and 'unity and solidarity'.[58] Although some of these contributors were not members of the Singapore Grocers' Guild, they were prominent Ethnic Chinese businessmen affiliated with the guild,[59] and their progressive ideas and insights would have an impact on its members. In Penang, the awareness of the relative backwardness of Ethnic Chinese and their traditional practices in early 1960 prompted some of the members of the Penang General Merchants Association to suggest that 'Ethnic Chinese business and industry have to catch up with time [and] reform obsolete practices'.[60] Among the proposed reform of obsolete practices included 'protracted bargaining' (*taojia huanjia*) and 'long opening hours'. The 'protracted bargaining' was considered to be a waste of time which was a burden on management, while the shortening of trading hours would help conserve energy.[61]

Employer–Employee Cooperation and the Ethnic Chinese Business), Qiu Zhanghe, 'Huaqiao shangye de tuanjie jingzhen he baozhang' (The Spirit of Unity and Its Guarantee of the Ethnic Chinese Business), Liang Junan, 'Jiaqiang tongye de tuanjie' (Strengthen the Cooperation among the Grocers), Feng Jiaju, 'Huaqiao shangye yu qiantu' (Ethnic Chinese Business and Its Future), Ke Tian, 'Nanyang huaqiao yuanyu de jiangji diqei' (The Economic Status of the Ethnic Chinese in Southeast Asia), in *Xinjiapo Zahuo hang sishisan zhounian jinian tekan* (Souvenir Magazine of the Celebration of 43rd Anniversary of the Singapore Grocers' Guild) (Singapore, Xingzhou Zahuo hang, 1950), pp. 21–5, 64–73.

59. Liang Bin was a leader of the Hong Kong Guang Yi Shanghui (Hong Kong Grocers' Guild), while Huang Shufen was a prominent Cantonese businessman and a leader of the Singapore and Johor Cantonese communities.

60. See Chen Xiting, 'Gongshangye ying yingtou ganshang shidai' (Ethnic Chinese Business and Industry Must Catch Up with Time), and Qian Chenxiang, 'Xiang benhui tongye jin yiyan' (A Proposal to the Members of Penang General Merchants Association), in *Bincheng Lianshang gonghui kaimu jinian ji zhounian huiqing hebian tekan, 1959–1960* (Penang Lean Seong Kong Hoay [General Merchants Association] Inaugural Ceremony and First Anniversary Combined Souvenir, 1959–1960), pp. 91–2, 94.

61. Qian Chenxiang, ibid., p. 94.

Informal Ethnic Chinese Business Organisations

Informal Ethnic Chinese business organisations consisted mainly of two types: mutual-aid societies and businessmen's clubs. They invariably played a supporting role for Ethnic Chinese businessmen in their business activities.

Mutual-aid Societies

The mutual-aid societies in the Ethnic Chinese communities grew out of the desire for mutual assistance in times of crisis. The uncertainty of business and the nature of early Chinese immigrant society provided no guarantee for the perpetuation of wealth. The fluctuation of fortunes in the business world brought fears of collapsing businesses and subsequent misery. Wealth was not ever-lasting and dependable; it could dissipate overnight leaving families devastated. Mutual-aid societies therefore began to form in the major cities in Singapore and Malaysia to meet these fears. In Singapore, The Kheng Teck Society (Kheng Teck Whay) came into existence in 1831,[62] while in Malacca, The Kheng Leong Society (Kheng Leong Huay) was founded in 1891,[63] followed by The Ghee Kiat Society (Ghee Kiat Huay) in later years.[64] The early members of these societies were mostly businessmen, but as time went on the societies were opened up and broadened their social base to include most of the adult Chinese.[65] The Kheng Teck Society was the earliest and

62. See David K.Y. Chng & Lim How Seng, 'Xinjiapo Qing De Hui yanjiu' (The 153-Year Old Kheng Teck Association of Singapore), in *Asian Culture*, no.5 (Singapore, Singapore Society of Asian Studies, April 1984), p. 54.

63. The Society claimed it was registered on 19 August 1891. See 'Rules, Bye-laws and General Objects of Kheng Leong Huay and Kheng Leong Huay Mutual Aid Section, Malacca', cover page, revised in September 1957. I have this document in my possession.

64. The 'Rules of Ghee Kiat Huay, Malacca' do not indicate when the Society was founded. When I acquired the pamphlet in 1970s, I was informed that the Rules were probably amended in 1939. I suspect the Society could have been founded before the First World War.

65. In the revised 'Rules of the Kheng Leong Huay', membership is open for

most important of these. Singaporean scholars Lim How Seng and David K.Y. Chng have made a careful study of this organisation and have thrown light on its origins, structure and operation. They have identified the thirty-six founders of the Society and examined its internal structure,[66] and Lim How Seng has further investigated its ideology, functions, social and historical significance.[67] Lim and Chng's studies have established the following: the Society was established by thirty-six Ethnic Chinese merchants in 1831 in Singapore; all founders of the Society were merchants of Southern Fujianese origins, and some of them were leaders of the Hokkien *bang* in Singapore with strong connections to Malacca; the Society was primarily a mutual-aid and welfare organisation for Ethnic Chinese merchants; and members of the Society, though English-educated, were imbued with strong Confucian values and loyalty to the Qing government.[68]

What is relevant to our study is the main function of this Society and its implications. With the foresight of the founders who contributed $100 (Spanish dollars) each, the Society had a flying start with its main objective of mutual aid.[69] The impressive $3,600 fund was invested in property, which gave a steady return. By 1914,

persons of Chinese race of either sex; but the revised 'Rules of Ghee Kiat Huay' confines membership to all Chinese of male sex over 20 years of age. See above documents.

66. See David K.Y. Chng & Lim How Seng, op. cit., pp. 60–5.
67. See Lim How Seng, 'Qing De Hui: Xinjiapo huashang huzhuhui de zuzhi yu yunzuo' (The Kheng Teck Association: The Dynamics of a Chinese Merchants' Mutual-Aid Organisation in Singapore), in *Asian Culture*, no.17 (Singapore, Singapore Society of Asian Studies, June 1993), pp.154–67.
68. See Lim How Seng, ibid., pp.158–65; David K.Y. Chng and Lim How Seng, op. cit., pp. 58–65.
69. The $100 contribution was a large sum of money at the time. In the middle of the nineteenth century, an average agricultural worker in Singapore earned $3 to $4 a month, and his annual income did not exceed $50. This contribution represented two years' income of an average worker. See Yen Ching-hwang, *A Social History of the Chinese in Malaysia and Singapore*, p. 144.

the Society had seven shops, the rental from which accounted for most of the income of $33,136.[70] The strong financial position of the Society enabled it to fulfil its main objective of helping members and their families in times of crisis. Members or non-members (presumably members' relatives or friends) could obtain loans from the Society by mortgaging of land titles or jewellery when they were in financial difficulties. When a member's livelihood was threatened by sickness, the Society would render support with a sickness allowance. More importantly, the Society would take care of member's family if he died in poverty; his widow and children would receive a monthly allowance until they could stand on their own feet; and children of the deceased members were eligible for scholarship or loans.[71] In the period between 1907 and 1928, the Society spent on average over thirty percent of its annual income on welfare, the bulk of which went to members' benefits. [72]

Two important implications are to be noted in relation to the Ethnic Chinese business activities. Firstly, this informal business organisation acted as modern insurance company, providing unemployment and sickness benefits as well as widow pension. This insurance policy would free Ethnic Chinese businessmen's fear of destitution in times of crisis, and reduce their level of worry and stress. This in turn would improve their focus on doing business, and provide them with a spirit of risk-taking which was necessary if their businesses were to succeed. Secondly, this informal organisation provided them a useful contact point where they could meet to exchange business ideas, market information, recruit labour and so on.

70. See Lim How Seng, 'Qing De Hui: Huashang huzhuhui de zuzhi yu yunzuo', op. cit., pp. 160–62; see also the same article in Lim How Seng, *Xinjiapo huashe yu huashang* (Ethnic Chinese Society and Ethnic Chinese Businessmen in Singapore) (Singapore, Singapore Society of Asian Studies, 1995), pp. 114–17.

71. Ibid., p. 161; pp. 116–17.

72. Ibid., pp. 161–62; pp. 117–18.

Businessmen's Clubs

Traditional Ethnic Chinese businessmen's clubs assumed the form of a social club, providing a meeting place and facilities for businessmen to meet after hours. In addition, they also had important business significance. Traditional Ethnic Chinese businessmen have gained a reputation of doing business in an informal way: no formal negotiation sessions, a valuing of verbal promises and no formal contract signed. This informal approach displays a sharp contrast with the way business is done in the West, and sometimes has been dubbed 'the Chinese way of doing business'. This informal approach is the product of the Chinese perception of the business relationship. In their view, the business relationship is an integral part of a total relationship. The Ethnic Chinese would do business not with adversaries but with friends, relatives and people of the same district or province, whom they could trust. A successful business relationship was a long-term and a lasting one, and this traditional attitude made businessmen's clubs important in the building of such relationships.

These clubs assumed names such as *ting* (pavilion), *yuan* (garden) and *xuan* (a porch or a side room), or the more modern term *jilobu* (club). Song Ong Siang's *One Hundred Years' History of the Chinese in Singapore* has listed at least four of such clubs in nineteenth century Singapore, including Ban Chye Ho Club, Cheng Kee Hean Club, Choon Guan Hock Club and Kim Ban Choon Club.[73] Available Chinese sources add another four businessmen's clubs in Singapore in that period: the Chui Huai Lim Club, the Shulin Yuan Club, the Xiao Tao Yuan (Hsiao T'ao Yuan) Club and the Ee Hoe Hean Club.[74] These clubs appeared

---

73. See Song Ong Siang, One Hundred Years' History of the Chinese in Singapore (Singapore, University of Malaya Press, 1967), pp. 98, 259, 291, 476, 552.
74. Song Ong Siang in his book lists a Chinese club in Kampong Java without a name. I have now identified it to be the Shulin Yuan Club that in 1890 hosted a dinner in honour of Qing visiting dignitary, Admiral Ting Juchang, who led a Chinese fleet to visit Singapore in April 1890. See *Lat Pau*, 15 April 1890, p.5; for the Chui Huai Lim Club, see 'Juihua lin jilobu' (The Chui Huai Lim Club), in Pan Xingnong (ed), *Malaiya Chaoqiao tongjian* (The Teochews in Malaya), pp. 343–44. For the existence of the Xiao Tao

to be founded by wealthy businessmen with strong dialect and regional affiliation.[75] For instance, the Chui Huai Lim Club, probably the earliest Ethnic Chinese businessmen's club, was said to be founded in 1849 for Teochew businessmen by Tan Seng Poh (Chen Chengpao), a well-known Teochew opium farmer in Singapore and Johore.[76]

Perhaps a better-known and more established businessmen's club was the Ee Hoe Hean Club founded in Singapore in 1895. The founders of the club were mostly Hokkien rich merchants such as Lim Ho Puah (Lin Heban, father of famous entrepreneur Lim Peng Siang), Tan Cheng Siong (Chen Jenxiang, father of famous banker Tan Chin Tuan), Lee Cheng Yan, Tan Jiak Kim and Gan Eng Seng.[77] The club aimed to bring both Chinese- and English-educated Hokkien businessmen together for recreational and social purposes.[78] It is clear that in its early stages, from 1895 to 1922, membership of the club was confined to Hokkien businessmen. It was not until 1923 when Tan Kah Kee (Chen Jiageng), the renowned Ethnic Chinese entrepreneur and community leader, became the *zongli* (chairman or director) of the club that it was opened for Chinese businessmen of

Yuan Club, see Yen Ching-hwang, *The Overseas Chinese and the 1911 Revolution: With Special Reference to Singapore and Malaya* (Kuala Lumpur, Oxford University Press, 1976), p. 55; for the Ee Hoe Hean Club, see C.F.Yong (Yong Ching Fatt), *Zhanqian Xinghua shehui jiegou yu lingdou chen chutan* (Chinese Community Structure and Leadership in Pre-War Singapore) (Singapore, South Seas Society, 1977), p. 31.

75. See Pan Xingnong, ibid., p. 343.
76. Ibid.; for identifying Tan Seng Poh as a big opium farmer in the region, see Song Ong Siang, *One Hundred Years' History of the Chinese in Singapore*, pp. 131-32; Carl A. Trocki, *Prince of Pirates: The Temenggongs and the Development of Johor and Singapore, 1784-1885* (Singapore, Singapore University Press, 1979), pp. 143–44; Carl A. Trocki, 'Tan Seng Poh', in John Butcher and Howard Dick (eds), *The Rise and Fall of Revenue Farming* (New York, St. Martin's Press, 1993), pp. 249–54.
77. See C.F. Yong, op. cit.,p. 31.
78. Ibid., pp. 31–2; Lim How Seng, 'Yi He Xuan Jilobu shilue' (A Short History of the Ee Hoe Hean Club), in Huang Yihua et.al. (eds), *Yi He Xuan jiushi zhounian jinian tekan* (Souvenir Magazine of the Celebration of 90th Anniversary of the Ee Hoe Hean Club, Singapore) (Singapore, Ee Hoe Hean Club, 1985), p. 37.

other dialect groups.[79] Under the leadership of Tan Kah Kee in the period between 1923 and 1947, the club was reformed with a new community spirit. It banned opium-smoking on the premises, encouraged punctuality and hygiene in social gatherings, and set up a small library.[80] When Tan Kah Kee was actively involved in China politics in 1920s and 1930s, the Ee Hoe Hean Club was turned into the headquarters for the mobilisation of the Ethnic Chinese in Southeast Asia in resisting the Japanese invasion of China in both the Jinan Incident (1928) and the Overseas Chinese National Salvation Movement (1937–1941).[81] However, the high political profile of the Ee Hoe Hean Club after 1923 did not distract it from its original function of providing recreational and social facilities for businessmen. These activities included opium-smoking (before 1923), playing mahjong,[82] drinking and feasting. More importantly, the club, like many other Ethnic Chinese businessmen clubs, provided a relaxed environment in which businessmen, both Chinese- and English-educated, could mix. They chatted and exchanged useful business information, and informally negotiated business deals; indeed, a great deal of business was done through these informal contacts.

Several conclusions can be drawn from this study. First, traditional Ethnic Chinese business organisations provided important institutional support for Ethnic Chinese business by monopolising certain lines of trade and providing training grounds for prospective entrepreneurs. Second, traditional Ethnic Chinese business organisations were a mechanism through which *Bang* (dialect- and

79. C.F. Yong, op. cit., p. 33; Lim How Seng, ibid., p. 38.
80. Lim How Seng, ibid.
81. C.F. Yong, op. cit., pp. 34–36; Lim How Seng, ibid., pp. 38–40; Yen Ching-hwang, 'The Response of the Chinese in Singapore and Malaya to the Tsinan (Jinan) Incident, 1928', in *Journal of the South Seas Society*, vol.43 (Singapore, South Seas Society, 1988), pp. 1–22; C.F. Yong, *Tan Kah-Kee: The Making of an Overseas Chinese Legend* (Singapore, Oxford University Press, 1987), pp. 160–67.
82. A very popular form of Chinese gaming — and it was still popular when I visited the Club in the 1990s.

geographically-based entities) perpetuated their control over business lines. *Bang* monopolies to a certain extent disadvantaged consumers, but guaranteed profit margins and generated competition in business activities. Third, traditional business organisations were a significant factor accounting for the dynamics of Ethnic Chinese businesses and were partly responsible for the dominance of the Ethnic Chinese in business, especially in Southeast Asia. Fourth, traditional Ethnic Chinese business organisations contain progressive elements which help to transform them and make them relevant to the modern world by changing or adding to their traditional functions. Just like many other Ethnic Chinese kin and dialect organisations, they are capable of modernising Ethnic Chinese business. Fifth, the formal and informal business organisations (guilds, mutual-aid societies and businessmen's clubs) complemented each other, and helped to mould the special character of Ethnic Chinese business.

CHAPTER 4

The Wing On Company in Hong Kong and Shanghai, 1907–1949: A Case Study of a Modern Overseas Chinese Enterprise*

The rapid economic growth of the Four Asian Little Dragons — Taiwan, South Korea, Hong Kong and Singapore — has puzzled many observers, and has altered the perception of the role of Confucianism in economic development. Confucianism has in the past been considered to have retarded China's modernisation, and Confucian values and institutions were believed to be incompatible with modernisation. Due to this new economic development, however, historians have begun to ask how, if Confucianism has retarded China's modernisation, the Four Little Dragons, which have been influenced strongly by Confucian values, could have achieved such remarkable economic success.

To answer this question, some sought explanation in the performance of government and its policies, some in the role of foreign

*   This chapter was first published inYen Ching-hwang, *Studies in modern Overseas Chinese History* (Singapore, Times Academic Press, 1995), pp. 196-236.

capital, and some in the cultural traits of the communities. However, there can be no single factor responsible for the remarkable economic success of these states. This complex phenomenon must be the result of the interplay of several key factors, such as government policy, foreign investment, cultural values and traits, and entrepreneurship.

The elevation of Hong Kong and Singapore to two of the Four Little Dragons also attracted the attention of scholars to the importance of the economic performance of the Overseas Chinese communities. This factor has not received sufficient attention in the past because it was believed that Chinese communities had assumed a subsidiary role in the colonial economies, and that their impact was limited. Perhaps this belief is right in a historical sense, but it hardly does justice to the Chinese during the post-colonial period in Southeast Asia and after the Second World War in East Asia. Overseas Chinese economies contained the seeds of fast economic growth, and had undergone drastic transformation. This was partly as a reaction to the new political environment in Southeast and East Asia, in which political pressure on the Overseas Chinese communities was greater than before, and also because new economic opportunities opened up during the postwar era. Because of these new political and economic challenges, many of the old Overseas Chinese enterprises, which were strongly family-based, were transformed into modern corporate companies.

Overseas Chinese entrepreneurs played an important role in the process of transformation of their enterprises from family-based companies into modern business conglomerates. When, in the second half of the nineteenth century, the Western colonial governments in Southeast Asia engaged in rapid economic development, some talented Overseas Chinese grasped the opportunity to found their family-based enterprises. Men like Oei Tjie Sien and his son Oei Tiong Ham of Java[1], Yap Ah Loy of Kuala

---

1.   See J. Panglaykim and I. Palmer, *Entrepreneurship and Commercial Risk: The Case of a Schumpeterian Business in Indonesia* (Singapore, Nanyang University, 1970); J. Panglaykim and I. Palmer, 'Study of Entrepreneurship in Developing Countries: The Development of One Chinese Concern in Indonesia', in *Journal of Southeast Asian Studies*, vol. 1, no. 1 (March, 1970), pp. 85–95.

Lumpur, and Chang Pi-shih of Penang and Sumatra[2] are just few such entrepreneurs of this generation.

Using the Wing On company in Hong Kong and Shanghai as a case study, this chapter seeks to examine a modern Overseas Chinese enterprise and the role of Overseas Chinese entrepreneurs in its success story. As the Wing On Company in Hong Kong is a modern conglomerate, its success has wider implications for the way in which many similar Overseas Chinese companies may have contributed, to a certain extent, to the economic miracles of Hong Kong and Singapore.

The Kwok Brothers

The Kwok brothers, principally Kwok Lock (also known as James Gocklock) and Kwok Chin (also known as Philip Gockchin) came from the Chuk Sau Yuen village (romanised in Mandarin as Chu Hsiu Yuan), Hsiang Shan district (modern day Chung Shan district) of Kwangtung province. Kwok Lock was born in 1874 and was the second among six brothers, while Kwok Chin was the third, born in 1880. Their father, named P'ei Hsun, was a middle-class peasant who tilled his own land with the help of his children.

Chuk Sau Yuen, a small village in the Hsiang Shan district, was predominantly inhabited by people with the surname Kwok, and most villagers were peasants.[3] The village was no different from millions of other rural villages in South China, and most of its inhabitants were rice farmers supplementing their income by growing vegetables and fruit, and by fishing. What made Chuk Sau Yuen different from many other villages was its proximity to Macao, the

---

2.   For works on Yap Ah Loy, see S.M. Middlebrook, 'Yap Ah Loy', in *Journal of Malayan Branch of The Royal Asiatic Society*, vol. 24, pt. 2 (1951, an independent issue); Wang Chih-yuan, *Yeh Teh-lai chuan* (A Biography of Yap Ah Loy) (Kuala Lumpur, 1958); for works on Chang Pi-shih, see Michael Godley, *The Mandarin-Capitalists from Nanyang: Overseas Chinese Enterprise in the Modernization of China, 1893–1911* (Cambridge University Press, 1981)

3.   See 'Chuk Sau Yuen: A Rural Village of the Chung Shan District', in *The Wing On Life Assurance Company Limited Golden Jubilee Book 1925–1975* (Hong Kong, 1975), pp. 20–21.

earliest Western enclave in South China. The village was a part of a larger geographical unit, the Hsiang Shan district, which was constantly exposed to Western influence because of its closeness to the Portuguese colony of Macao. The emergence of Macao as an international port in East Asia since its founding in the sixteenth century benefited Hsiang Shan tremendously, and it served as a window for the Hsiang-Shanese to the outside world. The Chinese population of Macao in the early nineteenth century was predominantly Hsiang-Shanese,[4] so the villagers in Hsiang-Shan were kept well-informed about the colony. Visiting their home villages during Chinese festivals, the Macao Chinese brought news about the prosperity of the colony, the strange looks and costumes of foreigners, and above all about the employment opportunities in the colony and beyond. Macao, for centuries, attracted tens of thousands of Hsiang-Shanese to work in the colony, and stirred the imagination of many thousands more about the outside world.

Of course, there was also an ugly side to this Portuguese colony. In the early 1830s Macao appeared to be a paradise for European adventurers, drug smugglers, slave dealers, gamblers and prostitutes.[5] With its excellent trade networks with Southeast Asian ports and the existence of a powerful underworld, Macao emerget in 1856 as the centre of the inhumane coolie trade.[6] This thriving trade had sustained the prosperity of the colony for about two decades since its emergence. The cruel treatment of the coolies in

---

4.   The majority of the 30,000 Chinese in Macao in 1835 appear to have been Hsiang-Shanese. See Yeh Hsien-en, 'Ming-Ch'ing chu-chiang san-chiao-chou shang-jen yu shang-yeh huo-tung', in *Chung-kuo shih yen-chiu*, no. 2 (1987).

5.   See A.L. Knt, 'Contribution to an Historical sketch of the Portuguese settlements in China, principally of Macao; of the Portuguese envoys and ambassadors to China, of the Catholic missions in China; and of the papal legates to China', in *The Chinese Repository*, vol. 1 (May 1832 – April 1833), pp. 403–4

6.   For the study of circumstances leading to the rise of Macao as the centre for the coolie trade, see Yen Ching-hwang, *Coolies and Mandarins: China's Protection of Overseas Chinese During the Late Ch'ing Period 1851–1911* (Singapore, Singapore University Press, 1985), pp. 52–56.

the *baracoons* in Macao awaiting export was well-known to people of the neighbouring districts, including the inhabitants of Hsiang Shan. The image of Macao was further tarnished by frequent kidnappings of local people, with the victims being sold to the *baracoons* in Macao. At the time of Macao's emergence as the centre of the coolie trade, kidnapping became so rife in areas around Macao and Canton that there was a public outcry against the kidnappers and the trade.[7]

Despite this image, Macao still served as the inspiration to many Hsiang-Shanese, and the Western influences transmitted through Macao affected the attitudes of many Hsiang-Shanese. Those who aspired to become the new mandarins pursued their studies overseas, such as Yung Wing, a Hsiang-Shanese who studied in the West and became the first Chinese to graduate from an American university, later returning to China to become a mandarin.[8] Others aspiring to be rich and powerful, including famous Hsiang-Shanese Cheng Kuan-ying, Tong King Sing and Hsu Yun,[9] succeeded in becoming influential compradors.[10]

Kwok Lock and Kwok Chin brothers could have followed the same path as Yung Wing had they had the connections with Christian missionaries. Alternatively, they could have become prominent compradors like Cheng Kuan-ying, Tong King-sing or Hsu Yun had they had rich or influential relatives in the business world on the China coast. However, the Kwok brothers were destined to become Overseas Chinese entrepreneurs. What made them prominent was a combination of circumstances and the personal qualities of diligence, insight and perseverance.

7. See 'Translation of a Chinese Placard in Canton respecting Coolie Barracoons at Macao', in FO 97/102A (1856), pp. 88a–88b.
8. For the career of Yung Wing, See Yung Wing's autobiography entitled *My Life in China and America*, (New York, 1909).
9. See biographies of Cheng Kuang-ying, Tong King-sing and Hsu Yun, in Hsu T'i-hsin (ed), *Chung-kuo ch'i-yueh chia lieh-chuan* (Biographies of Chinese Industrialists) vol. 1 (Beijing, Ching-chi jih-pao, 1988), pp. 34–70.
10. For the study of comprador class, see Yen-ping Hao, *The Comprador in Nineteenth Century China; Bridge between East and West*, (Cambridge, Massachusetts, Harvard University Press, 1970).

Socio-economically, the Kwok family were middle-class peasants. The grain produced from the family-owned land was enough to feed the members of the family, but there was little surplus for lean years. Like in many other peasant families in Hsiang Shan, the Kwok boys helped to till the family land, as well as attending the local village school (*Shih-ssu*) for their elementary education. Both Kwok Lock and Kwok Chin appear to have received seven years of traditional education in their home village.[11] Like many other village boys in Hsiang Shan, the young Kwoks must have heard numerous fascinating stories about the outside world, in which land was fertile and plentiful and gold could be picked up from the roadside. They must have cherished the hope of becoming rich and wealthy by making money overseas.

At the age of eighteen, Kwok Lock, the future Overseas Chinese entrepreneur and a founder of the Wing On company, left his home village for Australia as a result of a flood in Hsiang Shan. With HK$280 in his pocket, he arrived in Sydney as a free immigrant in 1892.[12]

The other founder of Wing On, Kwok Chin, took slightly different route from his second brother. In 1894, at the age of fifteen and with the encouragement of his father, Kwok Chin accompanied a relative to Honolulu to try his luck.[13] With the relative's introduction, he got a job with a legal firm as an office boy, providing him with the leisure hours to learn English and the local Hawaiian dialect. After a year, he changed his job and worked for the British Consulate. Kwok Chin's exposure to foreigners provided him with not only the opportunity to learn the English language, but also with an insight into the manners and habits of foreigners which would be useful for his future enterprises in Sydney and Hong Kong.[14] After another year's service with the British Consulate, Kwok Chin decided to try his luck in business. He had

---

11. See Kwok Chin, *Yung-an ching-shen chih fa-jen chi ch'i chang-ch'eng shih-lueh* (The origins of Wing On Spirit and its Development) (Hong Kong, 1961) hereafter referred to as 'Autobiography'.

12. See Chu Lung-k'an, 'Hsuai-hsien yin-chin ch'iao-tzu te Kuo Lo' (Kwok Lock — The Industrialist who used Overseas Chinese Capital, in Hsu T'i-hsin (ed), *Chung-kuo ch'i-yueh chia lieh-chuan*, vol.2, pp. 208–9.

13. See Kwok Chin, Autobiography, p. 2.

saved some money and started a small business, but his luck did not carry the day.[15] After spending three years in Hawaii he returned home, got married and fathered two children. He then decided to try his luck again overseas, and left his home village for Sydney in 1899 to join his second brother.[16]

The Origins of the Wing On Company

Had Kwok Chin stayed in Hawaii and developed his business there, the history of the Wing On company would have been entirely different — indeed it might not have come into existence at all. The arrival of Kwok Chin paved the way for the close cooperation between the two brothers in their entrepreneurial pursuits. Long before their arrival in Sydney, their eldest brother, Kwok Ping Fai, (romanised in Mandarin as Kuo Ping-fei), had accompanied relatives to work in Melbourne, and then in 1882 to Sydney on business.[17] Not too long after the arrival in Sydney of Kwok Lock in 1892, Kwok Ping Fai died from an illness. Kwok Lock had to work as a shop assistant for Wing Sang & Company, which was partly owned by his cousin, George Kwok Bew, (romanised in mandarin as Kuo Piao).[18] Wing Sang & Company was the first Chinese fruit and vegetable wholesale store in Sydney. Founded in 1890 by a group of Hsiang-Shanese in Sydney, it handled a large section of the banana trade with Queensland and Fiji.[19] Wing Sang succeeded in the banana trade and later expanded into the import–export business, making handsome profits from these businesses. In 1894 one of its founders and proprietors, Ma Ying piu (romanised as Ma Ying-piao) decided to start the famous Sincere & Company (known

14.   Ibid.
15.   Ibid.
16.   See Kwok Chin, Autobiography, pp. 3–4.
17.   Kwok Chin, Autobiography, p .4; Chu, 'Hsuai-hsien yin-chin ch'iao-tzu te Kuo Lo', in Hsu T'i-hsin (ed), *Chung-kuo ch'i-yueh chia lieh-chuan*, vol. 2, p. 208.
18.   See Chu, op. cit., p. 209.
19.   See C.F. Yong, *The New Gold Mountain: The Chinese in Australia, 1901–1921* (Adelaide, Raphael Arts, 1977), p. 56.

in Chinese as *Hsien Shih kung-ssu*) in Hong Kong with the money he had made in Sydney.[20] The young shop assistant Kwok Lock must have been impressed by the success of Wing Sang, and at the same time was quickly learning how to handle the same kind of business. With few years' work experience and savings, and together with two good friends, Leung Chong (romanised as Liang Ch'ang) and Ma Cho Seng (romanised as Ma Tsu-hsing), he founded the Wing On Fruit Store (*Yung-an kuo-lan*) on 1 August 1897. The initial capital of the company was only 1,400 Australian pounds.[21] In the following year, three of his young brothers, Kwok Yik Fai (romanised as Kuo I-fei), Kwok Yuen Fai (romanised as Kuo Yuan-fei) and the youngest, Kwok Ho Fai (romanised as Kuo He-fei), joined him in Sydney, and Kwok Ho Fai assisted him in the fruit store.[22] When Kwok Chin arrived in Sydney in 1899, all of the Kwok brothers were reunited overseas, and his arrival helped to strengthen the foundation of their business in Sydney.

The founding of the Wing On Fruit Store in Sydney began a new chapter in the Kwok brothers' success story, and was the harbinger of Kwok Brothers' future business empire in Hong Kong and China. Although in the same line of business as Wing Sang & Company, the Wing On Fruit Store did not become a fierce competitor, but rather a close business partner of Wing Sang. The banana trade was a lucrative business in which the Hsiang-Shanese in Sydney occupied predominant position. As early as the 1880s, the Chinese became the principal banana cultivators in North Queensland.[23] They marketed their produce in Australia in 1890s through an effective network of distribution agencies in Sydney, Melbourne, Adelaide and Perth.[24] Both Wing Sang and later Wing On were two major agencies.

20. See *Hsien–shih kung–ssu erh–shih wu chou–nien chi–nien ch'ih*, (The Souvenir Magazine of the Silver Jubilee Celebration of the Sincere Company), (Hong Kong, shang-wu yin-shu kuan, 1924).

21. See Kwok Chin, Autobiography, p. 4; Chu, op. cit., p. 209.

22. Kwok Chin, Autobiography, p. 4.

23. See C.F. Yong, 'The Banana Trade and the Chinese in New South Wales and Victoria, 1901–1921', in *ANU Historical Journal, 1965–1966*, vol. I, no. 2, p. 28.

24. See C.F. Yong, *The New Gold Mountain*, op. cit. p. 48.

As the scope for all types of business was wide, there were plenty of opportunities for everyone, which perhaps partly explains why Wing On was not Wing Sang's business rival. Another factor which may help explain the close co-operation between Wing On and Wing Sang was their geographical and kinship ties. All of the proprietors of the two companies came from the neighbouring villages of Hsiang Shan, and spoke the same dialect; and of course one of Wing Sang's proprietors was Kwok Lock's cousin.[25] In addition, as Kwok Lock had worked with Wing Sang for several years, he must have felt indebted to Wing Sang and particularly to his cousin. Since the conflict of interest was minimal and the kinship ties were strong, the Wing On and Wing Sang companies worked closely together in the banana trade, and attempted to expand their interests to direct cultivation of bananas in the Fiji islands. In 1902, Wing On and Wing Sang, together with another Hsiang-Shanese controlled fruit store, Wing Tiy (romanised as Yung T'ai) went into partnership to form a company named Sang On Tiy (romanised as Sheng Yung T'ai) which undertook the cultivation of bananas in Fiji. The name of the new company, Sang On Tiy, resulted from combining the last name of the three companies, and served as a clear indication of the close cooperation between the three fruit stores in their common venture. Young and enterprising Kwok Chin, who had worked with Wing On for some time, was appointed manager of Sang On Tiy. The company had 350 acres of cultivated banana plantations, and managed to supply the Sydney stores with some 10,000 bunches of bananas fortnightly.[26]

The Founding of Wing On in Hong Kong

What really motivated the Kwok Brothers to found the Wing On company may not be fully known, due to a lack of reliable information. Late Ch'ing Overseas Chinese nationalism, which played a part in the contribution of Overseas Chinese entrepreneurs such as Chang Pi-shih,

---

25. See Chu, op. cit., p. 209.
26. See C.F. Yong, *The New Gold Mountain*, op, cit., p. 49; C.F.Yong, 'The Banana Trade', op. cit., p.28; Kwok Chin, Autobiography, p. 5.

Chang Yu-nan and Ch'en I-hsi to the economic modernisation of China, did not seem to have a significant impact on the Kwok Brothers.[27] Although no trace of Overseas Chinese nationalism can be found in Kwok Chin's autobiography, it is reasonable to suggest that the Kwok brothers must have heard of Chang Pi-shih, Chang Yu-nan and Ch'en I-hsi and their deeds in China, and this may have inspired them to undertake a major Overseas Chinese enterprise in Hong Kong. However, the Kwok brothers had nowhere near the wealth of Chang Pi-shih, Chang Yu-nan and Ch'en I-hsi. Indeed, the relatively small capital that the Kwok brothers possessed in 1907 perhaps explains, in part, why they founded a relatively modest enterprise like Wing On instead of undertaking larger enterprises like the railways in south China built by the two Changs and Ch'en I-hsi.

What motivated the Kwok brothers to found a modern department store in Hong Kong seems to have been the enormous economic potential of Hong Kong Chinese society. Hong Kong, a westernised city, prospered under British administration. It was geographically close to the home district of the Kwok brothers, and was much better located than Sydney between the Eastern and Western worlds. Most of the people in Hong Kong were Chinese from the southern part of Kwangtung, and Cantonese was the *lingua franca* of the population. These Chinese, though they retained many of their traditional values, were more exposed to foreign influences than their compatriots in China. As a result, a modern Western-style department store would have a better chance of succeeding in

27.   For the Overseas Chinese contribution to late Ch'ing economic modernisation, see Yen Ching-hwang, 'The Overseas Chinese and Late Ch'ing Economic Modernization', in *Modern Asian Studies*, vol. 16, no. 2 (1982), pp. 217–232; for Chang Pi-shih's contribution, see Michael Godley, *The Mandarin-Capitalists from Nanyang*, (Cambridge, 1981); for Chang Yu–nan's contribution, see Yen Ching-hwang, 'Chang Yu-nan and Chaochow Railways, 1904–1908' in *Modern Asian Studies*, vol. 18, no. 1 (1984), pp. 119–135; for Ch'en I-hsi's contribution, see Liu I-tsun, Cheng Teh-hua & Lucie Cheng, 'Hua-ch'iao, Hsin-ning tieh-lu yu T'ai-shan' (Overseas Chinese, Hsin Ning Railways & The T'ai Shan District), in *Hua–ch'iao lun–wen chi*, vol. I (Canton, 1982), pp. 304–340.

Hong Kong than in Chinese cities such as Canton or Shanghai. To the Kwok brothers, this venture was a calculated risk which might eventually produce immense profits.

Neither the founders nor the descendants of the Wing On company like to acknowledge openly their debt of inspiration to the Sincere Company which was founded seven years earlier than theirs, but some of the leaders of the Wing On have privately admitted that the Wing On founders were influenced by Ma Ying-piu, the founder of the Sincere Company in Hong Kong.[28] Ma Ying-piu, a Hsiang-Shanese from a village neighbouring the Kwok brothers' home village, founded the first modern Chinese department store in Hong Kong in January 1900.[29] Four years' struggle in overcoming the initial problems began to bring the company success. By 1904, it started to make a profit and distributed dividends to the shareholders.[30] Given the fact that there existed close contacts between the Hsiang-Shanese back home and Hong Kong on the one hand, and the Hsiang-Shanese in Sydney on the other, Ma Ying-piu's success in his department store must have been known to the Kwok brothers, and perhaps inspired them to found a similar one in Hong Kong where opportunities were better still than in Sydney.

Whatever their motives and influences, the Kwok brothers' decision to found a department store in Hong Kong changed their lives and future, and led them to join the rank of Ma Ying-piu as early Overseas Chinese entrepreneurs. The Kwok brothers' involvement in the banana trade and the import–export business not only provided them with insight into business world, but also prepared them for the founding of Wing On. Their social and business networks

28.　See my interview with Dr. Russel Kwok, director and general manager of the Wing On Company, Hong Kong, on 11 December 1990 at the Wing On Centre, 211 Des Voeux Road, Central, Hong Kong.

29.　See 'Hsien-shih kung-ssu erh-shih wu nien ching-kuo shih' (Twenty-five years of the Founding of the Sincere Company), in *Hsien-shih kung-ssu erh-shih wu chou-nien chi-nien ch'ih* (The Sincere Company Limited: Twenty Fifth Anniversary, 1900–1924) (Shang Wu, Hong Kong, 1924), *Chi Chai* (records) column, p. 1.

30.　Ibid., p. 2.

in Sydney and Fiji proved to be extremely useful in floating capital for the proposed department store in Hong Kong, and a sum of HK$160,000 was raised among the Hsiang-Shanese in Sydney.[31] Kwok Chin, who had some knowledge of the English language as well as business acumen, was entrusted by the group to carry out the actual task of founding the department store in Hong Kong. Returning to Hong Kong in 1907, he rented a shop at 167 Queen's Road, Central as the premises for the new company, and the name Wing On (Yung An) which means 'eternal peace', was chosen. The store was officially opened on 28 August 1907.[32]

Teething Problems

Any modern enterprise needs the backing of capital to succeed. Even with the flow of capital, an enterprise encounters the problems of staff, management and marketing. The sum of HK$160,000 as starting capital for Wing On was by no means huge, but it gave the company a modest start. A five-year contract for the shop premises was signed, and more than ten people were employed. By the time rent and wages were paid, the level of recurrent capital was low. The form of partnership from which the Kwok brothers raised their initial capital was traditional, and it inhibited the company from tapping wider sources of capital from within the community, causing a shortfall which humbled Wing On and handicapped its proper development.

Wing On, as a modern enterprise, could not afford to be run in a traditional Chinese way. The Kwok brothers had learned how to use modern bank facilities in Sydney to overcome the problem of capital shortfalls. They quickly extended their social tentacles to

31. See Kwok chin, Autobiography, p. 6. Another source claimed that a sum of HK$150,000 was raised as the starting capital for Wing On. See Liu T'ien-jen, 'Pen kung-ssu erh-shih wu chou-nien chih ching-kuo' (The Historical Records of Wing On in the last Twenty Five Years), in *Hsiang-kang Yung-an yu-hsien kung-ssu nien-wu chou-nien chi-nien lu* (The Wing On Company Limited, Hong Kong: In Commemoration of 25th Anniversary, 1907–1932) (T'ien Hsing Press, Hong Kong, 1932), *Shih Lueh* (History) column, p. 1.
32. See Kwok Chin, Autobiography, p. 6.

the high society of Hong Kong, in which useful contacts were made. They got to know Robert Ho Tung, a powerful Chinese comprador and a wealthy merchant in Hong Kong.[33] With the support of Ho Tung, the Kwok brothers obtained their first big loan of HK$600,000 from the Hong Kong and Shanghai Banking Corporation.[34] This loan, almost four times its initial capital, helped Wing On to overcome its financial difficulties and provided additional capital for expansion. The company would have been in a sorry state had this capital not been forthcoming, and the story of Wing On would have been very different. The loan was repaid promptly according to the agreement. Now with a good reputation in financial circles, Wing On had no difficulty in obtaining more loans from the Hong Kong and Shanghai Bank and other financial institutions.[35] This ability to obtain loans from banks assured the flow of capital to Wing On for further development.

Wing On was a modern department store which practised a 'one price' policy, contrary to the traditional Chinese practice of hard bargaining. The absence of remarks about Wing On having problems in its early stages, either in Kwok Chin's autobiography or in Wing On's *Twenty Fifth Anniversary Magazine,* can be interpreted as suggesting that the 'one price' policy did not encounter any serious problems. Perhaps the Chinese shoppers in Hong Kong had been gradually accustomed to this practice by the Sincere Company seven years ago.[36]

Wing On also avoided another potential problem by not employing female shop assistants. The Sincere Company had done so in its early days, despite the fact that Chinese society still held a woman's place to be in the family rather than in business. This new practice had been dropped by Sincere because of strong social resistance, to the extent

33. See Ho Wen-hsiang, *Hsiang-kang chia-tsu shih* (History of Some Powerful Families in Hong Kong) (Hong Kong, 1989), p. 11.
34. See Kwok Chin, Autobiography, p. 6.
35. Ibid.
36. For the problems caused by the 'one price' policy encountered by the Sincere Company, see 'Hsien-shih kung-ssu erh-shih wu nien ching-kuo shih', in *Hsien-shih kung-ssu erh-shih wu chou-nien chi-nien chih,* p. 1.

that the business of the company had been harmed.[37] Presumably Wing On had the advantage of learning by the mistakes made by Sincere, and avoided adopting a practice which might otherwise have hampered its growth.

Success in tiding over the problems of the company in its early stages should partly be attributed to the stability of the leadership. Two years after Wing On came into existence, Kwok Lock arrived in Hong Kong from Sydney to join the company. He was made chairman, and Kwok Chin retained his position as general manager. Another partner, Tu Tse-wen (also known as David Jackman) was made deputy general manager.[38] The arrival of Kwok Lock and Tu Tse-wen greatly strengthened the leadership of the company at the top, and together with Kwok Chin they formed a strong team. Kwok Lock, who had business acumen and had accumulated immense experience in Sydney, was a charismatic leader. He was warm and honest,[39] and was a good public relations man who had made useful contacts and improved Wing On's public image. Meanwhile, his brother Kwok Chin was relatively quiet, but good at administration and planning; they seemed to complement each other.[40] Tu Tse-wen, who had himself accumulated ample business experience in Australia, was also a good and efficient administrator. He assisted Kwok Chin to manage the company and planned for its expansion. This three-man team obviously worked well and complemented each other in personality and skills.

37. Ibid, pp. 1–2.
38. Kwok Chin, Autobiography, p. 6.
39. It was claimed by a writer that Kwok Lock returned £500 to the bank in Australia, which had mistakenly overpaid him. See Chu, 'Hsuai-hsien yin-chin ch'iao-tzu te Kuo Lo' (Kwok Lock — The Industrialist Who used Overseas Chinese Capital), in Hsu T'i-hsin, (ed), *Chung-kuo ch'i-yueh chia lieh-chuan*, vol. 2, pp. 209–210.
40. See 'Interview with Dr. Russel Kwok, Director and General Manager of the Wing On Company, Hong Kong, on 11 December 1990 at the Wing On Centre, 211 Des Voeux Road, Central, Hong Kong'.

The Structure of the Company

Traditional Chinese firms were based on partnership or sole proprietorship. Sole proprietorship would take the form of family ownership. Families owned and managed the firm, and recruited its staff mainly from their members or relatives. When the proprietor or his family members or relatives were unable to manage the firm, he would hire a full-time manager known as *Chang-kuei* (literally, 'holder of counter') who would take charge of the running of the business.[41] Partnership was a multiple ownership of a firm by several partners. It could take the form of near-equal share partners, or of a mixture of major and minor partners. These partners were usually friends, relatives or persons of same locality. Obviously, the organisation of the partnership was based on kinship, friendship and geographical ties. Usually, the major partners would assume control over the firm personally, or would recommend their trusted relatives to fill the post of manager.

One striking characteristic of traditional Chinese firms was the close connection between the ownership and the management. The control and running of the firm were done either by the owners by their trusted relatives; there was little or no chance for the development of the professional managers of modern times. The absence of a professional managerial class does not mean the lack of specialisation and dynamism. Given the right leadership at the top, traditional Chinese firms were capable of massive expansion and growth. Wellington K.K. Chan in his study of the Jui-Fu-Hsiang company in Peking has clearly demonstrated how a traditional firm was capable of expanding to twenty-five branches with about one thousand staff at its height in around 1925.[42] The dynamism of Jui-Fu-Hsiang was very much connected with the able leadership of Meng Lo-ch'uan (1850–1939) who, together with his chief assistant Meng Chin-hou, developed a highly personalised system of management which

---

41. For a discussion of the structure of traditional Chinese firm, see Wellington K.K. Chan, 'The Organizational Structure of the Traditional Chinese Firm and Its Modern Reform', in *Business History Review*, vol. LVI, no. 2 (Summer 1982), pp. 219–222.
42. Ibid, pp. 222–223.

achieved a high degree of centralisation and control of this large enterprise. Meng Lo-ch'uan maintained his centralised control over the firm through a personalised network of trusted subordinates and a formal structure of meetings and written reports. He selected his branch managers personally on the basis of ability and loyalty. He required regular written reports from his branch managers, and personally conducted two major meetings each year attended by all branch managers and his chief assistant to review the progress and strategy of the business. Jui-Fu-Hsiang was thus run in the traditional Chinese way, with a strong leadership at the top. Meng Lo-ch'uan was an autocratic, paternalistic and astute businessman, and treated his business as his private estate and his staff as his children. He was also innovative. His innovation ensured the company's success in a changing political environment and changing market conditions. Under his leadership, the company seized opportunities to branch out into new lines of business and achieved dramatic growth. To reward his staff's loyalty and hard work, he developed a system of bonus shares which were to replace the traditional *jen-li* shares for the hired manager.[43]

Wing On was not a traditional Chinese company like Jui-Fu-Hsiang in Peking, nor was it a completely westernised modern company. Like the Sincere company founded by Ma Ying-piu in 1900, it was a company that combined both traditional Chinese and modern Western elements. This hybrid structure was the Kwok brothers' creation, based on their education, personal experience and traditional values. Both Kwok Lock and Kwok Chin had keenly observed and borrowed modern Western practice in doing business in Sydney, and Kwok Chin in particular had acquired some knowledge about the West while he was working as an office assistant in a legal firm and the British Consulate in Honolulu. However, none of them had received any formal Western education, nor had they worked in a Western enterprise like Chinese compradors had on the China Coast. Even had they desired to run a completely westernised modern company, they were incapable of doing so. On the other hand, the traditional education they received in their home village, the

---

43. Ibid., pp. 224–225.

predominantly Chinese environment in which they lived in Sydney and the Confucian value system under by they were influenced led them to retain some traditional Chinese attitudes towards the running of a business. This was most obviously reflected in the way they treated and trained their staff.

Wing On started with the traditional form of partnership. Each partner contributed a sum of capital and helped with the running of the business. The Kwok brothers were the major partners, and the minor partners of the company included Tu Tse-wen, Kuo Hsien-wen and Liang Fan-nan.[44] Starting with HK$160,000 as initial capital, the company's traditional form of partnership expanded its base by enlarging the number of partners. By 1912, the partnership was expanded and the capital of the company had been increased to HK$600,000.[45] However, this traditional form of partnership proved in time to be inadequate in acquiring new capital in order to remain competitive in retail business and to achieve rapid growth. The company was thus changed from a partnership to a modern Western public liability company in 1916, with a capital of HK$2,000,000. Control of the company, however, still remained in the hands of Kwok brothers and their fellow Hsiang-Shanese.

Little is known about the early structure of the Wing On company. With slightly more than ten employees to start with, Wing On appears to have had a simple two-tier structure of management and general staff, with strong close links between ownership and management. Both Kwok Lock and Kwok Chin were heavily involved in the running of the business. With the broadening of the partnership at the beginning of the Republican era and the change of the company from private to public ownership, Wing On underwent substantial changes in structure. By 1932, when the company celebrated its twenty-fifth anniversary, it was a large conglomerate with many branches in Hong Kong, Shanghai, Canton, Southeast Asia, Australia and the United States. At that time, the parent company in Hong Kong was distinguished by its three-tier

44. See Kwok Chin, Autobiography, p. 6.
45. See Liu T'ien-jen, 'Pen kung-ssu erh shih-wu chou-nien chih ching-kuo', in *Hsiang-kang Yung-an yu-hsien kung-ssu nien-wu chou-nien chi-nien lu, Shih-lueh* column, p. 2.

structure and by having a modern outlook. A board of directors was headed by a chairman who carried the title *tsung-chien-tu*. The directors were elected by shareholders. Like modern company, the board was responsible for making major decisions and produced an annual report for the shareholders signed by the *tsung-chien-tu*. Kwok Lock, one of the original founders, remained as the *tsung-chien-tu* for at least the first twenty-five years.[46]

Under the board of directors were the management and the general staff. The management, which was responsible for implementing the policy laid down by the board, was headed by a general manager with a Chinese title of *ssu-li* and by a deputy general manager with the Chinese title *fu-ssu-li*. In 1932, the management of the parental company in Hong Kong consisted of a general office (*tsung-wu pu*), a cashiers' office (*tsung-shou-chih pu*), a purchasing office (*pan-fuo pu*), a general accounting office (*chung chang-fang*), a bills and cost accounting office (*hsi chang-fang*), a shares office (*ku-wu pu*), and an estate office (*tsu-wu pu*). The management came under the strong domination of Kwok Chin, who became the general manager of the company throughout Wing On's history. The overlapping between ownership and managerial responsibility may not be too desirable in a modern multinational conglomerate nowadays, but in Chinese society in Hong Kong before the Second World War, this overlapping gave the managers additional authority to run the company. As many Chinese employees in Overseas Chinese communities have little concept of public ownership,[47] Wing On's employees after 1916 still viewed the company as the Kwok family's controlled enterprise, and Kwok Chin's general managership still commanded the authority of ownership. This gave him extra power to run the company in the way he saw fit.

46.   See 'lists of the Chairman and Directors of the Board of Wing On Company of Hong Kong', in *Hsiang-kang Yung-an yu-hsien kung-ssu nien-wu chou-nien chi-nien lu*, Shih-Lueh column, pp. 12–16.

47.   Gordon Redding, in his study of overseas managers, has found that overseas Chinese employees have more respect for ownership than for managerial responsibility. See Gordon Redding, *The Spirit of Chinese Capitalism*, (Berlin & New York, Walter de Gruyter, 1990) pp. 158–59.

The general rank and file of staff at Wing On were grouped together under the control of the trading department, which was the company's specialisation. They were divided into groups and attached to various sub-departments dealing in particular commodities. Each sub-department was under the control of a head, and the staff of that sub-department were trained to conduct sales and to provide customers with excellent service. By 1932 there were fifty sub-departments covering a wide range of commodities from throughout the world. They included sub-departments for general goods and services such as furniture, chinaware, electrical appliances, gold jewellery, hardware, groceries, men's wear, ladies wear, money exchangers, medicine, music, optical, perfumery and photo supplies. They also included sub-departments for highly specialised commodities, from blankets, buttons, handbags and umbrellas to handkerchiefs and towels, to Chinese and European shoes.[48]

The success story of the Wing On company would not be complete if the company's policy on staff training were not explored. The company's attitude towards its staff was fundamentally paternalistic and moralistic, qualities which also characterised many modern Japanese enterprises.[49] This was by no means a historical coincidence, but rather the product of blending Confucian and Western cultures, of mixing the Confucian values of paternalism and moralism with the Western values of pragmatism and inquisitiveness. The Kwok brothers consciously tried to blend these two cultures in order to succeed in a westernised society such as Hong Kong, as had the Japanese entrepreneurs during and after the Meiji period — and it worked.

Wing On's attitude towards its staff derived from the traditional Chinese concept of family and the Confucian concept of mutual responsibility. In the eyes of the Kwok brothers the company was a big

48. See Liu T'ien-jen, 'Pen kung-ssu erh-shih-wu chou-nien chih ching–kuo', in *Hsiang-kang Yung-an yu-hsien kung-ssu nien-wu chou-nien chi-nien lu*, *Shih-lueh* column, pp. 4–5; see also the English summary of this article, p. 4.

49. For paternalism in the management of Japanese industry, see Solomon B. Levine, *Industrial Relations in Postwar Japan*.

family unit, they were the heads of that family and the employees were members of this large extended family. The Kwok brothers were morally obliged to look after the interests of the employees and, in return, the employees were to work their utmost for the interests of the company. The Kwok brothers seemed to be strong believers in moulding the characters of their staff through moral and intellectual cultivation. Kwok Chin in his autobiography clearly spelled out that employees should be inculcated with the traditional Chinese values of hard work, thrift, loyalty, sincerity, uprightness and trustworthiness; and that character-building should start with the senior staff of the company who would set examples for their subordinates to follow.[50] Kwok Chin also believed in the use of talent and the development of the intellectual standards of his employees. He emphasised merit as the only principle for appointment and promotion in the company.[51] This of course was not a traditional Chinese value, but a modern Western principle for running a large business organisation. Kwok Chin saw fit to adopt this principle for the Wing On.

In accordance with the principles of moral and intellectual cultivation of the employees, Wing On set up two separate departments for moral education (*teh-yu pu*) and intellectual cultivation (*chih-yu pu*). The former conducted a weekly lecture for staff. Prominent members of society in Hong Kong or overseas were invited to deliver lectures in an attempt to inculcate moral values into the minds of the employees as well as improving their knowledge. The latter organised English night classes and set up newspaper reading rooms. For those employees who had no previous English education, English night classes provided them with an excellent opportunity to learn a foreign language, which was of increasing importance in this British colony.[52] In addition, the department of intellectual cultivation also founded a drama troupe and a music ensemble for the recreation of the employees.[53]

50. See Kwok Chin, Autobiography, pp. 27–8.
51. Ibid, p.27.
52. See Liu T'ien-jen, 'Pen kung-ssu erh-shih-wu chou-nien chih ching-kuo', in *Hsiang-kang Yung-an yu-hsien kung-ssu nien-wu chou-nien chi-nien lu, Shih-lueh* column, p. 5.
53. Ibid.

In addition to moral and intellectual cultivation, the Wing On company also founded a department of physical education which was to take care of the physical well-being of the employees. The department organised and promoted Chinese martial arts, football and swimming in the belief that a good moral and intellectual mind must be complemented by a healthy body. A combination of virtues and physical health would make a perfect employee who would make important contributions to the success of the company. As swimming became an increasingly popular outdoor sport in Hong Kong, the company went out of its way to promote swimming as part of employee's physical health. The company formed a swimming club and erected a swimming shed in North Point, of which employees and their family members were encouraged to take advantage. A free car service was even provided nightly after business hours, between the company offices and the North Point swimming shed.[54]

The Wing On Company in Shanghai

Wing On would have been relatively insignificant in Overseas Chinese history and the economic history of China had it not expanded into Shanghai, the hub of trade, business and finance in China, and grown to become the leader of the four largest Chinese department stores in China. What precisely motivated Kwok brothers to found their company in Shanghai is uncertain. No direct comments can be found in Kwok Chin's autobiography, and the explanation given in the company's *Twenty Fifth Anniversary Magazine* for the founding of a Wing On branch in Shanghai is vague. It stated that 'Shanghai is one of the four largest markets in China. Its location is central. It is the financial centre of China where Chinese and foreign merchants concentrated. To follow the trend, the company founded a branch in Shanghai in 1917'.[55] What we can extract from this statement are two relevant points: the immense business potential offered and the trend of setting up Chinese companies in Shanghai. Shanghai emerged

---

54. See Liu T'ien-jen, op. cit., p. 6 and the English summary, p. 6.
55. See Liu T'ien-jen, op. cit., in *Hsiang-kang Yung-an yu-hsien kung-ssu nien-wu chou-nien chi-nien lu*, *Shih-lueh* column, p. 8.

as a centre of commerce in the 1840s, and by the end of the nineteenth century it became China's foreign trade entrepot and financial centre.[56] Shanghai was also the city in which wealthy foreign and Chinese merchants concentrated. In 1899 there were an estimated 10,000 Chinese compradors in China,[57] and at least half of them were in Shanghai. Since Chinese compradors and other types of merchants in Shanghai were rich, the purchasing power of their family members must have been enormous. At the same time, their taste for foreign imported goods had been quickly developed in Shanghai and other Treaty ports. This is clearly reflected in the increased import of foreign luxurious commodities such as perfume, cosmetics and carpets; the import of high-quality perfume and cosmetics into Shanghai, for instance, increased from 50,405 *taels* in 1894 to 319,822 *taels* in 1911, a sixfold increase in volume.[58] The value of the import of luxurious carpets, tablecloths and bedroom items rose from about 200,000 *taels* in 1904 to about 1,000,000 *taels* in 1911.[59] The Kwok brothers, who were schumpeterian-style entrepreneurs, must have quickly realised the great potential of Shanghai for making wealth. Their constant pursuit of profits drove them to look for new locations for expansion, and their insight into the business world led them to recognise Shanghai as the best venue for the expansion of Wing On outside Hong Kong.

With regard to the trend of setting up Chinese large department stores in Shanghai, the Wing On *Twenty Fifth Anniversary Magazine*

56. See Tang Zhan-chang (ed) *Shang-hai Shih* (A History of Shanghai) (Shanghai, 1989) pp. 359–83; Liu Hui-wu, *Shang-hai chin-tai shih* (A Modern History of Shanghai) vol. 1 (Shanghai, 1985), pp. 222–30; Shang-hai she-hui k'o-hsueh-yuan Ching-chi yen-chiu so (ed), *Shang-hai tui-wai mo-i* (Shanghai Foreign Trade, 1840–1949) vol. I, (Shanghai, 1989), pp. 155–203.

57. See Yen-p'ing Hao, *The Comprador in Nineteenth Century China: Bridge between East and West* (Cambridge, Massachusetts, Harvard University Press, 1970), p. 102.

58. See Shanghai Pai-fuo kung-ssu et al. (eds), *Shanghai chin-tai pai-fuo shang-yeh shih* (A History of Department Stores of Modern Shanghai) (Shanghai she-hui k'o-hsueh-yuan, Shanghai, 1988), p.100, hereafter referred to as 'Shang-yeh shih'.

59. Ibid.

was unspecific. Perhaps it meant that new opportunities for native Chinese capitalists during the First World War period were good. Due to the deep involvement of the Western powers in the war, the position of Western capitalists in China had been greatly weakened. This gave excellent opportunities for native Chinese capitalists to expand their economic activities in the Treaty ports. More specifically, these opportunities were first quickly seized by Ma Ying-piu, who set up the first large Chinese department store in Shanghai in 1914.[60] The founding of the Sincere Company in Shanghai and its initial success must have inspired the Kwok brothers and other native Chinese capitalists.

In 1915, the second year of the First World War (also the second year of operation for the Sincere Company in Shanghai), the Kwok brothers began their preparations for the founding of the Wing On company in Shanghai. The successful expansion of the partnership of the Wing On in Hong Kong in 1912 gave the Kwok brothers much confidence in raising the huge capital needed for the proposed company. The transformation of Wing On in Hong Kong from a partnership into a public company in 1916 further strengthened their confidence in raising capital from among the general public. With HK$2,500,000 targeted as capital for the proposed company, the Kwok brothers invested HK$670,000 worth of shares, while the bulk of the capital was raised from among the Overseas Chinese.[61] The floating of company stock was not without problems, but with the Kwok brothers' experience and reputation among the Overseas Chinese, and with the help of their business associates in Hong Kong and Sydney such as David Jackman, Sun Chih-hsing, Li Yen-hsiang, Lin Tse-shen, Yang Chin-hua and Ou-yang min-ch'ing, the proposed Wing On branch in Shanghai overcame its difficulties and raised the targeted sum.[62]

---

60. See 'Hsien-shih kung-ssu erh-shih-wu nien ching-kuo shih' (A History of the Founding of the Sincere Company), in *Hsien-shih kung-ssu erh-shih-wu chou-nien chi-nien ch'ih* (The Sincere Company Limited: Twenty Fifth Anniversary 1900–1924) *Shang-wu*, Hong Kong, 1924, *Chi Tsai* column, p.3.

61. See Chu Lung-k'an, 'Shuai-hsien yin chin ch'iao-tzu teh Kuo Lo', in Hsu T'i-hsin (ed), *Chung-kuo ch'i-yueh chia lieh-chuan*, vol. 2, p. 211.

62. See Kwok Chin, Autobiography, p. 8; Shang-yeh shih, p. 104.

With much of the capital assured, Kwok Chin and his younger brother Kwok Yik Fai left for Shanghai in July 1917 in an attempt to acquire a suitable site for the proposed branch. In October of the same year, a large block of land of 8.732 acres in Nanking Road, Shanghai was found. It was located opposite the Sincere Company and had immense business potential. Kwok Chin signed a thirty-year lease with the owner, a rich British real estate merchant, at 50,000 silver *taels* per year.[63] The acquiring of the site in Nanking Road prompted Kwok Lock to go to Shanghai to take charge of the construction of the project with the help of his brother Kwok Yik Fai. After more than a year's construction, a modern six-storey building was completed. The appearance of the Wing On building was similar to that of the Sincere Company, but its interior design was superior: it was more spacious, brighter and had more room for customers to move around.[64]

As the preparation for the opening of the Wing On branch in Shanghai shifted into top gear, many experienced senior staff of the head office in Hong Kong were sent to Shanghai. Yang Hui-t'ing, a director of Wing On in Hong Kong and a close business associate of the Kwok brothers, was appointed general manager, and he was aided by Ma Chu-hsing, another experienced businessman who assumed the position of deputy general manager.[65] The head office also gathered the best and most up-to-date commodities and despatched them to Shanghai for the grand opening. In addition, the Kwok brothers also adopted the modern business strategy of making full use of the media, and widely publicised the grand opening of Wing On in most of the Shanghai newspapers. The large eye-catching advertisements for the grand opening appeared continuously in Shanghai Chinese newspapers for a fortnight, and the political elite and leaders of the community were invited to attend the function. On 5 September 1918, the Wing On branch in Shanghai was officially opened for business, and the building was packed with invited

---

63. See 'Shang-hai shih Huang-p'u ch'u huang-ti ch'an kuan-li chi tang-an' (The Archives of the Bureau of Property Management of the Huang P'u Area of the Municipality of Shanghai), cited by Shang-yeh shih, p. 104

64. See Shang-yeh, shih, p. 105

65. See Kwok Chin, Autobiography. p. 9.

dignitaries and well-wishers. The grand opening was a great success, and successfully promoted the new company as a top class Chinese emporium which emphasised quality and fair prices. The stock, which was expected to be sold in months, was cleared within three weeks. Apart from selling good quality imported goods throughout the world, the Wing On branch also ran hotel, restaurant, amusement park and money savings businesses.[66]

The success of the Shanghai branch was expected. It can be measured clearly in terms of turnover and net profit. In 1918, the first year of Wing On's operations, its turnover was $1.58 million with a small net profit of $15,000. The modest success for the first year was obviously due to the short trading period (about four months) and the cost of offsetting the huge expenses involved in the preparation of the grand opening. In 1919 the net profit of the company rose steeply to $620,000, with a massive turnover of $4.556 million for that year.[67] The business of the Wing On company continued to grow spectacularly, from an annual turnover of $4.556 million in 1919 to $6.999 million in 1921, $8.153 million in 1923 and the remarkable figure of $9.78 million in 1925, more than double the turnover in 1919. The net profit also rose rapidly from $620,000 in 1919 to $724,000 in 1921, $1,016,000 in 1923 and $1,103,000 in 1925, just short of double the 1919 figure.[68] The growth of the Wing On business was sustained and had reached its peak in 1931 with an annual turnover of $13.637 million and a net profit of $2,475,000, double the net profit figure of 1925.[69] By this time, the Wing On company had already emerged as the leader of the four large Chinese emporia in Shanghai, namely the Wing On, the Sincere Company, the Hsin Hsin Company and the Ta Hsin Company.

The success of the Wing On company in Shanghai was not accidental. It was the result of a combination of various factors:

---

66. See Chu Lung-k'ang, op. cit., in Hsu Ti-hsin (ed), *Chung-kuo ch'i-yueh chia lieh-chuan*, p. 209.
67. See 'Shang-hai Yung-an kung-ssu li-nien ying-yeh nger chi yin-li ch'ing-k'uang' (The Table of Annual Turn-overs and Net Profits of the Wing on Company of Shanghai), in Shang yeh shih, p. 151.
68. Ibid, pp. 151–152.
69. Ibid.

foresight, planning, organisation and circumstances. The foresight and experience of the Kwok brothers had contributed to the planning, management and the strategy of running the Wing On branch in Shanghai. The major policies of the branch were made by the board of directors in the head office in Hong Kong. The Shanghai branch, in view of its importance, had a chairman with the title of *chien-tu*, and under him were the general manager and deputy general manager. The chairmanship of the branch was first held by Kwok Lock himself, who was also the chairman of the board of directors of the head office, and it later passed to Kwok Bew, the cousin of the Kwok brothers, who had returned to China from Sydney.[70]

The organisation of the Wing On branch in Shanghai was modelled after the head office in Hong Kong. The company was divided into the administrative and trading arms under the control of a general manager and his deputy. The two arms were sub-divided into departments with specialised functions, and there was a clear line of authority vertically organised from top to bottom. It was certainly very efficient, and met the standards of a modern large Western company.

The success of the Wing On branch was partly due to its policies on buying, marketing and borrowing. As a large emporium which sold commodities from all over the world, Wing On's policy-makers were quick to find out that the best buying policy for the company was to have direct access to the factories and to cut out the middlemen. This gave Wing On a competitive edge. To by-pass the foreign agencies in Shanghai, Wing On sent people directly to foreign countries in order to import certain goods which had great potential in the Chinese market. Sole agency rights were sought from overseas producers which would guarantee a high profit margin in Shanghai. Special purchasing agents in foreign countries were also sometimes appointed by Wing On to import a variety of goods which would sell locally.[71]

The Kwok brothers seem to have developed certain techniques in purchasing goods. Kwok Chin in his autobiography proudly reveals the secret of his success in this aspect, emphasising his

70. See ibid., p. 175; Kwok Chin, Autobiography, p. 9.
71. See Shang-yeh shih, p. 128–130.

principle that 'you buy when the price of goods is up, not when the price of goods is down'.[72]

Marketing was an area which was most crucial to the success of Wing On. The Kwok brothers, who had spent time overseas and observed how Western business was done, were most impressed by Western business practices, especially their way of treating customers. This was in contrast to the traditional Chinese way of treating customers, which was passive and unfriendly and inhibited sales. The Kwok brothers were highly aware of this fact, and were determined to change this attitude among Wing On staff. Kwok Chin in his autobiography clearly shows how much effort was required in order to do this. He observed that the attitude of the Chinese shop assistants in Shanghai was better than that in Hong Kong, but was worse when compared with the shop assistants in Japan.[73] This, he explained, was due to the character of the Chinese and their lack of training.[74] Therefore, Wing On shop assistants were trained to treat customers as guests who brought business to the company and on whose patronage their jobs depended. Customers were greeted with courteous greetings of 'good morning' or 'good afternoon', and the Western concept that 'customers are always right' was inculcated into the minds of the staff of Wing On. In accordance with this principle, customers were always treated with courtesy and friendliness, even when no sale was made, the customers were thanked for coming,[75] The establishment of a good relationship between Wing On and its customers was important to its success. It retained old customers and attracted more and more new ones because satisfied customers tended to spread the good word among their relatives, friends and acquaintances.

One of the successful marketing strategies that the Kwok brothers adopted was the introduction of credit sales. Of course the concept of credit was not modern — it existed in traditional business practice in China — but indiscriminate credit sales would lead the business to

72. See Kwok Chin, Autobiography, p. 28.
73. Kwok Chin, Autobiography, p. 25.
74. Ibid.
75. Kwok Chin, Autobiography, p. 26.

collapse due to insurmountable bad debts. The modern concept of credit sales, which induced customers to spend more than they intended, was supported by a credit assessment system. Since most of the customers of Wing On in Shanghai belonged to the upper-middle and upper classes, the risk of bad debt was relatively low. When the Shanghai Wing On branch came into operation in September 1918, credit was introduced, and within five years of its operation the number of credit customers grew to more than 4,000.[76] The Kwok brothers also adopted a policy of treating Chinese and foreign credit customers differently in accordance with their customs. The credit bills of foreign customers were settled once a month, while the credit of Chinese customers was repaid three times a year: before the Dragon Boat Festival (around June), the Moon Festival (around September) and Chinese New Year (around January or February).

The success of credit sales was clearly reflected in their proportion to the total turnover of the company. In 1935, the income from credit sales was $1,278,000 (*fa pi*) which was about 14.3 percent of the total turnover ($8,964,000 *fa pi*). In 1939, income from credit sales increased to $4,508,000 *fa pi*, accounting for 24.5 percent of the total turnover of $18,371,000 *fa pi*.[77]

Added to Kwok brothers' marketing strategy for Wing On in Shanghai was the sale of gift vouchers (*li chien*, literally translated as 'a gift ticket'). The origin of this gift voucher was probably Western, and it was practised by the parent company in Hong Kong before the founding of the Wing On branch in Shanghai. As in Hong Kong, Shanghai's Chinese population had become more westernised and they came under the increasing influence of Western practices of gift giving. The introduction of gift vouchers by Wing On invariably increased turnover, broadened the social base of customers and facilitated the marketing planning. At the same time, the company had the advantage of using cash on credit without paying interest for it. Because of the reputation and prestige of Wing On among consumers, and its wide range of goods available to choose from, gift

76. See Chu Lung-k'an, op. cit., in Hsu T'i-hsin (ed), *Chung-kuo ch'i-yeh chia lieh-chuan*, vol. 2, p. 211–12.
77. See *Shang-yeh shih*, pp. 135–36.

vouchers sold by the company were very popular. The vouchers were well-designed and attractive; they looked like bank notes and had a value range of $1, $2, $5, $10 and $50. They suited all types of customers for all functions, and their popularity is indicated in the rapid increase of sale of vouchers by the company. Sales were worth $458,000 *fa pi* in 1935, and increased to $600,000 *fa pi* in 1938. In 1939 they increased dramatically to $1,126,000 *fa pi* and reached $2,639,000 *fa pi* in 1940.[78]

In addition, the Wing On company in Shanghai also started mail order and home delivery services. As Wing On's reputation travelled beyond the boundaries of Shanghai, it greatly appealed to the Chinese upper class members of other cities. In around 1920 the company set up a mail-order department handling orders from other cities. Goods were advertised in Chinese newspapers in other major cities, and customers ordered from as far as Mukden and An Tung in the northeast, Sian and T'ung Kuan in the northwest, Ch'engtu in the southwest and Foochow in the south.[79] The home delivery service was mainly done through telephone orders, which suited the wealthy Chinese in Shanghai. As most of them were not worried about the price, the convenience of home delivery helped develop their appetite for more goods.[80]

The success story of the Wing On company in Shanghai and Hong Kong will not have been fully told if the Kwok brothers' ingenious use of Overseas Chinese capital for the benefit of the company is not explored. With their contacts with the Overseas Chinese in Sydney, Honolulu and Hong Kong, the Kwok brothers realised that there was a big pool of Overseas Chinese capital untapped. This consisted of the savings of individual Overseas Chinese who, after many years' toil, desired to bring their money home for regular family expenditure, for buying property or building houses. With their strong peasant mentality, most Overseas Chinese at that time did not trust modern banks or post offices, but rather only those whom they knew had

78. See the figure compiled from the account books of the Shanghai Wing On branch, in Shang-yeh shih, pp. 137–38.
79. See Shang–yeh shih, p. 138.
80. Ibid.

good reputations. The Kwok brothers also realised that many of their fellow Hsiang-Shanese were spread widely throughout the world, in Australia, Southeast Asia, North America and Hong Kong, and much of their individual savings could be mobilised to the benefit of Wing On. Wing On's remarkable business success enhanced the reputation of the Kwok brothers, and attracted many depositors. In the early stage of the Wing On operation in Hong Kong, these depositors were mainly local Hsiang-Shanese as well as Hsiang-Shanese from Australia and the United States. Their deposits with Wing On were a sign of trust in the Kwok brothers and the convenience that Wing On could provide them in remitting money back home. In the early days, the Overseas Chinese had no concept of banking interest, and their deposit of money with a person or company was mainly for security reasons. This was why Wing On had paid little or no interest to those depositors and could freely use their savings for further development.[81] The management of early deposits seems to have come under the control of the cashier's office, until the number of depositors increased and a separate department of savings and remittance was set up to handle this business.[82]

In the case of the Wing On branch in Shanghai, mobilisation of this scattered capital started with the commencement of the company in September 1918, but there was no formal department which handled the matter, and all deposits and savings accounts were managed by the cashier's office. It was not until 1921 that a separate department of finance was set up. The depositors in Shanghai were different from those in Hong Kong; many were Cantonese or Overseas Chinese from Hong Kong and Macau who might not be Hsiang-Shanese, but who were none the less proud of Wing On's success and were prepared to deposit money with Wing On.[83] The finance department was divided into savings and commercial affairs, and the former dealt with ordinary savings, while the latter handled fixed deposits and other types of commercial accounts. By 1929 the

81. See interview with Mr M.C. Kwok, 8 November 1990 in Hong Kong.
82. See interview with Dr Russell Kwok, the grandson of Kwok Chin and the general manager of Wing On, in Hong Kong on 11 December 1990.
83. See Shang-yeh shih, pp. 163–64.

department was so successful that it acquired semi-independent status within the structure of the company. It had $1,000,000 in reserve, and set up a major sub-branch in the H'ung K'ou area, at which business grew rapidly. At the peak of business in 1931, funds deposited with the finance department reached $6,400,000.[84] Much of the funds accumulated in the finance department were used by the Wing On company as operating capital. For instance, the deposits at the H'ung K'ou branch in 1929 amounted to $1,430,000, of which $1,420,000 was injected into the company's liquid capital while only $10,000 was kept in the finance department. In 1930 the deposits of the H'ung K'ou branch increased to $1,999,000, the bulk of which was used by the company with only $37,000 kept in the department.[85]

The mobilisation of overseas-Chinese scattered capital for Wing On was an important innovation of the Kwok brothers. The normal way of obtaining capital through bank loans would have resulted in high interest payments, while their innovation provided them with cheaper capital for the development of their. The Kwok brothers' success was determined by their ability to use geographical and community ties for economic purposes. They had first acquired the confidence and trust of their fellow Hsiang-Shanese based on geographical ties, and later widened it to include those who spoke Cantonese and those who came from the Kwantung province as a whole. The Kwok brothers were also active in community affairs, and with the success of Wing On in Hong Kong they emerged to become leaders of the local Hsiang-Shanese community. They helped the Hong Kong Hsiang-Shanese Chamber of Commerce (which later became the Hong Kong Chung-Shanese Chamber of Commerce) to acquire a club house, and Kwok Chin was at one stage its president.[86] He was also the president of the Pan Overseas Hsiang-Shanese Relief Association (*Chung-shan h'ai-wai t'ung-hsiang chi-nan tsung-hui*). In relation to the welfare of the Hsiang-Shanese back home, the Kwok

84. Ibid., p. 164.
85. Ibid., p. 166.
86. See Kwok Chin, Autobiography, p. 22; Liu T'ien-jen, 'Pen kung-ssu erh-shih wu chou-nien chi ching-kuo', in *Hsiang-kang Yung-an yu-hsien kung-ssu nien-wu chou nien chi-nien lu*, Shih-lueh column, p. 6.

brothers donated a large sum of money to build schools and to construct a motor road linking the area with the outside world.[87] In addition, they were generous in donating money to help local schools and hospitals as well as other charity organizations in Hong Kong. Kwok Chin was particularly active: he was elected director of Po Leung Kuk, a charitable organisation known in Hong Kong for its protection of women and children; he was elected to the position of deputy director (*fu tsung-li*) of the famous T'ung Wah Hospital of Hong Kong;[88] and became the president of the Hong Kong Chinese Chamber of Commerce (*Hsiang-kang hua-shang tsung-hui*). He was also elected to sit on various boards of management for several Chinese schools in Hong Kong.[89]

The Kwok brothers' active involvement in the local Chinese community and the welfare of their home village, though time consuming, brought them fame and social status. This in turn gave them special credentials in the community, and gained for Wing On continuous patronage from local Hsiang-Shanese as well as from the general public. The brothers would not fit the romantic description of the so-called 'community-centred entrepreneurs' who were supposed to sacrifice their self-interest for the sake of the community.[90] They were self-aggrandising rather than self-sacrificing, and their enterprise had undoubtedly benefited from their involvement in the community. In this sense, the Kwok brothers were overseas-Chinese entrepreneurs who knew how to use the geographical, kinship and other social ties available to them for

---

87. See Kwok Chin, Autobiography. pp. 22–3.
88. Tung Wah Hospital was the leading social organisation in Hong Kong, and its leadership was accepted by the local community as leaders of the entire community. For the early history of Tung Wah and its status in the Chinese community in Hong Kong, see Elizabeth Sinn, *Power and Charity: The Early History of the Tung Wah Hospital, Hong Kong* (Hong Kong, Oxford University Press, 1989).
89. See Kwok Chin, Autobiography, p. 22.
90. For a discussion of this topic, see W. Mark Fruin, 'From Philanthropy to Paternalism in the Noda Soy Sauce Industry: Pre-Corporate and Corporate Charity in Japan', in *Business History Review: Special Issue on East Asian Business History*, vol. LVI, no. 2 (Summer 1982), pp. 168–69.

economic purposes. At the same time, they were philanthropic in an overseas-Chinese tradition, and tried to strike a balance between self-interest and community welfare.

Diversification

Diversification is the key to rapid expansion of any modern business enterprise. The advantages of diversification in the areas of marketing and investment of surplus capital cannot be denied. The Kwok brothers seem to have realised the importance of diversification for the Wing On company. The first step of Wing On's diversification was the expansion into real estate. This was not a fully-fledged operation aimed at making Wing On into a leading real estate company. Instead the Kwok brothers, especially Kwok Chin, felt that acquisition of some valuable real estate in Hong Kong would be to the company's advantage. When the company was founded in Hong Kong in 1907, it had rented the shop in Queen's Road as its premises, but this was too small for future development. After two years' operation, the Wing On company had rented premises in Des Voeux Road, Central, for five years with the option of extending for another fifteen years.[91] Early success of the company confronted the Kwok brothers with problems of rapid expansion or diversification. The company could have taken the course of rapid expansion by opening more branches throughout Hong Kong and renting premises for that purpose. Instead, the Kwok brothers chose to diversify. In accordance with this strategy, the company started buying up properties in the area of the rented premises in Des Voeux Road. It acquired a row of shops from 207 to 235 Des Voeux Road, and another row from 104 to 118 in Connaught Road, Central, as well as a property in Connaught West which was developed into a godown for the company. In all, more than thirty shops were acquired by the company with a total area of more than 40,000 square feet.[92]

---

91. See Kwok Chin, Autobiography, p. 6.
92. See Liu T'ien-jen, 'Pen kung-ssu erh-shih wu chou-nien chi ching-kuo', in *Hsiang-kang Yung-an yu-hsien kung-ssu nien-wu chou-nien chi-nien lu, Shih lueh* column, p. 3.

In the first step of diversification, Wing On was obviously very successful. The properties acquired appreciated rapidly in value due to the growth of the population and business in Hong Kong. At the same time some properties were used as company godowns or as premises for company-owned hotels such as the Ta Tung Hotel, and many of the shops acquired were let out to collect rental. As the demand for shops in the Hong Kong business centre increased, the rental also increased substantially over the years, contributing to the cashflow of the company. The fact that Wing On had to set up a separate department, the estate office, within its structure of administration indicates the importance of rental in its annual income.

Wing On's most important diversification was its move into new types of business, such as finance and manufacturing. What gave the Kwok brothers the idea of venturing into the world of finance is uncertain. None of them had special knowledge in this area, nor did they have any training. Perhaps their success in using Overseas Chinese capital had given them insight into the area of finance. Their first was the founding of Wing On Insurance Company in 1915 ,which specialized in fire and shipping insurance. With the First World War in progress, they came to realise that many Chinese trading ships on the China coast needed insurance as a safeguard against possible loss in the war. The insurance company encountered some problems in its initial stage. With its limited capital of HK$610,000, it had difficulty competing with other large Western insurance companies for clients. Kwok Chin, in his autobiography, attributes the company's shortage of capital and the unfamiliarity of the Chinese with the insurance industry as two major problems encountered in the company's early days.[93] However, with the help of its business associates and friends, the company overcame its initial difficulties and succeeded in increasing its capital and setting up agents in most of the major cities in China.

Life insurance, which gained its popularity in the West after the First World War, was another important area for the Kwok brothers' financial attempts. Life insurance companies already

---

93.   See Autobiography, p. 14.

existed in Hong Kong and coastal cities of China, but most of them were Western-owned. It was seen as an emerging industry with a bright future ahead, and the Kwok brothers started floating stock and recruiting talent for the endeavour. They founded the Wing On Life Insurance Company in Hong Kong in April 1925 with a paid up capital of HK$1,537,000.[94] However the company initially encountered problems due to a lack of confidence in the local Chinese for a Chinese-owned insurance company.[95] The efforts of the staff and the Wing On spirit sustained the company for more than a decade. The postwar period saw the growth of the Wing On life insurance business, and it subsequently developed and spread to other major cities in Southeast Asia[96]

The climax of Kwok brothers' financial venture was reached in 1931 when the Wing On Bank was established in Hong Kong. They had from their early days in Hong Kong realised the importance of banking in business. If Wing On wished to grow in leaps and bounds, it had to become larger and more powerful in both the financial and business worlds. The registered capital of the Wing On Bank was HK$5,000,000, and the bank had also registered with the new Kuomintang government in Nanking which would facilitate its operation in central and southern China. The Wing On Bank was opened on 19 September 1931 and was operated like other normal banks, handling business transactions, mortgages, loans, savings and remittance. It also set up safe deposit boxes for customers which soon gained popularity with the local wealthy Chinese.

With the reputation of Wing On, the new bank had a good start. It gained a number of customers, and within two years attracted more than HK$2,000,000 in deposits. In 1936 it purchased its own building, and in 1937 established a branch in Yaumatai for the convenience of the customers in the Kowloon area. The bank underwent a very difficult period during the Japanese Occupation, but quickly revived after the

---

94. See *The Wing On Life Assurance Company Limited Golden Jubilee Book, 1925–1975* (Hong Kong, 1975) p. 6.
95. See Kwok Chin, Autobiography, p. 15.
96. Ibid., p. 16.

Second World War, when deposits with the bank increased rapidly to over HK$30,000,000.[97]

Another major area of Wing On's diversification was manufacturing. It was quite remarkable for the Kwok brothers to go into an area of business about which they knew very little. Perhaps they realised the importance of manufacturing in the modern business world as an important source of wealth. With their business acumen, they must have realised that the retreat of the West from China during the First World War provided an excellent opportunity for the Chinese national *bourgeoisie* such as themselves.[98] It was a historical accident rather than a planned act that when a knitting factory owned by a Western company in Hong Kong collapsed, the Kwok brothers took it over in 1919 and changed its name to Wai San Knitting Factory. The factory used to produce underwear, especially the Eagle brand singlet which had enjoyed good reputation. The name 'Wai San', which literally meant 'reform', signified the change of ownership and the 'reform' the Kwok brothers were going to take. They proceeded to take over all the machinery and produced a variety of underwear for both domestic and foreign markets.[99]

The biggest manufacturing enterprise the Kwok brothers undertook was the founding of the Wing On Textile Manufacturing Company in Shanghai in June 1921.[100] The idea of undertaking a large scale textile manufacturing enterprise came as the result of Kwok Chin's visit to Shanghai in the early 1921. This was the year that saw the continuing intensification of anti-Japanese feelings in Shanghai and other major Chinese coastal cities, in the wake of the May Fourth movement in

---

97. See Kwok Chin, Autobiography, pp. 17–8.; see also Liu T'ien-jen, op. cit., in *Hsiang-kang Yung-an yu-hsien kung-ssu nien-wu chou-nein chi-nien lu*, p. 10.
98. See the discussion of the emergence of a Chinese national bourgeoisie in Marion Levy and Shih Kuo-heng, *The Rise of the Modern Chinese Business Class* (New York, International Secretariat, Institute of Pacific Relations, 1949).
99. Se Liu T'ien-jen, op. cit., in *Hsiang-kang Yung-an yu-hsien kung-ssu nien-wu chou nien chi nienlu*, p. 11.
100. See Kwok Chin, Autobiography, p.10.

mid-1919. Japanese goods were burnt as an expression of hatred against the Japanese for their military and economic aggression in China. For those far-sighted Chinese, to roll back Japanese economic imperialism in China was to encourage the Chinese manufacturing industry in order to protect China's economic interests. Kwok Chin's visit to Shanghai in early 1921 was timely. He must have been impressed by the enthusiasm of the burgeoning Chinese nationalism and the prospect of capturing a vast growing market in the textile industry. In his autobiography Kwok Chin that explains he and his brother, Kwok Lock, decided to found this textile company due to the backwardness of the Chinese manufacturing industry and the spilling of economic interests into the hands of foreigners.[101]

With the acquisition of the Wai San Knitting Factory in Hong Kong, the Kwok brothers must have accumulated some experience in manufacturing cotton piece goods. This gave them the courage and confidence to set up a large modern textile manufacturing company in the hub of China's business and industry. The decision to found such an enterprise in Shanghai was timely. It struck the chord of Chinese nationalism, which was reflected in strong public support for the shares of the company. The capital of the company was first given as $3,000,000, but was shortly increased to $5,000,000 and then to $6,000,000 so as to meet the demands of enthusiastic supporters.[102]

When the Wing On Textile Manufacturing Company was founded in Shanghai, Kwok Lock was made the chairman of the board of directors; a younger brother of the Kwoks, Kwok Ho Fai, was appointed general manager; and he was deputised by another experienced businessman, Leung Chong. The selection of sites and the construction of the textile factory took about one and a half years to complete, when the first mill was established in Yangtzepoo, Shanghai and the company began its production in winter 1922. With the rise of Chinese economic nationalism and with Wing On's fine reputation, the Wing On Textile Company's

---

101. See Kwok Chin, Autobiography, p. 10.
102. See Liu T'ien-jen, op. cit., in *Hsiang-kang Yung-an yu-hsien kung-ssu nien-wu chou nien chi-nien lu*, p 9.

products, including yarn and cloth, received tremendous support among Chinese consumers both at home and abroad. The company continued to build its second mill at Woosung and the third mill at Markham Road, Shanghai. By 1931 the company had doubled its capital to $12,000,000 by capitalising its reserve for further expansion. By 1932, when the company entered its tenth year of existence, its three mills employed more than 14,000 workers and staff, and it possessed 2000 weaving machines with 240,000 spindles. The company produced a wide range of cotton piece goods, including its two most popular brands, 'Golden Wall' and 'Golden Coin'.[103]

Other areas of diversification undertaken by the Kwok brothers included a hotel business, godowns and amusement parks. The founding of Ta Tung Hotel in Hong Kong, and the starting of a restaurant business and the amusement park in and on top of the Wing On Building in Shanghai, were sidelines which were to support the main business of Wing On. The restaurant and the amusement park in Shanghai were to attract customers of the Wing On emporium, and the godown in Hong Kong was mainly to solve the problem of storage for the Wing On parent body in Hong Kong.

Many advantages accrued from diversification of business. One of these was the cushioning of economic and political effects on business. Had Wing On just concentrated on trading, it might have not been able to withstand the devastating impact of the world depression from 1929 to 1932. Instead, its diversification reduced the impact of the depression on Wing On to a minimum. The growing importance of the income from the properties in Hong Kong and Canton in Wing On's overall income further illustrates the benefits of diversification. In 1934 the income accrued from the properties in those two cities reached HK$5,558,246, or about a quarter of the total income for the year.[104]

---

103. See Kwok Chin, Autobiography, pp. 10–11; Liu T'ien-jen, op. cit., in *Hsiang-kang Yung-an yu-hsien kung-ssu nien-wu chou-nien chi-nien lu, Shih-lueh* column, p. 9.
104. See *Hsiang-kang Yung-an yu-hsien kung-ssu min-kuo nien-san nien fen tsung chieh-ch'ih* (The Balance Sheet of the Wing On Company of Hong Kong of the year 1934), p. 3.

Another obvious advantage of diversification was the cross pollinating of capital, where surplus capital in either the Wing On parent body in Hong Kong or the Wing On Company in Shanghai could be absorbed into the subsidiary companies. This solved problems both of surplus funds from the emporia and of the capital shortage of the subsidiary companies. This cross pollinating of capital was frequently practised by the Shanghai branch of Wing On. In the two-year period of 1930 and 1931, the company invested $600,000 in the Wing On Textile Manufacturing Company for expansion, and injected $310,000 into the Wing On Bank in Hong Kong, $425,000 into the Wing On Fire and Shipping Insurance Company, $300,000 into the Wing On Life Insurance Company in Hong Kong, and another sum of $202,000 into the general funds of the Wing On parental company in Hong Kong.[105]

The orthodox view that the Chinese lack entrepreneurship has gradually been revised. The views of Albert Feuerwerker, Marion Levy and Shih Kuo-heng no longer hold sway among the economic historians on modern China.[106] Yen-ping Hao, Thomas Rawski, Sherman Cochran and Wellington K.K. Chan have contributed significantly to the revision of this orthodox view by arguing the existence of Chinese entrepreneurship. Hao was the first to identify Chinese compradors on the China coast as schumpeterian entrepreneurs par excellence.[107] Thomas Rawski and Sherman Cochran have identified indigenous Chinese entrepreneurs[108], while Wellington K.K. Chan has vaguely

105. See Shang–yeh shih, p. 161.
106. See Albert Feuerwerker, *China's Early Industrialization : Shen Hsuan-huai (1844–1916) and Mandarin Enterprises* (Cambridge, Massachusetts, Harvard University Press, 1958), pp. 22–6, 58–9; Marion J. Levy Jr & Shih Kuo-heng, *The Rise of the Modern Chinese Business Class.*
107. See Yen-ping Hao, *The Comprador in Nineteenth Century China: Bridge Between East and West* (Cambridge, Massachusetts, Harvard University Press, 1970).
108. See Thomas Rawski, 'The Growth of Producer Industries, 1900–1971', in Dwight H. Perkins (ed), *China's Modern Economy in Historical Perspective* (Stanford, Stanford University Press, 1975), p. 208; and Sherman Cochran,

identified Ma Ying-piu, the founder of the Sincere Company in Hong Kong, as an Overseas Chinese entrepreneur.[109] However Chan has presented Ma Ying-piu as a modern reformer in the context of traditional Chinese business structure, rather than fully identifying Ma as a new type of Chinese entrepreneur.

This chapter, through a study of the Wing On companies in Hong Kong and Shanghai, shows how the Kwok brothers, Kwok Lock and Kwok Chin, belonged to a new type of entrepreneur in modern China, the Overseas Chinese entrepreneur. The Kwok brothers possessed the schumpeterian ideals: they were acquisitive, innovative and risk-taking, and fitted well the description of modern entrepreneurs. The definition of a modern entrepreneur as a contractor who served as intermediary between capital and labour,[110] can hardly do justice to an entrepreneur. J.W. Gough has rightly pointed out in his book that "To call him [entrepreneur] an 'intermediary' between capital and labour suggests the salaried official, the modern 'personnel manager' rather than the genuine entrepreneur".[111] An entrepreneur is not just an intermediary between capital and labour, but also a creator and perpetuator of a modern enterprise. He is a man who brings capital, labour and management together and creates an enterprise. He is personally involved in making decisions for the growth, expansion and perpetuation of that enterprise. An entrepreneur must be a man who possesses a capitalistic attitude: the love of money, the pursuit of profit, the courage to take initiatives and risks, and the determination to implement ideas. He must also possess foresight, business acumen

Big Business in China: Sino-Foreign Rivalry in the Cigarette Industry, 1890–1930 (Cambridge, Massachusetts, Harvard University Press, 1980), p. 214.

109. See Wellington K.K. Chan, 'The Organizational Structure of the Traditional Chinese Firm and Its Modern Reform', in *Business History Review: Special Issue on East Asian Business History*, vol. LVI, no. 2 (Summer 1982), pp. 218–35.

110. See *Shorter Oxford Dictionary* for a discussion of the definition of entrepreneur; and J.W. Gough, *The Rise of the Entrepreneur* (London, T.B. Batsford, 1969) pp. 9–17.

111. Ibid., p. 17.

and imagination that would contribute to the success of an enterprise. Apart from these personal qualities, he must also be able to lead, to communicate and to manage a successful enterprise.

The Kwok brothers met most of these criteria. They successfully mobilised scattered Overseas Chinese capital, and merged with labour and management to found the Wing On companies in Hong Kong and Shanghai. Throughout their lives, the Kwok brothers were actively involved in the running of the company, from the founding of the Wing On in Hong Kong in 1907 to its expansion and diversification. Almost every important decision was taken by the two brothers in conjunction with other business partners. Kwok Lock himself occupied the position of the chairman of the board of directors for over thirty years, and Kwok Chin was the general manager of the company for most of his life.

The Kwok brothers also possessed capitalistic attitudes. Like many other Chinese immigrants, they possessed a strong desire for material advancement. They had an intense love of money and were on a constant quest for profits. One of Kwok Chin's grandsons whom I interviewed in Hong Kong recalled that his grandfather in his retirement days still frequented the emporium, watching customers coming and going, and he enjoyed immensely the flourishing of business in the store.[112] This capitalistic attitude was also partly reflected in the brothers' constant search for opportunities for business expansion. The founding of the Wing On Company in Shanghai and the diversification of the company into new lines of business reflected the brothers' ability to take initiatives and risks. Although burgeoning Chinese nationalism provided opportunities for textile manufacturing, the political instability and military chaos in China in the 1920s and 1930s were potentially hazardous to any industry. The Kwok brothers' decision to go ahead with their plan to found the Wing On Textile Manufacturing Company in June 1921 was the result of a calculated risk.

In addition, they seem to have had enormous foresight and business acumen. This personal quality does not seem to have come from

---

112. See interview with Dr Russel Kwok, General Manager of the Wing On Centre on 11 December 1990.

education but rather from their acute observation and their ability to grasp new ideas and turn them to their advantage. Their observation of the success of Western department stores gave them the idea of running a similar one in the westernised Chinese society of Hong Kong. Kwok Chin seems to have benefited tremendously from a business trip to Europe, United States and Australia, and he concluded that the success of Western businesses rested on their more scientific methods, planning, organisation and experience.[113] This obviously had some impact on his style of running the enterprise. His foresight was further illustrated in his proposal for a textile company in Hong Kong during the postwar period. He predicted a bright future for textile manufacturing in Hong Kong due to the demand of this British colony after the devastation of the war. His scheme did not materialise due to internal problems at Wing On, but his prediction was proven correct when textile manufacturers enjoyed a boom in postwar Hong Kong.[114]

The Kwok brothers not only possessed most of the qualities of a modern entrepreneur, but also those of overseas-Chinese entrepreneurs. Being Overseas Chinese, who could be classified sociologically as marginal men, their desire for material advancement and the will to succeed were almost ingrained. Being overseas-Chinese entrepreneurs, they had the advantage of leading their enterprises to grow under an efficient colonial government and at the same time enjoyed preferential treatment from the Chinese government. From another perspective, the Kwok brothers also possessed all the qualities of an immigrant: the desire for material gain, the will to succeed and the capacity to work hard. Chinese virtues of thrift and diligence, combined with the qualities of the immigrant and an overseas environment, produced the enormous energy and dynamism which characterised their enterprises. This seemed to have occurred more often in the first generation of overseas-Chinese immigrants, and helps to explain why many overseas-Chinese enterprises were founded among the first generation, but expanded in the second generation.

113. See Kwok Chin, Autobiography, p. 68.
114. See Kwok Chin, Autobiography, p. 36; Wong Siu-Lun, *Emigrant Entrepreneurs: Shanghai Industrialists in Hong Kong* (Hong Kong, Oxford University Press, 1988), pp. 3–10.

As the Overseas Chinese were the products of two cultures, Chinese and Western, they had wider contacts with foreigners and were less steeped in traditional culture than their counterparts in China, and they adopted highly innovative and flexible approaches to business. This could be claimed to be the result of the blending of Chinese and Western cultures. The Kwok brothers' techniques of mobilising scattered Overseas Chinese capital, their ingenious marketing techniques, their training of staff and their management style, are all the illustrations of their successful blending of Chinese and Western cultures, and the result of a high degree of innovation and flexibility. In this perspective, Overseas Chinese entrepreneurship formed a new type of entrepreneurship in modern China. And it was partly the development of this Overseas Chinese entrepreneurship that explains the rise of Hong Kong and Singapore to the status of two of the Four Little Dragons.

CHAPTER

Tan Kah Kee and Overseas Chinese Entrepreneurship*

Discussion of entrepreneurship is more meaningful if it takes into account of different types of entrepreneurs. Although entrepreneurs share some common characteristics, such as risk-taking and innovation, they nevertheless vary according to their environments and time and their reactions to particular circumstances.[1] I have in the past attempted to define Overseas Chinese entrepreneurs and Overseas Chinese entrepreneurship.[2] This chapter presents a case study of Overseas Chinese entrepreneurship in Southeast Asia in the period before and after the First World War. Using a prominent entrepreneur, Tan Kah

---

*   Paper presented at the Chinese Studies Association of Australia Fifth National Conference held in Adelaide, 16–18 July 1997.

1.   For a general discussion of entrepreneurs and entrepreneurship, see Mark Casson (ed), *Entrepreneurship* (Aldershot, Edward Elgar Publishing Limited, 1990); J.W. Gough, *The Rise of the Entrepreneur* (London, T.B. Batsford, 1969); Peter F. Drucker, *Innovation and Entrepreneurship* (Oxford, Butterworth-Heinemann, 1994).

2.   See Ch. 4, last section.

Kee, as an example, it illustrates the process of how an Overseas Chinese entrepreneur is made, and highlights some salient aspects of Overseas Chinese entrepreneurship. Tan Kah Kee was one of the best known Overseas Chinese entrepreneurs in Southeast Asia and China in 1920s, and has become a legend in Overseas Chinese history.[3] Centred in Singapore and Malaya, his business empire extended to many parts of Southeast Asia and south China. A top Overseas Chinese capitalist, a Chinese patriot and a well-known Chinese educationist and philanthropist, he left his mark in modern Chinese history, and his impact is still being felt in Overseas Chinese communities and south China today.

Tan Kah Kee was not destined to become a modern Overseas Chinese entrepreneur. He was not brought up in a business

---

3. Tan Kah Kee published two volumes of his memoirs in Chinese in March 1946 entitled *Nan-ch'iao hui-i lu* (literally, 'Reminiscence of My Life and Activities in the Chinese Communities in Southeast Asia'; translated as 'Tan Kah Kee: An Autobiography') (Singapore, Nanyang Printing Company, 1946, two volumes, 422 pp.). The memoirs were reprinted in 1993 by the Tan Kah Kee International Society, headed by Professor Li Yen-che, a Nobel Prize winner in Chemistry, by the Global Publishing Company (River Edge, USA). The new edition contains some valuable correspondence between Tan Keng Hean and Tan Kah Kee in the period between 1923 and 1927. Tan Keng Hean was Tan Kah Kee's younger brother and his most trusted administrator of his educational and business enterprises. The memoirs record his life and his involvement in social activities, educational enterprises, politics in China and business activities. Since 1981, several works have been published on Tan Kah Kee in both Chinese and English. The most authoritative work is Dr C.F. Yong's, *Tan Kah-Kee: The Making of an Overseas Chinese Legend* (Singapore, Oxford University Press, 1987, 391 pp.). Dr Yong, who is attached to Flinders University, South Australia, has exhausted most of the source materials related to Tan Kah Kee in Chinese and English, and took ten years to complete his work. This has been regarded as the definitive work on Tan Kah Kee in any language. Dr. Yong's work has also been translated into Chinese and published in Singapore. Dr Yong has also published two books in Chinese related to Tah Kah Kee. The first is entitled *Chan-ch'ien Ch'en Chia-keng yen-lun shih-liao yu fen-hsi* (Tan Kah Kee in Prewar Singapore: Selected Documents and Analysis) (Singapore, South Seas Society, 1980, 182 pp.); the second is entitled *Ch'en Chia-keng yen-chiu wen-chi* (Collected

environment, nor was he educated and prepared for an entrepreneurial position. His success in business was due to the combination of his environment, the period in which he lived and his personal attributes. Tan Kah Kee was born in 1874 in Chi Mei village of T'ung An district in the southern part of Fukien province. Close to Amoy, an early Treaty port, T'ung An had been one of the districts in southern Fukien to export immigrants to Southeast Asia. With a rugged and mountainous landscape and vast coastline, T'ung An produced immigrants with the qualities of thrift, honesty, tenacity, adventure and independence .[4] These qualities helped to mould Tan Kah Kee's personality and prepared him to become an outstanding Overseas Chinese entrepreneur.

At the time Tan Kah Kee emerged as an Overseas Chinese entrepreneur, both China and Southeast Asia were undergoing rapid political and economic changes. The deteriorating economic conditions in late Ch'ing China compelled more and more Chinese in the south to

Papers on the Studies of Chen Jia Geng) (Beijing, Chung-kuo Yu I ch'u-pan she, 1988, 234 pp.)

In addition to Dr. Yong's work, five books in Chinese on Tan Kah Kee are: Wang Tseng-ping & Yu Kang, *Ch'en Chia-keng hsing-hsueh chi (Records of Tan Kah Kee' Educational Activities)* (Foochow, Fu-chien chiao-yu ch'u-pan she, 1981, 125 pp.); Ch'en Pi-sheng & Yang Kuo-chen, *Ch'en Chia-keng chuan (A Biography of Tan Kah Kee)* (Foochow, Fujian jen-min ch'u-pan she, 1983); Chung-hua ch'uan-kuo kui-kuo hua-ch'iao lian-ho hui, et.al. (eds.), *Hui-i Ch'en Chia-keng (In Memory of Tan Kah Kee)* (Beijing, Wen Shih tzu-liao ch'u-pan she, 1984, 316 pp.); Ch'en Pi-sheng & Ch'en I-ming (eds.),*Ch'en Chia-keng nien-p'u (The Chronology of Tan Kah Kee)* (Foochow, Fu-jian jen-min ch'u-pan she, 1986, 260 pp.); Yang kuo-chen, *Ch'en Chia-keng (Tan Kah Kee)* (Beijing, Jen-min ch'u-pan she, 1987, 158 pp.). A most recent work on Tan Kah Kee is an English translation with notes of Tan Kah Kee memoirs entitled *The Memoirs of Tan Kah Kee* (Singapore, Singapore University Press, 1994, 366 pp.). The editors and translators of this work are three Canadian scholars of the University of Toranto. They are A. H.C. Ward, Raymond W. Chu and Janet Salaff. The work is a good and reliable translation and is a great help to those scholars who have difficulty in reading Tan Kah Kee's original work.

4.   See C.F. Yong, *Tan Kah-kee: The Making of an Overseas Chinese Legend*, p. 16.

seek jobs and fortunes overseas, especially in Southeast Asia. Later, the collapse of the Manchu regime and the founding of the Republic in early 1912 ushered in a new era of political change, and offered millions of Chinese and Overseas Chinese new hopes of building a modern and powerful China. At about same time, the rise of the cash crop industry in Southeast Asia offered many new opportunities for Overseas Chinese entrepreneurs.[5] Tan Kah Kee was one of such entrepreneurs, who could fully exploit new business opportunities as they arose. In addition, his personal attributes played an important role in his success. Apart from the qualities of thrift, honesty, tenacity, adventure and independence shared by other fellow T'ung An people, he was known since he was young for his self-discipline. One of his sons recalled his lifestyle in Singapore as simple but highly regulated. He got up early at 5.30 am, and had breakfast at 6.30 am after fifteen minutes' exercise and a warm bath. At 6.45 am he left home to inspect his factories. He called a meeting of senior staff at 12.00 noon, and in the afternoon spent his time dealing with other business at head office. After 5.00 pm he returned home for dinner, and his evening was spent in the Yee Ho Hean, a businessmen's club in Singapore which was used for dealing with matters relating to Chinese communities or for social networking.[6]

Although Tan Kah Kee's grandfather and father were Overseas Chinese who did business in the Straits settlements, he did not benefit substantially from this family background. Like many Southern Fukienese immigrants, his father had another wife and children in Singapore, while Tan Kah Kee was brought up by his mother in T'ung An. He received traditional training in Confucian classics, reciting texts without comprehension.[7] This traditional form of education did not prepare him for becoming an entrepreneur, but laid the foundation for his further pursuit of knowledge in later life.

5. For the development of cash crop industry in Singapore and Malaya, see James C. Jackson, *Planters and Speculators: Chinese and European Agricultural Enterprise in Malaya 1786–1912* (Singapore, University of Malaya Press, 1968).

6. See Tan Kok Keng, 'Wo te fu-ch'in'(My Father, Tan Kah Kee), in *Hui-i Ch'en Chia-keng* (In Memory of Tan Kah Kee) p. 54.

7. See Tan Kah Kee, *Nan-ch'iao hui-i lu* (Autobiography), vol. 2, new edition, (River Edge, Global Publishing Co., 1993) p. 479.

At the age of sixteen, Tan Kah Kee arrived in Singapore for the first time in 1890. He worked in his father's rice shop, Soon Ann, as an apprentice. His father, Tan Kee Peck, had already established himself in Chinese business circles as a reputable merchant before Tan Kah Kee's arrival. Kee Peck's variety of business, including rice wholesaling and real estate, earned him a handsome income and social status in the Chinese community. Soon Ann was a typical Chinese family business concern, in which division of labour was non-existent and the management of the business was in the hands of a relative. This blurring of labour and management gave Tan Kah Kee a good overall training, as he was involved in all aspects of the business operation. Soon Ann was more than a typical Chinese urban shop: it was a wholesale establishment for rice imported from Thailand, Vietnam and Burma. It distributed to local rice retailers, and had a monthly turnover of S$20,000 with a handsome profit.[8] Tan Kah Kee demonstrated his business acumen and managerial competence at a very young age when he took over the entire operation of the rice business, and acted both as manager and treasurer of Soon Ann at the age of eighteen, when the manager had to leave Singapore for China in 1892.[9] He further benefited from his father's other diverse business operations, which gave him an insight into the operation of various types of business in the Singapore Chinese community.

Undoubtedly, Kah Kee's deep involvement in managing his father's business prepared him for entrepreneurial pursuits. He was quick to grasp new ideas in business, and emerged as a top player. The building of his business empire can be divided into three distinctive periods: foundation and growth from 1904 to 1913; diversification during the First World War between 1914 and 1918; and consolidation and expansion between 1919 and 1925.

After the collapse of his father's business in 1903 due to bad management, Tan Kah Kee was left with $7,000 capital and experience in business for a fresh start. The early foundations of his business empire were based on the production and distribution of

---

8.   See C.F. Yong, *Tan Kah Kee: The Making of an Overseas Chinese Legend*, p. 42.
9.   Ibid.

agricultural products. His familiarity with the rice business and pineapple canning gave him tremendous confidence and a competitive advantage. He founded a rice shop, Khiam Aik ('Modesty and Benefits') in 1904 for wholesale distribution of rice from Indo-China. He then founded rice mills in Thailand to ensure the supply. Rice was the basic diet of the Chinese, and the great demand for rice in Southeast Asia and coastal China ensured an expanding market and its profitability. In the same year, he founded two pineapple-canning factories and developed a pineapple plantation estate. Again, Tan Kah Kee was aware of the importance of the supply side of his business. Unlike rice, the pineapple-canning industry was export-driven, and any shortage of supply of pineapple would kill the industry. This vertical integration of industries became a trademark of Tan Kah Kee's business activities. During this period, Tan Kah Kee's resolute entrepreneurial qualitites were best illustrated by his decision to invest in rubber planting. Pioneered by Tan Chay Yan, a Hokkien planter from Malacca, rubber planting required large sums of capital and lengthy development periods, and had an unpredictable market.[10] Many of the wealthy Chinese businessmen in Singapore wavered over the profitability of commercial planting of rubber, but Tan Kah Kee took a daring step in this direction by investing a large sum in this new risky plantation industry.[11]

The second stage of Tan Kah Kee's business-empire building coincided with the First World War (1914–1918). The war presented Tan Kah Kee with both a crisis and an opportunity. The war ruined the lucrative Indian and European markets for his cooked rice and canned pineapple, resulting in severe loss of income, retrenchment of staff and the closure of his rice mills and pineapple canneries.[12]

10. For Tan Chay Yan's pioneering work in Malacca and the early development of Rubber, see Wu T'i-jen, *Je-tai ching-chi chih-wu — hsiang chiao shu* (Rubber — the Tropical Cash Crop) (Singapore, Kuang Hua Publishing Company, 1951) pp. 6–8; James C. Jackson, *Planters and Speculators: Chinese and European Enterprise in Malaya, 1786–1921*, pp. 211–18; J.H. Drabble, *Rubber in Malaya, 1876–1922: The Genesis of the Industry* (Kuala Lumpur, Oxford University Press, 1973), pp. 14–9.
11. See C.F. Yong, *Tan Kah-kee: The Making of an Overseas Chinese Legend*, p. 48.
12. Ibid., p. 50.

However, the war created a great demand for transport facilities and strategic war materials such as rubber, and with foresight, courage and luck Tan Kah Kee turned this to his advantage. He grasped the opportunity to found a shipping line and converted some of his pineapple canneries into rubber mills. He also produced tin plate to supply the war need. This diversification strategy and the plunge into the new rubber processing industry was a successful move, and earned him enormous profits: from 1915 to 1918 he made a net profit of $4.5 million.[13]

The third stage of Tan Kah Kee's empire building took place during the post-war period of 1919 to1925, during which time his business empire was further diversified and consolidated. With the end of the First World War, the political situation both in Singapore and abroad changed dramatically, and so did economic needs. Tan Kah Kee therefore also had to change his strategy in order to capture the opportunity for expansion. First, he restructured his business empire, incorporating all of his business enterprises into the Tan Kah Kee Company in 1919. The new company possessed a new structure and carried a limited liability, enabling him to chart a new course of action for his business empire. The main thrust of his business strategy was the venture into rubber manufacturing. The slump of rubber prices in the post-war period did not lead Tan Kah Kee to sell off his rubber estates and rubber mills. Instead, he believed that rubber still had a future if he could manufacture rubber products to satisfy growing consumer markets. In 1920 he transformed the Sumbawa rubber mill, his largest in Singapore, into a factory producing rubber raincoats, rubber sheets, rubber umbrellas, rubber sleepers, sports shoes, boots, tennis balls and a variety of rubber toys.[14] In 1922, he acquired several rubber mills in the Malay peninsula at a very cheap price, thus consolidating his control over rubber production. His strategy of vertical integration in order to control rubber production and manufacturing worked well, and by 1925 his business empire reached its peak and made a net profit of S$7.8 million.[15]

13.   See Tan Kah Kee, *Autobiography*, vol. 2, p. 500.
14.   C.F. Yong, op. cit., pp. 54–7.
15.   Tan Kah Kee, Autobiography, vol. 2, p. 505.

The Secrets of Tan Kah Kee's Success

Tan Kah Kee possessed neither an economics degree nor a MBA, but he emerged as an outstanding entrepreneur of his time. What were the secrets of his success? To understand these we need to focus on his management, including the source of his management ideas, his management structure and management style. His personal attributes certainly also had an important role to play, but they are subjective and cannot be measured; and in any case they were integrated into his style of management.

The Source of Tan Kah Kee's Management Ideas

The main source of Tan Kah Kee's management ideas appears to have been Confucian values, such as hierarchy, harmony, loyalty, reciprocity and collectivism. The influence of these values on him was most clearly demonstrated in the 'Rules and Regulations' produced for the branches of his public company (the Tan Kah Kee Company Pty Ltd.) in 1929. Designed as a reference document for branch executives, the 'Rules and Regulations' (*Chang-ch'eng*) were to promote Confucian core ideas among all staff and workers at the company. Confucian core values such as loyalty (*chung*), honesty (*kung*), propriety (*li*), benevolence (*jen*) and courage (*yung*) received prime exposure in the document.[16] Loyalty received a special emphasis because Tan Kah Kee perceived this to be most important. 'Loyalty' was meant in the broadest sense: it was due not just to the company, but was also to the entire Chinese business community and to the nation. At the same time, loyalty was also directed to a particular role, function or job which demanded the dedication of the individual.[17] For instance, the catch title of the first page of the

16. See Lim How Seng, 'Ch'en Chia-keng te ching-ying li-lian yu ch'i-yueh kuan-li' (The Entrepreneurial Ideas and Management of Tan Kah Kee), in Lim How Seng, *Hsin-chia-po hua-she yu hua-shang* (The Chinese Society and the Chinese Merchants in Singapore) (Singapore, Singapore Association of Asian Studies, 1995), pp. 155–56.
17. See *Ch'en Chia-keng kung-ssu fen-h'ang chang-ch'eng* (The Rules and Regulations of the Tan Kah Kee Company Pty Ltd) (Singapore, 1929) pp. 4–

document compares the role of a merchant to that of a soldier at war. A soldier defends his country with arms, while a merchant defends his country by pushing sales of national products. Conversely, if a staff member does not push sales of his national products with all his effort, he is like a soldier who fights the war reluctantly.[18]

Tan Kah Kee's promotion of loyalty among his staff was intentional, and perhaps acted as a last-ditch effort to save his company. The slide in his fortunes after 1926 saw the company go downhill, and the declining morale among staff needed a moral boost.[19] However Tan Kah Kee did not do this for personal gain, but instead aimed to save his company in order to support his non-profit making educational ventures in China — the Chi Mei Education Village and the Xiamen University.[20] Nevertheless, the importance placed on loyalty, a key Confucian value, illustrates how much Tan Kah Kee was influenced by Confucianism and was prepared to use it for management purpose.

Tan Kah Kee's management ideas do not just derive from Confucian values, but also from Western business practices. Western emphasis on quality of service and a good attitude towards customers, in contrast with traditional Chinese practice of neglecting them, impressed him, and the 'Rules and Regulations' contained many references to the proper way of treating customers.[21]

17. I wish to thank Dr C.F. Yong of Flinders University, South Australia for providing me with this document.
18. Ibid., pp. 1, 3.
19. For the decline of profit of the Tan Kah Kee Company Pty Ltd, see Tan Kah Kee, Autobiography, vol. 2, pp. 506–08.
20. For Tan Kah Kee's non-profit making educational enterprise in Fukien province, see Tan Kah Kee, Autobiography, vol. 1, pp. 10-28; Ch'en Pi-sheng & Yang Kuo-chen, *Ch'en Chia-keng chuan* (A Biography of Tan Kah Kee); Wang Tseng-ping & Yu Kang, *Ch'en Chia-keng hsing-hsueh chi* (Records of Tan Kah Kee's Educational Enterprise).
21. See 'The Rules and Regulations of the Tan Kah Kee Company Pty Ltd', pp. 21–5.

The Structure of Tan Kah Kee's Business Enterprises

The capacity of traditional Chinese family businesses to expand and grow is beyond doubt. The case of the Jui-Fu-Hsiang Company of Peking well illustrates this point. Originated in a small township in Shantung province of eastern part of China in the seventeenthth century, Jui-Fu-Hsiang was a family business owned by the Meng family, specialising in cloth for wholesale and retail. The company expanded rapidly after the 1870s, benefiting from buoyant foreign trade as result the opening up of China in the 1840s. At the height of its business in 1925, the company had 26 branches in Peking, Shanghai, Tsingtao and Chefoo, selling a variety of goods and employing 1,000 staff. [22] The two important factors for its success were its strong leadership at the top and an effective structure of organisation. [23]

Similarly, an important factor for the success of Tan Kah Kee's business empire was its effective organisational structure. Two stages of development in the management structure of the Tan Kah Kee empire can be discerned. The first stage lasted from 1904 to 1919, and the second stage from 1919 to 1934. The first stage was characterised by a decentralisation of management. There was no pyramid structure, and each business unit was placed under the control of a superintendent (*tsung-hsun*) who was appointed by and was directly responsible to Tan Kah Kee or his brother Tan Keng Hean. The superintendents had a great deal of power to run their particular units or factories, but their performance was subject to constant scrutiny by Tan Kah Kee himself.[24] However this rather simple structure, though effective, could not cope with a growing and diversifying business empire.

In the second stage, all of Tan Kah Kee's enterprises were incorporated into a large group of companies in 1919 under the name

---

22. See Wellington K.K. Chan, 'The Organizational Structure of the Traditional Chinese Firm and Its Modern Reform', in *Business History Review: Special Issue on East Asian Business History*, vol. 56, no. 2 (1982) pp. 222–26.
23. Ibid.
24. See Lim How Seng, 'The Entrepreneurial Ideas and Management of Tan Kah Kee', in Lim How Seng, *Chinese Society and Chinese Merchants in Singapore*, p. 157.

of the Tan Kah Kee Company Pty Ltd. A pyramid structure was adopted to control the entire operation, with a head office located at 1 River Valley Road, Singapore. A three-tier management hierarchy was installed. At the top of the hierarchy was a management board comprising Tan Kah Kee, his brother Tan Keng Hean and a small group of top managers, and it was responsible for the formulation of policies and decision-making. The second level of the hierarchy consisted of departmental heads who had direct control over various specific lines of company business in Singapore, Malaya and overseas, and who were responsible for executing the policies made by the management board. At the bottom of the hierarchy was a large group of staff in charge of various factories, rubber mills, plantation estates, branches and retail units. They had direct contact with the labour force, and were directly responsible for production, maintenance and sales.[25]

Although the structure of Tan Kah Kee Company was hierarchical, it was not rigid. There were neither physical barriers nor status symbols to project functional differences. For instance, in the head office at River Valley Road senior management staff were not allocated special rooms, and their offices were located in a big hall.[26] The absence of physical barriers projected an image of equality among senior and junior staff, and shortened the distance between superiors and subordinates; it also helped to generate a sense of solidarity and wholeness of the company under the same roof.

The structure of the branches was also hierarchical, each branch being placed under the control of a manager who was assisted by a deputy manager. Under them were a treasurer and a bookkeeper, and below this were the shop assistants and apprentices. However, the branch hierarchy was blurred by the remuneration system. The salary gap between the branch manager and an ordinary shop assistant was not vast. For instance, an A grade branch manager drew S$70 to S$100 per month, while an A grade bookkeeper or shop assistant was paid between S$40 and S$60, more than half of the salary of the manager.[27]

25. See C.F. Yong, *Tan Kah-kee: The Making of an Overseas Chinese Legend*, p. 61.
26. See Lim How Seng, op. cit., p.158.
27. See 'The Rules and Regulations of the Tan Kah Kee Company', pp. 40-1.

The control of the head office over branches and factories was effective and flexible. All branch managers, deputy managers, treasurers and bookkeepers were directly appointed by head office, while branch managers were only empowered to appoint shop assistants and apprentices. A check and balance system was also built into the branch structure to prevent abuse of power or corruption. The manager was entrusted with the overall responsibility of running the branch both internally and externally, and was responsible for supervising the financial affairs of the branch. The treasurer was to take care of entire financial operation of the branch under the supervision of the manager, and he had the right to report directly to head office if he saw the branch was not properly managed. [28] Control was further institutionalised by reports. All branches and factories were required to report to the head office every month on business and management, together with reports on finance, administrative and sundry expenses; every three months they were required to submit stock reports. [29] Under the operation of this system, instructions from head office were implemented without delay, while the business operations and financial situation of the branches were communicated to the top for appropriate decisions.

The Management Style of Tan Kah Kee

Like many other Overseas Chinese business enterprises, Tan Kah Kee's management style was characterised by a centripetal authority or 'paternalistic style of management'. Power and authority were concentrated at the top, and the decision-making process was top-down rather than bottom-up. The Confucian elitist concept of responsibility drove many Overseas Chinese entrepreneurs to over-burden themselves with executive and administrative duties. The foundation of Chinese 'paternalism' is based not on Western concepts of 'power' but on 'responsibility'. The Chinese owner–manager tends to make most of the decisions not because he enjoys making them, but because he feels obligated to run the business properly.

28.   Ibid, pp. 5–6.
29.   Ibid., p. 39.

Leadership and centripetal authority accounted much for the success of the Jui-Fu-Hsiang company of Peking, and they were also the key factors for the success of Tan Kah Kee's business. However, Tan Kah Kee was not as dedicated to business as Meng Lo-ch'uan of Jui-Fu-Hsiang, whose hobby was reading his companny's account books.[30] Nevertheless Tan Kah Kee devoted much of his time to building up his business empire. Rising early in the morning to inspect his factories and branches became a daily routine, and his regular meetings with staff and subordinates qualified him as a workaholic.[31] His dedication to business not only injected dynamism into the organisation, but also became a model for emulation among his staff and subordinates.

Tan Kah Kee's paternalistic style of management was inherently Confucian. Being influenced by Confucian Classics when he was young, he seems to have absorbed much of the Confucian value system, which he then unconsciously incorporated into his management thought. He and his brother Tan Keng Hean made most of the important decisions regarding the operations of his various enterprises before 1919; and he continued to do the same with the help of a small group of top managers of his company after 1919. Although this paternalistic style of management inhibited the active participation of workers in the management of the company, it nevertheless offered a strong leadership at the top.

The domination of ownership over management has been an important feature of modern and contemporary Overseas Chinese enterprises,[32] and it was conspicuously presented in Tan Kah Kee's style of management. Tan Kah Kee was a firm believer in Confucian elitism: a strong and dedicated leadership would lead to the success of any task. He did not believe in the Western style of democratic process, which he reckoned to be inefficient and time-consuming.

---

30. See Wellington K.K. Chan, op. cit. p. 222.
31. See Lim How Seng, op. cit., pp. 159–60.
32. See Yen Ching-hwang, 'Modern Overseas Chinese Enterprise: A Preliminary Study', in Yen Ching-hwang, *Studies in Modern Overseas Chinese History* (Singapore, Times Academic Press, 1995), pp. 245–46; Gordon Redding, *The Spirit of Chinese Capitalism*, (Berlin, Walter de Gruyter, 1990), pp. 158–59.

The traditional Chinese owner-manager style business suited his aspirations and personality. He believed that a strong leadership was predicated on the control of ownership, and this was why he safeguarded control by placing his family members in key management positions. When his Khiam Aik Company was registered as a liability company in 1916, he ensured his permanent control over the company by making himself and his brother Tan Keng Hean two out of the three permanent directors, whose approval was to be sought before any new directors could be added.[33] The collapse of his father's business taught him that control over the management was the key to success in business. He thus exercised strict control over his business operations; he was the owner-manager of most of his enterprises, and was the managing director when his enterprises came under the umbrella organisation of Tan Kah Kee Company in 1919.[34] Even when he was away in China busy with his non-profit making educational activities, he had his brother Tan Keng Hean at the helm of his business. He also appointed his sons to some major management positions, and his son-in-law, Lee Kong Chian, in a key position in his management hierarchy.[35]

In all probability the domination of ownership over management suits Chinese behaviour and values. Firstly, it gives the management more weight in running the business, and facilitates the enterprise's smooth operation. In a status- and power- conscious society like that of the Overseas Chinese community, a salaried manager carries less weight than an owner–manager because in the eyes of the staff and workers he is just one of them, and his power is limited. Secondly, the owner–manager is able to make decisions more quickly because he is responsible not only for the short-term profit and loss of the company, but also for the destiny of the entire enterprise. He alone will ultimately take the responsibility for the success or failure of the entire enterprise. Thirdly, unlike the salaried managers of some Western companies who carry little risk to their own financial positions and may make reckless

33. See Lim How Seng, op. cit., p. 157.
34. See C.F. Yong, *Tan Kah-kee: The Making of an Overseas Chinese Legend*, pp. 55, 62; Tan Kah Kee, Autobiography, vol. 2, p. 509. .
35. Ibid. p. 60; Tan Kah Kee, Autobiography, p. 162. .

decisions, the owner–manager has to be more cautious because his personal finance is at stake, and will probably also work harder for the success for the company as a result. Fourthly, the owner–manger is easier for staff and workers to identify and to invest their goodwill with. And in a web of complex human relationships like those in the Overseas Chinese community, the investment of goodwill in an owner–manager produces better and quicker results.

Like other modern and contemporary Overseas Chinese entrepreneurs, Tan Kah Kee's main strength of management lay in his ability to integrate traditional Chinese values with Western business practices, and Western principles of meritocracy with Chinese emphasis on personal connections, particularly relating to kinship, dialect and geographical ties. The deficiencies of Western meritocratic principles are revealed in a strong spirit of individualism and a lack of loyalty; while the traditional Chinese reliance on personal connections tends to generate complacency and nepotism. However, the combination of these two strengthen and complement each other. A manager recruited under this formula feels indebted to the employer and has sealed a strong bond with the company. His link with the company is not just hinged on financial rewards, but also on personal and moral grounds; and his loyalty to the company cannot easily be swayed by a higher financial reward from another company.[36] Tan Kah Kee was keenly aware of this advantage, striving to strike a balance between meritocracy and personal connections. In the selection of his managers and senior staff, Tan obviously favoured his relatives, kinsmen and fellow district men from T'ung An. His talent pool was not just confined to these men, however, but was extended to cover most southern Hokkien speakers and graduates of the Chi Mei and Xiamen university. For instance, in the Sumbawa manufactory, which employed more than 6,000 workers, he had six superintendents under the manager, five of whom were southern Hokkien speakers with only one coming from Anhwei province.[37] The managers and senior staff recruited on this formula worked

---

36. See Yen Ching-hwang, 'Modern Overseas Chinese Enterprises: A Preliminary Study', in Yen Ching-hwang, *Studies in Modern Overseas Chinese History*, p. 246.
37. Lim How Seng, op. cit., p. 158.

hard for Tan Kah Kee; they were bonded to him through dialect and geographical ties, and could not easily be poached by Tan's business competitors.

John Lorriman and Takashi Kenjo in their work draw a contrast between Western and Japanese management styles. Western management emphasises technical competence and strategies, while Japanese management focuses on training of staff and the unleashing of human energy.[38] Tan Kah Kee's approach to management was similar to that of the Japanese. He greatly emphasised moral power and the cultivation of the correct attitude of staff and workers. His exalted aim of using commerce to save China was inspiring and generated a strong sense of patriotism among his staff and workers, who had a clear purpose for working hard for the success of the company.[39]

One of the strengths of Western business practice is emphasis on marketing. The consumers' needs must be satisfied, and to meet this need, consumer behaviour has to be investigated and understood. However, consumer behaviour can be influenced and guided to certain products by the media. Although Tan Kah Kee had no such advanced marketing knowledge, he nevertheless knew that his competitive edge over other Chinese pineapple-canning manufacturers was his knowledge of overseas markets. Consuming prepared food from a can was a new concept, and it was not readily accepted by the Overseas Chinese even after they had been exposed to Western influences. But canned food had already become popular in the West at the turn of present century, and Tan knew pineapple canning would have a future if he could capture the vast European market. He kept himself well-informed about market demand, and made daily contact with European agency houses regarding overseas demands for every minute detail of size, shape and level of added sugar for canned pineapple.[40] The traditional Chinese business attitude was that

---

38. See John Lorriman and Takashi Kenjo, *Japan's Winning Margins: The Secrets of Japan's Success*, (Tokyo, Oxford University Press, 1996), pp. 82–3.

39. See 'The Rules and Regulations of the Tan Kah Kee Company, 1929', 'Preface' and pp. 1–8.

40. See C.F. Yong, op. cit., p. 45.

customers will always buy if you have something good to sell, but Tan knew this philosophy was no longer compatible with the fiercely competitive environment.

Tan Kah Kee also adopted the Western business principle of vertical integration, which he applied to his pineapple canning industry. In 1904, he invested in a pineapple plantation in order to ensure the supply of quality pineapple. He turned 500 acres of raw jungle land into a pineapple plantation which he named Fu Shan Yuan ('The Plantation Estate of Lucky Mountain').[41]

Tan Kah Kee and Overseas Chinese Entrepreneurship

The study of Tan Kah Kee's business practices has illustrated some of the salient features of Overseas Chinese entrepreneurship. The ability to bring capital, labour and management together to found an enterprise; a capitalistic attitude, with the courage to take initiatives and risks, the determination to implement ideas and the will to succeed; the ability to lead, to communicate and manage a successful enterprise — most of these features were reflected in Tan Kah Kee's entrepreneurship. But what contribution did Tan Kah Kee make to the development of Overseas Chinese entrepreneurship as a whole? What weaknesses can be identified? Will Overseas Chinese entrepreneurship stand the future test of time?

In comparison with other prominent Overseas Chinese entrepreneurs such as Ma Ying-piao of the Sincere company of Hong Kong,[42] the Kwok Brothers of the Wing On company of Hong Kong

41. C.F. Yong, Ibid., p. 46.
42. For a study of Ma Ying-piao and his founding of the Sincere Company, see Wellington K.K. Chan, 'The Organizational Structure of Traditional Chinese Firms and Its Modern Reform', in *Business History Review: Special Issue on East Asian Business History*, vol. 56, no. 2 (1982) pp. 229–35. For the history of the Sincere Company of Hong Kong, see 'Hsien-shih kung-ssu erh-shih-wu nien ching-kuo shih'(Twenty Five Years' History of the Sincere Company), in *Hsien-shih kung-ssu erh-shih-wu chou-nien chi-nien ch'ih* (The Souvenir Magazine of Silver Jubilee Celebration of the Sincere Company) (Hong Kong, Shang Wu Printing House, 1924), pp.1–5, 'Records' Section.

and Shanghai,[43] Oei Tiong Ham of the Dutch East Indies[44] and Chang Pi-shih of the Dutch East Indies and Penang,[45] Tan Kah Kee stands out starkly as a highly politically-motivated entrepreneur. He may not have had a strong political orientation when he started to build his business empire in 1904, but as rapid political change unfolded in China, Tan Kah Kee was more and more drawn into China's modern destiny, which became intertwined with his business activities. The uniqueness of Tan Kah Kee's entrepreneurship was that his businesses were linked by the broad and lofty overall objective of saving China through commerce. He aimed to make a

43. For a study of the Kwok brothers, principally Kwok Lock and Kwok Chin, and their founding of the Wing On Company in Hong Kong and Shanghai, see Yen Ching-hwang, 'The Wing On Company in Hong Kong and Shanghai: A Case Study of Modern Overseas Chinese Enterprise, 1907–1949', in Yen Ching-hwang, *Studies in Modern Overseas Chinese History*, pp. 196–236. For the history of the Wing On Company, see Liu T'ien-jen, 'Pen kung-ssu erh-shih-wu chou-nien chih ching-kuo' (History of the Wing On Company in the last Twenty-five Years), in *Hsiang-kang Yung-an yu-hsien kung-ssu nien-wu chou-nien chi-nien lu* (The Souvenir Magazine of Silver Jubilee Celebration of the Wing On Company of Hong Kong) (Hong Kong, T'ien Hsing Printing Company, 1932), *Shih-lueh* (history) column, pp. 1–4; Kwok Chin, *Yung-an ching-shen chih fa-jen chi ch'i chang-ch'eng shih-lueh* (The Origins of Wing On Spirit and Its Development) (Hong Kong, 1961).
44. For works on Oei Tiong Ham in English, see J. Panglaykim and I. Palmer, 'Study of Entrepreneurship in Developing Countries: The Development of One Chinese Concern in Indonesia', in *Journal of Southeast Asian Studies*, vol.1, no.1 (March, 1970), pp. 85–95; Yoshihara Kunio (ed), *Oei Tiong Ham Concern: The First Business Empire of Southeast Asia* (Kyoto, The Center for Southeast Asian Studies, Kyoto University, 1989, 231pp.). For works in Chinese, see Zhou Nanjing, *Feng-yu t'ung-chou: Tung-nan-ya yu hua-jen wen-t'I* (In the Same Boat Through the Storm: Southeast Asia and the Overseas Chinese) (Beijing, Chung-kuo hua-ch'iao ch'u-pan kung-ssu 1995), pp. 525–38.
45. For works on Chang Pi-shih in English, see Michael Godley, 'Chang Pi-shih and Nanyang Chinese Involvement in South China Railroads, 1896–1911', in *Journal of Southeast Asian Studies*, vol.4, no.1 (1973) pp.16–30; Michael Godley, 'The Late Ch'ing Courtship of the Chinese in Southeast Asia', in *Journal of Asian Studies*, vol. 34, no. 2 (1975), pp. 361–85; Michael

lot of money in order to finance his non-profit making educational enterprises in Fukien province, principally the Chi Mei Educational Village and the Xiamen University. Profit was not the aim in itself, but a means to an end.

However, the political orientation of his enterprise was a double-edged sword. On the one hand, his noble objectives aroused patriotism among his staff and workers and unleashed positive contributions from them; on the other, they invited jealousy and retaliation from British and Japanese business concerns. British business in Southeast Asia was weary of the growing economic power of the Chinese in British Malaya, and Tan Kah Kee's success in manufacturing in Singapore was taken as a threat rather than as a blessing. The uncooperativeness of British banks in dealing with the Tan Kah Kee Company in early the 1930s was a factor in the collapse of his business empire in 1934.[46] In an attempt to retaliate against Tan Kah Kee for his active involvement in the anti-Japanese Tsinan Incident movement in Singapore and Malaya,[47] the Japanese dumped cheap manufactured

Godley, 'Overseas Chinese entrepreneurship and Reformers: The Case of Chang Pi-shih', in Paul A. Cohen and John E. Schrecker (eds), *Reform in Nineteenth Century China* (Cambridge, Massachusetts, Harvard University Press, 1976) pp. 49–59; Michael Godley, *The Mandarin-Capitalists from Nanyang: Overseas Chinese Enterprise in the Modernization of China, 1893–1911* (Cambridge, Cambridge University Press, 1981). For works in Chinese, see Cheng Kuan-ying, *Chang Pi-shih chun sheng-p'ing shih-lueh (A Brief Biography of Mr Chang Pi-shih)*, in *Chin-tai chung-kuo shih-liao ts'ung-k'an*, series 75 (Taipei, n.d.); K'uang Kuo-hsiang, 'Chang Pi-shih ch'i-jen' (A Short Biography of Chang Pi-shih), in K'uang Kuo-hsiang, *Ping-ch'eng san-chi (An Anecdotal History of Penang)* (Hong Kong, Shih Chieh Book Store, 1958), pp. 97–107.

46.   See Tan Kah Kee, *Autobiography*, vol. 2, p. 511.

47.   For Tan Kah Kee's deep involvement in the anti-Japanese movement and boycotting Japanese goods in Southeast Asia after the Tsinan massacre, see Yen Ching-hwang, 'The Response of the Chinese in Singapore and Malaya to the Tsinan Incident, 1928', in *Journal of South Seas Society*, vol.43 (Singapore, South Seas Society, 1988), pp. 1–22; see also Yen Ching-hwang, *Community and Politics: The Chinese in Colonial Singapore and Malaysia* (Singapore, Times Academic Press, 1995), pp. 306–29; Yong Ching Fatt, *Chan-ch'ien Hsing hua she-hui chieh-kou yu ling-tou ch'en ch'u-t'an* (C.F. Yong,

goods on the Southeast Asian market with the intention of undermining the position of Tan Kah Kee's manufacturing enterprise.[48] Yet the political orientation of Tan Kah Kee's entrepreneurship did not make Tan Kah Kee less of an entrepreneur. His love of money was not less than that of other Overseas Chinese entrepreneurs, but it was aimed at serving China's national interests. Apart from this difference, his business acumen, innovativeness and other personal attributes match those of the other prominent Overseas Chinese entrepreneurs mentioned above.

The discussion of Overseas Chinese entrepreneurship is even more meaningful if we can assess its negative aspects. Certainly Chinese culture helps to mould Overseas Chinese entrepreneurs.[49] To deny this cultural influence would be tantamount to an assertion that Western culture has no influence on the behaviour of Euro-American politicians. However, a cultural perspective should not deny the negative aspects of Confucian culture and its impact on Overseas Chinese business behaviour. Confucian emphasis on family restricts the development of a family-based enterprise into a large conglomerate. Family orientation reinforced by kinship and geographical loyalty tends to produce a feeling of distrust in outsiders, and a propensity towards in-breeding, which gives rise to nepotism.[50] This produces centrifugal forces which tend to undermine the unity and solidarity of a commercial organisation, and prevent collaboration between and amalgamation of Overseas Chinese enterprises. The result of this is the proliferation of small and medium-sized businesses constantly engaging in price wars and fighting for an increase in market share.

    Chinese Community Structure and Leadership in Pre-War Singapore) (Singapore, South Seas Society, 1977), pp. 154–65.

48. See Tan Kah Kee, 'Wei-chi shih-pai tsai shih k'e-ch'ih' (Those who fear risking failure are the shameful ones), in *Tung-fang tsa-chih* (Eastern Miscellanies), vol. 31, no. 7 (Shanghai, 1934), p. 7.

49. For an exposition of this cultural influence on Overseas Chinese entrepreneurship, see J.A.C. Mackie, 'Overseas Chinese Entrepreneurship', in *Asian-Pacific Literature*, vol. 6, no.1, Manila, May 1992), pp. 43–5; Yen Ching-hwang, 'The Wing On Company of Hong Kong and Shanghai' and 'Modern Overseas Chinese Business Enterprise: A Preliminary Study', in Yen Ching-hwang, *Studies in Modern Overseas Chinese History*, pp. 196–254.

50. See Gordon Reading, *The Spirit of Chinese Capitalism*, p. 134.

Of course, some Overseas Chinese enterprises are becoming larger, but they are in the minority. Those enterprises which have grown to become modern conglomerates are under the constant stress of internal friction generated by the large size of the family and a lack of primogeniture. Wong Siu-lun has aptly described the process of the degeneration of a Chinese family enterprise in three generations,[51] and 'wealth will not last three generations' becomes a stigma in the Overseas Chinese communities.[52] The carving up of family wealth weakens the foundation of Overseas Chinese conglomerates and undermines the prospect of their expansion. Strong family orientation is the root cause of internal dissension, although disunity and lack of solidarity among Overseas Chinese could also due to the environment. Overpopulation in China produced a strong sense of competition and increased the survival instincts of individuals and families, who have to compete more fiercely than people in the West for jobs and business; and this intense competition undermines unity and solidarity.

The future for Overseas Chinese entrepreneurs and Overseas Chinese conglomerates is bright. Like Japanese and South Korean entrepreneurs, they are on the right track in integrating Confucian cultural values with Western business practices, and they have benefited greatly from combining the best of both worlds. Technological and information revolutions have made the world smaller, and globalisation of the world economy is growing. Free trade will call the shots in the twenty-first century, and competition among multinational companies will become more intense. In the future corporate competition, those companies which are able to integrate Western and Eastern cultures, will have the competitive edge. Confucian culture is rich in handling human relationships, but it lacks a strong sense of change, creativity and innovation; while Western culture emphasises the values of organisation and system, but lacks strong human bonds. The combination of the best of both cultures will produce a superior hybrid.

51. See Siu-lun Wong, 'The Chinese Family Firm: A Model', in *British Journal of Sociology*, vol. 36, pp. 58–72.
52. This stigma is still common in the Overseas Chinese communities. See John Naisbitt, *Megatrends Asia: The Eight Asian Megatrends that are Changing the World* (London, Nicholas Brealey Publishing Ltd, 1995), p. 17.

One of the positive signs for the growth of Overseas Chinese conglomerates is the training and preparation of future successors. Prospective Chinese tycoons have been sent to the West and Japan for education, and are exposed to advanced knowledge about business and management of the world. At the same time, they have built up contacts and personal networks with the future managers of Western and Japanese companies during their university education, and will greatly benefit from these connections when they take over the business empires from their fathers or uncles.

There are also signs that these prospective Overseas Chinese tycoons are increasingly interested in Chinese culture and will tap traditional Chinese values for the benefit of their conglomerates. As China emerges as a world economic superpower and one of the most important markets, and as Overseas Chinese communities in the Asia Pacific region also emerge as an important economic force, prospective Overseas Chinese tycoons cannot afford to ignore the vast China and Overseas Chinese markets for their future expansion. They will have to turn to traditional values and traditional Chinese social organisations to seek strength for their future development. By that time, they should have a balanced view of the world and a more balanced approach to the well-being of their business empires, and should benefit greatly from their efforts in the integration of Eastern and Western cultures.

PART II

CULTURE, EDUCATION AND POLITICS IN ETHNIC CHINESE SOCIETY

CHAPTER 6

Ethnic Chinese Culture in Southeast Asia: Continuity and Change*

The Formation of Ethnic Chinese Culture

For the convenience of this study, Ethnic Chinese culture is defined as the culture of the ethnic Chinese minority of Southeast Asia. The Chinese in Southeast Asia as an ethnic group is taken in terms of physical, cultural, social and economic differences from indigenous Southeast Asians;[1] while culture is understood as a set of beliefs, values and customs together with their outward expressions such as religion, education, language, dress, and cuisine.

---

*   This chapter was first published in Yu Chunghsun (ed), *Ethnic Chinese: Their Economy, Politics and Culture* (Tokyo, The Japan Times Ltd, 2000), pp. 221–247.

1.   See Fredrik Barth, 'Introduction', in Fredrik Barth (ed), *Ethnic Groups and Boundaries: The Social Organization of Culture Difference* (London, George Allen & Unwin, 1969), pp. 10–11; Charles Hirschman, 'The Meaning and Measurement of Ethnicity in Malaysia: An Analysis of Census Classification', in *The Journal of Asian Studies*, vol. 46, no. 3 (August 1987), p. 557.

The formation of the Ethnic Chinese culture in Southeast Asia was closely related to the history of Chinese trading activities and settlements in this region. The Chinese began to trade with Southeast Asia as early as the second century BC,[2] but trade did not start to grow until the seventh century AD.[3] It continued to grow and expand throughout the Song (960–1279), Yuan (1280–1368), Ming (1368–1644) and Qing (1644–1911) periods.[4] The earliest Chinese settlement in maritime Southeast Asia can be traced back to the tenth century AD on the island of Sumatra; an Arab visitor to the island in the year 943 recorded Chinese settlements in Palembang and neighbouring areas. Migration of the Chinese to the island was mainly due to the scourge of the notorious Huang Chao.[5]

Chinese political refugees increased in Southeast Asia after the fall of the indigenous Chinese Song Dynasty in the thirteenth century. These Song loyalists who refused to surrender to the new Mongol rulers in China took their families and followers to settle in mainland Southeast

2. See Hsu Yun-ts'iao, 'Hua Qiao', in *Yu Shukun, Nanyang Nianjian* (The Nanyang Annals) (Singapore, Nanyang Baoshe youxian gongsi, 1951), kui, p. 5.

3. An excellent study of China's early trade with Southeast Asia is Wang Gungwu, 'The Nanhai Trade: A Study of the Early History of Chinese Trade in the South China Sea', in *Journal of the Malayan Branch of the Royal Asiatic Society* vol. 31, pt. 2 (June 1958), pp. 1–135.

4. For China's trade with Southeast Asia and other parts of the world during the Song and Yuan periods, see Chen Gaohua, *Song, Yuan shiqi de haiwai maoyi* (China's Overseas Trade during the Song and Yuan Dynasties) (Tienjin, 1981); Chen Gaohua, 'Yuan dai de haiwai maoyi' (Overseas Trade of the Yuan Dynasty), in Lishi Yanjiu (Beijing, 1978), pp. 61–9; Li Donghua, 'Song Yuan shidai Quanzhou haiwai qiaotong de shengkuang (Quanzhou's Overseas Communication and Trade during the Song and Yuan Periods), in *Zhongguo haiyang fazhanshi lunwenji* (Essays of the Maritime History of China) (Taipei, Zhongyang Yanjiuyuan Sanmin zhuyi yanjiusuo, 1984), pp. 1–40. For China's expansion of foreign trade, including with Southeast Asia, see Li Jinming, *Mingdai haiwai maoyishi* (A History of the Foreign Trade of the Ming Dynasty) (Beijing, Zhongguo shehui kexie chubanshe, 1990).

5. See Hsu Yun-ts'iao, op. cit., in Yu Shukun (ed), *Nanyang Nianjian*, kui, p. 12.

Asia, especially in Annam (Vietnam) and Champa.[6] Chinese settlements in Southeast Asia grew in size and became more widespread over time; when, in the early fifteenth century, Admiral Zheng He visited the region, he witnessed Chinese settlements in parts of mainland and maritime Southeast Asia.[7]

Chinese political refugees continued to arrive and settle in Southeast Asia, especially after the fall of the Ming dynasty in 1644. Almost at about the same time, Chinese immigrants arrived in substantial numbers in response to new economic opportunities arising from European penetration in the region. The Dutch policy of inducing Chinese to man its domains in the East Indies resulted in the rise of Chinese settlements in Batavia.[8] At the same time, European economic penetration effectively linked Southeast Asia with international markets, and created new demands for Southeast Asian agricultural and mineral products. This in turn stimulated Chinese migration and settlement in the Southeast Asian region. The demand for gold, for instance, encouraged a large number of Chinese miners to emigrate and resulted in the creation of Chinese settlements in Pontianak (Borneo) and Bangka in the eighteenth century.[9] British

6. See Chen Zhutong, 'Yuandai Zhonghua minzu haiwai fazhan kao' (Notes on Overseas Expansion of the Chinese during the Yuan Dynasty), pt. 2, in *Jinan xuebao* (Journal of Jinan University) vol. 2, no. 2 (Shanghai, 1937), pp. 123–24.

7. See the records of Ma Huan and Fei Xin, two officials who accompanied Zheng to the region. See Ma Huan (annotated by Feng Chengjun), *Yingya shenglan jiaozhu* (Beijing, Zhonghua shuju, 1955), pp. 1–17; Fei Xin (annotated by Feng Chengjun), *Xingcha shenglan jiaozhu* (Beijing, Zhonghua shuju, 1954), pp. 1–43.

8. For the early Dutch policy of inducing Chinese to join its early settlements and the practice of collaborative policy with the Chinese, see Leonard Blusse, 'Batavia, 1619–1740: The Rise and Fall of a Chinese Colonial Town', in *Journal of Southeast Asian Studies*, vol. 12, no. 1 (A Special Issue on Ethnic Chinese in Southeast Asia, edited by C.F. Yong) (March 1981), pp. 159–78; Leonard Blusse, 'Testament to a Towkay: Jan Con, Batavia and the Dutch China Trade', in Leonard Blusse, *Strange Company: Chinese Settlers, Mestizo Women and the Dutch in VOC Batavia* (Dordrecht, Holland, Foris Publications, 1986), pp. 49–72.

9. For Chinese settlement in Pontianak, See Lo Xianglin, *Xi Polozhou Lo Fangbo deng sojian gongheguo kao* (A Historical Survey of the Lan-Fang Presidential

advancement in Southeast Asia since the late eighteenth century and its free trade policy attracted a number of Chinese economic immigrants to settle. Under the stimulus of rapid economic development in the region, a large number of Chinese labourers were induced or imported to mines and plantation estates in Southeast Asia.[10] By the beginning of the twentieth century, large modern Chinese settlements dotted many parts of the region.

Chinese immigrants, whether political or economic, invariably brought with them Chinese beliefs, values and customs to their new lands, and expressed them in various cultural forms such as Chinese temples, Chinese-style houses and shops, Chinese dress, cuisine, music, festivals and so on.[11] Although these cultural values and forms did not belong to Chinese high culture, they nevertheless preserved the core of Chinese tradition and constituted the backbone of Ethnic Chinese culture in Southeast Asia.

What made the Ethnic Chinese communities in Southeast Asia essentially different from indigenous communities were Chinese customs and traditions, and Chinese religion and education, which

System in Western Borneo Established by Lo Fang-Pai and Other Overseas Chinese) (Hong Kong, Zhongguo Xueshe, 1961); Wang Tai Peng, *The Origins of Chinese Kongsi* (Petaling Jaya, Pelanduk Publications, 1994) and Daniel Chew, *Chinese Pioneers on the Sarawak Frontier, 1842–1941* (Singapore, Oxford University Press, 1990). For Chinese mining settlement in Bangka, see Mary F. Somers Heidhues, *Bangka Tin and Mentok Pepper: Chinese Settlement on an Indonesian Island* (Singapore, Institute of Southeast Asian Studies, 1992), pp. 10–8.

10. For a discussion of the development of the tin and cash crop industries and their demand for Chinese labourers in Malaya, see Wong Lin Ken, *The Malayan Tin Industry to 1914* (Tucson, The University of Arizona Press, 1965); J.C. Jackson, *Planters and Speculators: Chinese and European Agricultural Enterprise in Malaya, 1786–1912* (Kuala Lumpur, University of Malaya Press, 1968). For the development of the tin and cash crop industries in the Dutch East Indies, see Mary F. Somers Heidhues, *Bangka Tin and Mentok Pepper*, p. 54; Jan Breman, *Taming the Coolie Beast: Plantation Society and the Colonial Order in Southeast Asia* (Delhi, Oxford University Press, 1990, second impression), pp. 50–64.

11. See Yen Ching-hwang, *A Social History of the Chinese in Singapore and Malaya, 1800–1911* (Singapore, Oxford University Press, 1986), pp. 10–21.

the immigrants unconsciously perpetuated. Born and bred in villages in the southeastern part of China, early Chinese immigrants had a strong desire to keep their customs. Being blindly loyal to their traditions, they did not see the need to change their customs and habits to suit local climates and conditions. This cultural tenacity was not just confined to the immigrants, but was also found among local-born Chinese, such as the Babas and Nyonyas in the British Straits settlements, the Peranakans in the Dutch East Indies and the Mestizos in the Spanish Philippines. Writing in 1879, a British observer, J.D. Vaughan, commented that 'The Chinese are so attached to the habits of their forefathers that notwithstanding an intercourse in the Straits for many generations with the natives of all countries, they have jealously adhered to their ancient manners and customs.'[12]

Indeed, early Chinese immigrants intended to keep all Chinese customs and habits. They wore Chinese-style clothes and hairstyles, ate Chinese food, consumed goods imported from China and built houses and shops in the Chinese style.[13] The most distinctive feature of the Chinese in the nineteenth century Southeast Asia was their hairstyle, the queue. Originally imposed on the Chinese by the Manchu conquerors, the queue was taken over by the Chinese as their hairstyle. Like their compatriots in China, the Ethnic Chinese considered their hair as an inseparable part of their body given by their parents, and thus developed a strong emotional attachment to the queue. It provided a common identity for all Ethnic Chinese regardless of their wealth and social status, and became a conspicuous symbol separating them from non-Chinese people. Although the queue was regarded by Europeans as a symbol of backwardness and an object for derision, and was considered by the anti-Manchu revolutionaries as the badge of Manchu servitude, it nevertheless became a symbol of Chinese

12.   See J.D. Vaughan, *The Manners and Customs of the Chinese of the Straits Settlements* (Taipei, Cheng Wen Publishing Company, 1971, reprint), p. 4.
13.   See Yen Ching-hwang, *A Social History of the Chinese in Singapore and Malaya*, pp. 16–7.
14.   See an article entitled 'Ping Shuo' (Protest against Injustice), published in *Lat Pau*, 3 December 1890, p. 1.

identity and pride in the nineteenth and early twentieth centuries.[14]

In the process of retaining their cultural identity, the early Ethnic Chinese consciously tried to keep alive traditional festivities. Most Chinese festivals were observed in their original forms. Despite climatic differences and local conditions, the Ethnic Chinese in nineteenth-century Southeast Asia followed strictly the dates of the festivals in the lunar calendar. These festivals included Chinese New Year; the birth of the Emperor of Heaven on the ninth day of the first moon (especially among the Hokkien Chinese); the *Yuanxiao* festival on the fifteenth day of the first moon; the *Qingming* festival in the third moon; the Dragon Boat festival in the fifth moon; the *Zhongyuan* festival (also known as the festival of the dead) on the fifteenth day of the seventh moon; and the Moon festival in the eighth moon.[15]

A leading Chinese sociologist has pointed out that the traditional Chinese festivities had important social role to play. They relieved monotonous routine life, refreshed after hard work and provided practical motivation. At the same time, they reinforced the social values of group spirit, optimism and harmony.[16] For the Ethnic Chinese communities at this time, traditional Chinese festivities served an even more important communal and cultural function: they provided a common focus for general participation. All the festivals fell on common days regardless of dialect difference, and the stories behind them were the same.[17] In the absence of the regular holidays held in Western societies, these festivities were taken by many Ethnic Chinese as

15. See Yen Ching-hwang, *A Social History of the Chinese in Singapore and Malaya*, p. 18.
16. See C.K. Yang, *Religion in Chinese Society* (Berkeley, University of California Press, 1967), pp. 94–6.
17. For instance, the story of the patriotic poet, Qu Yuan, who commited suicide in protest against the politics of the Chu kingdom, was behind the Dragon Boat Festival (Duan Wu Jie) for all Chinese. Similarly, the story of a beautiful fairy, Chang E, who ran away from her lover to the moon, was the story behind the Moon Festival for all Chinese. See C.S. Wong, *A Cycle of Chinese Festivities* (Singapore, Malaysia Publishing House Limited, 1967), pp. 120–27, 144–51.

days for celebration and rest, and to refresh themselves for the hard work ahead.[18] Culturally, the celebration of these festivities also rekindled their sense of Chinese identity and reinforced their emotional attachment to Chinese traditions.

Early Chinese immigrants in Southeast Asia were conscious of their religious needs in the new land. With unpredictable futures and hazardous voyages ahead, religious worship became an important part of their spiritual life. The majority of early Chinese immigrants were Buddhists of the Mahayana denomination. Mahayana Buddhism emphasised the power of prayer and taught that the salvation of individuals rested with prayer and worship rather than with personal suffering in life. Because of this, the early immigrants worshipped Buddha and other Buddhist deities in temples by burning joss paper and joss sticks. The import of a large quantity of joss paper and joss sticks into Southeast Asia in the early nineteenth century testifies to the importance of Buddhist worship in the Ethnic Chinese communities.[19] In addition, many beautiful and magnificent Buddhist temples dotted the landscape of Southeast Asia. A 1988 study of the Chinese community in Medan, North Sumatra, found the existence of at least twenty-five Chinese temples in that city.[20] The finding of another study of 1968 on the Chinese temples in Kuala Lumpur, Malaysia, is even more

18. For instance, the Chinese New Year celebration in Kuala Lumpur in January 1894 attracted a large number of Chinese mining coolies from the neighbouring tin-mining districts, Rawang and Serendah, in the state of Selangor. The coolies crowded the streets of the city and enjoyed themselves very much. See *Selangor Journal*, vol. 2, no.11 (Kuala Lumpur, January 1894) p. 163.
19. Between 1829 and 1830, 144 bales of joss-paper and 734 pounds of joss-sticks were imported into Singapore alone. See 'Statement of the Imports at Singapore during the Official year 1829–1830', in *Singapore Chronicle* (Singapore), 7 October 1830.
20. See Wolfgang Franke, 'Chinese Religion in Southeast Asia with Particular Consideration of Medan, North Sumatra', in *Journal of the South Seas Society*, vol. 43 (Singapore,1988), pp. 23–42, or his collected essays entitled 'Sino-Malaysiana: Selected Papers on Ming & Qing History and on the Overseas Chinese in Southeast Asia' (Singapore, South Seas Society, 1989), pp. 401–20.

astounding. There were at least 150 major and small Chinese temples in Kuala Lumpur (including Petaling Jaya).[21]

Polytheism characterised Ethnic Chinese religious life in Southeast Asia, Hong Kong and Taiwan. The so-called Buddhist temples found in Southeast Asia were for the worship not just of Buddhist deities, but also for Taoist and regional deities.[22] The polytheistic nature of Ethnic Chinese religion made the religious life more complex. The commercialisation of Ethnic Chinese communities since the end of the Second World War did not see the decline of Buddhism in the region. Instead, more and more Buddhist temples, and temples dedicated to different deities, flourished. Numerous popular religious sects arose in the Ethnic Chinese communities. These sects are of a syncretistic nature, blending Buddhism, Taoism and Confucianism together. One of these sects is the so-called 'Three-in-one Doctrine' (*Sanyijiao*), founded in the sixteenth century in Fujian province and introduced into Southeast Asia in the late nineteenth and early twentieth centuries. In Singapore and Malaysia in the 1960s there were quite a number of temples dedicated to this doctrine, and the followers were mostly Hinghua

21. See Choo Chin Tow, 'Jilongpo huaren shimiao zhi yanjiu' (Some Sociological Aspects of the Chinese Temples in Kuala Lumpur) (MA thesis, University of Malaya, 1968, in Chinese) p. 3. See also an article based on the thesis by the same author entitled 'Yibainian lai de Jilongpo huaren shimiao' (One Hundred Years History of the Chinese Temples in Kuala Lumpur), *in Xuelan E Zhonghua Dahuitang Chingzhu Wushisi Zhounian Tekan* (Souvenir Magazine of 54th Anniversary Celebration of the Chinese Assembly Hall of Selangor) (Petaling Jaya, Selangor, Life Printers Limited, 1977), pp. 616–31.

22. For instance, the earliest Chinese temple in Singapore and Malaysia, Cheng Hoon Teng (Qing Yun Ting, the temple of blue clouds) was dedicated to the worship of Guan Yin (Goddess of Mercy, a Buddhist deity). In addition, Guan Di (God of War and Prosperity, a Taoist deity) and Tian Hou (also known as Tian Fei or Ma Zu, Goddess of the Sea, a regional deity) were also worshipped in the temple. See Tan Cheng Lock (Chen Zhenlu), Cheng Hoon Teng Temple (Malacca, 1965), pp. 6, 14. For identifying Guan Di as a Taoist deity, see Kubo Tokutada (transl. Xiao Kunhua), *Dao Jiao Zhu Shen* (The Taoist Deities) (Chengdu, Shichuan Renmin chubanshe, 1988), pp. 170–72.

Chinese. [23] Another sect, the 'Doctrine of the True Void' (*Zhenkongjiao*) spread to Indonesia and Thailand, and is popular among the Hakka Chinese. Another even more widespread Chinese religious sect is 'The Moral Uplifting Society' (*Dejiaohui*) which not only blends Buddhism, Taoism and Confucianism together, but also incorporates some of the teachings of Islam and Christianity. It was first founded in China in 1939, but became popular among Hong Kong and Southeast Asian Chinese after the Second World War. [24]

The illiteracy of the majority of early Chinese immigrants in Southeast Asia did not lead them to desire strongly for education. But as the Ethnic Chinese communities became more mature, and a younger generation of Chinese was brought up in the new land, the need to educate the young was keenly felt. Three types of Chinese schools were established before the introduction of modern Chinese education at the beginning of the twentieth century: a traditional private school popularly known as *sishu*, community schools run by dialect or clan associations, and missionary schools. The traditional *sishu* predominated among them. Most of these early Chinese schools existed in the ports or cities of Southeast Asia; there were also a few in rural areas. In 1885, for instance, there was an estimated one hundred and fifteen Chinese schools founded in the Straits Settlements, fifty two in Penang, fifty one in Singapore and twelve in Malacca. [25]

Small enrolments and conservative teaching methods characterised these traditional Chinese schools. The majority of the

---

23. The Hinghua Chinese are from Fujian province. They speak a distinctive dialect unintelligible to Southern Fujianese (Hokkien). For the 'Three-in-one Doctrine' (*Sanyijiao*) see Wolfgang Franke, "Some Remarks on the 'Three-in-One Doctrine' and its Manifestations in Singapore and Malaysia", in Wolfgang Franke, *Sino-Malaysiana: Selected Papers on Ming & Qing History and on the Overseas Chinese in Southeast Asia, 1942–1988* (Singapore, South Seas Society, 1989), pp. 343–44.

24. See Chen Zhiming (Tan Chee Beng) (transl. Su Qinghua [Soo Khin Wah]), *Ma Xin Dejiaohui zhi fazhan ji qi fenbu yanjiu* (The Development and Spread of the Dejiaohui in Malaysia and Singapore) (Kuala Lumpur, Agents' Digest (M), 1991), pp. 17–8.

25. See 'Annual Education Report for the Straits Settlements for the year 1885', in *Straits Settlements Legislative Council Proceedings, 1886*, appendix 17, table E.

one hundred and fifteen Chinese schools in the Straits settlements in 1885 had less than twenty students, and some of them had only two.[26] The conservative teaching methods did not teach students to comprehend, but only to recite and memorise the texts.[27] The facilities and the quality of teachers in the *sishu* were generally poor, and the standard was low.[28] On the other hand, those schools run by dialect groups or clan associations had better facilities, better teachers and better standards.

The twin aims of traditional Chinese education in Southeast Asia were to exalt the moral principles of Confucius, and to acquire literacy skills. This was clearly reflected in the curriculum of the early schools. 'Trimetrical Classics' (*San zijing*) together with 'the Four Books' (*The Great Learning, The Mean, Analects* and *Mencius*), the *Commentary on the Four Books* by Zhu Xi, the great Song Confucian philosopher, and 'the Five Classics' (*Book of Poetry, Book of History, Book of Change, Book of Rites* and *Spring and Autumn Annals*) constituted the main texts for students in both *Sishu* and community schools.[29] 'The Four Books' and 'the Five Classics', which were the basic texts to prepare students for imperial examinations in China, did not serve the same function in the Ethnic Chinese communities; but rather, they were used to exalt the moral principles of Confucius. Thus, the Classics were instrumental in imparting Confucian values to students in order to benefit their adult lives.[30] As the majority of the immigrants were illiterate, literacy opened up a new world for students which would benefit them in trade and business.

The rise of modern education in China at the turn of the present century changed the direction of Ethnic Chinese education in Southeast Asia. As part of the Qing Government's political and social reforms, the age-old imperial examination system was replaced by a

---

26. Ibid.

27. See Lucius, 'State of Education Among the Chinese Settlers in Malacca', in *Indo-Chinese Cleaner, Quarterly* no. 11 (Malacca, January 1820), pp. 267–69.

28. See an editorial published in *Sing Po* (Star Daily) (Singapore, 9 January 1892), p. 1.

29. See Yen Ching-hwang, *A Social History of the Chinese in Singapore and Malaya*, p. 298.

30. Ibid.

modern education system based on the Japanese model (indirectly based on the American system). As a result, modern Chinese schools were founded in the Chinese communities in Southeast Asia. The first modern Chinese school in Southeast Asia was the Zhonghua School (Zhonghua Xuetang) in Penang.[31] Founded in March 1904 by a group of rich Chinese merchants led by Zhang Bishi — a renowned Ethnic Chinese entrepreneur and Qing bureaucrat — the school was to advance Confucian morality and to meet the needs of the local Chinese community.[32] In the following years, scores of modern Chinese schools were established in major ports and cities throughout Southeast Asia for the same purpose.[33] In contrast with traditional Chinese schools, modern Chinese schools in the Ethnic Chinese communities were larger in size and in a stronger financial position, had better facilities and teachers, and were of a higher standard. Their curriculum was more diversified and geared to equip students with modern knowledge. Apart from Confucian Classics, students were taught history, geography, foreign languages (English, Dutch, French or Spanish in their respective colonies) and mathematics.[34]

31. See *Penang Sin Pao* (Penang, 1 July 1904 and 4 July 1904); *Lat Pau* (Singapore, 30 December 1904).

32. Apart from Zhang Bishi, other prominent Chinese merchants included Foo Chee Choon (Hu Zichun, also known as Hu Guolian), Lin Kequan, Lin Juzhou, Liang Tingfang and Ng Kim Keng (Huang Jinqing). See an official document from the Ministry of Commerce to the Ministry of Education regarding the founding of the Zhonghua School in Penang by a group of Chinese gentry–merchants dated July 1906, in *Xuebu Guanbao* (The Gazettes of the Ministry of Education) vol. 9 (Beijing, 1st day of 11th moon of 32nd year of the Guangxu reign [16 December 1906]), pp. 46–7.

33. Scores of modern Chinese primary schools were established in British Malaya, including those in Singapore, Kuala Lumpur, Ipoh and Penang. In July 1908 it was also reported that more than fifty modern Chinese schools were founded in the Dutch East Indies with about 4,000 students. See two official reports published in the *Xuebu Guanbao* (The Gazette of the Ministry of Education), vol. 52 (Beijing, 1st day of 4th moon of 34th year of the Guangxu reign [30 April 1908]), p. 72 and vol. 60 (21st day of 6th Moon of 34th year of the Guangxu reign [19 July 1908]), p. 79.

34. One of the rare surviving documents relating to the curricula of modern Chinese schools in Southeast Asia is the curriculum of the Yingxin School of

The collapse of the Qing dynasty and the founding of the Republic in early 1912 saw modern Chinese education striding ahead. The new government restructured the school system, changed the curricula and re-oriented the objectives of the education system. Three important principles were enunciated: education for moral values, education for acquiring practical knowledge and education for the physical well-being of students.[35] The new Republican education system had a profound impact on the Ethnic Chinese communities in Southeast Asia. It boosted the spread of modern Chinese education in the region, and effectively incorporated Ethnic Chinese education into its orbit of influence. At the same time, the Chinese Government helped to provide qualified teachers, textbooks and curriculum supervision.[36]

The founding of the Nationalist Government in Nanjing in 1927 began a new chapter in the history of Ethnic Chinese education in Southeast Asia. With its close political connections with the Ethnic Chinese communities, the Nationalist Government placed a strong emphasis on Ethnic Chinese education. Ethnic Chinese leaders were recruited into the Overseas Chinese Bureau (Qiaowu weiyuanhui) which was set up partly to advise the government on the development of Ethnic Chinese education.[37] The Nationalist

Singapore, which was founded by the Jiaying Hakka community of Singapore. The Yin Sin School's curriculum was printed in a booklet published in Singapore in 1907. It contained the new subjects in addition to the study of traditional subjects like *Duching* (study of the classics). See Xia Pingyan, *Xinjiapo Yingxin Xuetang zhuogai jianming zhangcheng* (Modified Comprehensive Rules and Regulations of the Yin Sin School, Singapore) (Singapore, Yin Sin School, 1907), pp. 3–5.

35. See Li Guilin (ed), *Zhongguo Jiaoyushi* (A History of Chinese Education) (Shanghai, Shanghai jiaoyu chubanshe, 1989), p. 355; Colin Mackerras, 'Education in the Guomindang Period, 1928–1949', in David Pong & Edmund Fung (eds), *Ideal and Reality: Social and Political Change in Modern China, 1860–1949* (Lanham, University Press of America, 1985), pp. 153–54.

36. See Yen Ching-hwang, 'Zhanqien Xin Ma Minren jiaoyu' (Hokkien Chinese Education in Singapore and Malaysia before World War II), in Yen Ching-hwang, *Haiwai huarenshi yanjiu* (Study in Ethnic Chinese History) (Singapore, Singapore Society of Asian Studies, 1992), p. 294.

37. Famous Ethnic Chinese leaders from Southeast Asia such as Tan Kah Kee of Singapore, Deng Zeru of Malaya and Xiao Foucheng of Thailand were

Government's special attention resulted in a big push for modern education in the Ethnic Chinese communities in Southeast Asia: more Chinese schools were established, and the quality of education was improved. Important developments in both secondary and female education were also witnessed. Although the first Chinese high school in the region was established in Singapore following the impact of the May Fourth movement, a large number of secondary Chinese schools and girls' schools sprang up in the 1920s and 1930s.[38] All of these schools (primary and secondary) were integrated into the education system of China. The Nationalist Government helped to provide qualified teachers, textbooks and curriculum development, helped to train Ethnic Chinese teachers and offered financial assistance.[39]

These close educational connections subjected the Ethnic Chinese to the influence of China and ensured the perpetuation of Chinese cultural values in the Ethnic Chinese communities. Thus, Confucian moral values and modern Chinese values filtered through to the Chinese-educated elite in Southeast Asia.

The Stages and Forces of Change in Ethnic Chinese Culture

The tenacity of traditional Chinese cultural values expressed in Ethnic Chinese beliefs, customs, religion and education tends to lead to the misconception of an unchanged Ethnic Chinese culture

recruited as members of the Overseas Chinese Bureau of the the Guomindang Government in Nanjing. See Zhang Pengyuan & Shen Huaiyu (eds), *Guomin zhengfu zhiguan nianbiao, 1925–1949,* vol. 1 (Offices and Personnel of Republican China: The Nationalist Era, 1925–1949) (Taipei, Institute of Modern History, Academia Sinica, 1987), pp. 282–84.

38.   See Zhou Shenggao, *Haiwai huawen xuexiao jiaoyu* (Overseas Chinese Language Education) (Taipei, Qiaowu weiyuanhui, 1969), pp. 69–99, 111–55; Tay Lian Soo & Gwee Yee Hean, *Malaixiya, Xinjiapo huawen zhongxue tekan tiyao fu xiaoshi* (Chinese High School Souvenir Magazines of Malaysia and Singapore with School Histories) (Kuala Lumpur, Department of Chinese Studies, University of Malaya, 1975), pp. 9–10; Xu Shuwu, *Xinjiapo huaqiao jiaoyu quanmao* (The Overview of the Chinese Language Education in Singapore) (Singapore, Nanyang shuju, 1949), pp. 46–56.

39.   Xu Shuwu, op. cit., pp. 64–6.

in Southeast Asia. Western scholars who were ideologically influenced by the Cold War and regarded the Chinese in Southeast Asia as a political problem, tended to perpetuate the theory of the 'persistence of traditional Chinese culture' as a means of justifying their advocacy for the assimilation of the Ethnic Chinese into indigenous societies.[40] The persistence theorists and assimilation advocates of the 1960s were perhaps justified to certain extent, since they intended to help the newly independent countries in Southeast Asia to solve the 'Ethnic Chinese problem' on a short-term basis. But their perception of the Ethnic Chinese was coloured by Cold War ideology and the suspicion that the Ethnic Chinese were potentially 'fifth columnists' for the expansion of Communist influence in the region:[41] and they had difficulty seeing beyond the 1960s. This persistence theory is fallacious not just due to its ideological and period biases, but also due to its proponents' attitude towards culture.

The relationship between culture and society is a complex one, which I do not intend to debate here. However, for the purpose of this analysis, I take the view that culture is the product of a society during certain historical stages and circumstances, and that cultural change takes place in concomitance with historical and circumstantial changes. From this perspective, changes in culture are an inevitable process of history. I pointed out nearly a decade ago that forces for social change in the Ethnic Chinese communities worldwide were both internal and external. The internal forces included the divisions and conflict between Chinese dialect groups, between local-born Chinese and China-born Chinese, and between class within the Ethnic Chinese communities. Among the external

---

40. See G. William Skinner, 'Change and Persistence in Chinese Culture Overseas: A Comparison of Thailand and Java', in *Journal of South Seas Society*, vol. 16, pts. 1 & 2 (1960), pp. 86–100; Lea E. Williams, *The Future of the Overseas Chinese in Southeast Asia* (New York, McGraw-Hill Book Company, 1966), pp. 89-111.
41. The foremost exponent of this theory is Robert S. Elegant in his work entitled *The Dragon's Seed: Peking and the Overseas Chinese* (New York, St. Martin's Press, 1959).

forces were the impact of China's politics, the impact of the political, economic and cultural policies of the local governments, and the impact of social and political change in the world in general.[42]

The development of Ethnic Chinese culture in Southeast Asia can be divided into four stages: pre-1912; the period from 1912 to the end of the Second World War in 1945; post-war to the late 1960s; and the 1970s and beyond. Taking into consideration both internal and external forces, and in making these divisions I have adopted an 'Ethnic Chinese-centred' approach. The first stage covers the long period of early Chinese history in Southeast Asia stretching from late Ming to the fall of the Qing dynasty (from 1500 to 1911). This period saw the formation and early development of Ethnic Chinese culture. The second stage covers the founding of the new Chinese Republic in 1912 to the defeat of Japan in the Pacific War in August 1945. During this period, Ethnic Chinese communities in general, and those in Southeast Asia in particular, were pulled closer to China, and Ethnic Chinese culture was profoundly affected by the policies of the Republican Government in China. The third stage saw the retreat of Western colonial powers from Southeast Asia and the rise of newly independent states in the region. The new political and economic forces stimulated rapid change in Ethnic Chinese culture and saw a great shift from China-centred to locally developing cultures. The final stage, between the 1970s and the present, saw new political environments in East and Southeast Asia, the growing economic power of the Four Little Dragons, the opening up of mainland China as a potentially huge market, the rise of Ethnic

---

42. This view was expressed in a keynote speech delivered at the International Symposium on the Postwar Transformation of Overseas Chinese held in Xiamen, 25–28 April 1989. See Yen Ching-hwang, 'Cong lishi de jiaodu kan haiwai huaren de shehui biange' (Social Change in the Ethnic Chinese Communities from a Historical Point of View), in Guo Liang et. al. (eds), *Zhanhou haiwai huaren bianhua guoji xueshu yantaohui lunwenji* (The Postwar Transformation of Overseas Chinese: Collected Papers of an International Symposium) (Beijing, Zhongguo Huaqiao chuban gongsi, 1990), pp. 1–2.

Chinese business culture and a change in attitudes and policies of indigenous governments towards the Ethnic Chinese and Ethnic Chinese culture in the region.

The first stage, which lasted more than four hundred years, can be further divided into three phases: the first phase from 1500 to 1800; the second phase from 1801 to 1877, and the third phase from 1878 to 1911. In the first phase, Chinese settlements began to take shape but most of these settlements were small and of a transitory nature, and were scattered widely in different parts of Southeast Asia. Ethnic Chinese culture during this very early stage was in fact the southern Chinese culture of lower order. The so-called 'Vulgar Confucian Values' (which I prefer to call 'Popular Confucian Values') intertwined Buddhist, Taoist and folk values of rural China, and were retained by Chinese traders, immigrants and political refugees. The degree of retention of Chinese culture varied according to the nature and size of Chinese settlements. In larger settlements, or in those composed largely of political refugees, the retention of Chinese culture appears to have been stronger; while in settlements made up of illiterate immigrants and semi-literate traders the retention of Chinese cultural values appears to have been less. This can be illustrated by the fact that the Chinese settlement in seventeenth century Malacca, which consisted mainly of Chinese political refugees after the fall of the Ming dynasty in 1644, appears to have preserved many Chinese cultural values and traditions.[43] On the other hand, the large Chinese mining settlement in Pontianak (Borneo) in the eighteenth century,

43. For the Chinese settlement in Malacca in the seventeenth century, see Zhang Liqian, *Maliujia shi* (A History of Malacca, in Chinese) (Shanghai, Shangwu Printing Company, 1929). Cheng Hoon Teng temple (Qing Yun Ting), the earliest Chinese Buddhist temple in Singapore and Malaysia, which also acted as the administrative centre of the Chinese in early Malacca, has kept some original records, including 'Records of worship (*Jishibu*) 1809–1882' and 'Minutes of meetings (*Jilubu*) 1905–1930'. See Zheng Liangshu (Tay Lian Soo), 'Tingzhu shidai de Qingyunting ji huazu (Shang)' (The Cheng Hoon Teng Temple of Malacca and Chinese Society under the Administration of the Head of the Temple, Part 1), in *Asian Culture*, no. 4 (Singapore, Singapore Society of Asian Studies, October 1984), p. 24.

which consisted mainly of illiterate miners, does not seem to have left any original written records.[44] However, the degree of retention of Chinese customs and festivities would appear to be equally strong regardless of the nature of the Chinese settlements.

Two principal forces for change in Ethnic Chinese culture in Southeast Asia throughout its history are the need to adapt to the local environment, which I have termed the process of 'localisation'; and external pressure and stimuli. The former is a slow and imperceptive process of change, driven by survival needs and competition as a result of the physical growth of the Ethnic Chinese communities: while the latter is rapid, abrupt, dynamic and organised adaptation came naturally in the early stages. Although most of the Chinese communities in the first and second stages were made up of Chinese immigrants, some immigrants who succeeded in establishing bases overseas tended to stay and produce a second generation of Ethnic Chinese. Regardless of where their parents were born, the second generation who were born and bred in new environments tended to miss out on some Chinese traditions as result of adapting to local conditions.[45] They were unconsciously involved in the localisation process and found themselves comfortable with the new mixed values and practices.

44. The famous Lanfang Gongsi does not seem to have left any original written records. Even the main documents for the study of this organisation, 'Lanfang gongsi lidai niance' (The Annals of the Lanfang Gongsi), was told verbally by Ye Xianyun. See Lo Xianglin, *Xi Polozhou Lo Fangbo deng sojian gongheguo kao* (A Historical Survey of the Lan-Fang Presidential System in Western Borneo, Established by Lo Fang-Pai and Other Overseas Chinese) appendix 2 (Hong Kong, Zhongguo Xueshe, 1961), pp. 137–46.

45. The gradual loss of Chinese culture was noted by the Chinese cultural nationalists in the region. Their fear was best expressed by the editor of *Sing Po* (Star Daily), a leading Chinese language newspaper in Singapore in 1891. He stated that 'Chinese immigrants married local girls and brought up children to learn Western language so as to have contacts with foreigners. These local-born Chinese are at a loss when asked to read Chinese characters or books. After tens and hundreds of years, they will forget their Chinese dialects as well. By that time, several hundred thousand Chinese will degenerate to become barbarians, spreading their hair over their shoulders, and buttoning their garments on the left side' (*Sing Po*, 27 July 1891), p. 1.

Traditional Chinese values and customs gradually diminished as this process continued and the Ethnic Chinese produced more and more generations locally. This process of localisation became more rapid when Chinese immigrants married indigenous women and produced a generation of mixed-blood Chinese known as Babas and Nyonyas in Malaysia and Singapore, Peranakans in Indonesia and Mestizos in the Philippines.[46]

In the third and fourth stages, these changes surfaced prominently in the Ethnic Chinese communities in Southeast Asia. Rapid changes in the political and economic environments in the region speeded up the process of localisation, which was facilitated by the cease in the flow of fresh migrants from Mainland China after 1949. The process of localisation included two familiar concepts, acculturation and integration. The majority of the Ethnic Chinese in Southeast Asia after the Second World War were local-born, and unconsciously entered into the process of acculturation. Cultural values and customs inherited from their parents had to be constantly adjusted to meet local conditions and accommodate the values and habits of the new environments, so producing a set of mixed values and habits. At the same time, the Ethnic Chinese had shifted their horizons from China to Southeast Asia as time passed, and developed

46. For studies on the Babas and Nyonyas, see Tan Chee Beng 'Baba and Nyonya: A Study of the Ethnic Identity of the Chinese Peranakan in Malacca' (unpublished PhD thesis, Cornell University, May 1979); John R. Clammer, *Straits Chinese Society* (Singapore, Singapore University Press, 1980); Png Poh Seng, 'The Straits Chinese in Singapore: A Case Study of Local Identity and Socio-Cultural Accomodation', in *Journal of Southeast Asian History*, vol. 10, no. 1 (March, 1969), pp. 95–114. For a study on the Peranakans in Indonesia, see Leo Suryadinata, *Peranakan Chinese Politics in Java, 1917–1942* (Singapore, Singapore University Press, 1981). For a study on Chinese Mestizos in Philippines, see Edgar Wickberg, 'The Chinese Mestizo in Philippine History', in *Journal of Southeast Asian History*, no. 5 (March 1964), pp. 62–100. For a more recent study on mixed-blood Chinese in Southeast Asia, see G. William Skinner, 'Creolized Chinese Societies in Southeast Asia', in Anthony Reid (ed), *Sojourners and Settlers: Histories of Southeast Asia and the Chinese* (Sydney, Allen and Unwin, 1996), pp. 51–93.

a Southeast Asian-centred mentality.[47] This process of integration was particularly conspicuous in the political arena after many Southeast Asian countries had achieved their modern statehood in the period between late 1940s and mid 1960s.

The forces of external stimuli and pressure were perhaps most dynamic in the development of Ethnic Chinese culture in Southeast Asia. It emerged in the last phase of the first stage, and swept through the second and third stages, and converged with the localisation force in the last stage. The rise of reform and revolutionary movements in the last decade of the nineteenth century in China constituted the most important stimuli for changes in the Chinese communities in Southeast Asia. The movements led respectively by K'ang Yu-wei and Dr Sun Yat-sen caused rapid changes in the Ethnic Chinese communities, including their cultural values and customs. K'ang Yu-wei's political and social reformism, experimented in China in the famous Hundred Days' Reform in 1898, spilled over to the Ethnic Chinese communities in the region. The Confucian revival movement inspired by K'ang's reformism and led by a Western-educated Chinese medical practitioner, Dr Lim Boon Keng, started in Singapore and Malaya, and spread widely to the Dutch Indies, Thailand and Burma.[48] The movement was aimed at making Confucianism a modern religion capable of modernising and unifying China, and at

---

47. For a study of this process of change of political identity of the Chinese in Singapore and Malaya during the post-war period, see Chui Kuei-ch'iang, *Xin Ma huaren guojia rentong de zhuanbian, 1945–1959* (Changing National Identities of the Chinese in Singapore and Malaya, 1945–1959) (Xiamen, Xiamen daxue chubanshe, 1989).

48. For the Confucian Revival movement in Singapore and Malaya, see Yen Ching-hwang, 'The Confucian Revival Movement in Singapore and Malaya, 1899–1912', in *Journal of Southeast Asian Studies*, vol. 7. no. 1 (1976), pp. 33–57; for the rise of Confucianism in the Dutch East Indies, see C.A. Coppel, 'The Origins of Confucianism as an Organized Religion in Java, 1900–1923', in *Journal of Southeast Asian Studies*, vol. 12, no. 1 (1981) pp. 179–95, and Leo Suryadinata, 'Confucianism in Indonesia: Past and Present', in Leo Suryadinata, *The Chinese Minority in Indonesia: Seven Papers* (Singapore, Chapman Enterprise, 1978), pp. 33–62.

'Confucianising' the Chinese overseas.[49] Partly taking his cue from K'ang Yu-wei, Dr Lim Boon Keng together with another Western-educated Chinese professional, Song Ong Siang, crusaded against foot-binding and opium-smoking and carried out reforms of traditional Chinese customs in the Straits Chinese communities in Singapore and Malaya.[50] The response to the rise of the Chinese reform movement resulted in the introduction of more modern schools and the education of girls, the publication of many pro-reform Chinese newspapers and a change in attitudes towards women and their role in society.

The impact of the rise of the revolutionary movement led by Dr Sun Yat-sen was even mightier and more pervasive in the Chinese communities in Southeast Asia. The arrival of a number of revolutionary refugees in Southeast Asia at the turn of the twentieth century saw a greater impact of revolutionary ideas on the Ethnic Chinese communities. For the first time, a large number of the Ethnic Chinese were exposed to an intensive barrage of revolutionary propaganda, and were organised in support of revolutionary actions in south and south-western China.[51] The response of the Ethnic

49. See Yen Ching-hwang, ibid., pp. 55–7.
50. For a recent study on Lim Boon Keng and Song Ong Siang's involvement in this reform, see Lee Guan Kin's PhD thesis entitled 'Responding to Eastern and Western Cultures in Singapore: A Comparative Study of Khoo Seok Wan, Lim Boon Keng and Song Ong Siang' (Department of Chinese Studies, Hong Kong University, 1997), Chs. 5 & 6, pp. 110–60.
51. For the activities of the Chinese revolutionaries in Singapore and Malaya, see Yen Ching-hwang, *The Overseas Chinese and the 1911 Revolution: With Special Reference to Singapore and Malaya* (Kuala Lumpur, Oxford University Press, 1976); for the activities of the Chinese revolutionaries in Vietnam and Java, see Lu Shipeng, 'Yuenan huaqiao dui Xinhai guoming zhi gongxian' (The Contribution of the Vietnamese Chinese to the 1911 Revolution) and Liao Jianyu (Leo Suryadinata) 'Xinhai guoming yu Zaowa huaren — chutanxing yanjiu' (A Preliminary Study of the Chinese in Java and the 1911 Revolution), in *Xinhai guoming yu Nanyang huaren yantaohui lunwenji* (Collection of Essays presented to the International Symposium on the Chinese in Southeast Asia and the 1911 Revolution) (Taipei, Center of International Relations, Cheng Chi University, 1986), pp. 274–93, 387–400.

Chinese in Southeast Asia to the 1911 revolutionary movement was all-pervasive. It cut across dialect and class boundaries, directly or indirectly involving many.[52] The profound impact of this mighty movement on Ethnic Chinese culture was obvious. Whole communities were pulled towards China and developed a China-centred culture. Dialect barriers were weakened and a common Chinese identity emerged. Traditional values of loyalty to the emperor, filial piety and male domination were also weakened; and at the same time new ideas of altruism, martyrdom, equality and freedom slowly surfaced,[53] helping to shape the new cultural outlook of the Ethnic Chinese in the region.

Perhaps the most important external impact on the culture of the Southeast Asian Chinese was made by the May Fourth movement. Begun as a patriotic anti-imperialist political movement in China, it was transformed into a mighty cultural and social movement in modern Chinese history. Its crusade against traditional Chinese values, social institutions and practices had a profound impact on society in China,[54] as well as exerting a tremendous influence on the cultural life of the Ethnic Chinese in Southeast Asia. It stimulated modern Chinese literary activities, imparted modern Chinese values to the Chinese communities and strengthened a China-centred culture in Southeast Asia. Under the stimulus of the May Fourth movement, Chinese intellectuals in Southeast Asia began to promote modern Chinese literature, using *baihua* (vernacular Chinese language) instead of classical language to write novels, prose and poetry. They published their works in local Chinese newspapers which introduced modern Chinese literature to the region.[55] New values emerged in China during

---

52. Yen Ching-hwang, *The Overseas Chinese and the 1911 Revolution*, pp. 262–86.
53. Ibid., p. 290.
54. For a standard work on this famous movement, see Chow Tse-tsung, *The May Fourth Movement: Intellectual Revolution in Modern China* (Stanford, Stanford University Press, 1967, paperback).
55. For instance, the modern literary movement in the Singapore and Malaya region commenced as a result of the impact of the May Fourth movement. See Fang Xiu, *Mahua xinwenxue shigao* (A History of New Literature of the Chinese in Malaya), vol. 1 (Singapore, Shijie shuju, 1962), p. 2.

the post May Fourth period such as utilitarianism, pragmatism, youth pro-activism and a new attitude towards women,[56] and these were transmitted to the Chinese communities in Southeast Asia through newspapers and magazines. The impact of these new ideas was especially conspicuous in the lifting of women's social status and their role in society. The traditional view of women's roles in family and society had been challenged. By the 1930s more radical feminist views received increased exposure in the media. Topics such as 'cultivation of a modern female', 'the dilemma of a modern women: between career and family', 'my ideal type of modern female', 'women after marriage', 'the posture of a modern woman', 'how to be a modern woman', 'how to get rid of the yoke of marriage imposed on women', 'a career guide for women' and 'advice to women on health' appeared in a major Chinese newspaper in Singapore which had a wide circulation in Malaya and other neighbouring areas.[57]

Also as a result of the impact of the May Fourth movement, the publication of modern Chinese newspapers increased considerably in Southeast Asia. In Singapore, for instance, twenty-one newspapers and magazines were published in four decades from 1881 to 1920. However the number of the newspapers and magazines jumped to eighty-five in just one decade, from 1921 to 1930.[58] The majority of Chinese publications in the 1920s and 1930s appear to have been China-oriented, drawing public attention to problems in China.[59] This strengthened the 'China-centric' view of the Ethnic Chinese in Southeast Asia.

The China-orientation was further strengthened by Japan's large-scale aggression towards China in the 1930s. Japan's continuous pressure on China since 1915 and the declaration of the notorious 21 Demands posed a serious threat to China as a nation. Japanese

56. Chow Tse-tsung, *The May Fourth Movement*, pp. 254–65, 289–96.
57. See *Nanyang Siang Pau* (The Nanyang Daily), Singapore, June to November 1934.
58. See Wong Hong Teng, *Xinjiapo huawen ribao shelun yanjiu, 1945–1959* (A Study of the Editorials of Chinese Dailies in Singapore, 1945–1959) (Singapore, Centre for Research in Chinese Studies, Department of Chinese Studies, National University of Singapore, 1995), p. 25.
59. Ibid., pp. 28–9.

aggression in 1919, 1928, and 1931 made Japan the most feared imperialist power in the eyes of the Chinese, both at home and abroad. The famous Marco Polo Bridge Incident on 7 July 1937 then triggered an all-out Japanese invasion of China. In response to this unprecedented national crisis, the Southeast Asian Chinese were mobilised under the leadership of Tan Kah Kee (Chen Jiageng) of Singapore to support China's war of resistance[60] This anti-Japanese mobilisation activated a flood of Chinese publications in Southeast Asia aimed at the salvation of their motherland. For instance, many Peranakan Chinese newspapers which appeared in the 1930s in the Dutch East Indies were due to the impact of this anti-Japanese war, and anti-Japanese sentiment was strongly expressed by many of them in the second half of the 1930s.[61] In Singapore and Malaya, these publications not only increased in number, but also concentrated their attention on attacking the Japanese invaders and supporting the patriotic salvation movement launched in Southeast Asia.[62] The flourishing of these politically motivated activities greatly rekindled Chinese identity and strengthened the relationship between the Chinese in Southeast Asia and those in their motherland.

Ethnic Chinese Culture and Identity

Apart from in Singapore, Ethnic Chinese culture in Southeast Asia is a sub-culture. This is because Ethnic Chinese communities do not constitute the mainstream of Southeast Asian societies. Being a minority, the Ethnic Chinese in Southeast Asia feel invariably insecure and

---

60. See Stephen M.Y. Leong, 'Sources, Agencies and Manifestations of Overseas Chinese Nationalism in Malaya, 1937–1941' (unpublished PhD thesis, University of California, Los Angeles, 1976), pp. 249–338; Tan Kah Kee (Chen Jiageng), *Nanqiao Huiyi Lu* (Reminiscence of My Residence in Southeast Asia), vol. 1 (River Edge, USA, Global Publishing Co, 1993), pp. 57–87.

61. See Leo Suryadinata, 'A Short History of the Chinese Press', in Leo Suryadinata, *The Chinese Minority in Indonesia: Seven Papers* (Singapore, Chapmen Enterprise, 1978), pp. 133–34.

62. See Shu Yun-ts'iao (Hsu Yun-ts'iao) & Chua Sher-koon (eds), *Xin Ma huaren kang Ri shiliao* (Malayan Chinese Resistance to Japan 1937–1945 — Selected Source Materials) (Singapore, Wenshi chuban Co Ltd, 1984), pp. 13–106.

ambiguous about their identity, and this sense of insecurity propels them to adapt to the fast-changing political and economic environments in the region.

The changing identities of the Southeast Asian Chinese were most marked after the Second World War. In retrospect, the war gave rise two new trends in the transformation of Chinese identity in Southeast Asia. Firstly, most Southeast Asian Chinese suffered great brutality under Japanese rule between 1942 and 1945. They invariably developed a closer attachment to their place of abode, since many of them helped defend these lands against Japanese invasion with their blood. This growth of local sentiment led to the development of a local identity during the post-war period. Secondly, the rise of indigenous nationalist movements in Southeast Asia increasingly required the Ethnic Chinese to identify with the interests of the country of domicile instead of with their motherland in China. The retreat of the Western powers from Southeast Asia and the cease of Chinese emigration from Mainland China after late 1949 further freed the Chinese communities from powerful external influences.

It would be erroneous to assume that Southeast Asian Chinese communities were a uniform entity or that their responses to the changing political and economic conditions were identical. In reality, the cultural changes in Southeast Asian Chinese communities varied in accordance with place, size of the community, the degree of assimilation and the government's policy towards them. In countries such as Singapore and Malaysia, where the size of Chinese community is large, the degree of assimilation is minimum, and the policy towards Chinese people is tolerant and accommodative, Ethnic Chinese culture survives better and shows signs of growth. In countries such as Thailand, Indonesia, Philippines, Vietnam and Burma, however, where the size of the Chinese community is proportionally small, the degree of assimilation is greater, and the government's policy is less tolerant, Ethnic Chinese culture has diminished rapidly.

Professor Wang Gungwu's theory of the multiple identities of the Southeast Asian Chinese is historically correct,[63] but it seems this

---

63.   See Wang Gungwu, 'The Study of Chinese Identities in Southeast Asia', in Jennifer Cushman & Wang Gungwu (eds), *Changing Identities of the Southeast*

theory is losing strength as time passes. More and more attention has been focused on the political and ethnic identity of the Chinese in the region. Generally speaking, political or national identities after the Second World War became stronger as the political situation in Southeast Asia changed, and the decline of Chinese national identity speeded up the process of local identity. Except for a very small number of elderly China-born Chinese, the overwhelming majority of Southeast Asian Chinese would undoubtedly identify themselves as Singaporeans, Malaysians, Indonesians, Filipinos, Vietnamese and so on.[64] This trend continues to strengthen and will eventually lead all Southeast Asian Chinese to identify themselves with their countries of domicile.

The rise of China as a global power and the increasing investment of Southeast Asian Chinese in China in recent years will not reverse this trend. [65] The theory of 'resinification' of Ethnic Chinese in Southeast Asia, entertained by some observers in the region and by some Western scholars, is largely ungrounded, being, as it is, based on suspicion and fear of China. On the contrary, China in its recent past has attempted to cultivate good relations with many of the Southeast Asian countries, and has long adopted the policy of encouraging the Ethnic Chinese to embrace local citizenship. The most obvious example of this was China's initiative in solving dual citizenship problems with the Indonesian Government in 1955.[66] China in fact has moved much closer to ASEAN

Asian Chinese Since World War II (Hong Kong, Hong Kong University Press, 1988), pp. 7–16.

64. See for instance the comments on Leo Suryadinata's paper by Tan Chee Beng, in Leo Suryadinata (ed), *Ethnic Chinese as Southeast Asians* (Sydney, Allen & Unwin, 1997), pp. 25–32; Tan Chee Beng, 'Nation-Building and Being Chinese in a Southeast Asian State: Malaysia', in Jennifer Cusman & Wang Gungwu (eds), *Changing Identities of the Southeast Asian Chinese Since World War II*, pp. 139–60.

65. See Leo Suryadinata, 'Ethnic Chinese in Southeast Asia: Overseas Chinese, Chinese Overseas or Southeast Asians?', in Leo Suryadinata (ed), *Ethnic Chinese as Southeast Asians*, pp. 15–20.

66. For details of this agreement signed in Bandung, Indonesia, see Donald E. Wilmott, *The National Status of the Chinese in Indonesia, 1900–1958* (Ithaca, Cornell University Southeast Asian Program, 1961).

countries in recent years, and has recently come out in support of the ASEAN governments' efforts to stabilise their currencies by promising not to devalue the renminbi.[67]

Ethnic Chinese political identity is not likely to become a problem, and should not be perceived as one. No thinking Ethnic Chinese in Southeast Asia would entertain the idea of advancing China's political interests in the region at the expense of their countries of abode. Nor should Ethnic Chinese economic identity be perceived as a problem in Southeast Asia. Prospective Southeast Asian Chinese investors, no matter how strong their feelings for their ancestral land in China, will not invest in China unless they have a chance to make a profit. Their decision to invest is determined purely by profit and market potential; and in this they have a competitive advantage over other investors because they are familiar with Chinese language and culture.

What should be focused on in Southeast Asia is Ethnic Chinese identity. This consists of two important components: physical identity and cultural identity. As far as the Ethnic Chinese are physically identifiable from indigenous and other ethnic groups, Ethnic Chinese identity will persist, and will do so for a long time to come. The process of physical integration is slow and imperceptible. The governments of Southeast Asian countries can only help to speed up the process of inter-marriage by providing incentives or by helping to remove certain social impediments; they cannot pass legislation forcing people to inter-marry.

Cultural identity is the key to the retention of Ethnic Chinese identity in Southeast Asia. Ethnic Chinese culture persists in this region despite inter-ethnic contacts and economic interdependence with the indigenous people. Ethnic Chinese culture is particularly strong in the countries where the Chinese are not a negligible minority; in Singapore and Malaysia Ethnic Chinese identity is strong because Ethnic Chinese culture is well-entrenched.[68]

67. For instance, President Jiang Zemin in December 1997 in Kuala Lumpur declared this stand, and it was further reinforced by other Chinese leaders such as Vice-Premier Zhu Rongji, Premier Li Peng and Vice-Premier Li Lanqing.
68. For the entrenchment of Ethnic Chinese culture in modern Singapore and Malaysia, see Tong Chee Kiong, Ho Kong Chong and Lin Ting Kwong,

What should be observed is that Ethnic Chinese culture is not identical with that of Mainland China or Taiwan. Ethnic Chinese culture, in terms of beliefs, values, customs and cultural expression, is coloured by a strong local Southeast Asian character. The localisation of Ethnic Chinese culture in Malaysia is a case in point. This process has been termed as the 'Malaysianisation' of Chinese culture (*Malai xiyahua*). It started long before the independence of Malaya in 1957 and the formation of Malaysia in 1963. What should be emphasised here is that in pre-independence Malaya and in Malaysia the process was slow and imperceptible, and was the natural result of the Ethnic Chinese interacting with the local environment and expectations. However, the process of 'Malaysianisation' was accelerated after 1963. In response to increasing pressure from the government, both economically and culturally, since 1971, the Chinese in Malaysia founded cultural organisations and promoted traditional cultural activities such as lion dances, dragon dances, Chinese calligraphy and painting classes, Chinese poetry recitation, Chinese folk dances, Chinese cuisine, Chinese tea-drinking and Chinese music.[69]

In the process of reviving traditional Chinese culture, the integration of traditional forms with local needs in Malaysia was

---

'Traditional Chinese Customs in Modern Singapore', in Yong Mum Cheong (ed), *Asian Traditions and Modernization: Perspective from Singapore* (Singapore, Centre for Advanced Studies, National University of Singapore and Times Academic Press, 1992), pp. 82–100; Tan Chee Beng, 'Nation-Building and Being Chinese in a Southeast Asian State: Malaysia', in Jennifer Cushman & Wang Gungwu (eds), *Changing Indentities of the Southeast Asian Chinese since World War II*, pp. 146–47.

69. See Guo Rende, *Fengyu nizhou ying zhaoyang: Malaixiya huaren wenhua xiehui de huigu yu zhanwang* (Against the Storm for Welcoming the Rising Sun: Prespect and Retrospect of the Chinese Cultual Association of Malaysia), in Fu Sunzhong & Lai Guanfu (eds), *Wenhua Shinian: Huaren Wenhua Dahui Shizhounian jinian huodong* (A Decade of Culture: Ten Years' Anniversary Celebration of the Symposium of Malaysian Chinese Culture) (Kuala Lumpur, Malaixiya Zhonghua Dahuitang Lianhehui, 1995), p. 189; also other articles written on Chinese music, tea-drinking, drama, literature, painting and so on.

attempted. The result was the birth of a new cultural form with a distinctive local flavour. The founding of a drummers' troupe in June 1988 known as *Niansi Jielinggu* (Twenty Four Festivals Drum) is a good example. It was inspired by the role of a large drum in Chinese festivities and its impact on the audience. Traditionally, festivities were preceded by a lion dance or dragon dance, and one or two big drums were played by two to four drummers interchangeably. The impact of the drumming in creating a festive atmosphere was tremendous. Inspired by the power and influence of the big drums, two Chinese artists, Chen Huichong and Chen Zaifan from Johor Bahru, formed a troupe of nine drummers. This was later expanded to twenty drummers with twenty big drums, each engraved with Chinese calligraphy, and the Twenty Four Festivals Drummers' troupe has since performed at the opening ceremony of major festivals in Malaysia.[70] However, it should be pointed out that over-emphasis on performance and exhibition of traditional Chinese culture may risk the new 'Malaysianised' Chinese culture remaining superficial and lacking real substance, as one observer has warned[71]

Yet the localisation of Ethnic Chinese culture in Southeast Asia does not make Ethnic Chinese less Southeast Asian and more Chinese, nor does it make them less capable of being integrated. Rather, it enriches Southeast Asian culture in general. Southeast Asia has long been the meeting place between East and West; and it is a melting pot for different cultures which produces a hybrid culture of its own. In the past, Southeast Asian culture has proven its remarkable

70. See Chen Zaifan, 'Niansi jielinggu: bianqian shi weiyi bubian de changtai' (Twenty Four Festivals Drum: Change is the only Unchanged Phenomenon), in Fu Sunzhong & Lai Guanfu (eds), *Wenhua Shinian*, pp. 157–65.

71. See He Qiliang (Ho Khai Leong), 'Wenhua Mahua: Lueshuo Mahua wenhua rentong de kunyou he fugui' (Cultural Malaysian Chinese: Dilemma and Restoration of the Malaysian Chinese Cultural Identity), in Lin Shuihao (Lim Chooi Kwa) & He Guozhong (eds), *Zhonghua Wenhua Zhilu: Zhonghua Wenhua Maixiang Nianyi Shiji Guoji Xueshu Yantaohui Lunwenji* (The Road for the Chinese Culture: Collection of Essays for the International Symposium on the Chinese Culture Marching Towards 21st Century) (Kuala Lumpur, The Federation of Chinese Assembly Halls in Malaysia, 1995), p. 245.

capacity to absorb foreign cultures, such as that of the traditional Chinese (in Vietnam), of the Indians (in Thailand, Cambodia, Malaysia and Indonesia), of the Arabs (in Malaysia, Indonesia, Brunei) and of the West (throughout most of the countries in the region); and I believe that it can also accommodate and absorb modern Chinese culture. In the past decades, the intense politicisation of Ethnic Chinese culture by Western scholars and indigenous ultra-nationalists tends to colour it in a narrow political perspective. All of these prejudices will fade away, however, as the Ethnic Chinese language (Mandarin) is transformed into an emerging commercial language in Asia and as China moves to identify itself with the interests of Southeast Asian nations.

Conclusion

The formation of Ethnic Chinese culture in Southeast Asia was closely related to the history of Chinese trading activities and settlements in the region. Chinese traders and immigrants brought along to the new land their beliefs, values and customs together with cultural expressions such as styles of temples and buildings, dress, music, cuisine and festivals. Distinctive Chinese dialects and Chinese system of education strengthened the retention of Chinese values and customs. Chinese immigrants had strong desire to keep everything Chinese regardless of the new climatic and economic environments. They entered into an unconscious process of perpetuating Chinese tradition in Southeast Asia.

The development of the Ethnic Chinese culture in Southeast Asia went through four different stages: pre-1912 period; the period from 1912 to the end of the World War II in 1945; the post-war to 1960s; and the 1970s till now. Two principal forces propelled the Ethnic Chinese culture to change: the force of adaptation and adjustment; and the force of responding to external stimuli. The localisation force diminished Chinese customs and values. The responding force, on the other hand, was mightier than localisation. As the result of China's political and cultural impact, Southeast Asian Chinese culture became modern, dynamic and pro-active.

The decline of Chinese national identity and the rise of indigenous nationalism after the Second World War speeded up the transformation of Ethnic Chinese political identity in the new states in Southeast Asia. The overwhelming majority of Southeast Asian Chinese after 1960s have identified themselves as Malaysians, Singaporeans, Indonesians, Filipinos, Vietnamese etc. This trend continues and will eventually lead all Southeast Asian Chinese to identify themselves with the countries of domicile. Ethnic Chinese political identity should not become a problem ; nor should the Ethnic Chinese economic identity be perceived as a problem in Southeast Asia. However, Ethnic Chinese identity is to a certain extent problematic. Ethnic Chinese identity consists of physical and cultural identities. Physical identity would persist for a long time to come. Southeast Asian governments could help to speed up the process of inter-marriage by providing incentives or help to remove certain social impediments. Ethnic Chinese cultural identity is the key to the retention of the Ethnic Chinese identity in Southeast Asia. It continues to persist despite inter-ethnic contact and economic interdependence. In Singapore and Malaysia, Ethnic Chinese culture is well-entrenched. But this culture is different from the Chinese culture found in Mainland China and Taiwan, and has possessed local Southeast Asian flavour. Traditional and modern forms of Chinese culture have adapted to local conditions to serve the needs of local Chinese communities.

The problem of Ethnic Chinese identity is hinged on the Chinese-Indigenous inter-racial relationship. To resolve this problem, the Ethnic Chinese not only should always regard themselves as Southeast Asians first and Ethnic Chinese second, but should also be aware of the feelings of the indigenous people; and they should be prepared to help the indigenous people whenever necessary. On the part of the indigenous Southeast Asians, they should accept the Ethnic Chinese as legitimate members of the Southeast Asian nations; and should also accept that the Ethnic Chinese are physically and culturally different from them and have the rights to preserve their beliefs, values and customs, language and education. In a multi-racial and multi-cultural Southeast Asia, each ethnic group must have rights and responsibilities as well as willingness to accept each other's differences.

CHAPTER 7

Hokkien Immigrant Society and Modern Chinese Education in British Malaya, 1904–1941

Late Qing Educational Reform

The greatest impact on the rise of modern Chinese education in British Malaya was made by the late Qing educational reform. Humiliated by Japan in the First Sino-Japanese war (1894–95) and impressed by Japanese modernisation, some Qing high-ranking officials, such as Zhang Zidong, saw educational reform as an effective means of self-strengthening. However, reforms had to be conducted within an overall institutional reform which his predecessors in the self-strengthening movement failed to grasp.[1] Zhang's plan for educational reform was contained in his famous treatise, *Quanxuepian* (Exhortation of Education) published in 1898,[2] which had an impact on some senior

1. See William Ayers, *Chang Chih-tung and Educational Reform in China* (Cambridge, Massachusetts, Harvard University Press, 1971), pp. 152–95.
2. See Zhang Zidong, *Zhang Wenxiang gong quanji* (The Complete Works of Zhang Zidong) (Taipei, Wenhai chubanshe, 1963), vol. 6, pp. 3702–50.

bureaucrats and later provided a theoretical basis for the Manchu educational reform after 1901.

Manchu institutional reform at the turn of the twentieth century was made possible by rapidly changing political circumstances and the dwindling fortunes of the court. The Empress Dowager Cixi, the *de facto* ruler of the court, fled Beijing for Sian in October 1900 as the result of the occupation of the capital by Allied forces following the disastrous Boxer uprising. As well as being obligated under the peace treaty and to recover support for the crumbling dynasty, the Empress Dowager accepted the memorial presented by Zhang Zidong and Liu Kunyi, another high-ranking official, to carry out educational reform. In September 1901 an edict was issued to this effect. Provincial governments were instructed to convert old private academies and community schools into modern schools. Those reform-minded officials were active in carrying out the edict. For instance, Zhang Zidong established at least eleven new schools of various kinds between 1901 and 1902 in Hunan and Hubei provinces, where he was the governor-general. He further established more modern schools in Jiangsu and Jiangxi between 1903 and 1904 when he took charge of these two provinces.[3]

By 1904, the Qing dynasty had already established a modern education system based on the Japanese model. It had an integrated structure, from primary school up to high school and university. To control and manage the new education system, a Ministry of Education was established in 1905.[4]

The impact of Qing educational reform was transmitted to Chinese immigrant communities overseas through Qing diplomats and immigrant leaders who had close relations with the court. In the case of British Malaya, the person who was instrumental in the establishment of the first modern Chinese school in the region was none other than Zhang Bishi (Chang Pi-shih, also known as Zhang Zhenxun and popularly known in the West as Thio Thiau Siat). Zhang, a Hakka,

---

3.   See Zhu Shoupeng (ed), *Shierchao donghualu, Guangxi chao* (The Donghua Records of the Twelve Reigns of the Qing Dynasty, Guangxi Reign), (Taipei, Wenhai chubanshe, 1963), vol. 9, pp. 5426–27.

4.   Ibid.

was a Chinese community leader in Penang and Batavia, and a wealthy tycoon with a variety of businesses to his credit.[5] He was made the first Chinese vice-consul in Penang in March 1893[6] and rose rapidly in Qing official hierarchy, being made China's Imperial Commissioner to promote business in Southeast Asia in 1905. Zhang's dual positions as an immigrant community leader and a Qing official enabled him to play the leading role in bringing modern Chinese education to the region. In 1904, with the support of a group of wealthy Chinese merchants, he founded the Zhong Hua School, the first of its kind in the Chinese immigrant communities of Southeast Asia.[7] The founding of this modern Chinese school was a great success, attracting a number of students. It started with two hundred and forty students in May 1904, organised into eight classes. The school was run by a headmaster with twelve teachers who were all recruited from China,[8] and placed under the control of a management board with fourteen directors. They were further classified into two superintendents, six directors and six deputy directors, all of whom were elected to the board from among wealthy Chinese merchants in Penang.[9] The curriculum of the school was a combination of traditional and modern

5. For a biography of Zhang and his involvement in China's economic modernisation, see Michael Godley, *The Mandarin-capitalist from Nanyang: Overseas Chinese Enterprise in the Modernization of China, 1893–1911* (Cambridge, Cambridge University Press, 1981).

6. See Yen Ching-hwang, *Coolies and Mandarins: China's Protection of Overseas Chinese during the Late Ch'ing Period* (1851–1911) (Singapore, Singapore University Press, 1985), p. 171.

7. See Penang *Sin Pao*, 1 July 1904; *Lat Pau*, 30 December 1904.

8. See 'The Origins of the Founding of the Zhong Hua School drafted by Hu Guolian & Lin Juzhou, the two superintendents of the Board of Management of the School', as an appendix to 'The Report of the Vice-Consul Dai Chunyong of Penang for the 34th year of Guangxu Reign (1908)', in 'The Records of the Qing Chinese Vice-Consulate of Penang', 'Despatches', Volume 6 (manuscript).

9. See *Xuebu guanbao* (The Gazette of the Ministry of Education of the Qing Government) vol. 9 (1st day of 11th moon of 32nd year of the Guangxu Reign [16 December, 1906]); 'Minutes of the Penang Chinese Town Hall' (Pingzhang gongguan) vol. 2, (manuscript).

syllabuses, integrating Chinese and Western learning. Traditional Chinese subjects such as 'self-cultivation' (*xiushen*) and 'study of the Confucian Classics' (*dujing*), modern subjects such as Chinese language, history and geography, and Western subjects such as a foreign language (English), mathematics and physics were made compulsory for students.[10]

It is significant to note that this first modern Chinese school in British Malaya was to serve as the beachhead for the modernisation of Chinese immigrant society. The study of modern subjects helped open the eyes of young Ethnic Chinese and made them see the world differently from those of their parents' generation. The modern content of the subjects was not yet linked to a meaningful nation-building, but the vague idea emerged of educating children to become modern adults who had to understand history, geography, mathematics and physics. What should be noted further is that the school acquired strong community support as well as the endorsement of the Chinese government. The former was important because the school could not sustain its growth without strong financial backing; while the latter ensured the supply of teachers and teaching materials for the running of the school.

The impact of the founding of the Zhong Hua School on the Chinese immigrant community in the region was profound. From 1905 to 1911 a number of modern Chinese schools were founded in British Malaya. These included the Ying Sin Primary School (May 1905),[11]

---

10. See Tan Yeok Seong (Chen Yusong), 'Malaiya huawen jiaoyu farenshi' (The Commencement of the History of the Chinese Education in Malaya', in Gao Xin & Zhang Xizhe (eds), *Huaqiaoshi lunji* (Essays on the History of Overseas Chinese) (Taipei, Guofang yanjiuyuan, 1963), pp. 136–37; also see Tan Yeok Seong, *Yeyinguan wencun* (The Literary Collections of Yeyinguan), vol. 2 (Singapore, South Seas Society, 1984), pp. 242–44; Tay Lian Soo (Zheng Liangshu), *Malaxiya huawen jiaoyu fazhanshi* (A History of the Chinese Education in Malaysia), vol. 1 (Kuala Lumpur, Federation of Chinese Teachers' Associations of Malaysia, 1998), pp. 101-02.

11. See Xie Pinfeng, 'Yin Sin xuexiao shilue' (A Brief History of Yin Sin School), in Lin Zhigao (ed), *Singzhou Ying Ho huiguan yibai sishiyi zhounian jinian tekan* (Souvenir Magazine for the Commemoration of 141 years Anniversary

the Yang Zheng, Duan Meng and Dao Nan primary schools (all founded in 1906) in Singapore;[12] and the Confucian Primary School and the Kuen Cheng (Kun Zheng) Girls' School (both founded in 1907) in Kuala Lumpur.[13] The majority of these schools were founded by different Chinese dialect groups.[14]

Belonging to the major dialect group in Singapore, the Hokkiens were aware of the importance of modern education for their children in competition with other dialect groups. They were financially more powerful than their counterparts in Malacca and Penang, partly due to the rise of Singapore as a leading international port in the region since the second half of the nineteenth century.[15] More importantly, Singapore had a number of high profile Hokkien leaders who were

of the Singapore Yin Ho Association) (Singapore, Yin Ho Association, 1965) p. 15.

12.   *Yang Zheng xuexiao jinxi jiniankan* (Souvenir Magazine for the Commemoration of Golden Jubilee Celebration of the Yang Zheng School, Singapore) (Singapore, Yang Zheng School, 1956), p. 31; *Lat Pau*, 19 April 1906, pp. 8, 10; Li Gushen & Lin Guozhang (eds), *Xinjiapo Duan Meng xuexiao sanshi zhounian jiniance* (Souvenir Magazine for the Commemoration of 30th Anniversary of the Founding of the Tuan Mong School) (Singapore, Duan Mong School, 1936); Lin Yun (ed), *Daonan xuexiao chuangxiao liushi zhounian jinian tekan* (Tao Nan School 60th Anniversary Souvenir, 1906–1966) (Singapore, Dao Nan School, 1966), pp. 25–8.

13.   See 'Xiao Shi' (History of the Confucian School), in *Sili Zun Kong zhongxue gaochuzhong biye tekan, yijiu liuwu nian* (The Souvenir Magazine of Graduation of the Senior and Junior Middle Three, 1965 Batch) (Kuala Lumpur, 1965) p. 6. Zheng Bangying in his article on the history of the Kuen Cheng school claims the school was founded in the 33rd year of the Guangxu reign of the Qing dynasty. At the same time, he converted that year to 1908 in the solar calendar. This is an obvious error: the 33rd year of Guangxu was 1907 rather than 1908. See Zheng Bangying, 'Benxiao jianshi'(A Brief History of Kuen Cheng School), in Kun Cheng *Liushi nian: Kun Cheng nuxiao liushi zhounian jiniankan* (Sixty Years of Kuen Cheng: Souvenir Magazine of the 60th year anniversary of the Kuen Cheng School) (Kuala Lumpur, 1968), p. 11.

14.   See notes 11 and 12.

15.   See Wong Lin Ken, 'Singapore: Its Growth as an Entrepot Port, 1819–1941', in *Journal of Southeast Asian Studies*, vol. IX, no. 1 (Singapore, March 1978), pp. 50–84.

also the leaders of the entire Chinese community on the island. Their lead in the quest for modern Chinese education guaranteed success. Under the leadership of Goh Siew Tin (Wu Shouchen), in 1906 the Hokkien community founded the Dao Nan Primary School (Daonan xuetang) which was opened in April 1907.[16] The preparatory committee for the establishment of the school was set up in 1906, with its first meeting convened on 8 November. The committee comprised of some influential wealthy merchants whose support was crucial for the success of this project. It raised a sum of $40,000 for initial expenses, with pledges of monthly contributions from Hokkien shops and companies.[17] Renting the Siam House in North Bridge Road as its premises, the school started its classes in April 1907 with ninety students. Ma Zhengxiang, a Hokkien scholar, was appointed first headmaster together with eleven other teachers in the same year. All of the teachers except one were native Hokkiens, and most of them appear to have been recruited from China.[18] With the strong financial support of the Hokkien community and small classes, the early results of the school were excellent. This gave confidence to Hokkien parents who might otherwise have sent their children to local English schools. The popularity of the school is reflected in the rapid growth of student numbers, which increased to 182 in 1908 and to 296 in 1909; by 1911, the school had 304 students.[19]

The school was placed under the control of a management board with forty directors who were elected by the Hokkien community. Most of them were rich merchants who possessed social status as well as financial power. Goh Siew Tin, for instance, was elected the first chairman of the board. He was a wealthy merchant with high

16. See *Lat Pau*, 16 April 1907, p. 8; 23 April 1907, p. 3; 2 May 1907, p. 8.
17. See Lin Yun (ed), *Daonan xuexiao chuangxiao liushi zhounian jinian tekan*, p. 25.
18. The list of teachers of the Dao Nan School in 1907 does not indicate where they were recruited. Given the shortage of teachers of the time, it is reasonable to suggest that the majority of them were recruited in China. See 'List of Headmasters of Daonan School' and 'List of Teachers of Daonan School', ibid., pp. 46–7.
19. Ibid., p. 44.

social status and political influence, and was the first president of the newly-founded Chinese Chamber of Commerce of Singapore.[20] Two other known merchants involved in the founding of the Dao Nan School were Lee Cheng Yan (Li Qingyan) and Teo Sian Keng (Zhang Shanqing), both wealthy import–export merchants. Lee was the leader of the Eng Choon (Yongchun) sub-Hokkien dialect group in Singapore, while Teo was a director of the Singapore Chinese Chamber of Commerce.[21]

The involvement of wealthy Hokkien merchants in the founding of first modern Hokkien school set an example for the active involvement of the merchant class in the promotion of modern Chinese education. With wealth, status and community spirit, the merchants were in the best position to undertake such a task. In return, they acquired additional recognition of their leadership status in Chinese immigrant society. This pattern of active merchants' participation in education continued throughout the period, ending with Tan Kah Kee's founding of Xiamen (Amoy) University in 1921 and Tan Lark Sye's founding of Nanyang University in 1953 in Singapore.

Republican Educational Reforms in China

The founding of the Republic in early 1912 brought a new educational system to China. Although the late Qing educational reform had brought changes in the structure of the school system and in curricula, the reform was not thorough. Further, education was still geared to the preservation of the dynasty, and the ideas of loyalty to the emperor and respect for tradition were still alive. The founders of the new Republic were the revolutionaries who

20. See Yen Ching-hwang, 'Ch'ing China and the Singapore Chinese Chamber of Commerce, 1906–1911', in Leo Suryadinata (ed), *Southeast Asian Chinese and China: the Politico-Economic Dimension* (Singapore, Times Academic Press, 1995), pp. 142, 155.

21. See *Su Xiaoxian, Zhangzhou shishu lu Xing tongxianglu* (The Directory of the Zhangzhou People in Singapore) (Singapore, 1948), pp. 59, 63; 'Minutes of the Singapore Chinese Chamber of Commerce', vol. 1, pp. 1–2 (manuscript); Yen Ching-hwang, *A Social History of the Chinese in Singapore and Malaya, 1800–1911* (Singapore, Oxford University Press, 1986), pp. 183, 208.

were more exposed than their predecessors, the scholar–gentry, to foreign influences. They credited in part the rise of the Western powers and the emergence of Japan to the introduction of modern education. In their eyes, education was an instrument for nation-building, the key to wealth and power in a new China. When Dr Sun Yat-sen was inaugurated as the provisional president of the new Republic in early 1912, one of the early tasks he undertook was the establishment of a new education ministry. He appointed Cai Yuanpei, a well-known educationist, to be the first education minister.[22] Cai's achievements as education minister rested with his new ideas and his consolidation of a modern education system introduced in the late Qing period. He pointed out that the traditional 'loyalty to emperor' and 'respect for Confucius' were no longer compatible with the spirit of the new Republic. They should be replaced by new values of the 'morality of citizens, militant nationalism, utilitarianism, globalism and aestheticism'.

Cai's views were incorporated in the government's education principles announced in September 1912.[23] Cai's achievements included the promulgation of the educational ordinance in May 1912 in which the inadequacies and imbalance of the Qing educational reform were corrected. It consisted of changing the name for schools from *xuetang* to *xuexiao* and the title of headmaster from *jiandu* to *xiaozhang*; replacing Qing textbooks with new republican textbooks; removing the study of the Classics from the curriculum; abandoning the link between education and bureaucracy; introducing co-education at primary level; and making high school education the standard for general education.[24] The change in the nomenclature of the schools and personnel may seem trivial, but it nevertheless gave a sense of newness and a departure from traditional China. The abolition of the study of the Classics and the replacement of Qing textbooks with new ones were designed to free Chinese children from

---

22. See Li Guilin (ed), *Zhongguo jiaoyushi* (A History of Chinese Education) (Shanghai, Shanghai jiaoyu chubanshe, 1989), p. 354.
23. Ibid., p. 355.
24. Ibid., pp. 354-55; Cyrus H. Peake, *Nationalism and Education in Modern China* (New York, Howard Fertig, 1970), pp. 75–6.

old frames of mind that encouraged students to look back to the past rather than forward to the future. The introduction of co-education was intended to remove gender barriers and ease traditional discrimination against women in the Chinese society. Making high school compulsory was aimed at lifting China's education and literacy standards, as a popular belief among the Republicans at the time was that literacy was the key to national strength and democracy.

An outstanding achievement of the early Republican period was the promulgation of the '1912-1913 school system, known as the *renzi kueichou* school system.[25] The new initiatives formalised the structure of the education system. The entire length of education was eighteen years, divided into three different stages: primary education (seven years), secondary education (four years) and tertiary education (seven years). Both primary and tertiary were subdivided into two difference phases: junior primary and senior primary education; and preparatory and normal tertiary education. In addition, two ancillary systems relating to vocational and teacher training were attached. The former was divided into elementary and secondary schools; and the latter was subdivided into medium and higher normal schools.[26] Even more significant was the reform of school curricula. In September 1912, the Ministry of Education promulgated the new curricula for all schools. In the junior primary schools, the subjects 'self-cultivation' (*xiushen*), Chinese language (*guowen*), mathematics (*xuanshu*), handicraft (*xougong*), drawing (*tuhua*), music (*gechang*) and physical education (*tichao*) were offered. An extra sewing (*fongren*) class was added for female students. At the senior primary level, Chinese history and geography were added with the extra subject of agriculture (*nongye*) for male students. In the secondary schools, in addition to those subjects taught at senior primary, new subjects such as foreign languages, advanced mathematics (*suxue*), physics, chemistry, the legal system (*fazhi*) and economics were introduced. For girls' schools, horticulture (*yuanyi*) and home economics (*jiashi*) were added.[27]

25. *Renzi* was the year of 1912 in the Chinese calendar, while *kueichou* was the year of 1913 in the Chinese calendar.
26. Li Gueilin, op. cit., p. 356.
27. Ibid., p. 358.

Two important points need to be noted in this curriculum reform. Firstly, the removal of the study of the Classics from both primary and secondary education freed young minds from the profound influence of Confucianism and some feudal values. It helped to prepare the Chinese to accept the new Republican values in order to build a new nation. Secondly, the introduction of natural science and technical subjects helped create a modern civil society in which the citizens could participate rationally in moulding a new China.

Another major step in the Republican educational reform took place in 1922, a decade after the first major reform. The main thrust of the reform was in the structure of education: the entire length of education was shortened from eighteen to sixteen years. Primary education was reduced by one year from seven to six years; secondary education was increased from four to six years; while tertiary education was restricted to four years for liberal arts and teacher training degrees, and five years for professional degrees such as law and medicine. Primary education was subdivided into four years of junior primary and two years of senior primary; and secondary education was subdivided into junior and senior with three years each. The new system was promulgated by the president of the Beijing government, which was under the control of the Beiyang warlords.[28] Political instability and chaos at that time does not seem to have deterred the reform initiatives. Perhaps the warlord regime in Beijing also shared with the Republicans the idea of using education to strengthen the nation.

What motivated the reform were also partly the social and economic needs of the time. After the First World War, China saw the return of Western economic influences, and the need for literate workers in the industry was greatly felt. The reduction of primary education from seven to six years facilitated the spread of literacy, and workers with six years' education were able to perform their jobs satisfactorily in modern factories. This change helped to pave the way for the development of modern Chinese industry. The

28. See Mao Lijui & Shen Guanqun (eds), *Zhongguo jiaoyu tongshi* (General History of Chinese Education), vol. 5 (Jinan, Shandong jiaoyu chubanshe, 1988), pp. 79–83.

division of secondary education into two stages served different purposes. The new system provided those students who were not inspired to pursue academic studies at university with the flexibility to switch to technical education after completing three years at junior secondary school. The 1922 educational reform, known as the 'renshu system',[29] became the cornerstone of the modern Chinese education system. It was later retained and practised in China by the Nanjing Government, which came into power in 1927. The system also appears to have been adopted by the Ethnic Chinese, including those in British Malaya.

Strong support of the Southeast Asian Chinese for the 1911 Revolution predestined their close educational ties with China.[30] After the founding of the Republic, the government, both central and provincial, became interested in promoting Ethnic Chinese education. The governments in Fujian and Guangdong, the two provinces that provided most of the Ethnic Chinese in Southeast Asia, sent officials to tour the region for this purpose. In 1913 the Beijing Government also involved Chinese diplomats in arranging for the protection and promotion of Ethnic Chinese education. Since the founding of the Nanjing regime in 1927, China further strengthened its educational ties with the Ethnic Chinese. In 1929, an Ethnic Chinese Education Planning Committee was established within the bureaucratic structure of the Ministry of Education. The committee was charged with the responsibility of planning and consulting over Ethnic Chinese education.[31] Due to its close political ties with the Ethnic Chinese, the Guomindang (Kuomintang, the Nationalist Party), which established the Nanjing regime, broadened its base of support by recruiting a number of Ethnic Chinese leaders into its party structure, forming the Overseas Chinese Affairs Committee (*Qiaowu weiyuanhui*).

29. *Renshu* was the year of 1922 in the Chinese lunar calendar.
30. For their close political relations, see Yen Ching-hwang, *The Overseas Chinese and the 1911 Revolution: With Special Reference to Singapore and Malaya* (Kuala Lumpur, Oxford University Press, 1976); Lee Lai To (ed), *The 1911 Revolution — The Chinese in British and Dutch Southeast Asia* (Singapore, Heinemann Asia, 1987).
31. See Mao Lijui & Shen Guanqun, op. cit., p. 366.

Some leading Ethnic Chinese leaders, such as Deng Zeju and Tan Kah Kee of British Malaya and Xiao Focheng of Thailand, were recruited into the committee.[32] They were able to provide up-to-date information which would help the Guomindang and its government to formulate appropriate policies and strategies to handle Ethnic Chinese education.

The Development of Modern Chinese Education

Modern Chinese education in British Malaya achieved its most remarkable growth during the Republican period between 1912 and 1941. It would not be an exaggeration to claim that without the development of this period, modern Chinese education would not have made the achievements that it has in the region today. Three factors were responsible for such rapid growth. Firstly, the founding of the new Republic in 1912 raised high hopes that China would emerge as a rich and powerful state, and modern education was seen as a means of fulfilling the requirements of modern statehood. Secondly, the Republican government, particularly the Nanjing regime, had integrated Ethnic Chinese education into its education system. The Chinese government was able to help solve problems with the supply of teachers and textbooks, and to provide advice when needed. Thirdly, the new cultural movement unleashed by the May Fourth movement in 1919 emphasised the importance of education as a means of salvation for China. This theme received good exposure in the Chinese newspapers in British Malaya, and inspired and encouraged people to take action and to found modern Chinese schools.[33]

The development of modern Chinese education in this period can be divided into two phases: the first phase from February 1912 to February 1919; and the second from March 1919 to December

32. See Chang Peng-yuan & Shen Huai-yu (eds), *Minguo zhengfu zhiguan nianbiao, 1925–1949* (Lists of the Officials of the Government of the Republic of China, 1925–1949), vol. 1 (Taipei, Institute of Modern History, Academia Sinica, 1987), p. 282.
33. See Mao Lijui & Shen Guanqun, op. cit., pp. 15–53; *Nanyang Siang Pau* (The Nanyang Daily, Singapore), February, 11 to 14 March 1924.

1941. The former was characterised by the rapid growth of primary schools, while the latter was marked by the introduction and growth of secondary education. The euphoria of the founding of the new Republic, combined with the efforts of Republican educational missions, resulted in the flourishing of modern primary schools in British Malaya. In the first phase, at least nineteen main schools were founded in the region, including six schools in Singapore and thirteen in the Malay Peninsula.[34] What should be noted is the spread of Chinese schools to small towns such as Kampar, Sungei Patani and Province Wellesley where Chinese children had access to modern Chinese education. This helped to bridge the gap between city and town in the area of educational services.

Compared with the late Qing period, modern Chinese schools in British Malaya during the Republican period were financially stronger. General awareness of the importance of education encouraged rich Chinese merchants to donate generously to Chinese schools. Most late Qing schools had to rent their premises and the basic equipment for teaching was inadequate, while the schools during this later period were better equipped and some of them had

34. They included the Aitong School (1912), Guangfu School (1916), Nanhua Girls' School (June 1917), Nanyang Girls' School (August 1917), Xingya School (Spring 1918) and Guangyang School (February 1918) in Singapore. In Malaysia, they included the Zhonghua School in Muar (April 1912); Xinmin School of Sungei Patani, Kedah (1912); Peiyuan School in Kampar, Perak (1912); Kuanrou (Foon Yew) School in Johor Bahru (January 1913); Siuqi School in Taiping, Perak (Spring 1913); Zhonghua School in Seremban, Negri Sembilan (July 1913); Peifeng School in Malacca (July 1913); Xunren School in Kuala Lumpur (1914); Zhongling School in Penang (February 1917); Zhonghua School in Kelantan (February 1918); Rixin School in Province Wellesley (1918); and Huaqiao School in Kluang, Johor (1918). See *Xu Suwu, Xinjiapo huaqiao jiaoyu quanmao* (The Overview of Chinese Education in Singapore) (Singapore, Lianshu yinwu youxian gongsi, 1949), pp. 19, 29–31; Tay Lian Soo & Gwee Yee Hean, *Malaixiya Xinjiapo Huawen zhongxue tekan tiyao, fu xiaoshi* (Chinese High School Souvenir Magazines of Malaysia and Singapore, with School Histories) (Kuala Lumpur, Department of Chinese Studies, The University of Malaya, 1975), pp. 6, 12, 15, 173, 181, 186, 247.

even built their own premises.[35] This meant that these schools could undertake long-term planning, leading to improvement and expansion. Secondly, the curricula of the schools had also been modernised due to the impact of China's new education system. In line with this, study of the Classics was removed and new subjects introduced. Republican ideas and nationalist feeling were nurtured in the classrooms.

However the most important progress during this first phase of the Republican period (1912–1919) was made in the growth of female education. The first Chinese girls' school was founded in 1900 by Dr Lim Boon Keng in Singapore, but the school, the Singapore Chinese Girls' School, taught in English and so catered mainly for the Straits-born Chinese.[36] The first Chinese-language girls' school was founded in 1905 by Huang Dianxian, the daughter of Wong Ah Fook (Huang Yafu), a famous Cantonese business tycoon in Singapore and Johor.[37] We know nothing about this school except that it was named *Hua Qiao Nu Xiao* (Overseas Chinese Girls' School). With the impact of the activities of the reformists, led by Kang Yuwei, and the revolutionaries, led by Dr Sun Yat-sen, four other Chinese girls' schools were founded in British Malaya during the late Qing period, two each in Singapore and the Malay Peninsula.[38] The founding of the Republic in China lifted the status of women in Chinese society,

35. At least three Singapore Chinese primary schools — Dao Nan, Qi Fa and Duan Meng — built their own premises during this period. See Xu Suwu, op. cit., pp. 25–27; Li Gushen and Lin Guozhang (eds), *Xinjiapo Duan Meng xuexiao sanshi zhounian jiniance*, p. 14.
36. See Song Ong Siang, One Hundred Years' History of the Chinese in Singapore (Singapore, University of Malaya Press, 1967), p. 305.
37. See Xu Shuwu, op. cit., p. 46; Tay Lian Soo (Zheng Liangshu), 'Xin Ma huashe zaoqi de nuzi jiaoyu' (Early Female Education in the Chinese Communities in Singapore and Malaysia), in *Malaxiya huaren yanjiu xuekan* (Journal of Malaysian Chinese Studies), no.1 (Kuala Lumpur, Huazi Resource & Research Centre, 1997), p. 48.
38. The four schools were the Kuen Cheng Girls' School in Kuala Lumpur (September 1908), the Zhong Hua Girls' School in Penang (end of 1908), the Pei Gen Girls' School (1910) and the Zhong Hua Girls' School (1911) in Singapore. Xu Shuwu, ibid.; *Nanyang Zonghui Bao*

and gave female education in the Chinese communities a boost. At least five girls'schools in Singapore and eight in the Malay Peninsula were founded during this period.[39] What should be noted is that many of the founders of the girls' schools in British Malaya were merchants and intellectuals who were directly or indirectly associated with Sun Yat-sen's revolutionary movement.[40] The success of the Republican revolution in China gave them special encouragement in the founding of these girls' schools, for they had shared some revolutionaries' progressive ideas of equality of the sexes in their access to modern education .

The second phase of the Republican period (1919 to 1941) saw great advancements made in modern Chinese education in the region. The importance of this period rested not just with the increase in the number of Chinese schools, but also the strengthening of Chinese education as an viable alternative for Chinese children — the introduction of secondary education. Without Chinese secondary schools, modern Chinese education would have remained at primary level, and it would probably have faded away due to competition

(*The Union Times*, Singapore), 13 February 1909; Pin Zheng Xin Bao (Penang *Sin Poe*) (Penang, 8 January, 1909; Kun Cheng *Nuxiao liushi zhounian jinianka*, p. 76.

39.   The five girls schools founded in Singapore were the Chong Fu Girls' School (April, 1915), Chong Ben Girls' School (January 1916), Qiao Ying Girls' School (1916), Nan Hua Girls' School (June, 1917) and Nanyang Girls' School (August 1917). In the Malay Peninsula, there were the Pi Ju Girls' School (1912), Wu Nei Girls' School (1915), and the Zhong Hua Girls' School (1916) in Penang; Pei De Girls' School (1913) in Malacca; Hua Nan Girls' School (1918) in Muar, Johor; Qin Ye Girls' School (1916) in Ipoh, Perak and Jun Xiu Girls' School (1918) in Kampar, Perak; and the Kun Hua Girls' School (1917) in Seremban, Negri Sembilan. See Tay Lian Soo, op. cit., pp. 52-6; Xu Shuwu, op. cit., pp. 48–50.

40.   For instance, the Nanyang Girls School was founded by Tan Chor-nam, Teo Eng-hock and others who were closely associated with Sun Yat-sen's revolutionary movement in Singapore and Malaysia. See Tay Lian Soo & Gwee Yee Hean (eds), op. cit., pp. 247–48; Yen Ching-hwang, *The Overseas Chinese and the 1911 Revolution: With Special Reference to Singapore and Malaya*, pp. 91–4.

with English education. The beginning of this new phrase was marked by the founding of the Hua Qiao Zhong Xue (The Chinese High School) in Singapore on 21 March 1919. The school was to provide a much-needed secondary education for Chinese-educated students. Prior to this, Chinese students who completed six years of education and wished to pursue further study had to go back to China — and of course the distance and cost prevented many of them from doing so. The founding of the school was due partly to the efforts of the some far-sighted leaders such as Tan Kah Kee, who was deeply committed to the idea of using education to strengthen China and the Chinese race. With the support of a group of different dialect group leaders, he succeeded in founding the school in March 1919. It commenced its classes on 21 March with ten teachers and seventy-three students from different parts of Southeast Asia. Another eighteen students were added in September, making a total of ninety-one.[41]

The founding of the Singapore Chinese High School was a major step towards the construction of a viable modern Chinese education system in the region. It was a significant step that set an example for others to follow. In addition, the founding of the school broke down dialect barriers and promoted inter-*bang* co-operation in education.[42] Since the second half of the nineteenth century, the Chinese community in British Malaya was plagued by inter-*bang* rivalry and conflict.[43] Most of the modern schools founded during the late Qing period were very much *bang*-oriented, with restrictions on enrolment. Although this restriction was gradually lifted after

41. See *Nanyang Hua Qiao zhongxue jinxi jinian tekan* (Souvenir Magazine of Golden Jubilee Celebration of the Chinese High School of Singapore) (Singapore, The Chinese High School, 1969), p. 11; Xu Shuwu, op. cit., pp. 50–1; Tan Kah Kee, *Nanqiao huiyi lu* (The Memoirs of Tan Kah Kee) vol. 1 (River Edge, USA, Global Publishing Co, 1993, new edition), p. 30.
42. The term *bang* or *pang* literally meant a band, group or organisation. In the context of Ethnic Chinese history, *bang* is referred to a dialect group. It is the combined entity of dialect and regional identities.
43. See Yen Ching-hwang, *A Social History of the Chinese in Singapore and Malaya, 1800–1911*, pp. 194–98.

the founding of the Republic, the Chinese community had never had any real co-operation in the founding of schools. Tan Kah Kee's success in acquiring support from various *bang* leaders to found the first Chinese secondary school was a major breakthrough in modern Chinese educational endeavours.

Following in the footsteps of the Singapore Chinese High School was Zhong Ling High School which was founded in Penang in 1923. It was built on the campus of the Zhong Ling primary school, founded in 1917 by the Penang Philomatic Society (Ping Cheng yeshu baoshe), a reading club closely affiliated with Sun Yat-sen's revolutionary movement on the island.[44] The leaders of the Philomatic Society were mostly staunch supporters of Dr Sun Yat-sen, and shared many of his aspirations. They were well aware of the importance of modern education and its potential contribution to the modernisation of local Chinese society. Under the leadership of Koh Seng Li (Xu Shengli) and Ong Keng Seng (Wang Jingcheng), they convened a meeting and founded the Zhong Ling High School. The school was inaugurated on 20 January 1923, the first Chinese high school in the Malay Peninsula.[45] Following the example of Zhong Ling, six other Chinese high schools were established in British Malaya in the 1920s, all of them in the Peninsula except one, which was in Singapore.[46]

The peak decade for the development of the Chinese secondary education in British Malaya was the 1930s. It witnessed not only the sustained growth of schools but also an extension of secondary

44. For the close relationship between the Penang Philomatic Society and the Chinese revolutionary movement, see ibid., pp. 140, 260–64.

45. See Tay Lian Soo & Gwee Yee Hean (eds), op. cit., p. 164.

46. These high schools were the Yu Cai High School (January 1924), Duan Meng High School (January 1924) in Singapore, The Confucian High School (1924) in Kuala Lumpur, the Zhong Hua High School (July 1924) in Muar, the Kuen Cheng High School (1925) in Kuala Lumpur and the Pei Feng High School (1925) in Malacca. Ibid., pp. 19, 97, 105 and 284; Wang Zuo (ed), *Pei Feng wushinian: jinxi jinian tekan* (Fifty Years of Pei Feng: Souvenir Magazine of the Golden Jubilee Celebration) (Malacca, Pei Feng High School, 1963), p. 20; Tay Lian Soo, *Malaixiya huawen jiaoyu fazhanshi*, vol. 2, p. 288.

education. At least seven high schools were founded, three in Singapore and four in the Malay Peninsula.[47] However the most important development in this decade was the introduction of senior secondary education. All of the high schools founded in the 1920s were confined to junior secondary, which provided students with three years' education after the completion of six years of primary school. It was comparatively easier to provide teachers and resources for junior secondary students, but senior secondary education, which involved more intensive teaching and specialisation in subjects, required better-qualified teachers and equipment. Without the introduction of senior secondary education, Chinese-educated students would not have been able to pursue their tertiary education in China. To meet such a need, Au Boon Haw (Hu Wenhu), a Hakka community leader and Chinese medicinal tycoon in Singapore, took the lead in introducing senior secondary classes in the Nanyang Girls' High School in Singapore. He donated S$5,000 as the school's development fund, and a preparatory committee was established in 1930 to co-ordinate the work. A fundraising campaign was successfully launched with strong community support, and the school was physically extended to accommodate new senior classes. New equipment was purchased and a new library established.[48] The example set by the Nanyang Girls' High School was soon followed by other high schools in the region; in the period between 1930 and 1941, there were at least ten high schools offering senior secondary classes.[49]

The Chinese secondary education system had many problems. Two notable ones were small enrolments and the shortage of funds. Many Chinese high schools started with a small number of students, and enrolments then stagnated or declined. For instance, the Pei Yuan High School in Kampar, Perak started with a dozen students in 1941;

47.   These schools were the Nanyang Girls' High School (1930), the Gong Jiao (Catholic) High School (1937) and Zhong Zheng High School (1939) in Singapore; the Zhong Hua High School in Seremban (1934), Negri Sembilan; the Hua Lian High School in Taiping (1937); Zhong Hua High School in Kuala Lumpur (1939) and the Xie He Girls High School in Penang (1939).
48.   See Xu Shuwu, Xinjiapo huaqiao jiaoyu quanmao, p. 55.
49.   See Tay Lian Soo & Gwee Yee Hean (eds), op. cit., pp. 9–10.

the Kuen Cheng Girls' High School in Kuala Lumpur had only twenty students when it started its secondary classes; while the Zhong Hua High School in Seremban started with twenty-six students.[50] Even the first high school, the Singapore Chinese High School, had a rather poor record of growth. In just over one decade from 1919 to 1929, student numbers only doubled from ninety-one to one hundred and eighty.[51] Small enrolments meant less fees collected from students, and school coffers suffered a shortfall of income. In turn, the schools were unable to appoint more staff, and the need for specialisation in teaching was not met, resulting in a drop in the standard of education. Worst of all, the dwindling enrolments, along with the impact of a downturn in the economy of the Chinese community, took their toll in the Chinese high schools in British Malaya. For instance, the Duan Meng (Tuan Mong) High School in Singapore started a junior secondary class in January 1924 with small number of students, and was forced to discontinue in the following year as enrolments declined.[52]

Shortage of funds was the second major problem facing Chinese high schools. The problem was an inherent one. All the Chinese high schools were either supported by a particular *bang* or by the entire Chinese community, and this support was subject to the fluctuations of the fortune of *bang* and community. When the prices of rubber and tin — the two mainstays of the Malayan economy — were good and the community witnessed an economic boom, the support for Chinese high schools was strong; but financial support dissipated when the community was hit by an economic recession. Although government grants-in-aid for Chinese schools was introduced in 1923, the amount received from the government per student was small in comparison with the aid given to the English school students.[53] The staple income of a Chinese high school derived mainly from tuition and auxiliary

50. Ibid., p. 13.
51. See Wu Yishuang, 'Zhongxie jiaoyu yu Nanyang' (Secandary Education and Southeast Asia), in *Nanyang Siang Pau*, 1 January 1929, p. 3.
52. See Li Gushen & Lin Guozhang (eds), *Xinjiapo Duan Meng xuexiao sanshi zhounian jiniance*, pp. 21–2.
53. For instance, the Chinese schools in the Federated Malay States received $9.78 per student compared with the rates of $54 and $87.50 per student paid to the subsidised and government English schools.

fees charged to students, and also the monthly contributions promised by shops and trading companies. If these incomes were proven to be insufficient, the school had to raise funds from the general public by way of staging drama performances or concerts. Increasingly, schools had to depend on fundraising for their survival and expansion.[54]

To overcome the financial problems of the Chinese high schools, a contemporary observer in early 1929 suggested a levy on the commodities traded by the Chinese. The levy was to be based on the volume and value of the goods exported and imported, and it was to be raised by the *gonghui* (public associations).[55] The suggestion sounded good, but unfortunately it was impractical and unenforceable. The Chinese community in the late 1920s was still divided into *bangs*, though inter-*bang* differences had narrowed. Further, not all businessmen were enthusiastic about Chinese secondary education, though some of them were converted believers. Without the full support of the business community, the scheme would not have worked. The Chinese community had no power to impose a levy and enforce it successfully; therefore the proposal was never taken up.

The Hokkien Community and Modern Chinese Education

The Hokkien community was the earliest Ethnic Chinese community established in British Malaya. It first took root in Malacca, an international entrepot, in the fifteenth century, and Hokkien traders formed the backbone of a small Chinese community in Malacca in the sixteenth and early seventeenth centuries.[56] The number of Hokkien

See the 1929 'Annual Report of the Education Department of the Federated Malay States', cited in Tan Liok Ee, *The Politics of Chinese Education in Malaya, 1945–1961* (Kuala Lumpur, Oxford University Press, 1997), p. 21.

54. See *Nanyang Siang Pau*, 9, 13, 18, and 21 February 1924; 22 March 1924; 3, 14, and 30 April 1924; 1 and 20 May 1924; 26 and 27 February 1929; 5 and 18 April 1929; 27 December 1929.

55. See Wu Yushuang, 'Zhongxue jiaoyu yu Nanyang' in *Nanyang Siang Pau*, 1 January 1929, p. 3.

56. See Yen Ching-hwang, 'Early Fukienese Migration and Settlements in Singapore and Malaya before 1850', in Pin-Tsun Chang & Shih-Chi

grew rapidly after the founding of Penang in 1786 and Singapore in 1819.[57] The Hokkiens, being the earliest Chinese settlers in the region, entrenched themselves in trade, and had the lion's share of some important lines of business.

With its economic power, the Hokkien community played an active role in the promotion of modern education. In Singapore, the founding of the Dao Nan School in 1907 was the first step taken by the Hokkien community. It was among the best of the early modern Chinese schools, with a sufficient number of teachers, small classes and good teaching facilities.[58] Stimulated by the founding of the Republic in early 1912, the Hokkien community in Singapore founded another two modern Chinese schools: Ai Tong School in 1912 and the Chong Fu Girls' School in 1915.

The founding of the Chong Fu Girls' School was of some significance. The first modern Chinese language girls' school in Singapore, the Hua Qiao Girls' School, founded in 1905 by Huang Dianxian, appears to have used Cantonese as the medium of instruction,[59] and dialect barriers and the social rigidity of the time barred Hokkien girls from entering it. The founding of the Chong Fu Girls' School was thus intended to meet an urgent social need of the community. The founder of the school was Wang Huiyi

Liu (eds), *Essays in Chinese Maritime History*, vol. V., (Nankang, Taipei, Sun Yat-sen Institute for Social Sciences and Philosophy, Academia Sinica, 1993) p. 681; Emanuel Godinho de Eredia (transl. J.V. Mills), 'Eredia's Description of Malacca, Meridional India and Cathay', in *Journal of the Malayan Branch of the Royal Asiatic Society*, vol. 8, pt. 1 (1930), p. 19.

57. See the tables of percentage distribution of Chinese dialect groups in Penang and Singapore, in Mak Lau Fong, *The Dynamics of Chinese Dialect Groups in Early Malaya* (Singapore, Singapore Society of Asian Studies, 1995), pp. 100, 120.

58. See the beginning of this chapter.

59. Xu Shuwu in his book on Chinese education in Singapore mentions only that the school taught in Chinese. Given the social and linguistic environments of the time, it was most likely the language used was Cantonese rather than Mandarin. See Xu Shuwu, *Xinjiapo huaqiao jiaoyu quanmao*, p. 46; Tay Lian Soo, 'Xin Ma huashe zhaoqi de nuzi jiaoyu', in *Journal of Malaysian Chinese Studies*, no.1, pp. 47–58.

(Wang Hui-i) who was the Educational Superintendent of the Hokkien Association (Hokkien Huay Kuan) of Singapore and also the acting principal of the Dao Nan School. With his influence on educational matters, he was able to gain the support of the Hokkien Association to found the Chong Fu Girls' School. The school started its classes in April 1915 with over thirty pupils and a headmistress, Lin Shuqin, appointed from Xiamen, China.[60] Wang was a progressive intellectual, a reformist who supported Kang Yuwei's reform movement. A journalist working for *Jit Shin Pau* and the *Thien Nan Shin Pao* (both reformist mouthpieces in Singapore) and was actively involved in the Confucian Revival movement in Singapore,[61] Wang was probably influenced by Liang Qichao's attitude towards female education, and became a fervent advocate for female education in Singapore.

Dao Nan, Ai Tong and Chong Fu were the three main Chinese schools financed and controlled by the Hokkien Association in Singapore during the Republican and post-war periods. In addition, at least another eight private and public Hokkien schools existed in Singapore in around 1929, and they received financial subsidies from the Hokkien Association. All of these schools were in financial straits, and had to depend on monthly and special contributions from the community for their survival. As a result, the number of teachers and students declined, and the standard of education slipped.[62] In February 1929, a change of leadership in the Hokkien Association in Singapore altered the priorities of the Association, and an educational committee was established to oversee Hokkien education. The result of this was an extra financial subsidy given to these needy Hokkien schools.[63]

60.	Xu Shuwu, op. cit., p. 48.
61.	See Yen Ching-hwang, 'Overseas Chinese Nationalism in Singapore and Malaya, 1977–1912', in *Modern Asian Studies*, vol. 16, no. 3 (Cambridge, Cambridge University Press, 1982), pp. 404, 422.
62.	See the article entitled 'Xinjiapo Min qiao gexiao kaikuang' (A Bird's-eye View of the Hokkien Schools in Singapore) in Lim Meigong (ed), 'Jiaoyu zhoukan' (*Educational Weekly*), nos.12, 13 and 15, published in *Nanyang Siang Pau*, 3 April 1929, 10 April 1929 and 24 April 1929, respectively.

A number of Chinese schools were founded by the Hokkien community in the Malay Peninsula during the Republican period. In Kuala Lumpur, for instance, there were in existence at least four Hokkien schools before 1932, one of which was a girls' school.[64] Recession in the Malayan economy in the early 1930s as a result of world economic depression took its toll on Chinese education. One of the four Hokkien schools in Kuala Lumpur was closed, while the remaining three were in financial straits. From 1936 the Selangor Hokkien Association helped the three schools to tide over their financial crisis by providing monthly subsidies as well as allowing them to use the Association's premises for school activities.[65] The founding of the Zhong Hua High School in Kuala Lumpur in 1939 was a major step taken by the Selangor Hokkien community in promoting Chinese education. Inspired by burgeoning Ethnic Chinese nationalism and preparation for the reconstruction of China after the Second Sino-Japanese War (1937–1945), a group of wealthy Hokkien merchants in Kuala Lumpur led by Chen Rener, Huang Zhongji and Hong Qidu founded the school in July 1939. A known Hokkien educationist, Liang Lingguang, was appointed as the first principal.[66]

An important contribution of the Hokkien community towards modern Chinese education in British Malaya was the promotion of Mandarin as the medium of instruction and the weakening of dialect barriers. Dr Lim Boon Keng (Lin Wenqing), a well-known Hokkien community leader, was the first to promote Mandarin speaking in Singapore. Believing in language as an useful tool for nurturing Chinese

63. See *Nanyang Siang Pau*, 4 February 1929, p. 4; 13 February 1929, p. 3; 5 August 1930.

64. See 'Jilongpo Xuelane Fujian huiguan yishi jilu' (Minutes of the Selangor Hokkien Association, Kuala Lumpur) (manuscript), 1930-1932, p. 149.

65. Ibid., pp. 131 & 145; 1934–1937, p. 21; Guo Zhuzhen (ed), *Xuelane Fujian huiguan bainian jinian tekan, 1885–1985* (The Souvenir Magazine of Centenary Celebration of the Selangor Hokkien Association, Kuala Lumpur) (Kuala Lumpur, Selangor Hokkien Association, 1986), p. 56.

66. See *Xuelane Zhong Hua zhongxue fuxiao* tekan, 1946 (Souvenir Magazine of the Zhong Hua High School of Selangor for 1946). The page on the high school section was reproduced in the *Guo Zhuzhen*, op. cit., p. 72.

identity and national unity, he started the first Mandarin class in his house as early as 1898 for Straits-born Chinese.[67] In 1906 he convened a meeting of clan leaders and exhorted them to introduce Mandarin as a subject in the 'temple schools'.[68] His campaign for popularising Mandarin in Singapore helped contribute to the breakdown of dialect barriers in education.[69]

The popularisation of Mandarin in Chinese schools received a tremendous boost after the founding of the Republic in 1912. The Republic gave the Ethnic Chinese (including the Chinese in British Malaya) a new identity and new confidence in being a Chinese. The 1919 May Fourth movement in China further injected into the Ethnic Chinese a new nationalist vigour which was expressed partly in the use of Mandarin and the breakdown of dialect barriers. In this regard, the Hokkien community in Singapore appears to have taken the lead. In 1916 the Dao Nan School, the flagship of Hokkien education in Singapore, took steps to phase in the use of Mandarin as the medium of instruction by appointing a non-Hokkien principal, Xiong Shangfu, who was a native of Hunan province.[70] From 1920, Dao Nan further recruited a number of non-Hokkien teachers from China to strengthen the use of Mandarin in the school.[71]

The efforts of the Dao Nan in promoting Mandarin as the teaching medium in Chinese schools in British Malaya were exemplified by a constructive proposal put forward by the school to the conference on

---

67. See Khor Eng-hee, 'The Public Life of Dr. Lim Boon-keng' (unpublished BA Honours thesis, University of Singapore, 1958) p. 28; Lee Guan Kin, *Lin Wenqing de suxiang: zhongxi wenhua de huiliu yu maodun* (The Thoughts of Dr Lim Boon Keng: Convergence and Contradictions between Eastern and Western Cultures) (Singapore, Singapore Society of Asian Studies, 1990), pp. 64–5.
68. See 'Straits Budget', 18 July 1907.
69. See Yen Ching-hwang, *The Overseas Chinese and the 1911 Revolution: With Special Reference to Singapore and Malaya*, p. 289.
70. See 'Liren xiaozhang minglu' (List of Principals of Dao Nan School) in Lin Yun (ed), *Dao Nan xuexiao chuangxiao liushi zhounian jinian tekan*, p. 46.
71. These teachers came from diverse backgrounds, ranging from Guangdong to Jiangsu, Hunan, Hubei and Hebei provinces. See 'Liren jiaozhiyuan minglu' (A List of Teachers of Dao Nan School), in Lin Yun (ed), ibid., pp. 47–8.

Ethnic Chinese education in Southeast Asia, sponsored by the Jinan University of Shanghai, held in June 1929. The conference was well-attended by about ninety-seven China and overseas delegates.[72] Dao Nan's proposal was constructive and relevant, and had attracted the attention of the participants. In the proposal, three points are worth noting. Firstly, the Chinese government was to send experts to tour Southeast Asia to promote Mandarin in schools, and help train Mandarin teachers; secondly, night schools attached to existing Chinese schools were to be established in Southeast Asia to promote Mandarin speaking; thirdly, dialect and regional differences in education were to be weakened.[73] To deal with the knotty problems of dialect and regional barriers in the Chinese schools, Dao Nan also suggested an umbrella organisation named Jiaoyu zonghui (Educational Association) to be established in every city or territory in Southeast Asia, and the proposed association was to be supported and financed by the entire Chinese community. The association was then to distribute funds to various schools according to need.[74] We do not know how much of Dao Nan's proposal was adopted by the Chinese government, but it nevertheless contributed to the ideas for promoting Mandarin in the Chinese schools in the region.

Tan Kah Kee and Modern Chinese Education in British Malaya

Tan Kah Kee is an important name in modern Ethnic Chinese history. He is appropriately dubbed by Yong Ching Fatt (C.F. Yong), who has produced the best biography of him, as an 'Overseas Chinese legend'.[75] Tan was an entrepreneur, a business tycoon, a community leader, a philanthropist, an education promoter and a Chinese patriot. His non-profit making educational enterprises in Southern Fujian province

---

72. Reports about the conference were published in Nanyang Siang Pau, 27 June 1929, 2 July 1929 and 3 July 1929.
73. The proposal was published in the *Nanyang Siang Pau* before the delegates left for the conference in China. See *Nanyang Siang Pau*, 20 May 1929, p. 22.
74. Ibid.
75. See C.F.Yong (Yong Ching Fatt), *Tan Kah-kee: The Making of an Overseas Chinese Legend* (Singapore, Oxford University Press, 1987).

(including the famous Xiamen University), at the cost of much of his personal wealth, set a good example for the promotion of modern Chinese education in China and in the Ethnic Chinese communities. His deeds are widely known throughout South China and Southeast Asia, and have inspired other wealthy Ethnic Chinese to follow his example.

There was a good crop of academic works on Tan Kah Kee published in both Mainland China and overseas in the 1980s to honour his great contribution to modern Chinese education. These works include Wang Zengbing and Yu Gang, *Chen Jiageng Xingxue ji* (Tan Kah Kee's Contributions to Modern Education, Fujian jiaoyu chubanshe, Fuzhou, 1981); Chen Bisheng and Yang Guochen, *Chen Jiageng zhuan* (A Biography of Tan Kah Kee, Fujian renmin chubanshe, Fuzhou, 1983); *Huiyi Chen Jiageng* (Reminiscence of Tan Kah Kee, wenshi ziliao chubanshe, Beijing, 1984); and Chen Bisheng and Chen Yimin, *Chen Jiageng nianpu* (A Chronology of Tan Kah Kee, Fujian renmin chubanshe, Fuzhou, 1986). Outside China, Dr Yong Ching Fatt of Flinders University, South Australia, spent more than ten years exhaustively researching many of the original materials to produce his definitive work on Tan Kah Kee. He published a Chinese-language work on Tan Kah Kee in Singapore, entitled *Zhanqian de Chen Jiageng yanlun shiliao yu fenxi* (Tan Kah Kee in pre-war Singapore: Selected Documents and Analysis, South Seas Society, Singapore, 1980), and his English-language biography of Tan Kah Kee entitled *Tan Kah Kee: The Making of an Overseas Chinese Legend* (Oxford University Press, Singapore, 1987). These academic works shed much light on Tan's life, his business and community activities, his political aspirations and his contribution to the promotion of modern Chinese education.

Tan Kah Kee was born on 21 October 1874 in Jimei, a seaside village in Tong An district, Fujian province. Most villagers were both farmers and fishermen. The geographical location and proximity to Xiamen (Amoy), an early international port in southeastern China, moulded the attitudes and aspirations of Tong An folks for seafaring and overseas ventures. The Tong An people spread widely throughout Southeast Asia pursuing trade and wealth.[76] Tan Kah Kee's father, Tan

---

76. See Chen Bisheng & Chen Yimin, *Chen Jiageng nianpu* (The Chronology of Tan Kah Kee) (Fuzhou, Fujian renmin chubanshe, 1986), pp. 1–3.

Kee Peck (Chen qibai), migrated to Singapore and had early success in business. Tan Kah Kee received some traditional Confucian education in his home village, and later joined his father in Singapore to work as an apprentice in his father's shops.

What he learned from his father's business laid the foundation for his future success in business.[77] Tan started his own business in 1904, and step by step became actively involved in plantation, manufacturing and shipping, emerging as one of the most successful businessmen in Southeast Asia. At the peak of his business career between 1923 and 1925 he possessed an estimated S$10.8 million and had a large number of employees; in 1925, his rubber factory in Singapore alone employed over 1,400 workers.[78] With his enormous wealth, Tan Kah Kee was able to pursue his non-profit educational enterprises in Southern China. He began by founding a primary school in his home village as early as February 1913. His business success in later years propelled him to commit more of his personal wealth to the promotion of secondary and tertiary education in Southern Fujian. In 1917 he founded the famous Jimei High School, and then the Jimei Normal College and the Jimei Marine and Navigation College between 1918 and 1921. However his most famous educational enterprise was the founding of the Xiamen (Amoy) University in April 1921. His personal wealth sustained the university for about sixteen years until 1937 when it was taken over by the Nationalist government.[79] Indeed his deep commitment to these non-profit educational enterprises partly caused the collapse of his business empire in Southeast Asia in the 1930s.

Tan Kah Kee's involvement in promoting Chinese education in British Malaya appears to have been secondary to the rest of his non-profit making educational enterprises, but it was undertaken by him with equal enthusiasm. In 1906, only about two years after he had

77. See Tan Kah Kee, *Nanqiao huiyi lu*, vol. 2, p. 479.
78. Ibid., p. 505 ;C.F. Yong, *Tan Kah Kee: The Making of an Overseas Chinese Legend*, pp. 44-57.
79. See Wang Zengbing & Yu Gang, Chen Jiageng xingxue ji, pp. 24–45; Tan Kah Kee, *Nanqiao huiyi lu*, vol. 1, pp. 13–28; Chen Bisheng & Chen Yiming, *Chen Jiageng nianpu*, pp. 20–50.

started his own business, Tan had already begun to show interest in modern Chinese education in Singapore. When in that year the Hokkien community in Singapore began to found a modern Chinese school, the Dao Nan School, he was one of its 110 founding members and a member of the preparatory committee. He donated $1,000 dollars towards the cost of establishing the school. After the school was opened in 1907, he was elected a director of school board and later became one of its two auditors. In 1911, he began to demonstrate his leadership and enthusiasm in education, when he was elected chairman of the school board. He served in this capacity for ten years intermittently between 1911 and 1929.[80]

Apart from his commitment to Dao Nan in terms of his time and money, Tan was also generous in donating large sums of money to support the Ai Tong School and Chong Fu Girls' School.[81] In 1929, when he was elected to the position of the president of the powerful Hokkien Association of Singapore, he began to restructure the Association and alter its priorities. Emphasis on the promotion of modern education saw the injection of large sums of Association funds into the running of the Hokkien schools. It took over control of and directly financed the Ai Tong School and Chong Fu Girls' School, and provided subsidies for eight other lesser Hokkien schools which were in financial straits.[82]

Tan Kah Kee's most important contribution to the promotion of modern Chinese education in British Malaya was his leadership role in the founding of the Singapore Chinese High School (Hua Qiao Zhong Xue) in March 1919.[83] The high school, the first of its kind in the region,

---

80. Tan's chairmanship was between 1911–1912 and 1923–1920. See 'Zhaoqi liren zongli minglu' (A List of Chairmen of Directors of the Board of Dao Nan School during the Early Period), in Lin Yun (ed.), *Daonan xuexio chuangxiao liushi zhounian jinian tekan*, p. 45; C.F. Yong, *Tan Kah-kee: The Making of an Overseas Chinese Legend*, p. 87.
81. See Xu Shu-wu, *Xinjiapo huaqiao jiaoyu quanmao*, p. 29.
82. Xu Shu-wu, ibid., pp. 29, 48; *Nanyang Siang Pau*, 4 February 1929, p. 4, 13 February 1929, p. 3.
83. See 'Nanyang Huaqiao zhongxue jinxi jinian tekan', in Tay Lian Soo & Gwee Yee Hean, *Malaixiya, Xinjiapo huawen zhongxue tekan tiyao fu xiaoshi*, pp. 260–61.

set an example for others to follow, and had a profound impact on the introduction of Chinese secondary education in the region. What motivated Tan Kah Kee to take such significant step? In exploring this, we need to take into account the fact that his educational activities in British Malaya, though secondary to his efforts in Southern Fujian, were an integral part of his entire non-profit making educational enterprise. They were not motivated by personal gain, but by the lofty idea of using education as a means of strengthening China and the Chinese race.[84] This is his famous dictum of *jiaoyu jiuguo* (rescuing the nation through education).

An enquiry into the motives for and aspirations of Tan Kah Kee's promotion of modern Chinese education sheds light not only on the relationship between immigrant society and modern education, but also on the relationship between immigrants and their deep commitment to the well-being of their mother countries. Tan Kah Kee was an Ethnic Chinese nationalist and a Chinese patriot. Although he was not a political activist responding to Dr Sun Yat-sen's call for an anti-Manchu revolution, he was nevertheless a committed Chinese nationalist ready to help safeguard the sovereignty of his mother country. His deep involvement in the anti-Japanese movement in British Malaya as a result of the Jinan (Tsinan) Incident,[85] and his leadership in the 'Anti-Japanese and Relieve China' movement in Southeast Asia between

84. See Tan Kah Kee's speech at the meeting for fundraising for the founding of the Singapore Chinese High School, in Yong Ching Fatt, *Zhanqian de Chen Jiageng yanlun shiliao yu fenxi* (Tan Kah Kee in pre-war Singapore: Selected Documents and Analysis) (Singapore, South Seas Society, 1980), p. 27.

85. Jinan (Tsinan) was the capital of Shandong. In the process of aggression of China, Japanese army massacred a large number of the Chinese in Jinan in an attempt to stop the advancement of the Nationalist army into North China. For Tan's involvement in this anti-Japanese movement in Singapore and Malaya, see Yen Ching-hwang, 'The Response of the Chinese in Singapore and Malaya to the Tsinan Incident, 1928', in the *Journal of the South Seas Society*, vol. 43 (Singapore, South Seas Society, 1988), pp. 1–22; see also Yen Ching-hwang, *Community and Politics: The Chinese in Colonial Singapore and Malaysia* (Singapore, Times Academic Press, 1995), pp. 306–29.

1938–45,[86] demonstrated his clear political stand. Being a Chinese patriot, he was elated by the founding of the Republic of China in 1912, but was later saddened by Yuan Shikai's usurpation of power and the plunge of China into political turmoil and military chaos after Yuan's death in 1916.

It was against this background that Tan Kah Kee expounded his theory of *jiaoyu jiuguo*. This lofty idea was clearly revealed in Tan's speech to the community meeting organised for the purpose of raising funds for the proposed Chinese High School in Singapore in June 1918. In rather emotional tones, Tan called upon his compatriots to donate generously to Chinese education, for education could indirectly strengthen the nation, and 'preserve our cultural essence and to expound our national spirit'.[87] Drawing a contrast with Japan and Europe, he lamented the fact that China had ninety-six percent illiteracy against thirty percent in Japan and ten percent in advanced Western countries such as Britain, the United States, Germany and France. He also lashed out at the Chinese Government (the warlord government in Beijing) for its neglect of education and its preoccupation with internal fighting for power and personal gain. He urged the wealthy Ethnic Chinese to donate a small portion of their assets (three to five percent) to education — which, he believed, would not in any way diminish their wealth.[88] Indeed, Tan Kah Kee had discovered a meaningful role for Chinese immigrants to play in relation to their mother country. Many of the Ethnic Chinese were financially better off than their compatriots in China, and had the capacity to make such an important undertaking.

86. See Tan Kah Kee, *Nanqiao huiyi lu*, vol. 1, p. 64; C.F. Yong, *Tan Kah-kee: the Making of an Overseas Chinese Legend*, pp. 213–16; Ren Gueixiang, *Huaqiao dierci aiguo gaochao* (The Second High Tide of Overseas Chinese Patriotism) (Beijing, Zhonggong dangshi ziliao chubanshe, 1989), p. 63; Yen Ching-hwang, 'The Overseas Chinese and the Second Sino-Japanese War, 1937–1945', in *Journal of the South Seas Society*, vol. 52 (Singapore, South Seas Society, 1998), pp. 155–56.

87. See Tan Kah Kee's speech published in Guomin Ribao, 18 and 20 June 1918, reproduced in Yong Ching Fatt, *Zhanqian de Chen Jiageng yanlun shiliao yu fenxi*, pp. 26–7.

88. Ibid., p. 27.

Another less obvious but equally important motive for Tan Kah Kee's involvement in promoting modern Chinese education was his belief that education would improve the competitiveness of the Chinese in business. Being a far-sighted Ethnic Chinese entrepreneur,[89] Tan was at the forefront of competition with other foreign businessmen. He was keenly aware of the weaknesses of traditional Chinese business practices, and was of the strong belief that Ethnic Chinese businessmen had to improve their competitiveness for their future survival and growth. This line of thought was clearly revealed in his declaration for the inauguration of the *Nanyang Siang Pau*, a Chinese daily newspaper founded by him in Singapore in September 1923. Tan pointed out that the merchants of advanced nations were well equipped with knowledge of economics and commerce, and were able to deal with different types of business such as natural resources, manufacturing, navigation and transport, and banking and insurance. They also possessed a broad world view. These factors gave them competitive advantage and placed them in a leadership position in the business world.[90] He also deplored the ignorance of Chinese (including Ethnic Chinese) merchants, saying that '... they are ignorant of the principles of commerce, and are poor in general knowledge of doing business ... and they are at the mercy of God and fate ...'.[91] Tan then went on to explain his belief that the promotion of education was the best way to overcome the ignorance of Chinese merchants, and that it would indirectly improve their competitiveness in business.

These two noble motives undoubtedly shaped Tan Kah Kee's attitude towards the promotion of modern Chinese education both in China and in the Ethnic Chinese communities. What prompted him to start taking the lead in the founding of the Chinese High School in Singapore was a social need for Chinese secondary

---

89. For an investigation into Tan Kah Kee and the Ethnic Chinese entrpreneurship, see Yen Ching-hwang, 'Tan Kah Kee and the Overseas Chinese Entrepreneurship', in *Asian Culture*, no. 22 (Singapore, Singapore Society of Asian Studies, June 1998), pp. 1–13.

90. See Tan's inauguration declaration published in the *Nanyang Siang Pau*, 6 and 7 September 1923; see also Yong Ching Fatt, *Zhanqian de Chen Jiageng yanlun shiliao yu fenxi*, p. 35.

91. Ibid.

education. Prior to the founding of the school in 1919, there was no Chinese high school which could admit those who had completed six years of primary education. Some of the wealthy parents were able to send their children back to China for further study, but secondary education was denied to most of the Chinese children in British Malaya. Tan Kah Kee was also concerned about the future of Chinese education in the region. The absence of Chinese secondary education would have rendered primary education ineffective, and would have driven it into oblivion. Thus, the founding of a Chinese High School would stimulate the development of Ethnic Chinese education, and make it viable in immigrant society.[92] Again using advanced nations as an example, Tan Kah Kee warned his compatriots of the futility of having Chinese education at primary level only. This, he told them, would fail to equip the younger generation with the necessary knowledge and skills to earn a living.[93]

Tan Kah Kee's idea of founding a Chinese high school in Singapore began much earlier than 1919. In 1913, after he had successfully founded a primary school in his home village in Fujian (Jimei), he began to float the idea of founding a Chinese high school in Singapore. He wrote from Xiamen to the Singapore Chinese Chamber of Commerce asking for support, but his idea was turned down by the Chamber on the grounds that educational matters were not within its jurisdiction.[94] When Tan arrived in Singapore in the spring of 1913 he raised the idea again, but found no favourable response.[95] His idea became more concrete in 1917 when a feasibility study was conducted by Xiong Shangfu, the headmaster of the Dao Nan School, showing that over one hundred students were eligible for entry into high school.[96] Although

92. See Tan Kah Kee's speech for raising funds for the proposed Chinese High School published in the *Guomin Ribao*, 18 and 20 June 1918.

93. Ibid.

94. See 'Xinjiapo Zhonghua zongshanghui yishi jilu' (Minutes of the Singapore Chinese Chamber of Commerce), vol. 8 (manuscript, 1913–1916), p. 19.

95. See Yong Ching Fatt, 'Chen Jiageng yu changban Hua Zhong ersanshi' (Some matters on Tan Kah Kee and his founding of the Singapore Chinese High School), in *Sin Chew Jit Poh* (Singapore Daily), 7 July 1980.

96. See Guoming Ribao, 10 April 1917.

this finding was encouraging for Tan Kah Kee, community response was still feeble.

In May 1918, in a twist of events, Tan Kah Kee was called upon by the representatives of the Tong De (T'ung Teh) Reading Club, a front organisation for the Guomindang (Kuomintang or Nationalist Party) in Singapore, to take lead in founding Chinese high school in Singapore. With the support of the presidents of sixteen Chinese schools, Tan Kah Kee convened a public meeting on 15 June 1918, held at the premises of the Singapore Chinese Chamber of Commerce. The meeting was attended by fifty-five representatives of various groups, with Tan Kah Kee in the chair. He made a rousing and emotional speech appealing for support, and enunciated his objectives for founding the proposed Chinese high school as a strategy to help modernise China and to preserve Chinese cultural essence and spirit.[97] The meeting endorsed Tan's proposal to set up a Chinese high school with the official name *Xinjiapo Nanyang Huaqiao Zhongxue* (The Nanyang Overseas Chinese High School of Singapore). Tan was unanimously elected the provisional president with Lim Ngee Soon, a leader of the Teochew community in Singapore, as his deputy. A board of directors of the school was also formed with representatives from various dialect groups and Chinese primary schools.[98] Under the leadership of Tan and Lim, two five-man committees were set up to raise funds and to purchase a site for the school, Tan Kah Kee donated a sum of $30,000 out of a total of $675,262 raised. He continued to hold the position of president of the school intermittently from 1918 until 1934, when he was replaced by Lee Kong Chian (Li Guangqian), his son-in-law.[99]

What should be noted in Tan Kah Kee's leadership in founding the Singapore Chinese High School was his non-sectarian approach. Although he was a leader of the Hokkien *bang*, and was to some extent restricted by the *bang's* sectarian interests, he was struggling to break the dialect barriers in education. As a nationalist and a patriot, he saw

---

97. See C.F. Yong, *Tan Kah-kee: The Making of an Overseas Chinese Legend*, p. 89.
98. See 'Nanyang Huaqiao Zhongxue jinxi jinian tekan', in Tay Lian Soo & Gwee Yee Hean, *Malaixiya Xinjiapo Huawen zhongxue tekan tiyao*, p. 260.
99. See C.F.Yong, *Tan Kah-kee*, p. 89.

the bigger picture for China and the Ethnic Chinese communities. In his view, as education was a means for strengthening China and the Chinese race, efforts to promote Chinese education, especially the introduction of Chinese secondary education, should not be restricted to one particular dialect group. A united Ethnic Chinese society perhaps was a first step towards the creation of a modern and powerful China. Further, a non-sectarian approach to education would broaden the social base of modern Chinese education, and would guarantee the success of this first Chinese high school in the region. In pursuance of this approach, he contacted the presidents of the sixteen Chinese schools belonging to various *bangs* and invited them to join him as founders of the proposed high school. At the same time, the election of Lim Ngee Soon (Lin Yisun), a Teochew *bang* leader, as his deputy, and the election of various *bang* representatives to the board of directors of the school, projected a positive image of *bang* co-operation in this important community endeavour.

Tan Kah Kee's less known educational initiatives, which were also of some significance to modern Chinese education in British Malaya, were the founding of a marine and navigation school and a teachers' training college in Singapore. In May 1938 Tan Kah Kee's educational institutions in China were greatly affected by the Japanese occupation of Xiamen port and its neighbouring areas in southern Fujian. The Jimei Marine and Navigation College founded by Tan was forced to move into the interior of Fujian; and enrolment and standards at the college were badly affected. Tan Kah Kee proposed to found another marine and navigation school in Singapore to continue his efforts in the areas of fishery and navigation.[100] In November 1938, Tan made the official proposal. With the support of the Singapore Hokkien Association, the Singapore Marine and Navigation School came into being on 2 February 1939 with thirty-two students (twenty of whom came from Singapore, while the rest were from other parts of Southeast Asia). A former principal of the

---

100. See Yeap Chong Leng (Ye Zhongling), 'The Founding of Nanyang Overseas Chinese Marine and Navigation School by Tan Kah Kee' (in Chinese), in Yen Ching-hwang (ed), *Asian Culture* no.14: Special Issue on Ethnic Chinese Abroad (Singapore, Singapore Society of Asian Studies, April, 1990), p. 150.

Jimei Marine and Navigation College was appointed the first principal of the school, and seven teachers were recruited.[101] The school existed for three years until, due to financial difficulties of the Hokkien Association, it was closed in 1942.

Tan Kah Kee's founding of a teacher training college in 1941 was another of his educational enterprises in British Malaya. The Chinese schools in the region in the pre-war period were mostly dependent on China for their supply of teachers, but the Pacific war had cut off this important supply. The need for qualified teachers prompted Tan Kah Kee to start raising funds in February 1941 for a teacher training college in Singapore. An enthusiastic response in the Chinese community raised a sum of $360,000.[102] The college was opened on 10 October 1941(the national day of China) with 230 students.[103] It was closed after a few months' operation due to the Japanese occupation of Singapore in 1942. However in March 1947, after the war, the college was re-opened with the new name of Nan Qiao Girls' High School.

The impact of Tan Kah Kee's non-profit making educational enterprises in Chinese immigrant society in British Malaya can be discussed at three different levels: on his close relatives and fellow district men; on his friends and business associates; and on his employees, the graduates of the Jimei colleges and Xiemen University, and his fellow Hokkiens. Tan Kah Kee was a traditional type of leader, characterised by paternalism and dedication. Not only did he set a good example for others to follow, but he was also prepared to put the pressure on others to comply. His son-in-law, Lee Kong Chian, was one who closely followed in his footsteps in promoting Chinese education. Lee first worked for Tan Kah Kee, and later left to start his own business. He was proven to be a shrewd entrepreneur and succeeded in building up a business empire in British Malaya, giving him the nickname, 'king of rubber'.[104] In 1934 when Tan resigned from

---

101. Ibid., p. 153.
102. See *Nanyang Siang Pau*, 18 April 1941.
103. See Wang Zengbing & Yu Gang, *Chen Jiageng xingxue ji*, p. 69.
104. For details about Lee Kong Chian and his business empire, see Lim Haw Seng, 'Li Guangqian de qiye wangguo' (The Business Empire of Lee Kong

his presidency of the Singapore Chinese High School, he encouraged Lee to step into his shoes.[105] In 1936, Lee donated S$50,000 as a contribution to the purchase of 400 acres of rubber plantation, the income from which was used as the Xiamen University operation funds.[106] In 1941, when Tan raised large sums of money for the founding of the Singapore Marine and Navigation School, Lee also donated a sum of $110,000.[107] Lee also continuously supported Tan's non-profit making educational enterprise in southern Fujian. In the period between 1950 and 1961, he and Tan Lark Sye were reported to have contributed a sum of 8,800,000 renminbi to the rebuilding of the Jimei colleges and Xiamen University. He also donated generously towards the University of Malaya in Singapore, and to the Nanyang University (ten percent of total collections, a sum of over S$1,000,000). In addition he set up the Lee Foundation, which gives generously to education and cultural and welfare activities.

Apart from Lee Kong Chian, Tan Lark Sye was another person who was profoundly influenced by Tan Kah Kee's deeds. Tan Lark Sye, the founder of Nanyang University, Singapore, was Tan Kah Kee's fellow district man. He was born in Tong An district, Fujian in 1897. He came to Singapore in 1916, and worked for Tan Kah Kee's factory as a foreman before joining up with his brothers to start their own business. He made millions in rubber trading, and later built up a vast business empire in Singapore and Malaysia.[108] Tan Lark Sye was profoundly influenced by Tan Kah Kee's dedication to the promotion of modern Chinese education, and was prepared to

Chian), in Lim Haw Seng, *Xinjiapo huashe yu huashang* (Singapore Chinese Society and Ethnic Chinese Business) (Singapore, Singapore Society of Asian Studies, 1995), pp. 183-226; Zheng Bingshan, Li Guangqian Zhuan (A Biography of Lee Kong Chian) (Beijing, Zhongguo Huaqiao chubanshe, 1997).

105. See C.F. Yong, *Tan Kah-kee, The Making of an Overseas Chinese Legend*, p. 111.
106. See Tan Kah Kee, *Nanqiao huiyi lu*, vol. 1, p. 28.
107. C.F. Yong, *Tan Kah-kee*, p. 111.
108. For Tan Lark Sye's business empire, see Lim Haw Seng, 'Chen Liushi de qiye shijie' (The Business World of Tan Lark Sye), in Lim Haw Seng, *Xinjiapo huashe yu huashang*, pp. 227–63.

donate generously to the maintenance of the Jimei colleges and Xiamen University. Together with Lee Kong Chian, he contributed a sum of 8,800,000 renminbi towards the rebuilding of the Jimei colleges and Xiamen University in the period between 1950 and 1961.[109] In 1950 when the University of Malaya was founded in Singapore, Tan Lark Sye also donated a sum of S$300,000 to the university.[110] However, Tan Lark Sye's most important contribution to Chinese education in the region was his founding of Nanyang University in 1953. Undoubtedly inspired by Tan Kah Kee's example in founding of Xiamen University in Southern Fujian, in January 1953 he proposed founding a Chinese university in Singapore, the first of its kind in the Chinese communities in Southeast Asia. To this end, he donated the huge sum of S$5,000,000 as a building fund.[111] At the same time, the Singapore Hokkien Association, under his influence as president, also donated 500 acres of land in Jurong as a site for the university.[112]

The second group of people influenced by Tan Kah Kee's deeds was his friends and business associates. Of course many of them were wealthy Chinese businessmen and were capable of donating generously to Chinese education. They included Oei Tiong Ham (Huang Zhonghan), the renowned 'king of sugar' of Java, Zeng Jiangshui, a wealthy Hokkien merchant of Malacca, and Lim Ngee Soon (Lin Yisun), a wealthy merchant and a leader of the Teochew community in Singapore. These men were not only Tan Kah Kee's friends and business associates, but also relatives through marriage. Zeng was particularly supportive of Tan Kah Kee's endeavours. He donated S$10,000 to the medical faculty at Xiamen University in 1926, and in 1931 he donated another large sum of S$150,000 to the university's library and operation fund. In 1941, Zeng came up with another S$20,000 for Tan's project

109. See C.F. Yong, *Tan Kah-kee*, p. 111.
110. See 'Haiwai minban daxue pingdiqi: Chen Liushi yu Nanyang daxue' (Tan Lark Sye and the Nanyang University), in *Nanyang Siang Pau* (Malaysia), 6 January 1990, p. 9.
111. Xinjiapo Nanyang wenhua chubanshe (ed), *Nanyang daxue chuangxiao shi* (A History of the Founding of the Nanyang University) (Singapore, Xinjiapo Nanyang wenhua chubanshe, 1956), p. 26.
112. Ibid., p. 32.

to found the teacher training college in Singapore.[113] Oei Tiong Ham and Lim Ngee Soon also contributed financially to the founding of the Singapore Chinese High School, and the former donated a sum of S$100,000 for the construction of its main hall (the hall was later named after Oei Tiong Ham).[114]

The third group of Ethnic Chinese who were influenced by Tan Kah Kee included his former employees, graduates of the Jimei colleges and Xiamen University, and his fellow Hokkiens. Many of them had seen and heard of Tan Kah Kee's educational deeds, and were inspired by him to contribute to the promotion of Chinese education in the region. This influence has been sustained for many generations. In the 1970s, when Chinese education faced an unprecedented crisis in Malaysia, some of the Hokkien leaders came out to defend it and contributed significantly to its revival. They included Li Zhengfeng (Lee Seng Png) in Kuala Lumpur, Yang Jindian in Ipoh and Dato Tan Say Eng (Chen Shiyong) in Seremban, Negri Sembilan. Li Zhengfeng was elected president of the Zhong Hua High School in Kuala Lumpur in 1974, and under his leadership and with his generous donation, a huge sum of money was raised for the rebuilding of the high school. A new majestic building gave the school new life, marking the revival of the school with rapidly increasing enrolments. Li had worked as the Kuala Lumpur branch manager of Lee Rubbers Pty Ltd, and was inspired by both Tan Kah Kee and Lee Kong Chian's deeds in education.[115]

Like Li Zhengfeng, Yang Jindian was a dedicated promoter of Chinese education. As a Hokkien community leader in Perak, he had been active in promoting Chinese education in the state. In 1955, he

113. See *Lat Pau*, 23 February 1926; *Nanyang Siang Pau*, 20 November 1931; Tan Kah Kee, *Nanqiao huiyi lu*, vol. 2, p. 372.
114. See 'Nanyang Huaqiao zhongxue jinxi jinian tekan', in Tay Lian Soo & Gwee Yee Hean, *Malaixiya Xinjiapo huawen zhongxue tekan tiyao*, pp. 261–62.
115. See Chen Yushui's article on 'Li Zhengfeng and the Revival of the Zhong Hua High School', in *Nanyang Siang Pau*, Malaysia, 8 February 1990, p. 6. See also the same article reproduced in Zeng Yongsheng et.al. (eds), *Malaixiya Fujianren xingxue banjiao shiliaoji* (Historical Materials of the Promotion of Chinese Education by the Hokkiens in Malaysia) (Kuala Lumpur, The Federation of Hokkien Association of Malaysia, 1993), pp. 80–5.

raised a large sum of money for the construction of the Pei Nan High School, Ipoh, of which he was president. In the 1970s, when the Chinese education revival movement was launched in Malaysia, he led a fundraising drive for rebuilding the Yu Cai (Yuk Choy) Independent High School in Ipoh. He took up the position of chairman of the fundraising committee, which aimed to raise the sum of $5,000,000. In 1984 at the age of 70, he was made chairman of the construction committee and succeeded in building a majestic new building for the independent school. Yang attributed his enthusiasm for Chinese education to the influence of Tan Kah Kee.[116]

Dato Tan Say Eng (Chen Shiyong) in Seremban was another Hokkien leader who was inspired by Tan Kah Kee's deeds. Born in Eng Choon district, Fujian province in 1909, he came to British Malaya at the age of eighteen and later became a successful businessman. His enthusiasm in promoting Chinese education in the state of Negri Sembilan was reflected in his deep involvement in the running of the Chinese schools. He had been chairman and deputy chairman of the Managing Board of Chinese Schools in the state. He had also been the president, deputy president and treasurer of the Zhong Hua High School in Seremban, a leading Chinese high school in the state of Negri Sembilan.[117] He was also active in the Chinese educational revival movement in Malaysia in the 1970s. When Dato Tan first arrived in Seremban, he worked as a junior clerk in the Seremban branch of the Tan Kah Kee Company Pty Ltd. Greatly impressed by Tan Kah Kee's spirit of 'promoting education at the sacrifice of personal wealth', he took Tan Kah Kee as his role model in his efforts to promote modern Chinese education.[118]

116. See Zheng Wanfa's article on 'Yang Jindian and the Yu Cai Independent High School', in *Nanyang Siang Pau*, Malaysia, 7 January 1990, p. 8.; see also the same article reproduced in Zeng Yongsheng et.al. (eds.) ibid., pp. 128–29.
117. See *Dongzhong sanshi nian* (Thirty Years of the Federation of the Chinese School Presidents of Malaysia) (Kuala Lumpur, 1987), vol. 1, pp. 102–03.
118. See Xu Shiping's article on Dato Tan Say Eng and Chinese education, in *Nanyang Siang Pau*, Malaysia, 11 May 1990, p. 2.; see also the same article reproduced in Zeng Yongsheng et.al. (eds), op. cit., pp. 168–70.

Concluding Remarks

Like many other immigrant societies, Chinese immigrant communities in British Malaya retained strong cultural and emotional ties with their motherland, China. The rise of modern Chinese education in British Malaya between 1904 and 1941 was the result of these strong ties. Chinese immigrant society developed its independent attitudes and shouldered the burden of educating its younger generation without seeking much government help. Instead, modern Chinese education in British Malaya grew by leaps and bounds with the financial support of the community, although sectarian divisions did weaken its efforts.

Being the earliest dialect community and being in a strong financial position, the Hokkien community played a leading role in the promotion of Chinese education in the region. Tan Kah Kee, as a Hokkien community leader, entrepreneur and Ethnic Chinese nationalist, played a significant role in the promotion of Chinese education. His educational deeds both in southern Fujian and in Singapore set an example for the Chinese in Singapore and Malaysia to follow. Tan's work has inspired many generations of Chinese (both in South China and in the Chinese communities in East and Southeast Asia) to further promote modern Chinese education.

CHAPTER 8

Economic, Political and Social Change in the Chinese Communities in Malaysia and Singapore before the Second World War: A Historical Survey*

Creation of the Early Chinese Communities

Chinese immigration to Malaysia and Singapore resulted largely from push factors such as the agrarian problems of overpopulation, natural calamities and landlord exploitation. Tens of thousands of Chinese immigrants, driven by poverty and despair, migrated from the coastal provinces of China to Southeast Asia and America. The pull force was equally strong. European expansion in Southeast Asia since the beginning of the sixteenth century, and British advancement in the region with the founding of the first free port in Penang in 1786, marked a new era of Chinese immigration to Southeast Asia. British free trade policy in Penang, Singapore and later in Malacca greatly attracted Chinese immigrants to that part of the world.

---
* First published in Lee Kam Hing and Tan Chee-Beng (eds), *The Chinese in Malaysia* (Singapore, Oxford University Press, 2000), pp. 1-36.

Chinese immigration was not supported by the home government. In fact, the immigrants' departure from China was against the wishes of the government. It was not until 1893 that the imperial Chinese government lifted its ban on Chinese immigration overseas.[1] Two patterns of early Chinese immigration to Malaysia and Singapore can be discerned: kinship-based immigration and the credit-ticket system. Up against many possible adversities — the penalty for breaking imperial law, the oppressive Chinese mandarins, the hazardous voyage and the hostile environment in the new land — early Chinese immigrants fell back on kinship ties for mutual support. Once they had established a foothold in business overseas, they recruited relatives and kinsmen for their business operations. The other system, the credit-ticket immigration, met the need of tens of thousands of poverty-stricken immigrants. Without the support of kinsmen, many prospective Chinese immigrants received an advance passage provided by labour brokers (known in Chinese as *kheh-t'au*), captains of junks or labour agencies. Arriving at their destinations, the credit-ticket immigrants (popularly known as 'coolies') were sent off to mines and plantation estates as labourers. The employers paid the labour brokers the passage money that the immigrants owed and entered into a written contract with the immigrants for the repayment of their debts in the form of labour. After working for a fixed period of several years, credit-ticket immigrants were released from their obligations and were free to choose their own employment. This pattern of migration was popular and was responsible for bringing the majority of Chinese immigrants to Malaysia and Singapore before 1911.[2]

The coolie trade, a thriving immigrant trade characterised by its inhuman treatment of the coolies during recruitment and transportation, became the dominant pattern of Chinese

---

1.　See Yen Ching-hwang, *Coolies and Mandarins: China's Protection of Overseas Chinese during the Late Ch'ing Period* (Singapore, Singapore University Press, 1985), pp. 249–66; Chuang Kuo-t'u, *Chung-kuo feng-chien cheng-fu te hua-ch'iao cheng-ch'ih* (China's Overseas Chinese Policy during the Feudal Period) (Xiamen, Xiamen University Press, 1989), pp. 259–60.

2.　See British Colonial Office Records, CO, 275/41.

immigration after 1852. This trade was primarily under the control of foreign immigrant agencies, including the British, Spanish, German, French, American, Dutch and Portuguese.[3] Before 1876 there were at least six coolie agencies in the Treaty ports on coastal China, supplying coolies bound for Singapore. Three of these agencies were owned by Chinese: Hee Kee, Yeong Seng What, and Ty Chaong & Company. The first two were stationed at port Swatow in Kwangtung province and provided Teochew and Hakka immigrants. The third agency operated in Amoy, Fukien province and supplied southern Hokkien immigrants. Both Hee Kee and Yeong Seng What had branches in Singapore for receiving coolies, and the surplus was dispatched to Penang for dispersal to the mining states in the northwest of the Malay Peninsula and the plantation estates of the northeast Sumatra.[4]

The earliest Chinese settlement in Malaysia and Singapore can be traced back to the time of Malacca Sultanate in the fifteenth century. Strategically located in the Straits of Malacca, Malacca was a thriving entrepot for the exchange of products from China, India and the islands of Southeast Asia. It attracted Chinese traders who remained to conduct their business. This small but growing Chinese community played an important role in the foreign trade of the Sultanate. The leader of the Chinese community was appointed one of the four port officials, the *shahbandar*, to help administer the affairs of foreigners.[5] Presumably the Chinese *shahbandar* was expected to control the commercial activities of the Chinese residents, to regulate their behaviour and to act as an agent of the government in dealing with the Chinese population. Most of the

3.   See Wang Sing-wu, *The Organization of Chinese Emigration, 1848–1888: With Special Reference to Chinese Emigration to Australia* (San Francisco, Chinese Materials Center, 1978), pp. 355–60.
4.   See Yen Ching-hwang, *A Social History of the Chinese in Singapore and Malaya, 1800–1911* (Singapore, Oxford University Press, 1986), p. 7.
5.   See K.S. Sandhu, 'Chinese Colonization of Malacca', in *Journal of the Tropical Geography*, vol. 15 (1961), p. 5; K.S. Sandhu & Paul Wheatley (eds), *Melaka: The Transformation of a Malay Capital, c. 1400–1980* (Kuala Lumpur, Oxford University Press, 1983), vol. 2, p. 96.

Chinese there were southern Hokkiens from Changchow, and did not remain long in one place.[6]

Three patterns of Chinese settlement can be observed during the period from the end of the eighteenth to the first decade of the twentieth century: urban port settlement, mining settlement and rural agricultural settlement. Urban port settlement began with the small trading community in Malacca Sultanate in the fifteenth century, but grew rapidly after the British founded Penang in 1786 and then Singapore in 1819. British free trade policy attracted a large number of Chinese from neighbouring states in Southeast Asia and from China. The urban port setting linked the Chinese settlement with home ports in China. It was more exposed to outside influences and contacts, and enabled the Chinese immigrants to gain new economic opportunities. Urban port settlement also provided opportunities for the immigrants to mix with Europeans and other non-Chinese residents. Such contacts were useful because they enabled Chinese businessmen to expand their commercial activities.[7]

Chinese mining settlement began with the gold-mining centre in Bau, Sarawak, in the early nineteenth century. Having arrived from the Chinese gold mines in West Kalimantan in the mid-eighteenth century, the Hakka gold miners in Bau increased to about 600 in 1848.[8] Chinese immigrants in the nineteenth century opened up tin mines in Lukut and Sungei Ujung in Negri Sembilan, Larut in Perak, and Kuala Lumpur in Selangor. Chinese mining settlements were geographically less accessible, and members of the mining communities were less mobile in employment, making the settlements relatively close societies. Hakka miners in particular, united by a common dialect and

6. See Yen Ching-hwang, 'Early Fukienese Migration and Social Organizations in Singapore and Malaya before 1900', in Pin-tsun Chang and Shih-chi Liu (eds), *Chung-kuo h'ai-yang fa-chan-shih lun-wen chi (Ti wu chi)* (Essays in Chinese Maritime History), vol. 5 (Nankang, Academia Sinica, 1993), p. 681.
7. See C.M. Turnbull, *The Straits Settlements, 1826–67: Indian Presidency to Crown Colony* (London, The Athlone Press, 1972), pp. 10, 32.
8. See Daniel Chew, *Chinese Pioneers on the Sarawak Frantiers, 1841–1941* (Singapore, Oxford University Press, 1990), pp. 23–5.

strengthened by secret society brotherhoods, were tough, clannish and wary of outsiders.

Chinese rural agricultural settlement developed later in response to the rise of the cash crop industry in the second half of the nineteenth century. The growth of pepper and gambier plantations in early Singapore and later in Johor under the system of the *kangchu (Lord of the River)* in the nineteenth century represented a major pattern of Chinese rural agricultural settlement.[9] This pattern was repeated elsewhere in Malaysia, such as in the Hakka agricultural settlement in Kudat, North Borneo (Sabah) in 1883[10] and the Foochow agricultural settlements in Sarawak at the beginning of the twentieth century.[11]

The rural agricultural settlement was also a relatively closed and less exposed community. In this rural setting, the leaders of the settlement enjoyed greater power and authority than the leaders of the mining settlements. This was partly due to the agriculturists' greater degree of dependence on their leaders, who were usually directly responsible for their recruitment in China.[12]

The social and linguistic background of the immigrants and the nature of Chinese immigration determined the form of the early Chinese social organisations. Strong kinship ties in China led to the founding of early Chinese kinship organisations.[13] Linguistic

9. See A.E. Coope, 'The Kangchu System in Johore', in *Journal of the Malayan Branch, Royal Asiatic Society*, vol. 14, no. 3 (1936), pp. 247–63; Carl A. Trocki, 'The Origins of the Kangchu System, 1740–1860', in *Journal of the Malayan Branch, Royal Asiatic Society*, vol. 49, no. 2 (1976), pp. 132–55.

10. See K.G. Tregonning, *Under Chartered Company Rule: North Borneo, 1881-1946* (Singapore, University of Malaya Press, 1959), p. 132; Han Sin-fong, *The Chinese in Sabah, East Malaysia* (Taipei, The Orient Cultural Service, 1975), p. 33.

11. Daniel Chew, op. cit., pp. 143-57; Lau Tzy Cheng, *Huang Nai-shang yu hsin Fu-chou* (Wong Nai Siong and New Foochow) (Singapore, South Seas Society, 1979), pp. 1-37.

12. Lau Tzy Cheng, *ibid.*

13. See Yen Ching-hwang, 'Early Chinese Clan Organizations in Singapore and Malaya, 1819-1911', in *Journal of Southeast Asian Studies*, vol. 12, no.1 (1981), a special issue on Ethnic Chinese in Southeast Asia, edited by C.F. Yong, pp. 62–3.

differences and a strong sense of regional identity also encouraged immigrants to form their respective dialect associations,[14] and secret societies were set up for protection and mutual help. Obviously, there was often an overlapping of membership and leadership in these early Chinese kinship organisations, dialect associations and secret societies.

Hokkiens were very active in establishing kinship organisations. They founded the earliest Chinese clan association in Malaysia and Singapore — the Cheah Kongsi of Penang in 1820[15] as well as many other powerful kinship organisations in Penang and Singapore, such as the Khoo Kongsi, Yeoh Kongsi, Lim Kongsi and Tan Kongsi of Penang. Most of the early Chinese clan organisations in Malaysia and Singapore were localised lineages which restricted their membership to clansmen from the same village or district in China. Relationships among the members were clearly defined, and traditional obligations to kinsmen and the performing of religious rituals for the founders of the clans in China were also strictly observed.[16]

In contrast to the Cantonese and Hakkas whose clans were predominantly non-localised lineages, the Hokkiens' clans were mainly localised lineages. This was probably due to factors such as the Hokkien domination of early trade in the Straits settlements and the nature of the overseas environment. Hokkien domination of the Straits' early trade provided a sound foundation for the rapid growth of the Hokkien population. The continuous expansion of business overseas compelled Hokkien traders to recruit manpower from China, and more and more of their kinsmen were sponsored to come to Malaysia to staff their shops and business enterprises. The overseas environment, whether in urban ports, mining centres or plantation estates, posed a serious challenge to the new immigrants. In the urban ports where unfamiliar

14. Yen Ching-hwang, *A Social History of the Chinese in Singapore and Malaya*, pp. 35–7.
15. Yen Ching-hwang, 'Early Fukienese Migration and Social Organizations in Singapore and Malaya before 1900', in Pin-tsun Chang & Shih-chi Liu (eds), op. cit., p. 696.
16. Yen Ching-hwang, ' Early Chinese Clan Organizations in Singapore and Malaya, 1819–1911', in *Journal of Southeast Asian Studies*, vol. 12, no. 1, p. 67.

faces were encountered and many unintelligible dialects were spoken, the new immigrants were forced to depend more on kinsmen for economic and emotional support. When the need for kinship support was felt keenly and the number of kinsmen was sufficient to form an organisation, a localised lineage organisation was established to meet the need.[17]

The Hakkas, a minority group among the early Chinese, appear to have been very active in founding their dialect associations. They established the first Chinese dialect organisation in Malaysia and Singapore, the Chia-ying Hakka Association of Penang in 1801.[18] The Association assumed the name Yan-woh Kongsi, which has raised some doubts about its ethnic character.[19] The Hakkas continued to found some of the early Chinese dialect associations in Malacca, Penang, Singapore, Kuala Lumpur, Perak and Negri Sembilan.[20]

What made the Hakkas most active among the Chinese in founding dialect organisations in nineteenth century Malaysia and Singapore was probably the result of the interplay of several factors: minority insecurity, the nature of the Chinese *kapitan* system, strong group cohesion and their early organisational experience in West Borneo. The Chinese in Penang, Malacca and Singapore were predominantly made up of Hokkiens and Teochews. Linguistic differences made the early Hakka immigrants in these ports more aware of their minority status, and helped give rise to a sense of insecurity. This insecurity was exacerbated by the nature of the

17. Yen Ching-hwang, *A Social History of the Chinese in Singapore and Malaya*, pp. 77–8.
18. Wu Hua, *Ma-lai-hsi-ya hua-tsu hui-kuan shih-lueh* (A Short History of Chinese Associations in Malaysia) (Singapore, Tung-nan-ya yen-chiu so, 1980), p. 3.
19. Yen Ching-hwang, 'Early Hakka Dialect Organizations in Singapore and Malaya, 1801–1900', in *Ya-chou wen-hua* (*Asian Culture*) (Singapore, Singapore Society of Asian Studies) vol. 17 (1993), pp. 108–09; Chee Liew Seong, 'The Hakka Community in Malaya: With Special Reference to Their Associations' (MA thesis, University of Malaya, Kuala Lumpur, 1971), p. xxi; Leong Kok Kee, 'The Chia-ying Hakka in Penang, 1786–1941', in *Malaysia in History*, vol. 24 (1981), p. 40.
20. Yen Ching-hwang, 'Early Hakka Dialect Organizations in Singapore and Malaya, 1801–1900', in *Asian Culture*, vol. 17, pp. 109–10.

Chinese *kapitan* system in early Malaysia. Chinese *kapitans* were appointed by the British Government from the dominant dialect group among the Chinese population, and were given enormous power to control the security and welfare of the Chinese community.[21] Naturally, these *kapitans* tended to look after their own interests and those of their own dialect group — particularly as they were unlikely to be able to speak other Chinese dialects. The minority groups thus felt insecure, and could not count on the *kapitans* for support in times of need or crisis.[22]

The Hakkas were known to be the latecomers on the scene in South China. They moved from the north to the south through several waves of migration. From north and central China they moved down to the border of Kiangsi, Fukien and Kwangtung provinces. Many of them moved further into the eastern and southeastern parts of Kwangtung province,[23] where they were discriminated against partly because they were the latecomers, and partly because they were in the minority. As a result, they had to develop strong group cohesion in order to cope with the adverse conditions.

The unique organisational experience of the Hakkas in the west Borneo gold fields also contributed to their active founding of dialect associations. The early Hakkas in mid-eighteenth century Borneo were predominantly miners, and they belonged to a tough and well-organised group. They survived and prospered in a hostile environment under the protection of a sophisticated organisation, the *kongsi*, which was an economic, social and political entity.[24] The best known Hakka Kongsi

21. C.S. Wong, *A Gallery of Chinese Kapitan* (Singapore, Dewan Bahasa dan Kebudayaan Kebangsaan, 1964), pp. 9–26.

22. Yen Ching-hwang, 'Early Hakka Dialect Organizations in Singapore and Malaya, 1801–1900', in *Asian Culture*, vol. 17, p. 111.

23. Lo Hsiang-lin, 'Huang Ch'ao pien-luan yu Ling-hua shih-pi ch'un' (The Rebellion of Huang Ch'ao and the Shih Pi Village of Ling Hua) in Hsueh Tso-chih (ed), *Ke'-chia yen-yuan* (The Origins of the Hakkas) (Singapore, Ts'ung-wen ch'u-pan-she, 1991), pp. 119–25.

24. Wang Tai Peng, 'The Word Kongsi: A Note', in *Journal of the Malaysia Branch, Royal Asiatic Society*, vol. 52, no. 1 (1979), pp. 102–05; Wang Tai Peng, *The Origins of Chinese Kongsi* (Petaling Jaya, Pelanduk Publications, 1994), pp. 67–83.

Government, under the famous Lo Fang-po, served as the protector of Hakka immigrants on the island of Borneo.[25] Some of these Hakka immigrants then shared what they had learned from their experience in Borneo with the Hakka communities in the Straits settlements.[26]

The secret society, a major form of social organisation in early Chinese immigrant communities in Malaysia and Singapore, was not the preserve of any particular dialect group. The term 'secret society' has a negative and sinister connotation in modern times, but was not perceived as such by the Chinese settlers. In fact, secret societies were tolerated by the governments in the Straits settlements and the Malay states as the *de facto* power structure among the Chinese until 1889, when they were suppressed by the British in the Straits settlements.[27]

Since the early Chinese immigrants came predominantly from Fukien and Kwangtung where the Triad was prevalent,[28] they introduced this form of social organisation when they arrived in Malaysia and Singapore. The Triad, which was originally politically-oriented, developed into a powerful social organisation providing protection and mutual assistance. Cutting across kinship and class boundaries, it became a focal point of political action and a formidable

25. Lo Hsiang-lin, *Hsi-po-lo -chou Lo Fang-po teng so chien kung-ho kuo k'ao* (A Historical Survey of the Lan-Fang Presidential System in West Borneo) (Hong Kong, 1961); Barbara E.Ward, 'A Hakka Kongsi in Borneo', in *Journal of Oriental Studies* vol.1, no. 2 (Hong Kong, Centre of Asian Studies, University of Hong Kong, 1954), pp. 358–70.

26. M.L. Wynne, *Triad and Tabut: A Survey of the Origins and Diffusion of Chinese and Mohamedan Secret Societies in the Malay Peninsula, 1800–1935* (Singapore, Government Printing Office, 1941), pp. 76–7.

27. Wilfred Blythe, *The Impact of Chinese Secret Societies in Malaya* (London, Oxford University Press, 1969), pp. 3–4; Yen Ching-hwang, *A Social History of the Chinese in Singapore and Malaya*, pp. 110–28.

28. See Fei-ling Davis, *Primitive Revolutionaries of China: A Study of Secret Societies of the Late Nineteenth Century* (London, Routledge & Kegan Paul, 1977), pp. 56–71; Frederic Wakeman, Jr, 'The Secret Societies of Kwangtung, 1800–1856', in Jean Chesneaux (ed), *Popular Movements and Secret Societies in China, 1840-1950* (Stanford, Stanford University Press, 1972), pp. 1–42; Lien Li-ch'ang, *Fu-chien pi-mi she-hui* (The Secret Societies in Fukien) (Foochow, Fu-chien jen-min ch'u-pan-she, 1988), pp. 158–208.

challenge to the Confucian socio-economic order during the Ch'ing dynasty in China.[29]

Secret societies existed in the port cities such as Penang, Malacca and Singapore, in mining centres such as Bau, Lukut and Larut, and in agricultural settlements such as the various *kangkars* in Johor.[30] Being in a foreign land, the early Chinese secret societies found their political aims of overthrowing the Manchus less relevant, but their functions of protection and mutual assistance became more important in the new environments, requiring them to be integrated into the social structure of the Chinese communities.[31]

Economic Pursuits and Advancement

Entrepot Trade

Under the Malacca Sultanate, the Chinese brought in large quantities of Chinese products and exchanged them for Indian textiles and Southeast Asian spices, camphor, sandalwood, musk, seed pearls, batik material and carpets.[32] They set up trading organisations based on family or partnership, and by linking Malacca with other Southeast Asian

29. Jean Chesneaux, *Secret Societies in China in the Nineteenth and Twentieth Centuries* (Hong Kong, Heinemann Educational Books, 1971), pp. 80–107.

30. Mak Lau Fong, *The Sociology of Secret Societies: A Study of Chinese Secret Societies in Singapore and Peninsular Malaysia* (Kuala Lumpur, Oxford University Press, 1981), pp. 77–84; Wilfred Blythe, op. cit., pp. 250–61; P'an Hsing-nung, *Ma-lai-ya Ch'ao-ch'iao t'ung-chien* (The Teochews in Malaya) (Singapore, Nan-tao ch'u-pan-she, 1950), p. 42; Carl A.Trocki, *Prince of Pirates: The Temenggongs and Development of Johor and Singapore, 1784–1885* (Singapore, Singapore University Press, 1979), p. 105.

31. Yen Ching-hwang, *A Social History of the Chinese in Singapore and Malaya*, pp. 110–40.

32. Paul Wheatley, 'A City that was Made for Merchandise — the Geography of Fifteenth Century Malacca', in *Nanyang yen-chiu* (The Bulletin of the Institute of Southeast Asia), vol. 1 (Singapore, Nanyang University, 1959), pp. J5–J6; Paul Wheatley, *The Golden Khersonese: Studies in the Historical Geography of the Malay Peninsula before A.D. 1500* (Kuala Lumpur, University of Malaya Press, 1961), pp. 313–15.

ports and the ports of coastal China to form an effective trading network, the Chinese traders dominated trade with Southeast Asia.

The arrival of the European powers in the region weakened the position of the Chinese traders, although the Chinese were still able to hold their dominant position in Southeast Asian trade in the sixteenth and seventeenth centuries. This was because European traders were still restricted by the Chinese authorities in their China trade, and Chinese traders had good commercial contacts in the region.[33] It was only with British penetration into Southeast Asia at the end of the eighteenth century, which greatly altered the pattern of trade, that the dominant position of the Chinese traders was undermined. The founding of Penang and Singapore created new centres for entrepot trading activities, and British free trade policies revolutionised the concept of trade. The volume of entrepot trade expanded, but competition became keener, undermining the position of the Chinese traders. At the same time, British political dominance in the new ports favoured British and European merchants. The founding in Singapore of Guthrie & Company in 1821, Boustead & Company in 1828, John Buttery & Company in Penang and Sandilands Buttery & Company in Singapore in the 1830s, marked the beginning of British and European dominance of trade.[34] Most of these companies started as agency houses for companies based in London or Europe, but expanded quickly into entrepot trade and later extended into finance, shipping, mining and plantations.[35]

The growing dominance of European trade subordinated Chinese traders in the new entrepot trading system. However, a group of Malacca-born Chinese merchants emerged as 'middlemen' in the new system. Some of them were probably born of Malay

33. Anthony Reid, 'The Unthreatening Alternatives: Chinese Shipping in Southeast Asia, 1567–1842' (Paper presented to the Conference on Island Southeast Asia and the World Economy, 1790s–1990s, held at the Australian National University, Canberra, 24–26 November 1992), pp. 1–2.
34. G.C. Allen & A.G. Donnithorne, *Western Enterprise in Indonesia and Malaya: A Study in Economic Development* (London, George Allen & Unwin Limited, 1957), pp. 53–6.
35. Ibid.

mothers, but maintained many of their Chinese manners and customs; and many had received both English and Chinese education in the Anglo-Chinese College of Malacca.[36] Most of them spoke Malay as well as the Hokkien dialect, in addition to English. This linguistic ability, together with their exposure to Western culture, made them most suited to fill the position of middlemen. Some of them were employed by British or European firms in Singapore and Penang as staff or as business agents serving the trade between the Europeans and the indigenous people.[37] In addition, a small group of enterprising Chinese immigrants newly arrived from China founded companies and was involved actively in the entrepot trade. They likewise forged a close relationship with British and European companies.

The new trading system operating in the region had fundamentally a three-tier structure. The top of the structure was occupied by British and European merchants who imported Western manufactured goods and exported Southeast Asian produce. On the middle rung were Chinese traders who distributed Western goods and collected native produce for export to Europe. Chinese traders also imported Chinese produce and foodstuffs and exported island produce to China. At the bottom were the indigenous traders who brought native products to the new ports to exchange for Western and Chinese commodities.[38]

36. See Song Ong Siang, *One Hundred Years' History of the Chinese in Singapore* (Singapore, University of Malaya Press, 1967) pp. 30–1; Brian Harrison, *Waiting for China: The Anglo-Chinese College at Malacca, 1818–1843, and Early Nineteenth Century Missions* (Hong Kong, Hong Kong University Press, 1979), pp. 129–30.

37. See Twang Peck Yang, 'Chinese Maritime Trading Network and Organizations based in Singapore, 1820s-1960s' (Paper presented to the Conference on Island Southeast Asia and the World Economy, 1790s–1990s, held at the Australian National University, Canberra, 24–26 November 1992), p. 2.

38. Chiang Hai Ding, 'Sino-British Mercantile Relations in Singapore's Entrepot Trade, 1870–1915', in Jerome Ch'en & Nicholas Tarling (eds), *Studies in the Social History of China & Southeast Asia: Essays in Memory of Victor Purcell* (Cambridge, Cambridge University Press, 1970), pp. 249–56.

The opening of Singapore as a free port stimulated the Dutch to open up more harbours in the Archipelago as free trading ports.[39] With the emergence of these new ports, Chinese traders widened their scope of activity by setting up branches or partnerships. The commodities they traded were more varied and included Chinese foodstuffs and domestic items.[40] On their return, Chinese junks carried back a variety of the Straits and Archipelago produce.

Chinese entrepot traders were also more integrated into local and international trading systems. The middleman role of the Chinese traders in the nineteenth century was important, for Western-manufactured products could not have been effectively distributed without the Chinese and Western trade would have been hampered had there no Chinese compradors.[41]

The Chinese traders greatly benefited from this role. They established firm connections with Western merchants, and a network of collection and distribution among the local inhabitants in Southeast Asia. They also opened shipping lines to facilitate this operation. Some of them amassed great fortunes from the booming entrepot trade, and their companies became well-known business establishments in the local Chinese communities. Some of the major Chinese companies in nineteenth-century Malaysia and Singapore were Kim Seng & Company, Lee Cheng Yan & Company, and Kim Cheng & Company, who were among most active operators in the entrepot trade. The founder of Kim Seng & Company, Tan Kim Seng, was born in Malacca and emigrated to Singapore to take advantage of the opening of the new port. The company built up extensive business with several leading European firms in Singapore, such as

---

39. See Wong Lin Ken, 'Singapore: Its Growth as an Entrepot Port, 1819–1941', in *Journal of Southeast Asian Studies*, vol. 9, no.1 (1978), p. 58.
40. These included earthenware, flooring tiles, coping stones, paper umbrellas, Chinese confectionery, dried and salted fruits, dried vegetables, Chinese medicine, Chinese cloth and joss-sticks. See Wong Lin Ken, *The Trade of Singapore, 1819–69* (Singapore, An independent issue of the *Journal of the Malayan Branch, Royal Asiatic Society*, 1960), vol. 33, no. 4, p. 111.
41. See J. Thomson, *The Straits of Malacca, Indo-China and China, or Ten Years' Travels, Adventures and Residence Abroad* (London, Sampson Low, Marston, Low & Searle, 1875), pp. 11–3.

Boustead & Company and the Borneo Company.[42] By 1870 it had already set up a network of entrepot trade, and had branches in Malacca and Shanghai.[43]

Commercial Agriculture

A major branch of Chinese economic activity in nineteenth century Malaysia and Singapore was commercial agriculture. To break the Dutch monopoly of the spice trade and to find a stable source of income for the new government, Francis Light, the founder of Penang, encouraged the Chinese settlers to undertake pepper planting.[44] The new venture was essentially a joint European–Chinese enterprise. The European planters financed and controlled large pepper estates, while the Chinese owned smallholdings. European planters usually hired Chinese contractors to develop their estates with *sinkheh* (new immigrants) labour. The industry targeted Europe as its main market. However, the exclusion of Britain from European trade by the Napoleonic regime dealt a severe blow to the Penang planters. At the same time, Penang producers also failed to develop an alternative market in China. The production of pepper declined, although the industry did revive somewhat after the fall of Napoleon and the restoration of European markets in 1815. Unfortunately the revival was short-lived, following a sharp fall in pepper prices in London in 1817. In the mid-1820s, the Penang planters began to abandon pepper planting, and after a decade pepper trading almost ceased to exist.[45]

42. Wong Lin Ken, 'Singapore: Its Growth as an Entrepot Port, 1819–1941', in *Journal of the Southeast Asian Studies*, vol. 9, no. 1 (1978), p. 46; K.G. Tregonning, *Home Port Singapore: A History of Straits Steamship Company Limited, 1890–1965* (Singapore, Oxford University Press, 1967), p. 9.
43. Chiang Hai Ding, 'Sino-British Mercantile Relations in Singapore's Entrepot Trade, 1870–1915', in Jerome Ch'en & Nicholas Tarling (eds), op. cit., p. 258.
44. James C. Jackson, *Planters and Speculators: Chinese and European Agricultural Enterprise in Malaya, 1786–1921* (Kuala Lumpur, University of Malaya Press, 1968), p. 95; C.S. Wong, *A Gallery of Chinese Kapitans* (Singapore, Ministry of Culture, 1963), p. 13.
45. James C. Jackson, ibid., pp. 97–100.

Unlike the situation in Penang where pepper planting was a joint European and Chinese enterprise, in Singapore the planting of gambier and pepper was entirely in the hands of the Chinese; and almost ninety percent of the plantations were controlled by a single Chinese dialect group, the Teochews. With experience in planting, unlimited supply of cheap labour and the command of dialect and kinship influence as well as the coercive power of the secret society, Teochew planters had a better chance of success in commercial agriculture than the Chinese or European planters in Penang. By 1848, more than 10,000 Teochews were involved in planting and distributing gambier and pepper produce, and they monopolised the trade of these crops in both domestic and international markets. Indeed, many of the planters became rich and powerful in Chinese society in early Singapore.[46]

Chinese planters adopted the shifting method of cultivation, which promised a quick return but exhausted the land quickly. As a result, Chinese planters started to move from Singapore to Johor. Apart from its geographical proximity to Singapore, Johor offered other attractions. It had vast virgin lands, its population was small and its soil was rich in the river valleys. Furthermore, the Malay ruler, the Temenggong, wanted Chinese planters to help develop the state. Starting as early as the 1820s, and gaining momentum in the 1830s and '40s, the movement of Teochew planters from Singapore and Riau into Johor grew rapidly in the second half of the nineteenth century. By the early 1860s, there were 1,200 gambier and pepper plantations in Johor with a labour force of 15,000.[47] This movement of labour reached its peak in the early 1890s, with

46. See Siah U Chin, 'General Sketch of the Numbers, Tribes, and Avocations of the Chinese in Singapore', in *Journal of the Indian Archipelago and Eastern Asia*, vol. 2 (1848), p. 290; Yen Ching-hwang, 'Power Structure and Power Relations in the Teochew Community in Singapore, 1819–1930' (Paper presented at the First International Conference on Teochew Studies, held at the Chinese University of Hong Kong, 20–23 December 1993), pp. 9–12; Song Ong Siang, *One Hundred Years' History of the Chinese in Singapore*, pp. 19–20.

47. Carl A. Trocki, *Prince of Pirates: The Temenggongs and the Development of Johor and Singapore, 1784–1885*, pp. 88–91; James C. Jackson, op. cit., pp. 14–5.

an estimated 210,000 Chinese in Johor who were chiefly gambier and pepper planters.

What accounted for the remarkable success of Chinese commercial agriculture in Johor during this period was the introduction of the *kangchu* system. The *kangchu*, literally 'lord of the river', was the headman who leased the river settlement from the Malay ruler. The ruler delegated his authority to the headman with a *surat sungei* (river document). The headman was given administrative and legal powers, like a Malay *penghulu* (the headman of a village). This *kangchu* system was well suited to the conditions of nineteenth-century Johor. The *kangchu*, who brought with him capital and labour to develop the settlement, imposed no strain on state coffers. He was responsible for administering the settlement (or *kangkar*, literally meaning 'foot of the river'). He paid the rent or taxes of the entire settlement to the state, maintained law and order, constructed and maintained paths, and provided for the upkeep of river communications. To compensate him for his administrative duties, the state also granted him opium and gambling 'farms', together with other exclusive rights to pawnbroking, selling liquor, slaughtering pigs and selling pork — all lucrative sources of income for early Chinese settlements in Malaysia.[48]

This system suited the Chinese planters well. Ambitious Chinese planters who had capital and a labour force ran the settlement in their own way. Once they were given the authority from the Malay ruler, they ruled their *kangkar* single-handedly with the help of assistants. Since most Chinese planters were Teochews, kinship ties provided the foundation of their rule, sometimes reinforced by the coercive power of the secret society.

Sugar and tapioca were two other commercial crops in which the Chinese were actively involved. The former was planted mainly in Province Wellesley and Perak in the north of Malaya, while the latter was concentrated in the western part of the peninsula, including

48. See A.E. Coope, 'The Kangchu System in Johore', in *Journal of the Malayan Branch, Royal Asiatic Society*, vol. 14, no. 3 (1936), pp. 247–63; Carl A. Trocki, 'The Origins of the Kangchu System, 1740–1860', in *Journal of the Malayan Branch, Royal Asiatic Society*, vol. 49, no. 2 (1976), pp. 145–52.

the states of Malacca and Negri Sembilan. Chinese sugar planters had settled in Batu Kawan Island prior to the cession of Province Wellesley to the British in 1800. They opened up sugar estates in the mangrove-covered land and later extended to Bukit Tambun. The industry gained a firm foothold and began to expand during the 1820s and 1830s. By 1841, about 1,000 acres of land were under Chinese cultivation, producing 600 to 700 tons of sugar annually.[49] Soon, however, Chinese expansion was checked due to the arrival of European planters in the 1840s. The Europeans — British, French, and Dutch nationals — developed large sugar estates in southern Province Wellesley. With ample supplies of capital, superior technology and cheap Chinese immigrant labour, they gained supremacy in sugar planting. By the 1850s they had already wrested control of this thriving industry from the Chinese, and reduced the Chinese planters to smallholders.

The majority of the Chinese sugar planters were Teochews. Outmoded methods and a shortage of capital made the majority of Chinese planters uncompetitive. Those who survived the fierce competition were the innovators. One group, with access to capital from relatives, became smallholders and emphasised hard work. Cuts in the cost of production and the wise use of capital ensured their survival. A representative of this group was Kee Lye Huat, a Teochew immigrant whose company, Kee Poh Huat Kongsi in Sungei Bakap, thrived and prospered. Khaw Boo Aun represented a second type of innovator, adopting Western methods of production and management. He employed European superintendents, introduced Western machinery and also used political influence to consolidate his economic interests, enabling him to compete successfully with his European rivals.[50]

Tapioca production was almost entirely in the hands of the Chinese. The planting of tapioca started in Malacca around the

49. James C. Jackson, *Planters and Speculators*, pp. 128–29; Tan Kim Hong, 'Chinese Sugar Planting and Social Mobility in Nineteenth Century Province Wellesley', in *Malaysia in History*, vol. 24 (1981), pp. 24–5.
50. Tan Kim Hong, ibid., p. 31; C.S. Wong, *A Gallery of Chinese Kapitans*, pp. 81–3.

234 • The Ethnic Chinese in East and Southeast Asia:

1850s, when a decline in trade and mining activities in Malacca forced the Chinese in the state to look for other economic alternatives. They found tapioca promising, for it required smaller sums of capital, assured quick returns and encountered less competition. It was also an export industry that was less labour-intensive. In 1860, there were an estimated 1,000 acres of tapioca estates producing some 2,000 *pikuls* in Malacca. By the late 1860s tapioca planting increased ten-fold to 10,000 acres. The industry expanded rapidly in the 1870s and early 1880s, increasing from 19,900 acres in 1871 to a phenomenal 93,000 acres in 1882.[51] Soil exhaustion and increasing government hostility then caused Chinese planters to shift to Negri Sembilan. By 1888, the estimated land held by Chinese tapioca planters in Negri Sembilan amounted to 90,000 acres.

The success of the Chinese in the tapioca industry was due to a small group of Chinese capitalists in Malacca. They formed *kongsis,* and owned tapioca concessions and factories which processed tapioca roots into flour, flake and pearl. Planting was undertaken by Chinese contractors using cheap *sinkheh* labourers.[52]

The Tin-mining Industry

Tin mining had existed in Malaysia long before the arrival of the Chinese, but Chinese contribution to the development of this industry was remarkable. Throughout the nineteenth century, the Chinese provided most of the capital and labour, and greatly improved methods of production. Indeed, the pace of economic development in modern Malaysia would have been much slower had there been no active Chinese participation in the tin-mining industry.

Growing British influence in Malaya after the formation of the Straits settlements in 1826 created the conditions for economic expansion into the Malay states. The Chinese merchants in the Straits settlements who had accumulated large sums of capital were ready to take advantage of the new situation to invest in peninsular

51. James C.Jackson, *Planters and Speculators*, pp. 52–6.
52. Ibid., 73–5.

mines. At about the same time, the Malay political system in the western states was in decline. Power fell into the hands of territorial chiefs, the *orang besar-besar*. The system was further weakened by constant succession disputes.[53] In their struggle to preserve their power, the Malay chiefs were drawn into a contest for power, revenue and territorial expansion. This was a vicious circle: to acquire more power, they had to increase revenue; to increase revenue, they had to expand territorial control. Keen competition among rival Malay chiefs for new revenue led to constant conflict, particularly over mining land because it was a major source of wealth and power.

The first tin-mining town with a substantial number of Chinese miners was Lukut in the state of Selangor (later incorporated into Negri Sembilan). As early as 1815, Chinese miners had already arrived in Lukut, probably at the invitation of Raja Busu, a member of the Selangor royal family. Three years later, an estimated 200 Chinese miners came under the control of a Chinese *kapitan* appointed by the Sultan of Selangor. The number of Chinese miners grew, and the new settlement prospered. But a dispute over tax on export soured the relationship between Chinese miners and Raja Busu, and ended with the murder of the Raja and the closure of the mine in 1834.[54]

By the 1840s, several new tin-mining settlements populated by a substantial number of Chinese miners sprang up in Selangor, Perak, Negri Sembilan and Malacca. In the 1860s, these new settlements grew into prosperous mining centres with large Chinese populations. The Chinese population in Larut, Perak, was estimated at between 20,000 and 25,000 men in 1862.[55] It was largely through their efforts in the two decades from 1874 to 1895 that the Malayan tin-mining industry reached its peak. At that time, Malaya topped the ranking of world tin producers, accounting for 55 percent of the world's tin produce. During

---

53. See Khoo Kay Kim, *The Western Malay States, 1850–1873: The Effects of Commercial Development on Malay Politics* (Kuala Lumpur, Oxford University Press, 1975), pp. 22–8.

54. Wong Lin Ken, *The Malayan Tin Industry to 1914* (Tucson, The University of Arizona Press, 1965), p. 18.

55. Ibid., p. 27

this period, despite the active involvement of Western companies, the Chinese remained dominant.[56]

The success of the Chinese in the tin industry was due to a combination of various factors: ample supplies of capital from the Straits settlements, an unlimited source of labour from China, a well-disciplined labour force, cost-effective mining methods and entrepreneurship. Prior to British intervention in 1874, capital for the development of the mining industry came mainly from European and Chinese capitalists in the Straits settlements. Chinese capitalists such as Chee Yam Chuan, See Boon Tiong, Si Food Kee and Yeo Hood Ing came principally from Malacca. They made their wealth in trade, real estate, opium and liquor 'farms', and accumulated enormous capital for reinvestment. Many of them regarded tin mining as one of the big-business enterprises and a potentially important source of wealth. As a result they were actively involved in opening up tin mines in Selangor and Negri Sembilan.[57]

Overpopulation, natural calamities, the effect of the opening up of China after the Opium War and the impact of the Taiping Rebellion (1853–1864) created a huge pool of rural unemployed in southern China. Tens of thousands of poverty-stricken Chinese peasants looked for employment opportunities overseas. However, the ample labour supply did not just work to the advantage of the Chinese. Malay and European miners also had access to the Chinese labour market and could recruit workers for their mines. What was to the advantage of Chinese miners was their familiarity with Chinese dialects, customs and practices; and also their command of the secret societies, which helped to regulate and discipline the workforce.

The success of the Chinese was also due to their relatively superior methods of tin production. Prior to British intervention in Malaya, Chinese tin mining essentially used an open-cast system, in which a large oblong pit was excavated in the ground to a depth of 15

56. Ibid., pp. 148–50.
57. Khoo Kay Kim, op. cit., pp. 62–4; David K.Y. Chng, *Hsin-chia-po hua-jen shih lun-ts'ung* (Collected Essays on the Chinese in Nineteenth Century Singapore) (Singapore, South Seas Society, 1986), pp. 22–4.

to 25 feet. Production methods were improved by adopting superior Western technologies; for example the adoption of the steam pump enabled Chinese miners to mine at greater depths, resulting in the increase of productivity.[58]

Another major factor in the success of the Chinese in tin mining was entrepreneurship. Being marginal men, Chinese immigrants were highly motivated and prepared to work hard for their prosperity. Some of those who possessed business acumen, foresight and courage grasped the opportunity to develop the tin industry. The success stories of tin miners such as Foo Chee Choon, Yau Tuck Seng, Yap Ah Loy, Yap Kwan Seng and Loke Yew testify to their entrepreneurship. As Overseas Chinese entrepreneurs were the creators and perpetuators of a modern Overseas Chinese enterprise,[59] their ability to use capital, labour, technology and management skills in the tin-mining industry made them wealthy and powerful in the Chinese communities. Their contribution to the rapid economic development of modern Malaysia was undeniably significant.

Growth of Cultural and Political Identity

The Origins of Overseas Chinese Nationalism

Early Chinese immigrants in Malaysia and Singapore had little interest in politics. Brought up in villages in southern China where the gentry dominated social and political affairs, ordinary villagers had little participation in the political process. This village experience helped to mould Chinese immigrants' political attitudes in the new land; they were indifferent to and fearful of politics. Yet in the last decade of the nineteenth century and in the early twentieth century,

58. Wong Lin Ken, *The Malayan Tin Industry to 1914*, pp. 56–8.
59. See Yen Ching-hwang, 'Modern Overseas Chinese Business Enterprise: A Preliminary Study' (A paper presented at the International Conference on Chinese Diaspora: Their Legal, Political and Economic Status, held in San Francisco, 26–29 November 1992), p. 14. See also Yen Ching-hwang, *Studies in Modern Overseas Chinese History* (Singapore, Times Academic Press, 1995), pp. 247–49.

the Chinese in Malaysia and Singapore were actively involved in China politics. What transformed the political attitude of the early Chinese immigrants was the rise of nationalism among the Overseas Chinese. In Malaysia and Singapore it was expressed in a strong emotional attachment to the preservation of cultural identity, and concern for the political future of China. Emotional attachments to the home province in China stemmed primarily from strong kinship ties and ethnicity. Brought up in an intricate network of kinship and imbued with Confucian ideas of filial piety, the early Chinese immigrants were captives of the traditional Chinese family system to which their prime loyalty lay. Indeed, many of them lived simple and hard lives in order to remit the major part of their income to feed their family members in China.[60]

The Chinese in Malaysia and Singapore also expressed a strong desire to preserve their cultural identity. Nevertheless, this cultural identity was felt to be threatened by pervading Western and Malay cultures. The early Chinese immigrants faced various problems, one of which was marriage. Traditional Chinese customs and a government ban on female immigration prevented Chinese women from migrating to Malaysia and Singapore on a large scale, leading some early Chinese immigrants to marry local women. This produced a distinctive group of mixed descendants known as Babas and Nyonyas.[61] At the same time, many of the local-born Chinese were sent to English schools for their education. They were thus exposed to the influence of Western culture and came to accept Western values and customs, learning to place less emphasis on traditional Chinese values and the Chinese way of life.

To reverse this trend towards westernisation and 'Baba-isation', Chinese cultural nationalists launched two movements to restore

60. See Siah U Chin, 'Annual Remittances by Chinese Immigrants to Their Families in China', in *Journal of the Indian Archipelago and Eastern Asia*, vol. 1 (1847), pp. 35–6.

61. See Tan Chee Beng, 'Baba and Nyonya: A Study of the Ethnic Identity of the Chinese Peranakan in Malacca' (PhD Thesis, Cornell University, 1979), pp. 57–63; John R. Clammer, *Straits Chinese Society* (Singapore, Singapore University Press, 1980), pp. 2–11.

traditional Chinese values and customs at the end of the nineteenth and the beginning of the twentieth centuries. These were the Lo Shan She lecture movement and the Confucian revival movement. The former, which started in Singapore in 1881 and spread to Malacca, Penang and Kuala Lumpur in 1895, attempted to reassert traditional Chinese values.[62] Regular lectures were conducted on the first and fifteenth day of every lunar calendar month, at which were expounded the Sixteen Sacred Maxims of the Emperor K'ang-hsi. These contained many of the Confucian values of filial piety, loyalty to the clan, propriety and thrift, being law-abiding, rejection of false doctrines and the exaltation of 'right' learning.[63] The Confucian revival movement, on the other hand, was launched in Kuala Lumpur in September 1899 and then spread to Singapore, Malacca, Penang and later to the Dutch East Indies in the early years of the twentieth century. It provided a sharper focus for the reassertion of Confucian values in the Southeast Asian Chinese communities.[64] The public celebration of Confucius' birthday was encouraged, and Confucian schools and Confucian temples were established in an attempt to convert more Overseas Chinese to Confucianism.[65]

The efforts of the Overseas Chinese cultural nationalists were complemented by the works of the Ch'ing Consul in Singapore. One of the main objectives of the Consulate since its inception in

62. Yen Ching-hwang, 'Overseas Chinese Nationalism in Singapore and Malaya, 1877–1912', in *Modern Asian Studies*, vol. 16, no. 3 (1982), pp. 401–02.

63. Ibid.; Kung-ch'uan Hsiao, *Rural China: Imperial Control in the Nineteenth Century* (Seattle, University of Washington Press, 1967), pp. 186-88; G.T. Hare, *A Text Book of Documentary Chinese*, pt.1 vol. 2 (Singapore, Government Printing Office, 1894), pp. 92–3.

64. See Yen Ching-hwang, 'The Confucian Revival Movement in Singapore and Malaya, 1899–1912', in *Journal of Southeast Asian Studies*, vol. 7, no. 1 (1976), pp. 33–57; C.A. Coppel, 'The Origins of Confucianism as an Organized Religion in Java, 1900–1923', in *Journal of Southeast Asian Studies*, vol. 12, no.1 (1981), pp. 179–95; Leo Suryadinata, 'Confucianism in Indonesia: Past and Present', in Leo Suryadinata, *The Chinese Minority in Indonesia: Seven Papers* (Singapore, Chapman Enterprise, 1978), pp. 33–62.

65. Yen Ching-hwang, 'The Confucian Revival Movement in Singapore and Malaya, 1899–1912', p. 37.

1877 was to foster Overseas Chinese national consciousness. The Ch'ing Consul promoted the study of Chinese literature, patronised Chinese cultural activities and exalted traditional Chinese values. In 1882, Consul Tso Ping-lung helped organise and launch a literary society in Singapore named Hui Hsien She (The Society for the Meeting of Literary Excellence), the first of its kind in the Chinese communities in Southeast Asia. He acted as a patron and judge for essay and poem competitions.[66] Tso's successor, Consul-General Huang Tsun-hsien, continued to nurture Chinese cultural identity in the early 1890s. He patronised the Hui Hsien She and renamed it T'u Nan She, which literally means 'The Society for Approaching the South'. Huang also encouraged literary activities by offering awards for the winners of essay competitions. He further patronised the Lo Shan She lecture and the Confucian revival movements, and rewarded filial sons and chaste women for upholding Confucian values.[67]

The Ch'ing Consul also sought to nurture political loyalty towards the dynasty. On auspicious occasions such as birthdays of the Emperor and the Empress-Dowager, he gathered rich merchants and community leaders at the Consulate to perform a solemn ceremony of allegiance to the throne. On occasions such as visits by Ch'ing dignitaries, ordinary Chinese were mobilised to welcome the visitors and to express loyalty to the dynasty.[68]

Chinese Reformists and Revolutionaries

Political events in China at the end of the nineteenth and the beginning of the twentieth centuries had a great impact on the Overseas Chinese communities. The defeat suffered by China in the First Sino-Japanese War in 1894–95 encouraged reformists such as K'ang Yu-wei and Liang Ch'i-ch'ao to rejuvenate the tottering

---

66. Chen Mong Hock, *The Early Chinese Newspapers of Singapore, 1881–1912* (Singapore, University of Malaya Press, 1967), p. 115.
67. Ibid., pp. 115–16; Yen Ching-hwang, 'Overseas Chinese Nationalism in Singapore and Malaya, 1877-1912', p. 411.
68. Yen Ching-hwang, ibid., p. 410.

empire through the Hundred Days' Reform in 1898. However the failure of the reform forced K'ang and Liang to flee overseas to seek refuge, first in Japan and then in North America. With the support of the Chinese in Canada, K'ang founded the Pao Huang Hui (Emperor Protection Society) on 20 July 1899 in Vancouver.[69] On 1 February 1900 K'ang arrived in Singapore to mobilise local support to finance a planned revolt in central China. Before his arrival there was already a reform movement in the local Chinese communities in support of K'ang's cause. The leaders of this movement were Dr Lim Boon Keng, a Western-trained medical practitioner and newly converted Confucianist, and Khoo Seok Wan, a Chinese scholar and poet.[70] During his twenty-two month stay in Singapore and Penang, K'ang visited several major cities in Malaya and gained substantial support among wealthy Chinese merchants, including a prominent tin miner from Ipoh, Foo Chee Choon.[71] K'ang's presence greatly boosted the reformists in the region. An Emperor Protection Society branch was established in Singapore with Khoo Seok Wan as its president, and two Chinese newspapers, *Thien Nan Shin Pao* and *Jit Shin Pau*, were used for the reformist cause.[72] Using modern media and a front organisation named Hao Hsueh Hui (the Chinese

69. See L. Eve Armentrout Ma, *Revolutionaries, Monarchists, and Chinatown: Chinese Politics in the Americas and the 1911 Revolution* (Honolulu, University of Hawaii Press, 1990), pp. 47–8.

70. See Yen Ching-hwang, *The Overseas Chinese and the 1911 Revolution: With Special Reference to Singapore and Malaya* (Kuala Lumpur, Oxford University Press, 1976), pp. 42–3; Lee Guan Kin, *Lin Wen-ch'ing te ssu-hsiang: chung-hsi wen-hua te hui-liu yu mao-tun* (The Thoughts of Lim Boon Keng — Convergency and Contradiction between China and Western Culture) (Singapore, Singapore Society of Asian Studies, 1990), pp. 98–149.

71. See Jung-pang Lo, *K'ang Yu-wei: A Biography and a Symposium* (Tucson, University of Arizona Press, 1967), pp. 183–89; Yen Ching-hwang, ibid., pp. 98, 271.

72. See Feng Tzu-yu, *Hua-ch'iao ko-ming k'ai-kuo shih* (The Overseas Chinese and the Founding of the Republic) (Taipei, Shang Wu Printing Company, 1953), p. 74; Feng Tzu-yu, *Ko-ming i-shih* (Reminiscences of the Revolution of 1911), vol. 4 (Taipei, Shang Wu Printing Company, 1965), p. 145; Chen Mong Hock, op. cit., pp. 68–9, 75–80.

Philomatic Society), the reformists in Malaysia and Singapore promoted Chinese nationalism, the ideas of progress and reform, and loyalty to the captive Emperor Kuang-hsu.[73]

Despite setbacks in 1901 as a result of Khoo Seok Wan's defection, the reformists in Malaysia and Singapore recovered in 1905 and grew in strength. The movement's main organ, *Nanyang Tsung Hui Pao* (The Union Times) exerted considerable influence in the local Chinese communities. From 1907 to 1908 it engaged in a heated polemic with the *Chong Shing Yit Pao*, the main organ of the revolutionaries led by Dr Sun Yat-sen. Reformist influence declined markedly after 1909 following the death at the end of 1908 of Emperor Kuang-hsu, whom the reformists had vowed to protect.[74] Their activities nevertheless had created a new political consciousness among the Chinese in Malaysia and Singapore. However, the more durable impact of the reformists was in the area of education. Reformist leaders such as K'ang Yu-wei and Liang Ch'i-ch'ao believed that modern education was the key to China's modernisation. Both had been involved in setting up modern schools in the Chinese communities in Japan and North America. When K'ang was in Singapore and Penang he helped found a girls' school in Singapore, and started a teacher training class in Penang in which his followers could be trained and sent to work. Thus the reformists exerted considerable influence in the modern Chinese schools in the region.[75]

The Chinese revolutionaries appeared relatively late on the political scene of Malaysia and Singapore. Dr Sun Yat-sen, the leader of the Chinese revolutionary movement, came to Singapore five months after K'ang's arrival on the island. Following the defeat of the revolutionary uprising in Waichow, Kwangtung at the end of 1900, more Chinese revolutionaries arrived to seek refuge in the peniusula. Prominent

73. See *Jit Shin Pau* (Singapore) March to May 1900; Yen Ching-hwang, 'Overseas Chinese Nationalism in Singapore and Malaya, 1877–1912', pp. 420–23.

74. See Yen Ching-hwang, *The Overseas Chinese and the 1911 Revolution*, pp. 186–202.

75. See Lee Ah Chai, 'Policies and Politics in the Chinese Schools in the Straits Settlements and the Federated Malay States, 1786–1941' (MA Thesis, University of Malaya in Singapore, 1958), pp. 31–2.

among them was Yu Lieh, a revolutionary leader of Cantonese origin. Yu laid solid foundations for further revolutionary activities in the region. Yu and other early Chinese revolutionaries disguised their identities in order to carry out underground activities, principally among workers and secret society members. He was particularly active and founded a Chung Ho T'ang branch in Singapore.[76] He also travelled widely in peninsular Malaysia and recruited a number of followers who formed the basis of various Chung Ho T'ang branches in Kuala Lumpur, Penang, Perak, Johor and Seremban.[77] Yu usually spread the revolutionary message secretly, but in a more favourable environment like Kuala Lumpur he and Too Nam, another revolutionary leader, were able to preach openly the idea of republicanism.[78]

Before the arrival of the revolutionary refugees from China at the turn of the present century, there arose in Malaysia and Singapore a small group of local Chinese revolutionaries responding fervently to the dramatic events in China. The crushing defeat of China in the First Sino-Japanese war in 1895 led eighteen young Chinese in Malacca to form a political group known as 'The Eighteen Saviours' (Chiu Kuo Shih Pa Yu) in Tongkak in 1897. They pledged to work towards the overthrow of the Manchus in China. Their leader was Sim Hung-pek, a rich young merchant from Malacca.[79] Four years later in 1901, another small group of local Chinese revolutionaries emerged in Singapore. Its leaders were Tan Chor-nam and Teo Eng-hock, two wealthy young merchants. Both Tan and Teo first embraced the reformist ideas of K'ang Yu-wei and became supporters of Khoo Seok-wan, but their disillusionment with the reformists and the ineptitude of the Manchu government later persuaded them to support the revolutionaries. In 1903, both Tan and Teo emerged as converted

---

76. Chung Ho T'ang originated in Yokohama, Japan where it was founded as a social club by a group of Chinese workers and members of lower social class. It was turned into a revolutionary affiliated organisation.
77. Yen Ching-hwang, *The Overseas Chinese and the 1911 Revolution*, p. 45.
78. Ibid., p. 46; Ch'en Chan-mei (Chan Chan-mooi) 'Tu Nan hsien-sheng chuan-lueh' (A Brief Biography of Too Nam) in Ch'en Chan-mei (ed), *Tu Nan hsien-sheng ai-ssu lu* (Obituaries on Too Nam) (Kuala Lumpur, 1940), p. 9.
79. Yen Ching-hwang, *The Overseas Chinese and the 1911 Revolution*, p. 50.

revolutionaries, and became outspoken critics of the Manchu government. They used the Hsiao T'ao Yuan Club (Small Peach Orchard Club) as their meeting place for promoting republicanism and anti-Manchu ideas.[80] In the same year, the expatriate and local Chinese revolutionaries joined force and published a revolutionary newspaper named *Thoe Lam Jit Poh*, which openly advocated the overthrow of the Manchu government. Both Tan and Teo later became important Chinese revolutionary leaders in Southeast Asian region.

On 6th April 1906, Dr Sun Yat-sen arrived in Singapore from Europe en route to Japan. Sun gathered both expatriate and local Chinese revolutionaries and founded a branch of T'ung Meng Hui (The United League). Tan Chor-nam and Teo Eng-hock were elected chairman and deputy chairman of the branch respectively. Dr Sun, accompanied by Tan and other leaders of the Singapore branch, made a quick tour of peninsular Malaysia in an attempt to set up more branches. He founded a branch in Kuala Lumpur on 7 August 1906 with Loke Chow-thye as its chairman. The Kuala Lumpur branch attracted many members; prominent founding members included the veteran revolutionary Too Nam and his sons, and Chan Chan-mooi, a wealthy merchant. Sun's mission failed in Ipoh, as reformist influence there was too strong. He returned to Singapore but sent Tan Chor-nam and Lim Ngee-soon to Penang for the same purpose. A T'ung Meng Hui branch was founded in Penang with Goh Say-eng as the chairman and Ng Kim-keng as his deputy. In the following two years, T'ung Meng Hui branches were established in Seremban, Ipoh, Kuala Pilah, Muar and Kuantan.[81]

The founding of T'ung Meng Hui branches in Malaysia and Singapore marked a new chapter in the history of Chinese politics in

---

80. Tan Chor-nam (Ch'en Ch'u-nan) 'Wan-ch'ing-yuan yu Chung-kuo ko-ming shih-lueh' (Wan-ch'ing-yuan and the Chinese Revolution of 1911) in *Chung-hua min-kuo k'ai-kuo wu-shih-nien wen-hsien* (Documents of the Founding of the Republic of China for the Last Fifty Years) series 1, vol. 11 (Taipei, 1963), pp. 533-34; Teo Eng-hock (Chang Yung-fu) *Nan-yang yu ch'uang-li min-kuo* (Nanyang and the Founding of the Chinese Republic) (Singapore, 1933), p. 7.

81. See Yen Ching-hwang, *The Overseas Chinese and the 1911 Revolution*, pp. 92–100.

the region. The main task of the Chinese revolutionaries was to raise money to support the planned uprisings in the south and southwest of China. For this purpose, they mounted aggressive propaganda activities in a bid for support. Three major types of propaganda organisations were formed: newspapers, reading clubs and drama troupes. Newspapers were a powerful medium for transmitting the revolutionary message. Apart from the early *Thoe Lam Jit Poh*, the Chinese revolutionaries founded another four newspapers in peninsular Malaysia and Singapore between 1907 and 1911. These were the *Chong Shing Yit Pao* (Restoration Daily) in August 1907, and the *Sun Poo* (The Morning Daily), the *Kwong Wah Yit Poh* (The Glorious Chinese Daily) and the *Nam Kew Poo* (The Straits Chinese Morning Post). Except for the *Kwong Wah Yit Poh*, which was founded in Penang, all other revolutionary newspapers were published in Singapore. They attacked the Manchu Government, engaged in heated polemics with the reformists and promoted new revolutionary ideas. The Chinese revolutionaries established a score of reading clubs to help propagate the revolutionary message. Newspapers, books and magazines were made freely available, being deemed an effective means of reaching wider audiences, particularly the poorer section of the Chinese population. There were at least fifty-eight reading clubs set up in peninsular Malaysia and Singapore. Prominent among these were the Singapore Reading Club, the T'ung Teh Reading Club, the K'ai Ming Public Speaking and Reading Club in Singapore, and the Penang Reading Club (also known as the Penang Philomatic Society) in Penang. All of these reading clubs exposed their members to the maximum influence of revolutionary ideas and acted as recruitment centres for the T'ung Meng Hui branches. Some intensified their indoctrination programmes by sponsoring public talks given by prominent local or visiting revolutionary leaders.[82]

The revolutionaries also founded drama troupes to spread their radical messages among the less educated. Drama was one of the oldest forms of entertainment in rural China, and found wide acceptance among the illiterate masses. In November 1907 a drama troupe in Kuala Lumpur performed a play entitled *Hsu Hsi-lin*,

---

82.   Ibid., pp. 100–22.

which presented the story of a revolutionary martyr in the abortive uprising in Anching, Anhwei province. This marked the beginning of a series of revolutionary drama performances in Malaysia and Singapore. The visit of a revolutionary drama troupe from Hong Kong, Chen T'ien Sheng, at the end of 1908 greatly boosted revolutionary drama activities, and received a warm welcome from audiences in the large towns in the peninsula. Several local drama troupes with strong affiliations with revolutionary organisations emerged. Principal troupes were the Universal Love Troupe (Fan Ai Pan) and the People's Bell Troupe (Min To She) in Singapore, The Perak Welfare Troupe in Ipoh, the Anti-opium Drama Troupe (Chen Wu She) in Kuala Lumpur, and the Warning to the Age Troupe (Ching Shih Pan) in Penang. All of these troupes, under the guise of charity, performed many popular plays which praised martyrdom and dedication to revolution, and exposed the corruption and nepotism of the Ch'ing government.[83]

A major obstacle to the revolutionary movement was the reformist influence among the local Chinese. The reformists had arrived earlier and were well-entrenched in some social and cultural institutions. To overcome this, the revolutionaries were forced to start night schools and schools in suburban areas. This led to rivalry and confrontation between the two camps, which sometimes led to violent clashes.[84] The revolutionaries also mounted a large-scale attack on the ideological foundations of their opponents. A full-scale polemic took place in Singapore between the revolutionary organ, *Chong Shing Yit Pao*, and the reformist *Nanyang Tsung Hui Pao* from September 1907 to October 1908. Wang Ching-wei and Hu Han-min, two distinguished revolutionary leaders, came to the aid of the *Chong Shing Yit Pao*, while Sun Yat-sen contributed a couple of articles to the debate. Reformist literary heavyweights such as Ou Chu-chia and Wu Hsien-tzu, two disciples of K'ang Yu-wei, then arrived in Singapore to help the *Nanyang Tsung Hui Pao*. The polemic focused on the issues of revolution, a constitutional monarchy, the practicability of a revolution and the introduction of

---

83.   Ibid., pp. 122–27.
84.   Ibid., pp. 154–70.

a parliament.[85] Although none could claim a total victory, the polemic helped to clarify some fundamental issues held by both the revolutionaries and the reformists.

Between 1909 and 1912 the revolutionaries launched several uprisings in the south and southwest of China. The Chinese in Malaysia played a significant role in the preparation for the Canton March 29th Uprising in 1911. However an internal feud within the T'ung Meng Hui caused a sharp decline in the revolutionary influence in Malaysia and Singapore. A simmering anti-Sun movement world wide prompted Dr Sun to mobilise his loyal supporters in Penang in the preparation for the Canton Revolt. The Penang Conference on 13 November 1910 brought Malaysian Chinese into the limelight of the Chinese Revolution.[86] With the outbreak of the Wuchang Uprising on 10 October 1911, the Chinese in Malaysia and Singapore contributed substantially to the revolutionary actions in China, particularly to the establishment of revolutionary regimes in Kwangtung and Fukien.[87]

The activities of the reformists and revolutionaries greatly politicised the Chinese in Malaysia and Singapore. This heightened consciousness helped to unify the fragmented local Chinese communities, and a sense of unity emerged. Traditional ideas of loyalty to emperor, filial piety and inequality between sexes and between age groups were weakened, while new ideas of altruism, dedication, equality and freedom, unity and democracy gradually took root.

85. Ibid., pp. 186–200; Chui Kuei-chiang, 'Chung-hsing jih-pao: Hsin-chia-po T'ung-meng-hui te h'ou-she, 1907–1910' (Chong Shing Yit Pao: The Mouthpiece of the Singapore T'ung Meng Hui, 1907–1910) in *Hsin-h'ai ko-ming yu Nan-yang hua-jen yen-t'ao-hui lun-wen chi* (Essays of the International Symposium on Nanyang Chinese and the 1911 Revolution) (Taipei, Centre of International Studies, Cheng Chi University, 1986), pp. 143–51.
86. Yen Ching-hwang, *The Overseas Chinese and the 1911 Revolution*, pp. 231–38; Yen Ching-hwang, 'Penang Chinese and the 1911 Revolution', in Yen Ching-hwang, *Community and Politics: The Chinese in Colonial Singapore and Malaysia* (Singapore, Times Academic Press, 1995), pp. 296–97.
87. Yen Ching-hwang, *The Overseas Chinese and the 1911 Revolution*, pp. 238–43.

Changes in the Chinese Communities between the Two World Wars

Economic Change

The most important economic change affecting the Chinese communities in Malaysia and Singapore was the rise of the rubber industry. Commercial planting of rubber began prior to 1900; experimental planting first took place in 1877 in Singapore and Kuala Kangsar, Perak. H.N. Ridley's arrival in November 1888 as the Director of the Botanical Gardens in Singapore marked a new beginning. Due to Ridley's efforts and influence, two groups of planters undertook the first commercial experiments. In 1896 a Chinese planter, Tan Chay Yan, planted forty acres at Bukit Lintang, northeast of Malacca. At about the same time European planters, the Kindersley brothers, planted about five acres of Hevea at the Inch Kenneth coffee estate in Kajang, Selangor.[88] Tan in 1896 further developed a large tract of more than 2,000 acres in Bukit Ashaham, Malacca into a rubber plantation. Tan was the grandson of Tan Tock Seng, a wealthy Chinese philanthropist in Singapore, and the son of Tan Teck Guan, a wealthy Chinese planter in Malacca.

Tan Chay Yan's commercial venture inspired many Chinese planters in Malaysia and Singapore to follow suit. In 1898 Lau Boon Tit planted fifty-four acres of rubber in his Semenyih Estate in Ulu Langat, Selangor. Another wealthy Chinese planter in Malacca, Cheng Ch'eng-k'uai, developed an estate of more than one thousand acres near Labis, Johor, for the planting of rubber and sago. He also established two rubber estates, Ch'uan Hsing Shan and Ch'uan Ch'eng Shan, in Tenang, near Labis, which covered a combined land area of 3,000 acres. In Singapore, several Chinese were also involved in planting rubber, including Dr Lim Boon Keng, a famous medical practitioner and entrepreneur, and Teo Eng-hock and Lim Ngee Soon, two Teochew

88. See James C. Jackson, *Planters and Speculators*, pp. 211–18; J.H. Drabble, *Rubber in Malaya, 1876–1922: The Genesis of the Industry* (Kuala Lumpur, Oxford University Press, 1973), pp. 14–9; Wu T'i-jen, *Je-tai ching-chi chih-wu — hsiang chiao shu* (Rubber — the Tropical Cash Crop) (Singapore, Kuang Hua, 1951), pp. 6–8.

businessmen. But the most important step was taken by Tan Kah Kee in l906. On hearing of the enormous profits made by Tan Chay Yan, who sold his Bukit Ashaham estate for $2,000,000, Tan Kah Kee bought l80,000 rubber seeds from Tan Chay Yan and planted them in his Fu Shan estate in Singapore.[89] This marked the beginning of large-scale commercial rubber planting and the growth of rubber-related industries in Singapore.

What stimulated and sustained the enthusiasm of Chinese and European planters in rubber were rapidly rising prices for the commodity. The price of rubber in the London markets rose from $2.36 per kilogram in 1900 to $5.55 per kilogram in 1906.[90] Underpinning high prices in the international markets was the growing demand for natural rubber, used in the electrical, bicycle and automobile industries. Rubber was an indispensable raw material for these fast-growing new industries, and it helped transform the economy of Malaysia and Singapore as well those of the Chinese communities in the region. It linked the Chinese communities to the world markets, and therefore made them subject to the frequent fluctuation of prices, but also made many Chinese planters wealthy, and provided numerous jobs for the Chinese.

The period between l901 and l941 saw the rise of Chinese commercial banking. In the l830s, some British agency houses in the Straits settlements had already acted as representatives of British banks in Singapore. The opening of a branch office of the Union Bank of Calcutta in Singapore in l840 marked the beginning of European banking activities in Malaysia and Singapore.[91] A string of European banks followed suit, including the Chartered Mercantile Bank of India, London and China, which opened a branch in Penang in l859, the first of its kind in Malaysia. But the most important European bank with close business dealings with the Chinese communities in the

89. Tan Kah Kee (Ch'en Chia-keng), *Nan-ch'iao hui-i lu* (Autobiography) vol. 2 (Singapore, Nan-yang yin-shua she, 1946), pp. 403–04.
90. See Colin Barlow, *The Natural Rubber Industry: Its Development, Technology and Economy in Malaysia* (Kuala Lumpur, Oxford University Press, 1978), p. 25.
91. See Lee Sheng-yi, *The Monetary and Banking Development of Singapore and Malaysia* (Singapore, Singapore University Press, 1990), p. 35.

region was the Hong Kong and Shanghai Banking Corporation. It established a branch in Singapore in 1877, and another in Penang in 1884.[92] It had long been active in trade with China and became a mainstay of economic activities in the Far East. Many Chinese merchants in Hong Kong and on the China coast used its facilities to advance their business operations. The opening of its branches in Malaysia and Singapore linked the Chinese communities with the fast growing economy of coastal China.

However, many Chinese merchants were reluctant to use Western banking facilities, partly because of language barriers. The founding of the Kwong Yik Banking Company Limited in Singapore in 1903 marked the beginning of Chinese commercial banking in Southeast Asia.[93] The name 'Kwong Yik' (romanised in Mandarin as Kuang I) was literally meant to benefit the Cantonese people. It was founded by Wong Ah Fook who was a leader of the Cantonese communities in Johor and Singapore.[94] Four years later a second Chinese commercial bank in the Malaysian and Singapore region, the Sze Hai Tong Banking Company Limited, was founded by the members of the Teochew community in Singapore.[95]

In Malaysia, the first Chinese commercial bank, the Kwong Yik Banking Corporation Limited of Selangor, was founded on 15 July 1913 by a group of Cantonese. Cheong Yeok Choy, a well-known Chinese merchant and philanthropist, was elected first chairman of the board of directors. The authorised capital of the bank was $1,000,000, but the paid up capital was only $300,000.[96] This bank in Kuala Lumpur was to serve the interests of Cantonese business community. The second

---

92. See Chee Peng Lim et. al., 'The History and Development of the Hong Kong and Shanghai Banking Corporation in Peninsular Malaysia', in Frank H.H. King (ed), *Eastern Banking: Essays in the History of the Hong Kong and Shanghai Banking Corporation* (London, The Athlone Press, 1983), p. 352.
93. See Tan Ee-leong, 'The Chinese Banks Incorporated in Singapore and the Federation of Malaya', in *Journal of the Malayan Branch, Royal Asiatic Society*, vol. 26, no. 1 (1953), p. 114.
94. See Yen Ching-hwang, *The Overseas Chinese and the 1911 Revolution*, pp. 274–75.
95. Tan Ee-leong, op. cit., pp. 115–16.
96. Ibid., pp. 137–38.

Chinese commercial bank founded in Malaysia was the Bank of Malaya Limited of Ipoh (the Chinese name of the bank was the Chung Hsing Yin Hang of Ipoh) established in Ipoh in 1920. The bank went into liquidation in 1930 amidst a worldwide financial crisis.[97]

Another Chinese commercial bank in Singapore which had direct influence on the Chinese communities in Malaysia was the Ho Hong Bank Limited. It was founded by a wealthy Hokkien merchant, Lim Peng Siang, together with Dr Lim Boon Keng and Seow Poh Leng, in 1917. Lim Peng Siang was an outstanding Chinese industrialist, ship-owner and banker. The bank set up many branches in the peninsula including Malacca, Penang, Muar, Batu Pahat and Seremban. But the bank could not escape the impact of the world depression in the early 1930s: in 1932, Lim Peng Siang resigned from the chairmanship of the bank, and it was later amalgamated with the Overseas Chinese Bank.[98]

There were at least another seven Chinese commercial banks which came into existence in Malaysia and Singapore in the period between 1903 and 1941. They were the Bank of Communication (1912), the Oversea-Chinese Bank Limited (1919), Lee Wah Bank Limited (1920), Batu Pahat Bank Limited (1920), the Oversea-Chinese Banking Corporation (1932), Ban Hin Lee Bank Limited (1935) and the United Chinese Bank Limited (1935). Except for the Batu Pahat Bank and the Ban Hin Lee Bank in Penang, the rest were located in Singapore.[99]

A characteristic of these early Chinese banks was their close ties with Chinese dialect communities. This was clearly reflected in the founding of two Kwong Yik banks and the Lee Wah bank by a Cantonese group, the Sze Hai Tong Bank by a Teochew group, and the Ho Hong Bank and the Oversea-Chinese Banking Corporation by the Hokkiens. This close connection suggests that these banks were primarily intended to serve the interests of a particular dialect group. As time passed, this dialect demarcation gradually blurred and the banks' customers diversified. Since most Chinese commercial banks during this period were communally based, they operated in a

97.   Ibid., p. 139.
98.   Ibid., pp. 119–24.
99.   Ibid., pp. 124–32; Lee Sheng-yi, op. cit., pp. 39–40.

slightly different manner from banks governed by Western principles. Loan mortgages were based not on the assessment of property, but on the good faith arising from personal connections in the community. However the fluctuation of commodity prices undermined the viability of the banks and explains the collapse of some of these early Chinese commercial banks in Malaysia and Singapore.

The rise of modern Chinese commercial banks helped to transform the Chinese communities in the region. It lubricated Chinese economic activities, stabilised Chinese financial positions, stimulated export trade and gave rise to a group of professional bankers who increasingly played important roles in the economic and social well-being of the Chinese communities.

The First World War disrupted the import of manufactured goods to Southeast Asia and provided an excellent opportunity for local industries to develop. Some Chinese merchants in the Straits settlements ventured into manufacturing and other related industries, especially rubber and food processing. Some industries had existed in Malaysia and Singapore before the First World War. Tin smelting and pineapple canning were among the earliest Chinese industries in the region. In 1893 there were thirty-seven Chinese smelting houses in Perak and twenty-six in Selangor.[100] These were old-style industries using traditional Chinese methods of operation. The first modern Chinese tin-smelting company was the Seng Kee Smelting Works founded in Penang by Lee Chin Ho in 1898. With a capital of $100,000 the Seng Kee was equipped with modern furnaces, electrically driven appliances and a laboratory for testing ore samples.[101] It was taken over at the end of 1907 by the Eastern Smelting Company Limited, which was backed by a group of prominent Chinese tin miners in Perak and Penang who invested capital of up to $1,5000,000. It was able to compete with Western-owned smelters, and succeeded in refining substantial amounts of tin ore produced in Malaysia.[102]

100. Wong Lin Ken, *The Malayan Tin Industry to 1914*, pp. 156–57.
101. See J.W. Cushman, *Family and State: The Formation of a Sino-Thai Tin-mining Dynasty, 1797–1932* (Singapore, Oxford University Press, 1991), pp. 75–6.
102. See J.W. Cushman, 'Chinese Enterprise in Early Twentieth Century Penang', in *Asian Culture*, vol.14, 'A Special Issue on the Ethnic Chinese Abroad',

The first Chinese-owned pineapple-canning factory was probably established in Singapore by Tan Kee Pek, the father of the famous Chinese entrepreneur Tan Kah Kee. Tan Kee Pek owned some pineapple estates in Singapore and Johor, and made good profits in the canning industry. By the first decade of the 20th century there were more than ten Chinese-owned pineapple-canning factories on the island.[103]

The outbreak of the First World War brought both opportunities and misfortune to the Chinese industry in the region. The war practically devastated the pineapple-canning industry by cutting off its lucrative markets in India and Europe, resulting in the closure of many canneries in Malaysia and Singapore. But it also created immense opportunities for the export of processed rubber. Responding to this, Tan Kah Kee established two rubber-processing mills in Singapore between 1916 and 1917.[104] By 1918 there were an estimated seventy-two rubber-processing mills in Malaysia and Singapore. As demand for rubber increased during wartime, the price of processed rubber rose. The two rubber mills owned by Tan Kah Kee reported a profit of S$800,000 in 1918. Tan himself admitted he had made S$4,5000,000 during the war, making him one of the richest capitalists in Southeast Asia.[105]

The fall in rubber prices after the First World War forced Chinese industrialists to move into rubber-related manufacturing industries. At the forefront was Tan Kah Kee, who converted one of his largest rubber mills in Singapore into a rubber factory, a relatively uncharted course of action. His Sumbawa plant turned out a variety of rubber products such as raincoats, tennis balls, rubber umbrellas, sports shoes, rubber boots, sleepers and toys.[106] In addition, Tan also

     edited by Yen Ching-hwang (Singapore, Singapore Society of Asian Studies, 1990), pp. 84–5.

103. See A. Wright & H.A. Cartwright, *Twentieth Century Impressions of British Malaya: Its History, People, Commerce, Industries and Resources* (London, Lloyd's Greater British Publishing Company, 1908), p. 504.

104. See C.F. Yong, *Tan Kah-Kee: The Making of an Overseas Chinese Legend* (Singapore, Oxford University Press, 1987), p. 51.

105. Ibid., p. 52; Tan Kah Kee, *Nan-ch'iao hui-i lu* (Autobiography) vol. 2, pp. 411–12.

106. C.F. Yong, ibid., p. 57.

ventured into the production of tyres and tubes for the growing world motor car market.

Another Chinese-dominated industry in the years between the two world wars was the refining of coconut oil. Modern coconut oil refineries were established in Singapore and Penang, where the supply of copra was abundant. Cooking oil was produced for domestic consumption and export. In 1925, there were at least five coconut oil refineries in these two ports. Two major refineries in Singapore were owned by Lim Peng Siang, while two in Penang were owned by a Hokkien and a Cantonese respectively.[107]

Other manufacturing industries during this period concentrated on producing biscuits and soap. The three well-known biscuit makers were the Ho Ho Biscuit Company, Tan Kah Kee's Globe Biscuits and the Chung Hwa Biscuit Company, all located in Singapore. They used modern methods to produce good quality biscuits, which were intended to satisfy growing local markets as well as other overseas Chinese markets in Southeast Asia.

Overseas Chinese industry during this period began to change from traditional businesses, characterised by family ownership, small-sized operations and a mixture of unpaid family labour and wage labour,[108] to modern management. Some industries continued to be owned solely by families, but others had already changed to partnerships or joint stock companies. As the size of operation expanded the management was no longer able to rely entirely on close family members, but also relied on a mixture of kinship ties and professionalism. The Ho Hong group of companies sold shares to kinsmen and friends, but Lim Peng Siang and his brothers still controlled the operation of the companies. On the other hand the Tan Kah Kee company, under the sole ownership of the Tan family,

---

107. The two refineries in Penang were Ban Tuck Bee and Sun Ho Lung. See Li Ch'ang-fu, *Nan-yang hua-ch'iao k'ai-k'uang* (Present Conditions of the Overseas Chinese in Southeast Asia) (Shanghai, Hua Feng yin-shua-she, 1930), pp. 95–6.

108. See Linda Y.C. Lim & L.A. Peter Gosling (eds), *The Chinese in Southeast Asia, Volume 1: Ethnicity and Economic Activity* (Singapore, Maruzen Asia, 1983), p. 245.

enlarged and diversified its operations and moved into various types of industry. The company broadened its social base in the recruitment of staff; employees included relatives, kinsmen, fellow district men from T'ung An county, and also those from southern Fukien who spoke the same dialect. Increasingly, merit and professionalism became the important yardstick in the promotion system.[109] Thus, the integration of the traditional Chinese practice of personal connections with Western principles of meritocracy provided Overseas Chinese industry with cohesion, continuity and stability in its management.[110]

Political Change

The inter-war years witnessed a continuous upsurge of Overseas Chinese nationalism, and the birth of the Chinese Republic in early 1912 brought the Overseas Chinese closer to China. The Chinese in Malaysia and Singapore placed much hope on the new Chinese Republican government to lift the standing of China and to improve their status overseas. This hope was shattered however by the failure of the Second Revolution in 1913, resulting in Yuan Shih-k'ai's dictatorship. Dr Sun fled China to seek financial and political support from the Overseas Chinese, but his approach in converting the existing Kuomintang branches into the Chinese Revolutionary Party split the Kuomintang and divided the communities. However, Sun and his Chinese Revolutionary Party still retained the loyalty of the majority of Kuomintang members, and the main Kuomintang branches in Singapore, Penang, Kuala Lumpur, Malacca, Ipoh, Taiping, Seremban, Muar, Alor Star and Bentong were converted into the branches of the new party. Though weakened by

---

109. C.F. Yong, op. cit., pp. 60–1.
110. See Yen Ching-hwang, 'Modern Overseas Chinese Business Enterprise: A Preliminary Study', in Yen Ching-hwang, *Studies in Modern Overseas Chinese History*, pp. 246–47; Yen Ching-hwang, 'Tan Kah Kee and the Overseas Chinese Entrepreneurship' (Paper presented at the Chinese Studies Association of Australia 5th National Conference held in Adelaide, 16–18 July 1997), p. 10.

factionalism, the new party raised substantial funds to support Sun's activities in China.[111]

Following the May Fourth movement in 1919, the Kuomintang entered into a process of reorganisation and regained its vigour. The reorganisation of the fragmented party branches in Malaysia and Singapore in 1920 under the new Kuomintang revived Chinese political activities in the region. The main activity in the period between 1920 and 1925 was fundraising in support of the parent body in China.[112]

The reinvigorated Kuomintang was put to the test during the period between 1925 and 1930. Fearing the growing political strength of the local Chinese and their anti-British posture, Sir Laurence Nunns Guillemard, the Governor of the Straits settlements, banned the Kuomintang. In August 1925 the Kuomintang branches were ordered to dissolve, and their activities were made illegal. Despite this the party grew in strength. Its branches, operating in secret, spread widely, and its membership increased. In 1926, for instance, there were fifteen sub-branches of the Kuomintang in Selangor, in addition to its main branch in Kuala Lumpur. In January 1929 membership of the Kuomintang was estimated to be at 10,290 in Malaysia and Singapore, including 240 from Sarawak.[113]

The Kuomintang was revitalised by left-wing elements within the party. A group of pro-Communist graduates of the Whampoa Military Academy returned to Malaysia and Singapore in 1926, and radicalised Chinese politics. Known to the British authorities as the 'Main School' of the Kuomintang, many of them were Hainanese. They penetrated the lower socio-economic stratum of Chinese society by organising trade unions and night schools, which were used as vehicles to reach workers and the youth. The Left leadership, characterised by its youthful outlook and revolutionary ideas, was prepared to confront the British authorities. The Left was deeply implicated in the Kreta Ayer

---

111. C.F. Yong & R.B. McKenna, *The Kuomintang Movement in British Malaya, 1912–1949* (Singapore, Singapore University Press, 1990), pp. 32–6.
112. Ibid., p. 39.
113. Ibid., pp. 83–4, 87,94.

Incident on 12 March 1927 in Singapore, which resulted in six demonstrators being killed by the police.[114]

The domination of the Kuomintang in Malaysia and Singapore by the Left ended as the result of a final split in the alliance between the Kuomintang and the Communists in China in July 1927. At a meeting held in Canton in August of the same year, delegates of the Nanyang (Southeast Asia) branch of the Kuomintang adopted a policy of 'cleansing Communist influence' from the party. The weeding out of Communist elements resulted in the victory of the moderates, who were mainly of the old-guard of the Party. They focused on the politics of China and toned down its anti-British and anti-imperialist rhetoric.[115] But the event sharply divided Left and Right politics in the Chinese communities in Malaysia and Singapore. At the same time, as the Left penetrated trade unions and youth organisations they gradually shifted their focus from Chinese politics to local issues.

The continuous surge of nationalistic sentiment among the Overseas Chinese during this period was due to several factors: outrage against the Japanese in 1915, the anti-Japanese movement of 1919, the Tsinan Incident in 1928, the Manchurian Incident in 1931, and the 'Anti-Japanese and Rescuing China' movement between 1937 and 1941. All of these agitations targeted Japan, which had emerged after the First World War as an aggressive imperialist power posing the greatest threat to China. Japan's imposition of the notorious 'Twenty One Demands' on the Yuan Shih-k'ai Government in February 1915 outraged millions of Chinese, including those living overseas. The Chinese in Southeast Asia organized a boycott of Japanese goods and services, especially in Malaysia and Singapore.[116] This intense anti-Japanese sentiment climaxed in demonstrations and riots in Singapore and Penang between 19–21 June 1919 in the wake of the May Fourth movement. Japanese goods were burned, Japanese shops were looted

114. Ibid., pp. 85–8.
115. Ibid., pp. 88–9.
116. See Yoji Akashi, 'The Nanyang Chinese Anti-Japanese and Boycott Movement, 1908–1928: A Study of Nanyang Chinese Nationalism', in *Journal of South Seas Society*, vol. 23, nos.1 and 2 (1968), pp. 72–3.

and the lives of Japanese nationals in the two cities were threatened. Four people were killed, eight wounded and over one hundred and thirty people were arrested in the Singapore riot before the British authorities imposed martial law to restore order on the island.[117]

By the 1920s Overseas Chinese nationalism in the form of anti-Japanese sentiment became a powerful force in Chinese politics in Malaysia and Singapore. The anti-Japanese movement reached its peak in the period between 1937 and 1942 when Japan invaded China. Overseas Chinese throughout the world were organised to support China's struggle against Japanese aggression. In this global mobilisation of Overseas Chinese support, the Chinese in Malaysia and Singapore played a significant role. The Chinese in Southeast Asia were united under the leadership of Tan Kah Kee, the leader of the Hokkien community in Singapore. The Federation of China Relief Fund Associations of Southeast Asia (Nanyang ch'ou-chen tsung-hui) was founded to co-ordinate and channel the efforts of more than forty-five organisations throughout Southeast Asia. Fundraising was the main thrust of this mobilisation, and community leaders of different dialect groups were organised to raise funds by a variety of approaches.[118]

The most militant expression of Overseas Chinese nationalism in the region was boycott. Overseas Chinese nationalists had used this weapon against the Americans in 1905, and against the Japanese in 1908, 1915 and 1919. Following the Marco Polo Bridge Incident of July 1937, boycott was again used as a weapon to retaliate against the Japanese invasion of China. The boycott movement in Malaysia and Singapore took various forms: refusal to buy Japanese goods (including manufactured goods and foodstuffs), banning the sale of Japanese goods

117. See Tsui Kuei-chiang, 'H'ai-hsia chih-min-ti hua-jen tui wu-shih yung-tung te fan-hsiang (The Response of the Straits Chinese to the May Fourth movement) in *Journal of South Seas Society*, vol. 20, nos.1 and 2 (1965), pp. 13–5.

118. See Stephen M.Y. Leong, 'Sources, Agencies and Manifestations of Overseas Chinese Nationalism in Malaya, 1937–1941' (PhD thesis, University of California, Los Angeles, 1976), pp. 258–59; Hsu Yun-ts'iao & Chua Ser-koon (eds), *Hsin-Ma Hua-jen k'ang Jih shih-liao* (Malayan Chinese Resistance to Japan, 1937–1945: Selected Source Materials) (Singapore, Cultural and Historical Publishing House Pte Ltd, 1984), pp. 101–20.

by Chinese wholesalers and retailers, withdrawing labour from local Japanese companies, denying services to Japanese residents, and rejecting services from Japanese nationals, including dentists and prostitutes. The ban on the sale and distribution of Japanese goods was vigorously enforced by the so-called 'patriotic elements', who organised themselves into clandestine bodies such as the 'Red Blood Brigade'. This sometimes led to violence.[119]

The continuous upsurge of Overseas Chinese nationalism during the inter-war years greatly politicised the local Chinese communities. By participating in the anti-Japanese movements, the Chinese gained tremendous experience in techniques of mass mobilisation. At the same time, they had a greater appreciation than before of the strength of unity and solidarity among different dialect groups and social classes. This perhaps paved the way for the inter-dialect conciliations among the Chinese during the post-war period.

Social and Cultural Change

The inter-war years witnessed a variety of social and cultural changes, including the rise of Chinese education in Malaysia and Singapore. Modern Chinese schools spread throughout the region in the first decade of the twentieth century as a result of the Manchu push for reform. But the schools were confined to provide primary education, with a curriculum combining traditional subjects such as the study of Confucian Classics and 'moral self-cultivation' with modern subjects such as history, geography and English.[120] This curriculum produced students with a strong China orientation as well as reverence for the Confucian tradition.

The Republican government after 1912 restructured the Chinese education system, and took steps to integrate the Overseas Chinese into the mainstream of Chinese education in China. In the period between 1912 and 1919, there were at least nineteen modern Chinese

119. Stephen M.Y. Leong, ibid., p. 265.
120. See Yen Ching-hwang, *H'ai-wai hua-jen shih yen-chiu* (A Study of Overseas Chinese History) (Singapore, Singapore Society of Asian Studies, 1992), p. 290.

schools founded in Malaysia and Singapore spreading throughout major urban centres in the peninsula. Among them were the Foon Yew School (January 1913) in Johor Bahru, Pay Fong School (July 1913) in Malacca, Chung Hwa School (July 1913) in Seremban, Shun Jen School (1914) in Kuala Lumpur, Chung Ling School (February 1917) in Penang and Nanyang Girls' School (August 1917) in Singapore.[121] Many of the schools raised funds and built their own premises, and adopted curricula similar to their counterparts in China, dropping traditional subjects such as the study of Confucian Classics, and increasing modern content in keeping with the new spirit of republicanism and modernity.[122]

Inspired by the idea of using education for nation building, Tan Kah Kee founded the first Chinese high school in the region. Tan donated a large sum of money and gained strong support from a number of leaders of different dialect groups for the proposed project. The Chinese High School of Singapore was officially opened on 21st March 1919 with seventy-three students.[123] At the same time, the Chinese became more aware of the importance of secondary education following the May Fourth movement in 1919. Many Chinese community leaders believed that education could lift the general standard of literacy and help to retain Chinese cultural identity. Because of this, they were prepared to donate money for education, and enthusiastically supported the founding of Chinese secondary schools. Following in the footsteps of the Chinese High School of Singapore, the Chung Ling High School

121. See Tay Lian Soo & Gwee Yee Hean (eds), *Ma-lai-hsi-ya Hsin-chia-po hua-wen chung-hsueh t'e-k'an t'i-yao fu hsiao-shih* (Chinese High School Souvenir Magazines of Malaysia and Singapore with School Histories) (Kuala Lumpur, Chinese Department of the University of Malaya, 1975), pp. 8–10; Hsu Su-wu, *Hsin-chia-po hua-ch'iao chiao-yu ch'uan-mao* (The Overview of the Chinese Education in Singapore) (Singapore, Nanyang Book Store, 1949) pp. 29–32; Tseng Yung-sheng et. al. (eds), *Ma-lai-hsi-ya Fu-chien-jen hsing-hsueh pan-chiao shih-liao chi* (Historical Materials of the Founding of Chinese Schools & Contributions to Chinese Education by the Hokkiens in Malaysia) (Kuala Lumpur, Federation of Hokkien Associations of Malaysia, 1993), pp. 252–53.
122. See Yen Ching-hwang, *H'ai-wai hua-jen shih yen-chiu*, pp. 296–97.
123. See Tay Lian Soo & Gwee Yee Hean (eds), op. cit., pp. 260–61.

was founded in Penang in January 1923. It was expanded from the Chung Ling School founded in 1917 by the Chinese Philomatic Society of Penang, an organisation closely associated with Dr Sun Yat-sen's revolutionary movement. The leaders of the Society were impressed by the success of the Chinese High School of Singapore, and recognised the pressing need of local Chinese students for higher education. Under the leadership of Koh Seng Lee and Ong Keng Seng, the Chung Ling High School was opened on 20 January 1923, the first of its kind in peninsular Malaysia. In the 1920s six other Chinese high schools were founded, including famous high schools such as the Confucian Middle School (1924) and Kuen Cheng Girls' High School (1925) in Kuala Lumpur, and the Pay Fong High School (1925) in Malacca. Eight other secondary schools were established in the 1930s, two in Singapore and six in peninsular Malaysia. Most of these initially only provided three years of lower secondary education, but during the 1930s and early 1940s many of them expanded to include senior secondary education.[124]

The introduction of secondary education made Chinese education more competitive *vis-à-vis* English education, and more attractive to the parents who wanted a Chinese education for their children. They were no longer satisfied with six years of primary education, which was intended only to provide a basic minimum education for a largely illiterate workforce. It also met the needs of a group of Chinese parents who had formerly sent their children back to China for secondary education at enormous cost. More importantly, it assured the continuation and perpetuation of Chinese culture and identity in the Chinese communities in the region. However, it divided Chinese society into English- and Chinese-educated, and blurred the traditional dialect divisions of the Chinese communities.

Early reformist and revolutionary activities laid the foundation for the spread of literacy and the improvement of women's status in the Chinese communities in Malaysia and Singapore. Their propaganda media and organisations such as newspapers, magazines, schools, night classes and reading clubs invariably promoted literacy among masses.

124. Ibid., pp. 9–10.
125. Yen Ching-hwang, *The Overseas Chinese and the 1911 Revolution*, pp. 112–15, 158–60.

A number of illiterate workers were attracted to reading clubs and night schools, where they could improve their reading abilities,[125] and the rise of Chinese education during this period also increased the opportunity for Chinese children to be educated.

The spread of literacy can be seen from the phenomenal increase in the number of Chinese newspapers and magazines published in the region. A study shows that 291 Chinese newspapers and magazines were published in Singapore during the inter-war period (1914–1945), compared to twelve in the period between 1881 to 1913, an increase of more than twenty-four fold.[126] Increased literacy among the Chinese was also reflected in the increased number of Chinese children in schools. In 1924, there were 564 Chinese schools with 27,476 students in the Straits settlements and the federated Malay states, and this number rose to 996 schools with 86,147 students in 1938.[127] It is difficult to measure the percentage of literacy among the Chinese population; it appears that the majority of the Chinese in Malaysia and Singapore during this period were still illiterate, though the literacy was improved markedly among the young and the local-born Chinese.

One significant aspect of social change in the Chinese communities during this period was the change of attitude towards women and the improvement of their social status. Women were among the most oppressed groups in traditional Chinese society. They had low social status within the family, clan and community. They were deprived of the right to inherit property, to divorce and to receive an education. Their roles were confined to childbearing, domestic work and working in the family fields.[128] The traditional remark that 'women without talents

126. Wong Hong Teng, *Hsin-chia-po hua-wen jih-pao she-lun yen-chiu, 1945–1959* (A Study of the Editorials of Chinese Dailies in Singapore, 1945–1959) (Singapore, Department of Chinese Studies, National University of Singapore, 1995), p. 25.

127. See Tan Liok Ee, 'Politics of Chinese Education in Malaya, 1945–1961' (PhD thesis, University of Malaya, Kuala Lumpur, 1985), pp. 19–20.

128. See Lloyd E. Eastman, *Family, Field and Ancestors: Constancy and Change in China's Social and Economic History, 1550–1949* (New York, Oxford University Press, 1988), pp. 19–29.

are a virtue' summarised the attitude towards women. However, the rise of the reform movement in China at the end of the nineteenth century marked a radical change of attitude towards women and women's role in society. Liang Ch'i-ch'iao, a top leader of the reform movement, openly advocated education for women and the establishment of girls' schools. In Singapore a group of young educated Chinese elite, led by Dr Lim Boon Keng, founded the Singapore Chinese Girls' School in April 1899, the first of its kind among the Chinese communities in Southeast Asia.[129] The school opened in June with seven girls, and the number increased to 30 two months later. However, the school used English as the medium of instruction, and was primarily established for the young girls of the Straits-born Chinese. It experienced difficulties in finance and enrolment.[130] The first Chinese Girls' school using Chinese as the medium of instruction was the Hua Ch'iao (Overseas Chinese) Girls' School founded in Singapore in 1905 by a Cantonese woman named Huang Tien-hsien, which ceased to exist after ten years' existence.[131] The first Chinese Girls' school in Malaya was the Kuen Cheng Girls' School which was established in Kuala Lumpur in September 1908. The school was founded by Madam Wu Hsueh-hua and Mrs Chung Cho-ching (Yoshiko Watanabe, a Japanese national) with the financial support of Cheong Yeok Choy, a wealthy Chinese merchant in Kuala Lumpur. The school opened with twenty students, one headmaster and two teachers.[132]

---

129. Apart from Lim Boon Keng, other educated elite included Song Ong Siang, a prominent lawyer, and Khoo Seok-wan, a prominent Chinese scholar and a reformist leader. See Song Ong Siang, *One Hundred Years' History of the Chinese in Singapore*, pp. 305–06; Lee Guan Kin (Li Yuan-chin), *Lin Wen-ch'ing te ssu-hsiang: chung-hsi wen-hua te hui-liu yu mao-tun* (The Thoughts of Lim Boon Keng — Convergency and Contradiction between Chinese and Western Cultures) (Singapore, Singapore Society of Asian Studies, 1990), p. 67; Hsu Su-wu, *Hsin-chia-po hua-ch'iao chiao-yu ch'uan-mao*, p. 46.

130. Song Ong Siang, ibid.; Lee Guan Kin, ibid .

131. Hsu Su-wu, op. cit., pp. 46–7.

132. Cheng Pang-ying, 'Pen-hsiao chien-shih' (A Short History of the Kuen Cheng Girls' School) in *K'un-ch'eng liu-shih nien* (Souvenir Magazine of Sixtieth Anniversary of the Kuen Cheng Girls' School) (Kuala Lumpur, 1968), p. 11.

Political developments in China inspired women's education in the region. A score of Chinese girls' schools came into existence during the period between 1911 and 1945, including the Chung Hua Girls' School (September 1911), Chong Fu Girls' School (April 1915), Ch'ung Pen Girls' School (January 1916), Nan Hua Girls' School (June 1917), Nanyang Girls' School (1917), and The Hokkien Girls' School of Penang (March 1920; the school changed its name to Pin Hua Girls' School in 1951). Except for the last school, all the others were established in Singapore.[133] Many founders of these schools were former reformists or revolutionaries who shared a belief that women's education would strengthen China and the Han 'race'. Although not all Chinese parents were persuaded to send their girls to school, the schools nevertheless provided access to education for female Chinese children, and indirectly influenced the attitude of many Chinese towards women and their role in the society. This was reflected in the increase in the number of female students in school, the introduction of junior and senior middle education for girls, the increase of professional women in the workforce, the open discussion of the role of women and the new male–female relationship in society.

The rise of Chinese education and burgeoning Overseas Chinese nationalism in this period had an obvious impact on urban middle-class families. More and more Chinese parents saw the need to educate their girls and were willing to send their daughters to school. In January 1931 The Hokkien Girls' School of Penang was reported to have more than 760 students.[134] The introduction of secondary and teacher training classes also helped change the perception of women's social roles. For the first time, women's education opened up a new career path for women. Those who qualified as teachers locally or returned from China with tertiary qualifications became school teachers, whose profession was respected in the society. The increase in the number of female teachers and female clerks lifted their social status. At the same time, as a result of the impact of the

133. Hsu Su-wu, op. cit., pp. 47–55; Tay Lian Soo & Gwee Yee Hean (eds), op. cit., p. 169.
134. *Nanyang Siang* Pau, Singapore, 20 January 1931, p. 7.

May Fourth movement and the rise of the feminist movement in China in the 1920s, the traditional view of women's roles in family and society was challenged and debated in the Chinese media in Malaysia and Singapore. By the 1930s, more radical feminist views received increasing exposure in the media. Articles on the problems faced by women appeared in a major Chinese newspaper in Singapore which also enjoyed readership in Malaysia.[135] All these discussions helped to improve the image of women, their new social status and their roles in family and society.

Further changes at this time also occurred in social and class structures in the Chinese communities in Malaysia and Singapore. These took place during the inter-war period against a background of sustained growth of the Chinese population in the region. Despite two ordinances in 1928 and 1933, which restricted the number of Chinese male immigrants entering peninsular Malaysia and Singapore, the growth of the Chinese population was rapid. In the two decades from 1911 to 1931, the number of Chinese immigrants remaining in the region was estimated to be 792,615; while the total number of Chinese in Singapore increased from 219,577 in 1911 to 730,133 in 1947 — an increase of more than three times in three and a half decades.[136] One striking feature of this demographic change was the remarkable improvement of the female–male ratio in the Chinese population in the region. In the nineteenth century, the Ch'ing Government's restrictions on female migration resulted in an unequal sex ratio for the local Chinese communities. In Perak, for instance, the sex ratio among the Chinese was one female to 18.6 males, and about twenty

---

135. Topics such as 'cultivation of a modern female','the dilemma of a modern woman: between career and family', 'my ideal type of a modern female', 'women after marriage', 'the posture of a modern woman', 'how to be a modern woman', 'how to get rid of the yoke of marriage imposed on women', 'a career guide to women' and 'advice to women on health' were discussed in the newspaper. See *Nanyang Siang Pau*, June to November 1934.

136. See Victor Purcell, *The Chinese in Malaya* (Kuala Lumpur, Oxford University Press, 1967), p. 206; Maurice Freedman, *Chinese Family and Marriage in Singapore* (London, 1957), p. 25; Joyce Ee, 'Chinese Migration to Singapore, 1896–1941', in *Journal of Southeast Asian History*, vol. 2, no. 1 (Singapore, Department of History, University of Malaya in Singapore, 1961), p. 50.

percent of 4,687 females were involved in prostitution.[137] China's lifting of restrictions on female immigration at the beginning of twentieth century improved the ratio markedly. By 1911, the ratio was about one female to four males in peninsular Malaysia and Singapore. With the founding of the Chinese Republic in early 1912, the momentum of Chinese female immigration was further increased, and the ratio continued to improve. By 1921, the sex ratio among the Chinese in the peninsula and Singapore was recorded as 384 females to 1,000 males, about one to three.[138]

However, the most drastic change was due to the immigration ordinances of 1928 and 1933 which restricted the entry of Chinese male immigrants but not female immigrants. The result of this was a rapid increase in female immigrants, including a large number of female workers. By 1931, the ratio was improved to 513 to 1,000, and by 1947 the ratio reached 833 to 1,000.[139] This almost-balanced sex ratio helped to transform the Chinese communities from a sojourner society into a settler society. More and more families were established, and a permanent Chinese society with a distinctive Chinese cultural identity was thus born.

There was no substantial change in the social structure of Chinese society except in the rise of alumni and cultural organisations. Chinese society was still organised mainly along dialect and kinship lines, but its hierarchy was increasingly blurred by new organisations such as alumni and cultural bodies. There was a substantial increase in the number of dialect and kinship organisations during this period. For instance, there were only twenty-five identifiable dialect-based organisations in Singapore in almost a century from 1822 to 1910, while in less than three decades from 1917 to 1945 at least fifty-six dialect-based organisations were founded.[140]

137. *Perak Government Gazette*, vol. 4, no. 25 (1891), p. 723.
138. See Yu Shu-k'un (ed), *Nan-yang nien-chien* (The Nanyang Annals) (Singapore, Nan-yang yin-shua yu-hsien kung-ssu, 1951), pt. 10, 'Hua-ch'iao'(Overseas Chinese), p. 71.
139. Ibid .
140. See Wu Hua, *Hsin-chia-po hua-tsu hui-kuan chih* (Chinese Associations in Singapore) vol. 1 (Singapore, South Seas Society, 1975), pp. 194–96.

Two developments in Chinese social organisations in this period can be discerned: convergent and divergent. The convergent process brought together district-based dialect organisations, which converged at the top under an umbrella organisation. Most of the major dialect organisations representing the Hokkien, Teochew, Cantonese, Hakka and Hainanese were founded during this period. On the other hand, the divergent process moved downwards, forming village-based dialect or kinship organisations. The former reflected a desire for unity and solidarity of the geographically-based dialect groups in a rapid changing environment, while the latter was the result of rapid Chinese population growth and difficulties in maintaining the unity of district-based dialect organisations.

Within the structure of the dialect organisation, there was a trend towards democratisation. Control of the organisation was no longer in the hands of one or two prominent families, but rested with a popularly elected management committee. The founding of the Teochew Poit Ip Association of Singapore and the restructuring of the Hokkien Association of Singapore in 1929 are two examples.[141] At the same time, many of the dialect organisations developed closer ties with China. Operating as pressure groups, they were concerned for the well-being of the home districts or provinces in China. The rise of 'the Home Province Rescue Movement' (*Chiu-hsiang yun-t'ung*) by the Hokkiens in peninsular Malaysia and Singapore in the early 1930s was evidence of the commitment of the local Hokkiens to the welfare of their countrymen at home.[142] Many dialect organisations also actively supported China's resistance to the Japanese invasion in China. The Hokkien Association of Singapore under the leadership

141. See Yen Ching-hwang, 'Power Structure and Power Relations in the Teochew Community in Singapore, 1819–1930'(Paper presented at the First International Conference on Teochew Studies, held at the Chinese University of Hong Kong, 20–23 December, 1993), pp. 21–3; Yong Ching Fatt, *Chan-ch'ien Hsing-hua she-hui chieh-kou yu ling-tao-ch'en ch'u-t'an* (Chinese Community Structure and Leadership in Pre-War Singapore) (Singapore, South Seas Society, 1977), pp. 14–23.

142. 'Hsueh-lan-ngo Fu-chien hui-kuan i-shih chi-lu' (Minutes of the Hokkian Association of Selangor) (manuscript), 12 December 1932.

of Tan Kah Kee became the focal point for mobilising support of the Overseas Chinese in the region.

One notable feature in the development of Chinese social organisation during this period was the rise of alumni associations. An alumni association was a union of ex-students of a school. As most schools founded after 1912 did not restrict enrolment to a particular dialect group, alumni associations cut across dialect and kinship lines and served as bridges leading to a more united Chinese society. They organised social and recreational activities for members, fundraising for the school, and cultural and charitable activities for the community or China. One of the earliest alumni associations was the Nan Lu Alumni Association in Singapore founded in August 1918. The members were the alumni of the Tao Nan School founded in 1906 in Singapore by the Hokkien community. Apart from social and recreational activities for members, the association was also involved in fundraising for the founding of the Chinese High School and the Nanyang Girls' High School, and for the relief of flood victims in T'ientsin in China.[143] The alumni association became popular and attracted a number of members. In the 1930s there were at least ten alumni associations in Singapore and thirteen in Penang. The ten associations in Singapore had a combined membership of around 2,000.[144]

There was no fundamental change in the class structure of the Chinese communities in Malaysia and Singapore during this period. The general profile of the class hierarchy of Chinese society in the nineteenth century continued with some modifications. The merchant class (*shang*) still occupied top social stratum, followed in descending order by the educated elite (*shih*) and the workers (*kung*).[145] The *shang*

---

143. Lin Yun (ed), *Tao-nan hsueh-hsiao ch'ang-hsiao liu-shih chou-nien chi-nien t'e-k'an* (Tao Nan School 60th Anniversary Souvenir, 1906-1966) (Singapore, Tao Nan School, 1966), p. 29.

144. Yang Chien-ch'eng (ed), *San-shih nien-tai Nan-yang hua-ch'iao t'uan-t'i t'iao-ch'a pao-kao shu* (A Report on the Overseas Chinese Organisations in Southeast Asia during 1930s, based on Japanese Intelligence Sources in Taiwan) (Taipei, Chung-hua hsueh-shu yuan, 1984), pp. 99–100.

145. Yen Ching-hwang, *A Social History of the Chinese in Singapore and Malaya*, pp. 141-42; Wang Gungwu, 'Traditional Leadership in a New Nation: The

class was sub-divided into two groups: capitalists and general merchants. Chinese capitalists were financially affluent and socially powerful, and some of them even exerted political influence either locally or in China. They included exporters and importers, property owners, ship-owners, bankers, manufacturers, large plantation owners, tin-mining proprietors and major contractors. The merchants consisted of shopkeepers, general traders, and small plantation or factory owners. Although they were economically well-off, they commanded less influence and respect in society.

The *shih* class was also sub-divided into upper and lower groups. The former included professionals such as doctors, lawyers, engineers, government officers and interpreters; the latter consisted of Chinese school teachers, Chinese newspaper editors and reporters, and clerks in foreign and Chinese firms. The development of English education in this period increased the number of the English-educated elite who had received their professional training in medicine, law or engineering in the United Kingdom or Hong Kong. They had high income and high social status, and they enjoyed more prestige and respect than the members of the lower *shang* class in the Chinese communities. On the other hand, the rise of Chinese education and the spread of literacy resulted in a large increase in the number of Chinese school teachers and cultural workers. Some of them also commanded more respect than the shopkeepers and traders

The *kung* class, which occupied a lower position than the *shih* in the social order, was also sub-divided into two groups: artisans and general workers. The former consisted of tailors, carpenters, goldsmiths, blacksmiths, mechanics and cooks; the latter consisted of shop assistants, factory workers, plantation workers, mining workers and rickshaw pullers.[146] The number of these general workers increased because of immigration growth and the development of industry.

Chinese in Malaya and Singapore', in G. Wijeyawardene (ed), *Leadership and Authority: A Symposium* (Singapore, University of Malaya Press, 1968), p. 210.

146. See James F. Warren, *Rickshaw Coolie: A People's History of Singapore (1880–1940)* (Singapore, Oxford University Press, 1986), pp. 38–45.

At the bottom of the social hierarchy was a class consisting of unemployed workers, beggars and prostitutes. Their numbers increased in the wake of the world depression in the early 1930s. Without any support from the government, the urban unemployed had to depend partly on the support of clan or dialect organisations or squatting,[147] and many were reduced to begging for a living. Chinese society during this period became more fluid than in the nineteenth century. Both horizontal and vertical social mobility was made easier because of the spread of literacy, the rise of education and economic development. Rapid economic development during this period provided more jobs and a better means for members of the lower classes to climb the social ladder.

Since the independence of Malaya in 1957, the formation of Malaysia in 1963 and the independence of Singapore in 1965, the Chinese communities have responded to rapid political and economic changes. The majority of Chinese have acquired citizenship of Malaysia and Singapore, and have pledged loyalty to these two new nations. Further, as a result of the rapid political, economic and social changes in the 1960s, the Chinese communities have been globalised. More and more Chinese have sent their children to study in Britain, the United States, Australia, New Zealand and Canada, and they have developed useful cultural and economic links with the outside world. At the same time, the local Chinese economy has also adapted to the new economic policies. Chinese students returned from the West have helped to restructure traditional Chinese business; companies have been reformed, restructured and amalgamated into modern corporations. The result of this development is the rise of modern powerful Chinese conglomerates with natural ties with the region.

Some of the trends in the development of the post-independence period can be traced back to the period before the Second World War.

147. See Francis Loh Kok Wah, *Beyond the Tin Mines: Coolies, Squatters and New Villages in the Kinta Valley, Malaysia, c. 1880-1980* (Singapore, Oxford University Press, 1988), pp. 28–30.

The rise of new plantations and that of the financial and manufacturing industries in the pre-war era laid the foundations for rapid economic growth in the 1970s and 1980s. Overseas Chinese nationalism in the late 1930s paved the way for the rise of local-oriented politics. The politicisation of the Chinese communities and the techniques of mass mobilisation proved to be valuable in gaining support for local-oriented parties, such as the Malayan Chinese Association (MCA) founded in February 1949. The rise of modern Chinese education, the spread of literacy, and the improvement of women's status between the two world wars also helped to lay the groundwork for the development of a better-educated, more sophisticated and globalised Chinese society in Malaysia and Singapore.

CHAPTER 9

Power Structure and Power Relations in the Teochew Community in Singapore, 1819–1930*

The existence of some Teochews in Singapore before the landing of Raffles in 1819 enables the Teochews to claim that they were the earliest Chinese settlers on the island. Perhaps this claim is not too far from the historical truth. A small number of Teochews were involved in gambir planting before the arrival of the British.[1] These early Teochew planters appear to have come from the Riau islands of the Dutch East Indies rather than from China.[2] Chinese sources claim that a score of H'ai Yang Teochews (H'ai Yang was

---

*   This chapter was first published in Tay Lian Soo and Chang Chack-yan (eds), *Ch'ao-chou-hsueh kuo-chi yen-t'ao hui lun-wen chi* (Essays from the First International Conference on Teochew Studies), vol. 2 (Guangzhou, Jinan University Press, 1994), pp. 685–732.

1.   See Carl A Trocki, 'The Origins of the Kangchu system, 1740–1860', in *Journal of the Malaysian Branch of the Royal Asiatic Society*, vol. 49, pt. 2 (1976), p. 138.

2.   Ibid., pp. 136–138.

the ancient name of Ch'ao An district) settled in Singapore, but they were harassed by the local Malays, who killed some of these early Teochew settlers. The early Teochew community on the island was reinforced by the arrival of Teochews from Thailand, who concentrated in Shan Chai Ting where the earliest Teochew temple, Yueh H'ai Ch'ing temple, was built, and in the Boat Quay area which was gradually developed into a base for the Teochew community in Singapore.[3] Later the arrival of Wang Ch'in and Wang Feng-shun, who were famous Teochew navigators and became the leaders of this early community, further consolidated Teochew settlement.[4]

But these sketches of early Teochew history do not allow us to reconstruct the early Teochew settlement in Singapore satisfactorily. We do not know the size of this early Teochew settlement in the pre-British period, nor do we know about its structure. They also do not tell us whether the Wangs arrived on the island before or after 1819.

The founding of Singapore and its free trade policy attracted immigrants of all nationalities to the island to exploit the new opportunities. These included traders, shopkeepers, artisans, labourers and agriculturalists. The existence of the early Teochew settlement of the island made things easier for prospective Teochew immigrants in Southeast Asia and China, for they could receive more reliable information about the opportunities in the new port. Some of them could even rely on their relatives or fellow district men for help in the initial period;[5] and this saw the immigration of large numbers of Teochews from Riau, Thailand and China.

Teochew gambir and pepper planters had already established themselves in the Riau islands in the middle of the eighteenth century. Their numerical strength made them the most powerful dialect group among the Chinese under the control of their own *kapitan*.[6] The

3. See P'an Hsing-nung, *Ma-lai-ya Ch' ao-ch'iao t'ung-chien* (The Teochews in Malaya) (Singapore, Nan-tao ch'u-pan she, 1950), p. 40.
4. Ibid.
5. See Siah U. Chin (Seah Eu-chin), 'General Sketch of the Numbers, Tribes, and Avocations of the Chinese in Singapore' in *The Journal of the Indian Archipelago and Eastern Asia*, vol. 2 (1848), p. 287.
6. See Carl A Trocki, 'The Origins of the Kangchu System, 1740–1860', in

movement of a large number of Teochew planters from the Riau archipelago to Singapore has to be seen in the context of triangular relationship between Riau, Singapore and Johor. These three settlements, though not under one political entity, were seen in the eyes of the Teochew planters as integral parts of a larger economic unit. They were linked by accessible sea transport, and a network of planting, distributing and marketing gambir and pepper produce had been well-established among the Teochews. Further, good political ties had also been established with the Temenggong family of Johor.[7]

The coming of large numbers of Teochew immigrants greatly boosted the Teochew population and made the Teochew community the largest among the Chinese in early Singapore. By 1848, about three decades after the founding of the new settlement, Seah Eu Chin, the leader of the Teochew community, was able to claim 19,000 Teochews out of an estimated 40,000 Chinese population, the largest dialect group among the Chinese on the island.[8]

Although there were signs of a slowing down of Teochew population growth in the decades following 1848, the Teochew community nevertheless occupied the second position among the Chinese in Singapore. In 1881, they were 22,644 out of 86,766 Chinese in Singapore.[9] By this time, the Teochews had already lost

Journal of the Malaysian Branch of the Royal Asiatic Society, vol. 49, pt. 2 (1976), p. 138.

7. It was claimed that the Teochew planters in pre-British Singapore were induced by the Temenggong of Johor to develop gambir plantations on the island. Later, the Temenggong of Johor became the main patron of the Teochew planters in Johor. Ibid.; Carl A Trocki, *Prince and Pirates: The Temenggongs and the Development of Johor and Singapore 1784– 1885* (Singapore, Singapore University Press, 1979,) pp. 85–117.

8. According to this estimate, the 19,000 Teochews were followed by 9,000 Hokkiens, 6,000 Cantonese (Macao), 4,000 Hakkas (Keh), 1,000 Malacca Chinese (descendants of Hokkiens) and 700 Hainanese (Hailam). See Siah U. Chin (Seah Eu Chin), op. cit., p. 290.

9. See Table 4, 'Return of the Chinese Population, showing the Difference Tribes to which they Belong', 'Report on the Census of Singapore, 1881 by A P Talbot, Secretary of the Census Officers, dated 15th August 1881', in 'Straits Settlements Legislative Council Proceedings', appendix no. 29.

their dominant position in the composition of the Chinese population in Singapore, but still remained as a major dialect group in the Chinese community.

The Structure of the Teochew Community

The structure of the Teochew community in Singapore was not very different from the structure of other Chinese dialect groups on the island. The community was organised on the basis of geographical affinity, kinship ties and occupation.[10] In addition, there were organisations based on sworn brotherhood and cultural interests.

Teochew (Ch'aochou), from which the Teochews derived their name, was a prefecture of Kwangtung province in Ch'ing China. During the nineteenth century it consisted of nine districts: H'ai Yang (Ch'ao An), Ch'ao Yang, Chieh Yang, Ch'eng H'ai, Jao P'ing, H'ui Lai, P'u Ning, Ta P'u and Feng Shun.[11] Uneven migration from Teochew prefecture to Southeast Asia was responsible for the predominance of Teochew immigrants in Singapore from H'ai Yang and Ch'eng H'ai districts. Their predominance meant there was no sense of urgency to found a district-based dialect organisation. Rather, priority was given to the management of the Teochew Yueh H'ai Ch'ing temple and the burial of poor fellow-Teochews. This resulted in the founding of the Ngee Ann Kongsi around 1830.[12] For almost a century until its replacement in January 1929 by the

10. For the general social structure of the Chinese Community in Singapore, see Yen Ching-hwang, *A Social History of the Chinese in Singapore and Malaya, 1800–1911* (Singapore, Oxford University Press, 1986), pp. 35–84.
11. See Cheng Huan (compiled), 'Ch'ao-chou yen-ke chih-lueh' (Historical Changes of the Ch'ao Chou Prefecture), in P'an Hsing-nung (ed), *Hsin-chia-po Ch'ao-chou pa-i hui-kuan ssu-shih chou-nien chi-nien chih ch'ing-chu Hsin-chia-po k'ai-fuo pai wu-shih chou-nien t'e-k'an* (Souvenir Magazine of the Fortieth Anniversary of the Singapore Teo Chew (Poit Ip) Huay Kuan and the commemoration of the 150th Anniversary of the Founding of Singapore (Singapore, Teo Chew (Poit Ip) Huay Kuan, 1969), p. 142.
12. See 'Hsin-chia-po Ch'ao-shu she-t'uan chien-shih' (A Concise History of the Teochew Social Organizations in Singapore), in P'an Hsing-nung, ibid., p. 205.

Teo Chew (Poit Ip) Huay Kuan (The Teochew Eight Districts Association), the Ngee Ann Kongsi functioned effectively as an umbrella dialect organisation for the entire Teochew community in Singapore. Its control over the community was so complete that no other Teochew geographically-based organisation was founded until 1926, when the Teo Yeonh (Ch'ao Yang) Association of Singapore came into being.[13]

Clan Organisations

The founding of the Teochew Eighth Districts Association in January 1929 was undoubtedly a landmark in the history of the Teochew community in Singapore. The founding of this organisation signalled the end of the control of the Ngee Ann Kongsi over the Teochew community, and also marked the beginning of a more broad-based and more democratic dialect organisation for the Teochews in Singapore. It also successfully terminated the monopoly stranglehold over the Ngee Ann Kongsi by the Seah family, which lasted for nearly a century.[14]

During the period under discussion, four Teochew clan organisations appeared on the scene in Singapore. They were the Singapore Hoon Yong Kong See founded in 1865, the Singapore Teochew Kang Hay T'ng founded in 1867, the Singapore Teochew Sai Ho Association founded in 1879, and the Singapore Teochew

13. See Ch'en Chan-i, 'Pen hui-kuan chien-shih' (A Concise History of the Ch'ao Yang Association of Singapore), in Hsiao Ch'ing-wei (ed), *Hsin-chia-po Ch'ao-yang hui-kuan chin-hsi chi-nien t'e-k'an* (Souvenir Magazine of the 50th Anniversary of Teo Yeonh Association of Singapore) (Singapore, Teo Yeonh Association, 1976), p. 205.

14. For the founding of the Teochew Eighth District Association of Singapore and its complications, see 'Hsin-chia-po Ch'ao-shu she-tuan chien-shih and 'Letter from Mr Yang Chan-wen to the directors of the Singapore Teo Chew Poit Ip Huay Kuan and the Ngee Ann Kongsi dated 28th October 1965', in P'an Hsing-nung (ed), *Souvenir Magazine of the Fortieth Anniversary of the Singapore Teo Chew (Poit Ip) Huay Kuan and the Commemoration of the 150th Anniversary of the Founding of Singapore*, pp. 164, 205–206.

Lee Clan Association founded in 1890.[15] These early Teochew kinship-based organisations did not depart from the two general patterns of Chinese clan organisation in nineteenth century Singapore and Malaya.[16] Localised lineage, the first type, was based on strong kinship, geographical and dialect ties; its members claimed a common ancestry in the recent past, and came from the same village or several neighbouring villages of the same district. Non-localised lineage, the second type, embraced broader kinship, geographical and dialect ties; its members claimed relatively remote ancestry, and cut across the district boundaries but still spoke the same dialect.[17] The Singapore Hoon Yong Kong See fits in the first pattern of localised lineage. The Kong See was founded by Kuo clansmen from Fen Ke, Liu Lung, Ta Lung K'ang and Hou Kuo villages in the district of H'ai Yang (Ch'ao An); while the Singapore Teochew Sai Ho Association and the Teochew Lee Clan Association fall into the second category of non-localised lineages. They were founded by Lim clansmen and Lee clansmen respectively, who were not derived from a particular village or a few neighbouring villages of one district, but from many districts of the Teochew prefecture.[18]

The appearance of the Singapore Hoon Yong Kong See, the first Teochew clan organisation in Singapore, was of particular significance. The Kuo clan, which founded the Hoon Yong Kong See in 1865, was also one of the twelve clans from H'ai Yang and Ch'eng H'ai districts which founded the Ngee Ann Kongsi around

15. See 'A Concise History of the Teochew Social Organizations in Singapore', in P'an Hsing-nung (ed), op. cit., pp. 216–18; Huang Wu-ssu, 'Pen-t'ang shih-lueh' (A Short History of the Singapore Teochew Kang Hay T'ng), in Huang Shih-t'ung et. al. (eds), *Chao-chou chiang-hsia-t'ang chiu-shih wu chou-nien chi-nien t'e k'an* (Souvenir Magazine of Ninety Fifth Anniversary of the Singapore Teochew Kang Hay T'ng) (Singapore, 1962), p. A–5.

16. For a discussion of this topic, see Yen Ching-hwang, *A Social History of the Chinese in Singapore and Malaya, 1800-1911*, pp. 75–6.

17. Ibid.

18. See 'A Concise History of the Teochew Social Organizations in Singapore', in P'an Hsing-nung (ed), op. cit., pp. 217–18.

1830.[19] The reasons for the Kuo clansmen to found a separate social organisation outside the Ngee Ann Kongsi's power structure can be interpreted to be that some special needs of the Kuo clansmen, such as ancestral worship, could not be met by an umbrella organisation like the Ngee Ann Kongsi. However it may also have been because the Kuo clansmen were not satisfied with the power shared by them within the Ngee Ann Kongsi. As a result of the increase in Kuo clansmen in Singapore, they may have felt that their interests would be better served under a new kinship-based social organisation.

The founding of three Teochew non-localised lineages by the Ng, Lim and Lee clansmen can be interpreted as another sign of displeasure over the control of the Ngee Ann Kongsi by the twelve clans from H'ai Yang and Ch'eng H'ai. The founding of the Teochew Kang Hay T'ng by the Ng clansmen in 1867 was specified as being for the worship of a common ancestor, Ng Shiao San. Two of the three founders, who could clearly be identified as prosperous businessmen (both of them owned shops in Singapore), perhaps signalled the displeasure of some Teochew merchants with the monopoly of social power held by the twelve clans of the two prominent districts.[20] It has been claimed that the founder of the Singapore Teochew Sai Ho Association in 1879 was a group of three Lim businessmen which went by the name 'Sai Ho Kongsi', and that members were recruited not on an individual basis, but by the names of shops owned by Lim clansmen.[21] However, we do not know whether these Lim businessmen were from H'ai Yang or Ch'eng H'ai. If they were, they had probably been dissatisfied with the power they shared within the Ngee Ann Kongsi and therefore, like the Kuo clansmen, acted to found a kinship-based organisation to advance their self interest. If they did not come from the ruling clans within the Ngee Ann power structure, they had even more reason to be resentful of the monopoly of power by the Ngee Ann Kongsi.

19. Ibid., p. 205.
20. See Huang Wu-ssu 'Pen-t'ang shih-lueh' in Huang Shih-t'ung et. al. (eds.), op. cit. p. A–5.
21. Ibid., p. 217.

The founding of the Singapore Teochew Lee Clan Association in 1890 by the Lee clansmen with the name 'Lee Clan Kongsi'.[22] The Lee clan was not one of the twelve ruling clans of the Ngee Ann Kongsi, and its members had obvious reason to be dissatisfied with the way the Teochew community was run. They founded this non-localised lineage clan organisation to broaden their base of appeal, which would in turn enhance their power and influence considerably.

Secret Societies

The Teochew community was also organised on the basis of sworn brotherhood. The existence of Teochew secret societies in early Singapore is beyond doubt. In 1824, five years after the founding of the new settlement, Munshi Abdullah, a prominent Malay scholar and a protégé of Raffles, ventured into the jungle of the island near Tanglin Tuah where the headquarters of the Triad (T'ien Ti Hui) was located. He witnessed an initiation ceremony of new recruits of the Triad and, based on secondary information, he estimated Triad membership on the island to be about 8,000 strong.[23] Abdullah does not provide us with any information about the dialect composition of the Triad membership, but gives us some useful clues. He stated that all the Triad members lived deep in the jungle, and some of them owned plantations of pepper, gambir and other crops.[24] As the overwhelming majority of the pepper and gambir planters were Teochews in early Singapore,[25] it is reasonable to suggest that a number of Teochew

---

22. Ibid., p. 218.

23. See Munshi Abdullah, 'The Thian Tai Huey Society in Singapore', in *The Hikayat Abdullah* (transl. A.H. Hill), an independent issue of the *Journal of the Malayan Branch of the Royal Asiatic Society*, vol. 28, pt. 3 (June 1955), pp. 180–192. A slightly abridged translation of the section of the *Hikayat Abdullah* by T. Braddell is entitled 'Concerning the Tan Tae Hoey in Singapore', published in the *Journal of the Indian Archipelago and Eastern Asia*, vol. 6 (July and August 1852), pp. 545–55.

24. See *Hikayat Abdullah*, p. 180, 'Concerning the Tan Tae Hoey in Singapore', p. 545.

25. Seah Eu Chin in 1848 listed 10,000 Teochews and 400 Cantonese (Macao) gambir and pepper planters. In addition, he listed 200 Teochew and 100

planters were members of the Triad. Like other Chinese secret societies, the Teochew Triad was a well-knit organisation based on sworn brotherhood and reinforced by high degree of secrecy and strict rules. The initiation ceremony climaxed in the drinking of a mixture of each other's blood in wine, sealing the relationship between the new recruits and the organisation, and the sworn brotherhood cemented a new bond among members regardless of age and seniority.[26] This new relationship, which deviated from traditional kinship and geographical ties, gave the members of the Teochew lower classes a new identity and sense of belonging, and kept them together for protection and self-advancement. Although no social stigma was attached to the secret societies at this early stage in Singapore, they were nevertheless regarded by many Chinese as disreputable organisations. However, in a society where law and order were not yet firmly established, the coercive power of the secret societies was very effective in enforcing business contracts and collecting debts. The Teochew Triad was probably instrumental in ensuring smooth business operations for some rich Teochew planters, at the same time also protecting poor Teochew planting workers.

The founding of the Ngee Ann Kongsi as an umbrella organisation for the Teochew community did not eclipse the power and influence of the Teochew Triad, which competed with the Kongsi for the allegiance of the Teochews. The Triad with its unique functions not only survived the competition but also grew in strength by substantially increasing its membership in the following decades. By 1854, it was numerically strong enough to challenge a dominant Hokkien secret society, and caused a major disturbance in Singapore.[27]

Hokkien gambir and pepper dealers. See Siah U. Chin (Seah Eu Chin), 'General Sketch of the Numbers, Tribes, and Avocations of the Chinese in Singapore', in *Journal of the Indian Archipelago and Eastern Asia*, vol. 2 (1848), p. 290.

26. For details of the initiation ceremony of the Triad in early Singapore, see Munshi Abdullah, *Hikayat Abdullah*, pp. 185–86.

27. For the details of this secret society riot in Singapore, see W.L. Blythe, *The Impact of Chinese Secret Societies in Malaya: A Historical Study* (London, Oxford University Press, 1969), pp. 75–83; Leon Comber, *Chinese Secret Societies in Malaya: A Survey of the Triad Society from 1800 to 1900* (Singapore, Donald Moore, 1959), pp. 82–93.

The power and influence of the Teochew Triad grew unabated in the second half of the nineteenth century, and it was not until the suppression of the secret societies in 1889 that it ceased to become an important part of the structure of the Teochew community in Singapore. Modern studies have verified the importance of the Teochew Triad in nineteenth century Singapore. David Chng's study of a group of ancestral tablets deposited in a Chinese temple, She Kung Miao, in Lavender Street, Singapore, reveals that about fifty percent of the forty-eight tablets of the Ghee Hin (Triad) leaders belonged to the Teochews. These Teochew Ghee Hin leaders had been active in the Singapore and Johor area since the 1840s, including the famous Teochew leader Tan Kye Soon, who was the Chinese *kapitan* of Johor.[28]

Power Structure in the Teochew Community

Three types of power in the Teochew community can be identified: social power, informal political power and coercive power. Social power rested with social organisations such as dialect or clan organisations; informal political power depended on relationships with the British Colonial Government or with the Chinese Government; and coercive power depended on control of the secret society, the power of the underworld.

Social Power

The Teochew community, like the larger Chinese community in Singapore, was predominantly immigrant-based, forming a subordinate and urban community.[29] The fluidity of population movement, which characterises immigrant communities, gave rise to a strong sense of

---

28. See David Chng, 'She Kung Miao shen-tsu p'ai yen-chiu' (A Study of the Ancestral Tablets in the She Kung Temple), in David Chng, *Hsin-chia-po hua-jen shih lun-ts'ung* (Collected Essays on the Chinese in Nineteenth Century Singapore), (Singapore, South Seas Society, 1986), pp. 124–150.
29. See Yen Ching-hwang, *A Social History of the Chinese in Singapore and Malaya, 1800–1911*, p. 141.

sojournment and instability. This had direct bearing on their social power, for the fluctuation of immigrants weakened the grip of social organisations over their members.

Social power was pivotal in the power structure of the Teochew community in early Singapore. It rested with the Teochew dialect or clan organisations. At the pinnacle of this social power was the Ngee Ann Kongsi founded around 1830. The Kongsi was originally established to manage the public cemetery and the temple of the Teochew community,[30] but it developed to become the focus of power, covering most community matters. As religious worship and funeral burial occupied important positions in the lives of early Teochew immigrants, control over the running of the temple and cemetery provided the leaders of the Kongsi with enormous power over the lives of ordinary Teochews. The command of social power was predicated on the possession of economic power; in fact economic success determined the acquisition and continuity of social power. No leader could emerge and maintain his dominant social position without wealth. Wealth, therefore, underpinned social power. The process of acquiring wealth was theoretically equitable for all immigrants. Those who had some education, business acumen, the correct kinship and dialect ties, and the capacity to overcome certain social evils such as gambling, opium-smoking, drinking and prostitution, had a competitive edge over others in becoming wealthy and climbing the social ladder.[31] When successive generations were born, however, those children who were from wealthy families had an obvious advantage in the race for wealth.[32]

Like other Overseas Chinese leaders, the quest of Teochew leaders for wealth was vigorous. They made money from commercial agriculture, opium farming, cash crops and entrepot trade. Right from the very early days of Singapore, the Teochews' dominant position in gambir and pepper plantations provided them with

30. See 'Hsin-chia-po Ch'ao-shu she-t'uan chien-shih' in P'an Hsing-nung (ed), op. cit., p. 205.
31. For a discussion of this topic, see Yen Ching-hwang, *A Social History of the Chinese in Singapore and Malaya, 1800–1911*, p. 159.
32. Ibid., p. 160.

enviable wealth. For example, Seah Eu Chin made a large fortune out of planting gambir and pepper on large scale on the island around late 1830s.[33] Active Teochew participation in entrepot trade in early Singapore was evident in their substantial share in shop ownership in the Boat Quay area, an area marked by its bustling trade scene.[34] The trade network centred in Singapore guaranteed continuous profits for those Teochews who were actively involved in this entrepot trade. Importing rice and sugar from Thailand, tea, silk and dairy necessities from China, cotton goods from India, and birds' nests and other dried seafoods from the archipelago, the Teochews exported large quantities of gambir and pepper to China and Europe, and reaped handsome profits.[35]

This profit formed part of the basis of the economic power of the Teochew leaders. The wealth accumulated from commercial agriculture and entrepot trade provided a solid foundation for the Teochew leaders to bid for opium farms, a mainstay of revenue of the Colonial Government in Singapore and big business for Chinese capitalists on the island. The Teochew leaders in nineteenth century Singapore and Johor appear to have been active bidders for control of the opium farms. For unknown reasons, well-known leaders like Seah Eu Chin do not seem to have been involved in bidding for the opium farms,[36] but others such as Tan Seng Poh (brother-in-law of

33. See Song Ong Siang, *One Hundred Years' History of the Chinese in Singapore*, p. 20.
34. For a study on 83 Chinese shop houses located in the Boat Quay area, see David Chng, 'Pa-shih nien-tai te Wu Chi' (Boat Quay in 1880s), in David Chng, *Hsin-chia-po hua-jen shih lun-ts'ung*, pp. 1–11.
35. This impression is gathered from David Chng, ibid.; Song Ong Siang, op. cit., p. 20; Siah U, Chin (Seah Eu Chin), 'General Sketch of the Numbers, Tribes, and Avocations of the Chinese in Singapore', in *The Journal of the Indian Archipelago and Eastern Asia*, vol. 2 (1848), p. 290; Wong Lin Ken, *The Trade of Singapore, 1819–69*, an independent issue of the *Journal of the Malayan Branch of Royal Asiatic Society*, vol. 33, pt. 4 (December 1960), especially pp. 106–175.
36. Nothing is mentioned about Seah's involvement in opium farms. See Song Ong Siang, op. cit. pp. 19–20; P'an Hsing-nung (ed), *Ma-lai-ya Ch'ao-ch'iao t'ung-chien*, pp. 78–9.

Seah Eu Chin), Heng Bun Soon and Tan Hiok Nee were among those who were deeply involved in the operation of the Singapore and Johor opium farms. In fact, both Tan Seng Poh and Tan Hiok Nee, together with a Hokkien leader Cheang Hong Lim, formed a triumvirate controlling the so-called 'Great Opium Syndicate'. This group consolidated Singapore, Johor, Malacca and Riau opium farms and distilleries for a decade from 1870 to 1879, bringing tens of thousands of dollars into the coffers of both Tan Seng Poh and Tan Hiok Nee.[37]

The possession of immense wealth by the Teochew leaders would not be relevant to our discussion if the functions of their wealth were not examined. Their control over the planting and distribution of gambir and pepper gave them enormous power over ordinary Teochews. Both gambir and pepper were labour intensive commercial crops, employing many labourers in the process of planting and production. Seah Eu Chin's 1848 breakdown of Teochew occupations provides some clues for this investigation. Seah listed 10,000 Teochews as gambir and pepper planters, with another 200 Teochew dealers for these two commodities.[38] The combined number of 10,200 Teochews involved in gambir and pepper accounted for more than fifty percent of the total Teochew population (19,000) at that time.[39] Undoubtedly the bulk of these Teochew planters on Seah's list were labourers employed by Teochew capitalists to plant, harvest and produce both commodities, and they had to depend on their employers for their livelihoods. With the spread of gambir and pepper plantations from Singapore to Johor, the number of Teochews involved in these crops also increased rapidly. By 1870 the gambir and pepper business may have provided a living for an estimated 100,000 people living within a fifty-mile radius of Singapore,[40] and undoubtedly the majority of them were Teochews.

37. For an analysis of the rise of this great syndicate and the involvement of Teochew leaders, see Carl A Trocki, *Opium and Empire: Chinese Society in Colonial Singapore, 1800-1910* (Ithaca, Cornell University Press, 1990), pp. 117–148.
38. See Siah U Chin (Seah Eu Chin), op. cit. p. 290.
39. Ibid.
40. See Carl A Trocki, 1990, op. cit., p. 199.

Teochew plantation capitalists such as Seah Eu Chin and Tan Hiok Nee employed thousands of Teochew labourers in their plantation estates, and possessed much power over their employees in terms of employment, promotion and special remuneration. In an overseas environment like Singapore, this power was perceived by many Teochew employees to be absolute. The Teochew community, like the Chinese community in Singapore at large, was a relatively closed one. Ordinary Teochew immigrants were unable to find jobs freely outside the community. Their dependence on fellow Teochews to earn a living ensured the economic and social powers of the leaders over them. Once this economic power was translated into social power, the social power of the Teochew leaders became overwhelming. However, the expression of this economic power must be understood in the context of intricate interdependence between Teochew leaders and workers. The leaders were employers, heads of the dialect or clan organisations, while the workers were employees and rank and file members of those social organisations. They needed and complemented each other, but sometimes their interests were diametrically opposed and this led to tensions and conflicts.

Informal Political Power

In comparison with social power, the structure of informal political power was irregular and less overt. What determined the acquisition of this informal power from the British seems to have been a command of the English language, business or social contacts with the Europeans (especially the British), and wealth and power in the local Chinese community.

The possession of this power was less visible. It did not involve holding any substantive office, but was expressed in the possession of titles which entailed influence and prestige. Adequate command of the English language was the essential ingredient for acquiring this power. It is obvious that those Chinese leaders who could speak good English were able to communicate effectively with the British colonial authorities in Singapore, and were likely to gain the trust of the British. With some exceptions, those who spoke English were English educated, had been exposed to Western values and mores, and were more attuned to British rule. They were therefore favoured by the British authorities as instruments for the advancement of its interests on the island.[41]

Adequate command of the English language was essential but not sufficient for acquiring informal power. It had to be buttressed by business or social contacts and the possession of wealth and power in the local Chinese community. Business dealings with the Europeans, especially with the British, provided frequent opportunities for making contacts and gaining mutual understandings, and gave rise to a sense of closeness. The advancement of mutual business interests would draw Chinese leaders closer to the European community and gain the trust of the British. Continuous social contacts lubricated human relationships, and built a bridge of good will between them. However, all these would become less meaningful if the informal power aspirants did not possess sufficient wealth or power in their own communities, as this would dilute their credentials of community leadership.

In the early part of the history of Singapore when English-educated Chinese were rare, the command of adequate English was not deemed to be absolutely necessary for acquiring informal power. Those *de facto* Chinese community leaders who had business and social contacts with the Europeans and had demonstrated their trustworthiness were given informal political power by the British authorities. Seah Eu Chin's case is illustrative of this point. Seah Eu Chin, an early Teochew immigrant from China, had no way of gaining adequate command of the English language, although perhaps he acquired some fluency in English through his extensive business dealings with European firms.[42] However, his linguistic inadequacy did not deter him from acquiring informal power from the British. His enormous wealth and his firm control over the Teochew community must have impressed the British authorities in Singapore. Seah's business dealings and social contacts with Europeans further

41. See C F Yong, 'British Attitudes toward the Chinese Community Leaders in Singapore, 1819–1941', in C F Yong, *Chinese Leadership and Power in Colonial Singapore* (Singapore, Times Academic Press, 1991), pp. 291–92.
42. See Song Ong Siang, *One Hundred Years' History of the Chinese in Singapore*, p. 20.

improved his quest for informal political power. His high profile in business and social circles earned him a good reputation among the Europeans, and in 1840 he was admitted to the Singapore Chamber of Commerce, the forum for European and native business barons in Singapore.[43] Seah gradually emerged as a recognised leader of the entire Chinese community in Singapore. His knowledge of the Chinese community was regarded as authoritative, and was frequently sought by Europeans. This is indicated in two articles written by him in Chinese in 1847 and 1848, entitled 'Remittances made by the Chinese to their parents' and 'Numbers, tribes and avocations of the Chinese in Singapore'. These were translated and published in the prestigious *Journal of the Indian Archipelago and Eastern Asia* (volumes 1 and 2).[44] In 1851, Seah Eu Chin demonstrated his political allegiance to the British by organising a deputation of wealthy Chinese merchants, which greeted the visit of the Governor-General, Lord Dalhousie, to Singapore. This act was very much appreciated by Governor Butterworth, who wrote to thank him for his assistance in welcoming His Lordship.[45]

Once Seah Eu Chin's credentials as a leader of the Chinese community were established and his political allegiance to the British ensured, informal political power was readily given to him by the British colonial government in Singapore. From 1851 onwards he was frequently called upon to act as a grand juror, and in 1853 he was granted the coveted certificate of naturalisation. This gave him the status of naturalised British subject in the Straits of Malacca,[46] entitling him to enjoy British legal and diplomatic protection wherever he went. In 1867, when Singapore came under the Crown rule as part of the Straits settlements, he was honoured by the new governor, Sir Harry Ord, with the position of Justice of the Peace, becoming one of the first Chinese to receive such a distinction from the government.[47]

43.   Ibid.
44.   Ibid.
45.   See C B Buckley, *An Anecdotal History of Old Times in Singapore 1819–1867* (Kuala Lumpur, The University of Malaya Press), p. 151.
46.   See Song Ong Siang, op. cit., p. 21.
47.   Ibid.

Informal political power given by the Chinese Government rested not so much on linguistic ability, but rather on wealth and political allegiance to China. Before 1912 when China was under Manchu rule, wealth was the determining factor for the Chinese in Singapore to acquire informal power. The financial straits of the Ch'ing Government during the last quarter of the nineteenth century induced it to sell its honours among its overseas subjects. A wide range of Chinese brevet titles and brevet ranks were sold openly, with different prices listed in the newspapers.[48] This provided excellent opportunities for many wealthy Chinese to purchase Ch'ing honours. In the period between 1877 and 1912, at least 295 Chinese in Singapore and Malaya purchased Ch'ing brevet titles or brevet ranks for the purpose of either enhancing their social prestige or confirming their leadership status.[49]

Political allegiance to the Ch'ing government also helped Chinese leaders in Singapore to acquire informal power. The Singapore Chinese Chamber of Commerce, which was founded by a pro-Ch'ing Chinese leader, Chang Pi-shih,[50] became the headquarters of many pro-Ch'ing Chinese leaders in Singapore.[51] The Chamber was given substantial informal power by the Ch'ing government. It could by-pass the Chinese Imperial Consulate in Singapore and communicate directly with the Ministry of Agriculture, Industry and Commerce, and it was empowered to issue protective passes to its members when they wished to escort the coffins of their relatives back to China for burial.[52]

48. See *Lat Pau*, 24 October 1887, p. 5.
49. For a detailed discussion of this issue, See Yen Ching-hwang, 'Ch'ing's Sale of Honours and the Chinese Leadership in Singapore and Malaya (1877–1912)', in *Journal of Southeast Asian Studies*, vol. 1, no. 2 (September 1970) pp. 20–32.
50. For the founding of the Singapore Chinese Chamber of Commerce by Chang Pi-shih, see 'Hsin-chia-po chung-hua shang-wu tsung-hui teng-chi i-shih pu' (Minutes of the Singapore Chinese Chamber of Commerce) (manuscript), vol. 1, pp. 1–2.
51. See Yen Ching-hwang, 'Overseas Chinese Nationalism in Singapore and Malaya, 1877–1912', in *Modern Asian Studies*, vol. 16, no. 3 (Cambridge, Cambridge University Press, 1982), pp. 413–16.
52. See 'Hsin-chia-po chung-hua shang-wu tsung-hui teng-chi i-shih pu', Chi Yu year (1909), vol. 1, p. 144.

After the founding of the Republic in 1912, the deciding factor in acquiring informal political power shifted from wealth to political closeness to China. Those who had been closely associated with Sun Yat-sen's struggle with the Manchu government in Singapore, and those who were actively involved in the Kuomintang activities on the island, tended to possess more of this informal power.[53] However, political instability in China limited such power. The power of Sun Yat-sen and his close associates in the early Republican period was ephemeral, and was greatly circumscribed by Yuan Shih-k'ai's dictatorship. It was not until the Nanking decade from 1927 to 1937 that the Kuomintang became the main ruling power in China.

Informal power from the Chinese Government was expressed through two channels: appointment to a position in the Chinese Government which entailed power and influence in the mainland, particularly over the home provinces or districts; the power and influence wielded through close connections with the Chinese Government's agency in Singapore, the Chinese Consulate-General.[54]

Coercive Power

Coercive power in the Teochew community was organised but covert. The acquisition of this power hinged upon control of the Teochew

53. For details of Sun Yat-sen's political activities in Singapore and Malaya and the support he gained from the local Chinese, see Yen Ching-hwang, *The Overseas Chinese and the 1911 Revolution: With Special Reference to Singapore and Malaya* (Kuala Lumpur, Oxford University Press, 1976) pp. 88–144, 212–86. For the involvement of Chinese in Singapore in the Kuomintang and its front organisations, see C F Yong and R.B. McKenna, *The Kuomintang Movement in British Malaya, 1912–1949* (Singapore, Singapore University Press), especially pp. 22–43, 83–105.

54. For the activities of the Chinese Consuls in Singapore during the late Ch'ing period, see Wen Chung-chi, 'The Nineteenth Century Imperial Chinese Consulate in the Straits Settlements' (unpublished MA thesis, University of Singapore, 1964). For the activities of the Chinese Consul–General in Singapore during the Republican period, see Yeo Hwee Joo, 'The Chinese Consulate–General in Singapore, 1911–1941, in *Journal of the South Seas Society*, vol. 41, pts. 1 and 2 (1986), pp. 79–106.

secret societies. Chinese secret societies were well integrated into the social structure of the Chinese communities in nineteenth century Singapore and Malaya, and were instrumental in the advancement of personal and group interests.[55] The power of the secret society rested on its effective clandestine network and on brute force. Even before its official suppression by the British in Singapore in 1889, it had already operated secretly on the island, and was much feared by ordinary people and authorities. In the absence of effective political control over the Chinese communities in Singapore, the power of the secret society was used to regulate unruly Chinese immigrants, to facilitate business transactions and to enforce business contracts.

Unlike the Triad secret society in South China, which was more politically oriented and had been developed into a power centre from below resisting the formidable imperial power,[56] the power of the secret societies in Singapore assumed a more economic and social character. It was rarely used as a political tool against the British colonial government.[57] In the case of the Teochew community in Singapore, those who possessed this coercive power seem to have derived from the lower classes, were less educated and were likely to have been involved in manual work. Those who commanded this power enjoyed the power unchallenged, but it was exercised covertly. Coercive power holders had an advantage over non-coercive power holders, as people were more likely bow to pressure and threats from the underworld than to the establishment.

55. For a discussion on this issue, see Yen Ching-hwang, *A Social History of the Chinese in Singapore and Malaya, 1800–1911*, Ch. 4, 'Secret Society and Social Structure', pp. 110–128.
56. For discussion on this issue, see Jean Chesneaux, *Secret Societies in China in the 19th and 20th Centuries* (Hong Kong, Heinemann Educational Books Ltd, 1971), pp. 80–5.
57. Commenting on the Chinese secret societies in the Straits settlements in 1879, the Protector of Chinese, W.A. Pickering, claimed that 'no Society would dare to think of making a combined effort against the Government'. See W.A. Pickering, 'Chinese Secret Societies, Part 2', in *Journal of the Straits Branch of the Royal Asiatic Society*, no. 3 (1879), p. 11.

Power Pelations in the Teochew Community

The relationship between social power, informal political power and coercive power was not static, but dynamic and changing.

There was a close connection between social power and informal power. Those who possessed social power were tempted to use it to acquire informal power, and in turn, the possession of informal power consolidated an individual's social power. The reverse was also true. Those who already held informal power could also use it to gain social power in the Teochew community in Singapore.

The relationship between social power and coercive power, and between coercive power and informal power was ambiguous and changing. Social power holders did not necessarily need to develop any connection with secret societies in order to exercise their power and influence; but many coercive power holders were tempted to use that power to acquire social and informal power. Tan Kye Soon's life story is illustrative of how coercive power could be used to acquire social and informal power. Tan, a lower class Teochew, was a leader of the Ghee Hin in Singapore. In around 1844 Tan led a group of his followers to Johor, where he obtained in October a grant of land along the Tebrau River. Here he developed his gambir and pepper settlement, later known as the Tan Chu Kang (The River of the Tan House), and became the *kangchu* (master of the river) of the Tebrau settlement. This territorial base in Tebrau strengthened his coercive power over the local Chinese population, and he then used this power to acquire social and informal political power. He emerged as the leader of the Teochew community in Johor, and developed a close relationship with the Temmenggong of Johor, being made the Chinese *kapitan* as a result.[58]

---

58. This profile of Tan Kye Soon (or Tan Kee Soon) is reconstructed from the following sources. P'an Hsing-nung (ed), *The Teochews in Malaya*, pp. 42–3; Carl A Trocki, *Prince of Pirates: The Temenggongs and the Development of Johore and Singapore 1784–1885*, pp. 102, 104–106; Carl A Trocki, *Opium and Empire: Chinese Society in Colonial Singapore, 1800–1910*, pp. 106, 132, 139; Hsu Yun-ts'iao, 'Jo-fuo hua-jen to-chih shih' (A History of Chinese Settlements in Johor), in Ch'en Pao-chin et. al. (eds), *Hsin-shan Chung-hua shang-hui yin-hsi chi-nien t'e-k'an* (Souvenir Magazine of Silver Jubilee Celebration of the Chinese Chamber of Commerce of Johor Bahru) (Johor Bahru, 1970), pp. 193–201.

The Seah Family

What characterised power relations in the Teochew community in Singapore during this period was the hegemony of a dominant family based on the power of two districts. The family had perpetuated its control over social and informal political power for close to a century. This was the Seah family and its Ch'eng H'ai and H'ai Yang group.

The founder of the Seah 'dynasty' was Seah Eu Chin, an early immigrant from China. Eu Chin was born in Ch'eng H'ai district, Teochew prefecture in Kwangtung province in 1805, and came to Singapore in 1823. Like other early Teochew immigrants attracted to Singapore by its new opportunities, he was prepared to work hard for economic advancement. What distinguished him from his fellow migrants were his literacy and his business acumen, which gave him a competitive edge. He first worked as a clerk to several trading vessels, and established business contacts with the natives in the Malay Peninsula and the Riau Archipelago. At the age of twenty-five Seah started his own business in Kling Street and later in Circular Road as a commission agent, supplying the junks with provisions and trading in local produce. He then invested his money in real estate and gambir and pepper plantations, and became one of the most successful Chinese merchants in Singapore.[59]

By about 1830, although still young, Seah Eu Chin had already emerged as a successful merchant. He gathered a group of Teochews from his home district, Ch'eng H'ai, and a neighbouring district H'ai Yang (Chao An), to found the Ngee Ann Kun (romanised in Mandarin as I An Chin), the predecessor of the Ngee Ann Kongsi. Apart from the Seah family, the co-founders of the organisation were derived from other twelve clans from the two districts, including Tan (Ch'en), Chua (Ts'ai), Lim (Lin), Ng (Huang), Kuat (Kuo), Teo (Chang), Ngoh (Wu), Sim (Shen), Yeoh (Yang), Cheng (Tseng), Lau (Liu) and Heng

59. See Song Ong Siang, *One Hundred Years' History of the Chinese in Singapore*, pp. 19–20; 'She Yu-chin hsien-sheng (Mr Seah Eu Chin)', in P'an Hsing-nung (ed), *Ma-lai-ya Ch'ao-ch'iao t'ung-chien*, pp. 78–9.

(Wang).[60] Seah Eu Chin appointed himself director (*tsung-li*), and appointed a member of each clan as his deputy. They formed into a committee, controlling the entire operation of the Ngee Ann Kun (which was changed into Ngee Ann Kongsi in 1845).[61] His grip on the Ngee An Kun and later the Ngee Ann Kongsi was firm and probably autocratic, and, due to the important functions of the Ngee Ann Kongsi, his power over the Teochew community was absolute. As a result Seah, together with the other twelve deputy directors of the Kongsi, were popularly known among the Teochews as 'The Thirteen Bosses' (*Shih-san t'ou-chia*).[62]

The control of Seah Eu Chin's family over the Ngee Ann Kongsi for nearly a century was not accidental, but the result of a well-executed plan. Seah Eu Chin, a self-made capitalist and a man of foresight, saw the danger of his leadership status disappearing after his death. He realised that the perpetuation of the Seah family fortune, and its dominant status within the Teochew community and the Chinese community at large, hinged on the continuation of his work by his children. Some of them therefore had to be groomed to take over. Like the Chinese gentry in China, Seah employed private tutors for the education of his children. His second son, Seah Liang Seah, had shown talent in his studies and later displayed his business acumen. He was sent to Saint Joseph's Institution, a prestigious Catholic missionary school on the island,[63] to receive an English education which paved the way for his future success.[64] Liang Seah married at the age of

60. See 'A Concise History of the Teochew Social Organizations in Singapore', in P'an Hsing-nung (ed), *Hsin-chia-po Ch'ao-chou pa-i hui-kuan ssu-shih chou-nien chi-nien chih ch'ing-chu Hsin-chia-po k'ai fuo pai wu-shih chou-nien t'e-k'an*, p. 205.

61. See 'Letter from Mr Yang Chan-wen (Yeoh Chan Boon) to the Directors of the Singapore Teo Chew Poit Ip Huay Kuan and the Ngee Ann Kongsi dated 28th October 1965', in P'an Hsing-nung (ed), ibid., p. 164; Wu Hua, Hsin-chia-po hua-tsu hui-kuan chih (Chinese Associations in Singapore) vol. 1 (Singapore, South Seas Society, 1975), p. 62.

62. Ibid.

63. See C.M. Turnbull, *A History of Singapore, 1819-1975* (Kuala Lumpur, Oxford University Press, pp. 62–3.

64. See 'She Lian-ch'eng hsien-sheng' (Mr Seah Liang Seah: A Short Biography), in P'an Hsing-nung (ed), *Ma-lai-ya Ch'ao-ch'iao t'ung-chien*,

seventeen and after his marriage worked in his father's firm, Eu-chin & Company, as his father's secretary. At the same time, he was groomed by his father to take public office. In 1871, at the age of 21, Seah Liang Seah together with his father and his elder brother, Seah Cheo Seah, were invited to the ball at Government House for the celebration of Queen Victoria's birthday.[65]

By the time Seah Liang Seah succeeded his elder brother to become *tsung-li* of the Ngee Ann Kongsi and the *de facto* leader of the Teochew community in 1885,[66] the power and influence of the Seah family had reached its pinnacle. About two years before his ascendancy to the leadership of the Ngee Ann Kongsi, Seah Liang Seah was appointed as a temporary member of the Legislative Council of the Straits Settlements by the Governor, Sir Frederick Weld. His permanent status on the Council was confirmed in November of that year (1883), and he held this position until 1890 when he resigned due to the pressures of private business and ill-health. He was appointed as a Legislative Councellor in 1894 for a second time, but held the seat briefly and resigned in the following year as a protest against the unsympathetic attitude of the British Home Government which imposed a Military Exaction on Singapore.[67]

Seah Liang Seah was only thirty-three when he was appointed to this prestigious position by the Governor, and he must have gained a great deal of personal satisfaction from this coveted appointment. After the famous Hoo Ah Kay (Whampoa), he was only the second Chinese to be appointed to such a position. Although a non-official member of the Legislative Council did not carry much real power,

p. 81; Song Ong Siang, *One Hundred Years' History of the Chinese in Singapore*, p. 212.

65. See Song Ong Siang, op. cit., p. 162.
66. This conjection is based on the fact that Seah Cheo Seah died in that year. Seah Cheo Seah had taken over control of the Ngee Ann Kongsi probably some time in the late 1870s from Seah Eu Chin, whose health had become frail and later died in 1883. See Song Ong Siang, op. cit., p. 21; 'Letter from Mr Yang Chan-wen (Yeoh Chan Boon) to the Directors of the Singapore Teo Chew Poit Ip Huay Kuan and the Ngee Ann Kongsi dated 28th October 1965' in P'an Hsing-nung (ed), op. cit., p. 164.
67. Song Ong Siang, op. cit., pp. 213, 261.

the title nevertheless held a great deal of influence in government circles, as well as considerable prestige and honour in the Chinese community. The appointment was also a clear recognition of Seah Liang Seah's leadership status in the Chinese community at large. Indeed he emerged as one of the foremost Chinese leaders in Singapore, and developed a strong pro-British stance by leading Chinese merchants in pledging loyalty to the British Crown on various occasions.[68] He helped to found the pro-British Straits Chinese British Association in 1900 and became one of its leaders in the early period.[69]

Seah Liang Seah's acquisition of informal political power from the British Colonial Government reinforced his social power, consolidated his leadership positions in both the Teochew community and the Chinese community at large, and helped to perpetuate the hold of the Seah clan on the Ngee Ann Kongsi. This was partly reflected in the passing of the position of *tsung-li* of the Ngee Ann Kongsi to his son, Seah Eng Tiong (or Seah Eng Tong) probably in around the mid-1920s.[70]

Breaking the Seah Monopoly

The prolonged monopoly of the Ngee Ann Kongsi and the control of the leadership of the Teochew community by the Seah family caused tension and conflict within the community. Although some dissatisfied members within the Ngee Ann Kongsi power structure had founded

---

68. See for instance in February 1889, on the Jubilee celebration of Queen Victoria, Seah Liang Seah led a group of thirty-four wealthy Chinese merchants to present a statue of Her Majesty to the government and pledge absolute loyalty to the British Crown. Ibid. pp. 249–50.
69. See Yong Ching Fatt, 'A Preliminary Study of Chinese Leadership in Singapore, 1900–1941', in *Journal of Southeast Asian History* vol. 9, no. 2 (September 1968), pp. 262–64; see also C F Yong, *Chinese Leadership and Power in Colonial Singapore*, pp. 52–4.
70. The actual year that this succession took place is unknown. Seah Liang Seah died in 1925 at the age of 75, but he could have relinquished the position of *tsung-li* in favour of his son earlier than this. See 'She Lian-ch'eng hsien-sheng', in Pan Hsing-nung (ed), *Ma-lai-ya Ch'ao-ch'iao t'ung-chien*, p. 83.

four separate clan organisations since 1865,[71] there was no clear break with the Ngee Ann power brokers. However, after the turn of the twentieth century there arose a new group of wealthy merchants and bankers who demanded a share of the control of the Teochew community. This anti-Seah group joined hands across district boundaries to challenge Seah's monopoly. The leaders of this new group were Chua Tse Yung (Ts'ai Tzu-yung), Liao Cheng-hsing, and Tan Hun Chiu (Ch'en Yun-ch'iu).

Chua was born in Ch'eng H'ai in 1847. Before setting foot in Singapore in 1874 he had already established himself as a reputable merchant in Swatow and was active in Treaty port trade. After his arrival in Singapore, he set up a company, Ch'eng Fa, dealing in silk, porcelain and tobacco from China. He later specialised in rice and sugar trading, and became one of the most powerful rice and sugar merchants in Southeast Asia and Hong Kong.[72]

Liao Cheng-hsing took a different road to wealth and fame. He was born in H'ai Yang district in 1874, was much younger than Chua Tse Yung, and had a humble beginning as a hawker in Singapore. Combining hard work and thrift with business acumen, he went into business and succeeded in trading gambir and pepper. He also traded in European textile produce and later invested in rubber plantations.[73] In 1907, together with Huang Shung-t'ing and other Teochew wealthy merchants, Liao founded the Sze Hai Tong Banking and Insurance Company, one of the earliest Chinese banks in Singapore.[74]

71. See the first section of this chapter.
72. For a short biography of Chua Tse Yung, See 'Ts'ai Tzu-yung Hsien-sheng' (Mr Chua Tse Yung), in P'an Hsing-nung (ed), *Ma-lai-ya Ch'ao-chiao t'ung-chian*, p. 195. See also Koh Kow Chiang (ed), *T'ung-nan-ya jen-wu chih* (1965: Who's Who in Southeast Asia), Singapore, *Hsin Sheng yu-hsien kung-ssu*, 1965), p. A58.
73. For a short biography of Liao Cheng-hsing, see 'Liao Cheng-hsing hsien-sheng' (Mr Laio Cheng-hsing), in P'an Hsing-nung (ed), *Ma-lai-ya Ch'ao-ch'iao t'ung-chien*, p. 181; Koh Kow chiang (ed), *Tung-nan-ya jen-wu chih*, p. A62.
74. Liao Cheng-hsing is also romanised according to the Teochew dialect as Leow Chia Heng. It was this name that appeared in the history of the Sze Hai Tong Banking. For details, see Tan Ee-leong, 'The Chinese Banks incorporated in

Tan Hun Chiu, another H'ai Yang leader, was born in China. His father founded a company named Joo Hong in Boat Quay, dealing in pepper and gambir. Tan inherited his father's business and became a leading merchant in Singapore. He was a reformist leader in Singapore, supporting the cause of K'ang Yu-wei and Liang Ch'i-ch'ao. He was also a proprietor and the managing director of *Nanyang Tsung-hui Pao* (The Union Times), a prominent reformist newspaper in Singapore.[75]

What characterised the leadership of this new group was its strong China orientation. In contrast to the Ngee Ann group led by Seah Liang Seah and later his son Seah Eng Tong, who had received English education and taken a clear pro-British stance, most leaders of this group received some form of Chinese education, and their political allegiance was pro-China. Tan Hun Chiu was an important reformist leader in Singapore advocating reform of the Ch'ing Government, while Chua Tse Yung, and another member of the group, Lan Chin-sheng, were obviously supporters of the Manchu regime in China.[76]

The rise of this new group changed the power landscape and polarised the Teochew community. The community was increasingly divided into pro- and anti-Seah camps, and the ultimate development of this trend was the ending of the Seah family's hold over the Ngee Ann Kongsi in 1930. The power base of the group was the Tuan Meng School, founded in October 1906 as response to the call of the Ch'ing Government for the development of modern Chinese education in the overseas Chinese communities.[77] The absence of Seah Liang Seah, the leader of the Ngee Ann Kongsi, from the twenty-eight founders of the school suggests a clear break between this new group and the Ngee

Singapore and the Federation of Malaya', in *Journal of the Malayan Branch of the Royal Asiatic Society*, vol. 26, pt. 1 (July 1953), p. 115; 'Liao Cheng-hsing hsien-sheng', in P'an Hsing-nung (ed), *Ma-lai-ya Ch'ao-ch'iao t'ung-chien*, p. 181.

75. See a short biography of Tan Hun Chiu in Koh Kow Chiang (ed), *Tung-nan-ya jen-wu chih*, p. A58; Yen Ching hwang, *The Overseas Chinese and the 1911 Revolution*, p. 271.

76. See Yen Ching-hwang, *The Overseas Chinese and the 1911 Revolution*, pp. 157, 271; Yen Ching-hwang, 'Overseas Chinese Nationalism in Singapore and Malaya', in *Modern Asian Studies*, vol. 16, pt. 3, (July 1982), pp. 415–17.

Ann power brokers.[78] The new group appears to have had a firm control over the school, reflected in its control over the management board. Chua Tse Yung was elected chairman, Liao Cheng-hsing and Tan Hun Chiu were made his deputies, and Tan Hun Chiu was further appointed as the first principal of the school.[79]

The new group controlled the educational and probably cultural interests of the Teochew community, but it failed to topple the Seah family from its entrenched position in the Ngee Ann Kongsi, which still dominated most of the social and religious activities. However, the leaders of the new group tried a variety of approaches in their quest for power and leadership in the Teochew community. They were active outside the Teochew community, trying to gain recognition of their leadership status in the Chinese community at large. Even before taking control of the Tuan Meng School in October 1906, some of its leaders had already been actively involved in the founding of the Singapore Chinese Chamber of Commerce. In the first Chamber election in April 1906, Tan Hun Chiu was elected as one of the two presidents (*tsung-li*); Chua Tse Yung and two other leaders of the new group, Ch'en Teh-jun and Huang Shung-t'ing, were three of the ten vice-presidents (*hsueh-li*) and several other leaders of the new group were also elected as directors of the Chamber.[80] In the following year, Chua Tse Yung was elected president, and Laio Cheng-hsing

77. See Li Ku-shen and Lin Kuo-chang (eds), *Hsin-chia-po Tuan-meng hsueh-hsiao san-shih chou-nien chi-nien ch'ih* (Souvenir Magazine of the Thirtieth Anniversary of the Tuan Mong School in Singapore) (Singapore, 1936), p. 11; Yen Ching-hwang, *The Overseas Chinese and the 1911 Revolution*, p. 157.

78. Li Ku-shen and Lin Kuo-chang (eds), op. cit., p. 11; Li Ku-shen (ed), *Hsin-chia-po Tuan-meng chung-hsueh wu-shih chou-nien chi-nien t'e-k'an* (Souvenir Magazine of the Fiftieth Anniversary of the Tuan Mong High School of Singapore) (Singapore, 1956), p. 9.

79. See Li Ku-shen (ed), op. cit., p. 9; Huang Chin-ying (ed), *Tuan-meng chung-hsueh ch'i-shih chou-nien chi-nien k'an* (Souvenir Magazine of the Seventieth Anniversary of the Tuan Mong High School) (Singapore, 1977), p. 73.

80. See 'Hsin-chia-po Chung-hua shang-wu tsung-hui teng-chi i-shih pu' (Minutes of the Singapore Chinese Chamber of Commerce), manuscript kept by the Chamber in Singapore, vol. 1, pp. 2–3; *Lat Pau*, 19 April 1906, p. 3.

and Ch'en Teh-jun were elected vice presidents.[81] What should be noted here is that these leaders of the new group were recognised by the Chinese community at large, not only as representatives of the Teochew community but also as representatives of the broader geographical unit of Kwangtung community, of which the Teochew community was a part.[82]

While the new group failed to unseat the monopoly of Seah family over the Ngee Ann Kongsi in 1906, this was finally was achieved by another new group of Teochew leaders in 1927. This new group also consisted of a number of wealthy merchants, planters and bankers. The leaders of this group were Lim Ngee Soon (romanised in Mandarin as Lin I-shun), Li Wei-nan and Yeoh Chan Boon (Yang Chan-wen). Li Wei-nan, was born in Ch'eng H'ai district (the same district as the Seah family), Kwangtung, in 1880. He accompanied his father to Singapore at the age of sixteen, and worked for various Teochew companies in Singapore and Kuala Lumpur, where he began to show his talent and business acumen. He was recruited into the management team when the first Teochew bank, the Sze Hai Tong Bank, was founded in 1907, and emerged as a well-known banker in Singapore.[83]

81. See 'Minutes of the Singapore Chinese Chamber of Commerce' (manuscript) vol. 1, pp. 60–1.

82. In the structure of the Chinese Chamber of Singapore, members elected to the board were divided into two main groupings: the Hokkien Pang (known as Min Pang) representing people from Fukien province; the Kwangtung Pang (known as Yueh Pang) representing people from Kwangtung province. This was obviously divided according to geographical boundaries. Under this classification the Teochew community, or Teochew Pang, was a part of the Kwangtung community. See ibid.; 'Hsin-chia-po Chung-hua tsung shang-hui shih chi' (Historical Records of the Singapore Chinese Chamber of Commerce), in *Hsin-chia-po Chung-hua tsung shang-hui ta-sha lo-ch'eng chi-nien k'an* (Souvenir of the Opening Ceremony of the Newly completed Singapore Chinese Chamber of Commerce Building) (Singapore, 1964), pp. 150–60, 273–81.

83. See 'Li Wei-nan hsien-sheng' (Mr Li Wei-nan), in Koh Kow Chiang (ed), *Tung-nan-ya jen-wu chih*, p. A67.

Another leader, Yeoh Chan Boon, was born in Ch'ao An district (H'ai Yang) in 1881, and received a traditional Chinese education. His father came to Singapore to become a cloth merchant, founding a shop named Yu Ch'eng. Yeoh Chan Boon came to Singapore at the age of eighteen to continue his father's business, and later also moved into the business of trading local produce and jewellery. Yeoh, at the age of twenty-six, was one of the twenty-eight founders of the Tuan Meng School in 1906.[84]

The most prominent leader of this 1920s group was Lim Ngee Soon, who was the driving force behind the campaign to end the Seah family monopoly. Unlike Li and Yeoh, Lim was born in Singapore in 1879. His father came to Singapore from Ch'eng H'ai district, Kwangtung, and operated a Chinese grocery shop in Beach Road. Lim became an orphan at the age of eight, and was brought up by his maternal grandparents. He was both Chinese- and English-educated, which proved to be extremely valuable for his career and business. His maternal uncle, Teo Eng Hock (Chang Yung-fu) was a leading Chinese revolutionary in Singapore, supporting Sun Yat-sen's cause. Under his uncle's influence, Lim became an ardent revolutionary. He became a founding member of the Singapore T'ung Meng Hui (The United League, the major Chinese revolutionary party) in April 1906, and was made the publicity officer of the branch. At the age of twenty-seven he became Sun Yat-sen's confidant, and accompanied Sun to tour Malaya for the founding of various T'ung Meng Hui branches in the Peninsula.[85] Lim was also a successful businessman: he was a pineapple and rubber planter, a rubber manufacturer, a contractor and later a banker. With

84.　See 'Yang Chan-wen hsien-sheng' (Mr. Yeoh Chan Boon), in P'an Hsing-nung (ed), *Ma-lai-ya Ch'ao-ch'iao t'ung-chien*, p. 174; Li Ku-shen & Lin Kuo-chang (eds), *Tuan-meng hsueh-hsiao san-shih chou-nien chi-nien ch'ih*, p. 11.

85.　For the early revolutionary activities of Lim Ngee Soon, see Yen Ching-hwang, *The Overseas Chinese and the 1911 Revolution*, pp. 92-5, 98-9. For a general biography of Lim Ngee Soon, see Chu Po-wei, *Lin I-shun chuan* (A Biography of Lim Ngee Soon) (Shanghai, 1921); 'Lin I-shun hsien-sheng' (Mr. Lim Ngee Soon), in P'an Hsing-nung (ed), *Ma-lai-ya Ch'ao-ch'iao t'ung-chien*, pp. 103–05; Feng Tzu-yu, *Ko-ming i-shih* (Reminiscences of the Revolution of 1911) vol. 1, (Taipei, Shang-wu Publishing House, 1965), pp. 249–53.

his new-found wealth, Lim contributed generously to Sun Yat-sen's cause and became one of Sun's important benefactors. After the founding of the Republic in 1912, due to his close connections with the revolutionaries, he wielded enormous influence in China. He was appointed by Sun Yat-sen in 1916 as an adviser to Sun's new government in Canton, and in 1917 was appointed by the Ministry of Agriculture of the Peking government as an adviser.[86]

Now possessing informal political power from China, Lim Ngee Soon probably used that power to acquire social power in the Chinese community in Singapore. The forum for power play was the Singapore Chinese Chamber of Commerce. Whoever was elected to the important position of the Chamber would be accepted by the Chinese community at large as *de facto* leaders, and the president of the Chamber would be regarded as the supreme leader and the spokesman on major issues for the community. With the command of immense wealth and the political influence from China, Lim was elected President of the Chamber for the 13th batch (1921–1922) and later the 15th batch (1925–1926).[87]

In the power structure of the Chinese community in Singapore, a communal leader without a solid base in his own dialect community would be vulnerable. Lim Ngee Soon was well aware of this fact. His considerable political influence in China ebbed and flowed with the political fortunes of the Kuomintang, proving this source of informal political power to be rather unreliable. Lim was thus forced to turn his attention to the leadership of his own Teochew community. However, leadership ambition and self-interest may not explain satisfactorily Lim's campaign for unseating the Seah family's monopoly of the Ngee Ann Kongsi. After all, at the time he was elected president of the Singapore Chinese Chamber of Commerce in 1921 he was already the acknowledged leader of the Chinese community in Singapore. What infuriated him and his close associates was the fact that the accounts of the Ngee Ann

---

86. See P'an Hsing-nung, (ed), *Ma-lai-ya Ch'ao-ch'iao t'ung-chien*, p. 104; Chu Po-wei, *Lin I-shun Chuan*, p. 11.

87. See 'Hsin-chia-po Chung-hua tsung shang-hui i-shih pu' vol. 4 (1916–1921), pp. 153–55, and vol. 5 (1921–1926), pp. 133–35; *Hsin-chia-po Chung-hua tsung shang-hui ta-sha lo-ch'eng chi-nien k'an*, pp. 162-63.

Kongsi were never made public, nor were they even made available for public scrutiny.[88] This dissatisfaction was tolerated when the aging Seah Liang Seah was still alive, probably out of traditional Chinese respect for his age. But when the old man died in 1925 at the age of seventy-five, the Ngee Ann Kongsi mangement board elected his younger son, Seah Eng Tong to succeed him as the *tsung-li*.[89]

Seah Eng Tong's succession outraged many Teochew leadership aspirants and united them to take action. The anti-Seah campaign was in the making. The first shot was fired on 28 December 1927 when Lim Ngee Soon, together with another thirteen close associates, presented to Seah Eng Tong an open letter which was also published in Chinese daily newspapers in Singapore.[90] The letter questioned the right of the Seah family to monopolise the Ngee Ann Kongsi, and urged Seah to make public the monthly income and expenses, the properties and their addresses, and information about the structure of the Kongsi.[91] Seah Eng Tong refused to negotiate directly with the challengers, replying instead through his lawyer. Realising the struggle for the control of Ngee Ann Kongsi would drag on for a long time, the challengers prepared for a prolonged legal battle by raising reserved funds. At the same time, they adopted the strategy of isolating the Seah family and its supporters from the majority of the Teochews. They planned to found a broad-based dialect association to represent all Teochews in Singapore,[92] but realising that this would mean an all-out war between the two camps, the challengers kept the plan as a last resort.

88. See 'Letter from Mr. Yang Chan-wen (Yeoh Chan Boon) to the Directors of the Singapore Teo Chew Poit Ip Huay Kuan and the Ngee Ann Kongsi dated 28th October 1965', in P'an Hsing-nung (ed), *Hsin-chia-po Ch'ao-chou pa-i hui-kuan ssu-shih chou-nien chi-nien chih ch'ing-chu Hsin-chia-po k'ai fuo pai wu-shih chou-nien t'e-k'an*, p. 164.
89. See 'A Concise History of the Teochew Social Organizations in Singapore', ibid., p. 205.
90. See *Nanyang Siang Pao*, 29 December 1927, p. 4.
91. Ibid.
92. See 'Letter from Yang Chan-wen (Yeoh Chan Boon) to the Directors of the Singapore Teo chew Poit Ip Huay Kuan and the Ngee Ann Kongsi dated 28th October 1965', in P'an Hsing-nung (ed), *Hsin-chia-po Ch'ao-chou pa-i hui-kuan*, p. 164.

In the meantime, Lim Ngee Soon urged the Protector of Chinese in Singapore to intervene. With mediation by the Protector of Chinese, six representatives of each camp met in the Protector's office. Surprisingly, Seah Eng Tong took a rather conciliatory attitude, and agreed in principle to handing over the assets of the Ngee Ann Kongsi, and to the formation of a broad-based new management board.[93] The negotiation was aborted, however, because one of the Seah Eng Tong's brothers, Seah Eng Kun, together with some others, came out strongly against the move. The legal battle for the control of Ngee Ann dragged on.[94]

After hopes for a peaceful solution to the dispute were dashed, the challengers went all-out to isolate the Seah family and its supporters. In August 1928, forty prominent Teochews led by Lim Ngee Soon published in the newspapers their proposal to found a Teochew Association of Singapore, and urged all Teochews to attend a scheduled meeting to be held at the Singapore Chinese Chamber of Commerce on 15 September 1928.[95] More than 50 Teochews attended the meeting, which produced an interim committee to draft a constitution. On 2 February 1929, a second meeting was held to pass the constitution and produce an executive committee. Lim Ngee Soon was elected unopposed as president, and Li Wei-nan and Yeoh Chan Boon were elected his deputies. Thus, a broad-based and more democratic dialect organisation representing all Teochews in Singapore was inaugurated. The association was registered and approved by the government in the following month as the legitimate body representing all Teochews.[96]

The strategy adopted by the challengers had worked. It had isolated the Seah family and swung the support to the challengers.

---

93. See P'an Hsing-nung, 'I-an kung-ssu shih-mo' (Historical Changes of the Ngee Ann Kongsi), in 'Ngee Ann Kongsi Records' (manuscript) (microfilm kept at the National Archives, Singapore), p. 2a.

94. Ibid.

95. See 'Ts'ou she Hsin-chia-po Ch'ao-chou hui-kuan yuan-ch'i' (The Origin and Justification of the proposed founding of Singapore Teochew Association), in P'an Hsing-nung (ed), *Hsin-chi-po Ch'ao-chou pa-i hui-kuan*, p. 165.

96. Ibid.

Authorised by the new association, Lim Ngee Soon and his close associates mounted another legal challenge against the Seah family. Realising that they had lost support of the majority of Teochews and also the government's sympathy, the Seah family capitulated and prepared for a peaceful solution. On 8 September 1930, Seah Eng Tong handed over $58,269 together with the titles of twenty-one blocks of land to the new committee.[97] Thus, the monopoly of Seah family over the Ngee Ann Kongsi for nearly a century came to an end. The new group led by Lim Ngee Soon, Li Wei-nan and Yeoh Chan Boon continued to dominate the Singapore Teochew Eight Districts Association and the newly reformed Ngee Ann Kongsi, but their leadership was more open and democratically based.[98]

Conclusion

The Teochews were the earliest Chinese settlers in Singapore. They were economically powerful and numerically strong in early Singapore. The structure of the Teochew community was not very much different from other Chinese dialect groups, and was based on geographical, dialect, kinship ties and sworn brotherhood.

Three types of power existed in the Teochew community in Singapore: social power, informal political power and coercive power. Social power was pivotal in the power structure of the Teochew community, and rested on the control of the Teochew dialect organisation, the Ngee Ann Kongsi. Social power was predicated on the possession of economic power, which Seah Eu Chin and other leaders possessed. Informal political power was acquired through close connections established with the British Colonial authorities in Singapore or with the Chinese governments in China, while the structure

97. See P'an Hsing-nung, 'I-an kung-ssu shih-mo', in 'Ngee Ann Kongsi Records' (manuscript) pp. 3b-4a. See also a list of Ngee Ann properties in the appendix of 'I-chiu san-san nien I-an kung-ssu chu-chih fa-ling' (An Ordinance to Incorporate the Ngee Ann Kongsi, no. 5 of 1933), in 'Ngee Ann Kongsi Records' (manuscript).

98. See lists of office bearers of the Singapore Teochew Eight Districts Association from 1st to 8th batch, 1929–1942, in P'an Hsing-nung (ed), *Hsin-chia-po Ch'ao-chou pa-i hui-kuan*, pp. 194–95.

of coercive power was based on the ability to control Teochew secret society members in Singapore.

The relationship between social power, informal political power and the coercive power was not static, but dynamic and changing. There was a close relationship between social power and informal political power: they reinforced one another. The main characteristic of the power relations in the Teochew community during this period was the hegemony of Seah Eu Chin's family over the Ngee Ann Kongsi for nearly a century. The prolonged monopoly of the Seah family over the social power in the Teochew community caused tensions and conflicts. Due to rapid social and political changes in Singapore and China after the turn of the present century, new groups armed with economic and informal political powers began to challenge Seah's hegemony. This process was not completed until 1930 with the founding of the new Teochew Eight Districts Association and the ousting of the Seah members from their entrenched positions in the Ngee Ann Kongsi. From then onwards, the power structure in the Teochew community was placed on a more open and more democratic basis, and power relations were less rigid and more harmonious.

CHAPTER 10

Ch'ing China and the Singapore Chinese Chamber of Commerce, 1906–1911*

In the contest for political power in the Overseas Chinese communities during the late Ch'ing period, the efforts of the reformists and the revolutionaries have been well documented.[1] But the role of the Ch'ing government in this battle for overseas Chinese political allegiance has been neglected in the past, partly due to the assumption that its efforts in this regard had been made on its behalf by its overseas diplomatic establishments. By using as an example the Ch'ing government's relationship with the Singapore Chinese Chamber of Commerce, this

---

*   This chapter was first published in Leo Suryadinata (ed), *Southeast Asian Chinese and China: The Politico-economic Dimension* (Singapore, Times Academic Press, 1995), pp 133–160.

1.   See Yen Ching-hwang, *The Overseas Chinese and the 1911 Revolution: With Special Reference to Singapore and Malaya* (Kuala Lumpur, Oxford University Press, 1976); L. Eve Armentrout Ma, *Revolutionaries, Monarchists and Chinatowns: Chinese Politics in the Americas and the 1911 Revolution* (Honolulu, University of Hawaii Press, 1990); Lee Lai To (ed), *The 1911 Revolution — The Chinese in British and Dutch Southeast Asia* (Singapore, Heinemann Asia, 1987).

chapter aims to shed some light on this obscure aspect of the triangular contest for Overseas Chinese political support in the last decade of Manchu rule.

In Search of a Mechanism for the Control of the Overseas Chinese

A change in the Ch'ing government's emigration policy in 1893 ushered in a new era of close relationships with the Overseas Chinese.[2] The lack of a central body handling Overseas Chinese affairs left the implementation of the new policy to the individual diplomats concerned. However, what emerged after 1893 was a positive attitude among Ch'ing diplomats towards the protection of the Overseas Chinese, and they became more concerned with their well-being.[3] But this policy of forging closer ties with overseas subjects must have had a clear objective — it was either to exploit their economic potential or to acquire their political allegiance in order to consolidate the rule of the dynasty. In evaluating its new relationship with its overseas subjects, the Ch'ing government did not lose sight of the potential threat from the Overseas Chinese communities. It was aware of increasing anti-dynastic agitation among the Overseas Chinese mounted by the reformists and revolutionaries, led by K'ang Yu-wei and Sun Yat-sen, respectively.[4] The arrival of Chinese political refugees in the Overseas Chinese

2. For a discussion of Ch'ing change in its emigration policy and historical significance, see Yen Ching-hwang, *Coolies and Mandarins: Ch'ing Protection of Overseas Chinese during the Late Ch'ing Period* (Singapore, Singapore University Press, 1985) pp. 249–280; see also Chuang Kuo-tu, *Chung-kuo feng-chien cheng-fu te hua-ch'iao cheng-ch'ih* (The Overseas Chinese Policy of China's Feudal Governments) (Amoy, Amoy University Press, 1989), pp. 126–34.)
3. See Yen Ching-hwang, *Coolies and Mandarins*, pp. 281–82.
4. For the anti-dynastic agitation mounted by Kang Yu-wei and Liang Ch'i-ch'iao in the Overseas Chinese communities before 1901, see Jung-pang Lo, *Kang Yu-wei: A Biography and a Symposium* (Tucson, The University of Arizona Press, 1967), pp. 178–83; Ting Wen-chiang (ed), *Liang Jen-Kung hsien-sheng nien-p'u ch'ang-p'ien ch'u-kao* (A Draft of Chronological Records of Liang Ch'i-ch'iao) (Taipei, 1959), pp 99–140; Chang Peng-

communities after 1899 created a new problem for the Ch'ing government. Anti-dynastic agitation reached an intolerable level after the turn of the twentieth century, exemplified by the revolts in central and South China at the end of the 1900.[5] The Court was quick to identify the source of the threat and took measures to counter the insidious propaganda of its adversaries. An edict issued on 9 March 1901 (the nineteenth day of the first moon of the twenty-seventh year of Kuang-hsu) instructed Chinese ministers (ambassadors) in Europe and America to take immediate steps to defuse the agitation. Suitable diplomats were to be selected to tour the Overseas Chinese communities in order to expose the evil intentions of K'ang's and Sun's gangs, and to persuade the overseas subjects not to lend their support to the conspirators.[6] In response to the edict, the Chinese minister to London, Lo Feng-lu, took prompt action. He instructed his two subordinates, the Chinese Consul-General in Singapore and the Vice Consul in Penang, to quash the anti-dynastic agitation in the

yuan, *Liang Ch'i-ch'iao yu Ch'ing-chi ko-ming* (Liang Ch'i-ch'iao and the 1911 Revolution) (Taipei, Chung-yang yen-chiu-yuan, 1964), pp. 81–9. For early anti-dynastic agitation mounted by Sun Yan-sen and his supporters in the Overseas Chinese communities, see Feng Tzu-yu, *Hua-ch'iao ko-ming k'ai-kuo shih* (The Involvement of Overseas Chinese in the 1911 Revolution and the Founding of the Republic) (Taipei, Shang-wu yin-shu kuan, 1953), pp. 1–47; Feng Tzu-yu, *Ko-min i-shih* (Reminiscences of the 1911 Revolution), vol. 1 (Taipei, Shang-wu yin-shu kuan, 1965), pp. 4, 17–9, 22-3.

5.   For the analysis of the revolutionary revolt in Waichow, Kwangtung province in 1900, see Harold Z. Schiffrin, *Sun Yat-sen and the Origins of the Chinese Revolution* (Berkeley, University of California Press, 1968), pp. 214–54; for the reformist-engineered revolt in Hankow, central China in 1900, see Edmund S.K. Fung, The T'ang Ts'ai-ch'ang Revolt, in *Papers on Far Eastern History*, no. 1 (Canberra, Department of Far Eastern History, Australian National University, March 1970), pp. 70–114; Feng, Tzu-yu, *Chung-hua min-kuo k'ai-kuo ch'ien ko-ming shih*, vol. 2 (Taipei, shang-wu yin-shu kuan, 1954), p. 105; Feng Tzu-yu, *Ko-ming i-shih*, vol. 1, pp. 128–31.

6.   See *Ta Ch'ing te-tsung ching-huang-ti shih-lu* (Veritable Records of the Emperor Kuang-hsu of the Great Ch'ing Empire), vol. 479 (Ch'ang Ch'un, 1935), p. 3.

local Chinese communities, and then to proceed to tour Australia and Canada for that purpose.[7]

Ch'ing concerns about the reformist and revolutionary activities overseas were later expressed in its move to send emissaries to visit the Overseas Chinese communities. From 1907 to 1912, at least three major missions were sent to tour Southeast Asia, where the majority of the Overseas Chinese resided. The Yang Shih-chi mission of 1907,[8] the Wang Ta-chen mission of 1909,[9] and the Chao Chung-fan mission of 1911,[10] all attempted to promote industry and commerce among the Overseas Chinese, and to induce them to invest in China.[11] But one hidden objective which did not appear in their

7.   Ibid., vol. 488, p. 6b; 'Shih Ying Lo Feng-lu chih wai-pu Ying wai-pu i chu Lo Chung-yao fu Hsin-chin-shan i chieh-hsi tien' (Cable by the Chinese Minister to England, Lo Feng-lu, to the Ministry of Foreign Affairs relating to the obstruction of Lo Chung-yao's tour of Melbourne by the British Foreign Office) in *Ch'ing-chi wai-chiao shih-liao: Kuang-hsu ch'ao* (Historical Materials on Foreign Relations in the Ch'ing Period for the Kuang-hsu Reign), vol. 152 (original), p. 19, or reprint, vol. 5 (Taipei, Wen Hai, 1964), p. 188.

8.   For the details of Yang Shih-ch'i's mission to tour the Chinese communities in Southeast Asia, see *Ta Ch'ing te-tsung ch'ing-huang-ti shih-lu*, vol. 576 (original), pp. 10b–11a; Chu Shou-peng (compiled), *Kuang-hsu ch'ao tung-hua lu* (The Tung Hua Records of the Kuang-hsu Reign), vol. 5 (Peking, Chung Hua shu-chi, 1958), vol. 5, p. 91.

9.   For details of Wang Ta-chen's mission to tour Southeast Asia, see the memorial of the Ministry of Agriculture, Industry and Commerce to the Court, in *Cheng-chih kuan-pao* (Ch'ing Government Gazettes), vol. 17 (Taipei, 1965), p. 317.

10.   For the details of sending this mission, see the memorial of the Ministry of Agriculture, Industry and Commerce to the Court, in *Cheng-chih kuan-pao*, vol. 42, p. 98; see also the cable of the Chinese Ministry of Foreign Affairs to the Chinese Consul-General in Singapore dated 13 February 1911, in 'Wai-wu pu shou-fa tien tang' (Cable Records of the Ministry of Foreign Affairs), 3rd year of Hsuan-tung Reign (1911).

11.   See for instance, in the speech given by roving envoy Chao Ch'ung-fan to a group of about 60 wealthy Chinese merchants in Penang, Chao encouraged Overseas Chinese merchants to invest in China, and emphasised that they would receive protection from the Ch'ing Government, See *Penang Sin Pao*, 28 March 1911, p. 3. (Original newspaper kept in the Chinese Library, National University of Singapore).

publicised aims was to defuse the growing influence of the revolutionaries and reformists in the Overseas Chinese communities. It was this objective which was condemned by the revolutionaries, and the missions were sometimes met with strong hostility from Sun Yat-sen's supporters.[12] Despite this minor setback, the missions were successful. They succeeded in spreading the message of imperial grace, arousing nationalistic sentiment and gaining support for the dynasty among many Overseas Chinese, especially the rich.[13]

Chinese diplomats overseas were used to suppress anti-dynastic elements in the Overseas Chinese communities, but they had many constraints. They did not have the extra-territorial rights in foreign lands that the foreign diplomats had in China, nor could they apprehend any anti-dynastic ringleaders directly. They had to work through a complex and time-consuming extradition procedure before any rebels could be apprehended and duly punished. The kidnapping of Dr Sun Yat-sen in London by the Chinese embassy staff in 1896 created a diplomatic embarrassment for the Ch'ing government, and aroused the suspicion and vigilance of the British Government concerning the activities of Chinese diplomats in its colonies.[14] Further, diplomats and emissaries could not build up a sustainable support among overseas subjects. Long-term influence could only be acquired through influential local organisations, which could mobilise substantial support when needed. In search of a mechanism for the control of the Overseas Chinese, the Ch'ing government found that

12. See for instance, the mission of Yang Shih-chi in 1908 met with scathing attacks from the local revolutionary newspaper, the *Chong Shing Yit Pao*. See *Chong Shing Yit Pao*, 9 January 1908, p. 2 and 10 January 1908, p. 2; Yen Ching-hwang, *The Overseas Chinese and the 1911 Revolution*, p. 103.
13. See 'Memorial of Yang Shih-chi to the Court of the 2nd moon of 34th year of Kuang-hsu (March 1908)', in *Kuang-hsu chao tung-hua lu*, vol. 5, pp. 23–6; the same memorial also found in *Cheng-chih kuan-pao*, vol. 6, pp. 26–9.
14. For a detailed reconstruction of the kidnapping of Sun and its impact, see J.Y. Wong, *The Origins of An Heroic Image: Sun Yat-sen in London, 1896–1897* (Hong Kong, Oxford University Press, 1986). For Sun Yat-sen's own account of this episode, see 'Lun-tun pei-nan chi' (My Kidnapping in London) in *Sun Chung-shan chuan-chi* (The Complete Works of Dr Sun Yat-sen) vol. 1 (Beijing, Chung-hua shu-chi, 1981), pp. 49–86.

institutions such as the Chinese chambers of commerce were most suitable for that purpose.

Despite its foreign origins, the chamber of commerce as an institution grew rapidly in China at the turn of the present century. Some 800 organisations under the name chamber of commerce spread throughout China in the last decade of the Ching rule testified to its dramatic growth.[15] Far-sighted Chinese diplomat–reformers at the end of the nineteenth century saw that much of the strength of Western powers rested with trade and the activities of merchants. This prompted some of them to suggest boldly that merchants should rank top among the four classes of commoners in Chinese society, a radical proposal which would lift the lowly merchant social status above that of the scholars.[16] In the eyes of Chinese mercantilists like Hsieh Fu-cheng, the enormous strength and energy of Chinese merchants could be tapped for a national purpose if they were organised into an institution like the chamber of commerce.

This belated discovery of merchants' strength was put into practice when the Ministry of Commerce was founded in 1903.[17]

15. See Wellington K.K. Chan, *Merchants, Mandarins and Modern Enterprise in Late Ch'ing China* (Cambridge, Massachusetts, Harvard University Press, 1977), p. 213.

16. This view was expressed by Hsieh Fu-cheng, a well-known diplomat reformer who was the Chinese minister to Britain, France, Italy and Belgium. He expressed this view in his writings in 1890. See Hsieh Fu-cheng, Ying-chi-li yung shang-wu pi-fang ti shuo (British use of merchants for developing undeveloped lands) in Ting Feng-lin and Wang Hsin-chih (eds), *Hsieh Fu-ch'eng hsuan-chi* (Selected Works of Hsieh Fu-ch'eng) (Shanghai, Jen-min ch'u-pan she, 1987), p. 297. For an analysis of Hsieh's view, see Hu Chi-ch'uang, *Chung kuo chin-tai ching-chi ssu-hsiang shih ta-kang* (Outlines of History of Economic Thoughts of Modern China) (Beijing, Chung-kuo she-hui k'o-hsueh ch'u-pan she, 1984), pp. 121–23; Ma Po-huang (ed), *Chung-kuo chin-tai ching-chi ssu-hsiang shih* (A History of Modern Chinese Economic Thought), vol. 1 (Shanghai, Shang-hai She-hui k'o-hsueh yuan ch'u-pan she, 1988), pp. 239–42.

17. For the circumstances leading to the founding of the Ministry of Commerce, see Wellington K.K. Chan, *Merchants, Mandarins and Modern Enterprise in Late Ch'ing China*, pp. 161–65.

As the instrument to rejuvenate the faltering Ch'ing empire, the Ministry had a mammoth task, and it rested much hope on the proposed chambers of commerce to provide a focal point for commercial and industrial activities, and for the expansion of China's foreign trade.[18]

The Ministry drafted rules and regulations governing the procedures of establishment, functions and power of the proposed chambers, the power and duties of the leaders, and the chambers' relationship with the Ministry. The rules consisted of twenty-six articles and six supplementary articles, which were submitted for approval by the Court.[19] The Court's prompt endorsement enabled the Ministry to move speedily to found main chambers of commerce in major cities and minor ones in regional commercial centres. The first to appear were the Shanghai Chinese Chamber of Commerce and the Canton Chinese Chamber of Commerce, in 1904 and 1905 respectively.[20] The founding of these two Chambers set in motion the establishment of chambers of commerce throughout China and the Overseas Chinese communities.

The chamber was designed not only as a means of acquiring new national strength, but also as an instrument for the control of the emerging merchant class. The desire to control this class by the Ministry of Commerce was clearly reflected in the contents of

18. See Shang-pu chou ch'ien-pan shang-hui cheoh yi chien-ming chang-ch'eng ch'i (Memorial from the Ministry of Commerce to the Court relating to the founding of chambers of commerce and the proposed rules and regulations) in *Ta Ch'ing kuang-hsu hsin fa-ling* (New Statutes of the Great Ch'ing Empire during the Kuang-hsu Reign), vol. 16 (Shanghai, n.d.), pp. 30a–31.

19. Ibid., pp. 31–35.

20. For details of the founding of the Shanghai Chinese Chamber of Commerce in May 1904, see Hsu Ting-hsin and Ch'ien Hsiao-ming, *Shang-hai tsung shang-hui shih, 1902–1929* (A History of the Shanghai Chinese Chamber of Commerce, 1902–1929) (Shanghai, Shang-hai she-hui k'o-hsueh-yuan ch'u-pan she, 1991), pp. 58–9. For the founding of the Canton Chinese Chamber of Commerce, see Wellington K.K. Chan, *Merchants, Mandarins and Modern Enterprise in Late Ching China*, pp. 220–21; Edward J.M. Rhoads, Merchant Associations in Canton, 1895–1911, in Mark Elvin and G.W. Skinner (eds), *The Chinese City between Two Worlds* (Stanford, Stanford University Press, 1974), pp. 105–08.

314 • The Ethnic Chinese in East and Southeast Asia:
Business, Culture and Politics

its drafted rules and regulations. The rules required Chinese merchants and traders to register with the chamber in their own locality, and they were to be registered in accordance with their respective trade.[21] They were also required to register official documents with the chamber, including commercial contracts, mortgage documents, and land and property titles. All of these registered documents were to be stamped by the chamber for official recognition.[22] The legalisation of documents gave the chamber additional authority over the members, and it was further conferred judicial power in settling commercial disputes among members.[23]

The key to control of the chamber rested with the control of the leadership by the Ministry. Although the rules and regulations empowered the rank and file members to elect directors (*shang-tung*), the top officers of the chamber, the president (*tsung-li*) and the vice president (*hsieh-li*) were actually appointed.[24] The rules required the president to submit an annual report, and to report directly to the Ministry on important matters relating to commerce.[25] He was also entrusted with protecting the merchants, and was to act on their behalf in dealing with local officials; he had direct access to the Ministry when necessary.[26] In short, the Ministry saw the president of the chamber as a government appointee carrying out its new policies, and reflecting the opinions of the merchants from below. He was to be protector of merchants and an informant for the Ministry at the same time. In this context, the chamber of commerce as an institution was to be used as an effective mechanism both as a sounding board and as a control mechanism.

---

21 See article 18 of the rules and regulations, Shang-pu chou ting shang-hui chien-ming chang-ch'eng, 24th day of 11th moon of 29th year of Kuang-hsu (11th January, 1904), in *Ta Ch'ing kuang-hsu hsin fa-ling*, vol. 16, p. 33.
22. See article 19 of the rules and regulations, ibid.
23. See article 15 of the rules and regulations, ibid., p. 33.
24. See article 3 of the rules and regulations, ibid., p. 31a.
25. See article 8 of the rules and regulations, ibid., p. 32.
26. See article 7 of the rules and regulations, ibid.

Chang Pi-shih and the Founding of the Singapore Chinese Chamber of Commerce

The Ministry of Commerce was also aware of the importance of the Overseas Chinese merchants and their potential role in Chinas economic modernisation. In its drafted rules and regulations, the Ministry stated clearly that chambers of commerce would be established in the major Chinese communities in Southeast Asia, Japan and the United States after they had been widely founded and consolidated in China.[27] But there were no details relating to the power and functions of the proposed overseas chambers and the ways that these chambers should be established. This rather broad statement perhaps only indicates the interest of the Ministry in organising Overseas Chinese merchants into the new institution in the way their counterparts did in China.

The Ministry must have been aware, however, that overseas conditions were different from those in China. Firstly, the Overseas Chinese communities were not under the jurisdiction of the Ch'ing government, and the Ministry did not have direct authority over the Overseas Chinese. Secondly, Overseas Chinese merchants differed in their outlook and temperament from their counterparts in China, and they could not be easily coerced into forming the proposed new institution. They therefore needed someone who understood them and commanded their respect and trust to persuade them to organise into chambers of commerce. It was probably due to this consideration that Chang Pi-shih was chosen by the Ch'ing government for the founding of overseas chambers in Southeast Asia.

Chang Pi-shih's direct contribution to the founding of the Singapore Chinese Chamber of Commerce, the first of its kind in the Overseas Chinese communities worldwide, is well recognised. The official records of the Singapore Chinese Chamber of Commerce state as follows:

> Last winter (1905), *T'ai-p'u* Chang Pi-shih was instructed by the Court to investigate commercial affairs in South-east Asia. He and *Ch'ao-chang* Shih Chu-ching arrived in Singapore, and

---

27.   See article 25 of the rules and regulations, ibid.

used the Thong Chai Medical Institution as his temporary office. He gathered together respectable merchants of both Fukien and Kwangtung origins at the Institution. In his speech, he persuaded them to found a chamber of commerce for the purpose of unity of the entire Chinese community and the promotion of commercial affairs. He donated a sum of $3,000 to set an example for the merchants to follow. Those who attended the meeting were much encouraged by his words and prepared to support the proposed chamber of commerce. From the 22nd day of 11th moon of last winter (18 December 1905) till the 29th day of 1st moon of this spring (22 February 1906), six meetings had been called to draft the constitution for the proposed chamber which consisted of 12 sections ... At the same time, several name books had been distributed to the founding members of various *Pang* (dialect group) who were responsible to recruit members among shop proprietors of their respective *Pang*. More than 600 shop proprietors had signed their names and joined the proposed chamber. On the 22nd day of 2nd moon (16 March 1906), members of various *Pangs* of Fukien and Kwangtung origins gathered to elect Goh Siew Tin and Tan Hun Chiu as Presidents (*Tsungli*), Lim Boon Keng and nine others as Executives (*Hsiehli*), Teo Sian Keng and 39 others as Committee members (*I-yuan*).[28]

What can be derived from this important record about the founding of the Singapore Chinese Chamber of Commerce is as follows. First, Chang Pi-shih was the driving force behind the founding of the Chamber. He personally called the first meeting and donated $3,000 to set the whole thing in motion. Second, with Chang's efforts and solid support from Chinese merchants of various dialect groups, the Singapore Chinese Chamber of Commerce came into existence without problems. Third, the founding date of the Singapore Chinese Chamber of Commerce was on 16 March 1906

28. See Hsin-chia-po Chung-hua shang-wu tsung-hui i-shih pu (Minutes of Committee Meetings of the Singapore Chinese Chamber of Commerce) (manuscript) vol. 1, 1906–1909, pp. 1–2.
29. Ibid., p. 3.

in the solar calendar (the twenty-second day of the second moon of the Ping Wu year in the lunar calendar).

It is important to point out that the commonly accepted date of 15 March 1906 as the founding date of the Singapore Chinese Chamber of Commerce is a historical error. This is based on the wrong event and the wrong calendar. In the original minutes of the Chamber, the fifteenth day of the third moon was the date that the Chambers office started to operate temporarily at the Thong Chai Medical Institution.[29] This fifteenth day of the third moon of Ping Wu year was based on the lunar calendar, because the lunar calendar was adopted for recording Chamber events during the Ch'ing period. After the founding of the Republic in 1912, the solar calendar was slowly phased in. Later, the date of 15 March in the solar calendar was confused with the fifteenth day of the third moon in the lunar calendar.[30] In fact, the fifteenth day of the third moon, on which the Chambers temporary office started to operate at the Thong Chai Medical Institution, was not of great significance. However, the general meeting of Chinese merchants held on the twenty-second day of the second moon of the Ping Wu year in the lunar calendar (16 March 1906), at which the office bearers of the Chamber were elected, should be regarded as the founding date of the organisation.[31]

At the time when Chang Pi-shih took the initiative in helping to found the Singapore Chinese Chamber of Commerce at the end of 1905, he had already been recruited into the Ch'ing bureaucracy for more than a decade. Since his recruitment as the Chinese Vice

30. See Hsing-chia-po Chung-hua tsung shang-hui shih-chi (Historical Records of the Singapore Chinese Chamber of Commerce) and Yeoh Chan Boon (Yang Chan-wen) recorded by Liu Tien-feng, 'Chung-hua tsung shang-hui chang-shang shih' (The Vicissitude of the Singapore Chinese Chamber of Commerce) in *Hsin-chia-po Chung-hua tsung shang-hui ta-sha lo-cheng chi-nien kan* (Souvenir of the Opening Ceremony of the Newly Completed Singapore Chinese Chamber of Commerce Building) (Singapore, 1964), pp. 145, 150.

31. See Hsin-chia-po chung-hua shang-wu tsung-hui i-shih pu (manuscript) vol. 1, 1906–1909, p. 2.

Consul for Penang in March 1893,[32] he was a rising star in Ch'ing officialdom and a credible expert on China's economic modernisation. He had often been consulted by top Ch'ing officers like Li Hung-chang and Sheng Hsuan-huai on matters relating to mining, banking and railway construction.[33] His ascent of the Ch'ing official ladder achieved a filip in June 1903 when he was granted an imperial audience by the Empress Dowager Tz'u-hsi, who consulted him on the strategy of overall economic development for the empire.[34] He was immediately granted Third Rank Expectant Director of the Court of Sacrificial Worship (*San-pin ching-tang hou-pu*) with the additional honour of the title of vice president of a board (*shih-lang hsien*).[35]

In the following month (July 1903), Chang presented an important memorial to the Court outlining a twelve-point proposal for the overall

32. Chang was appointed by the Chinese minister (ambassador) for Britain, France, Italy and Belgium, Hsueh Fu-cheng, to that position. See Hsueh Fu-cheng, 'Despatch to the Tsungli Yamen relating to the appointment of the Vice Consul in Penang dated 20th day of 1st moon of 19th year of Kuang-hsu (8 March 1893)', in Hsueh Fu-cheng, *Chu-shih Kung-tu, tsou-shu* (Correspondence of My Diplomatic Mission to England, and my Memorials to the Court) vol. 2 (Taipei, n.d.) tzu-wen, pp. 25a–25b. For the circumstances leading to the setting up of the Chinese Vice Consulate in Penang, see Yen Ching-hwang, *Coolies and Mandarins: China's Protection of Overseas Chinese during the Late Ch'ing Period* (1851–1911), pp. 168–71.
33. See Michael Godley, *The Mandarin-capitalists from Nanyang: Overseas Chinese Enterprise in the Modernization of China 1893–1911* (Cambridge, Cambridge University Press, 1981), pp. 84–90.
34. See Ta Ching te-tsung ching-huang-ti shih-lu, vol. 516, p. 5b; Michael Godley, op. cit., p. 93.
35. Quoting reports from two Chinese newspapers in Singapore and Penang, Michael Godley claims that Chang Pi-shih was named a vice president of the Board of Trade (Ministry of Commerce). This claim is not supported in the Ch'ing official records; Chang does not seem to have held this position. Perhaps Chang's entitlement to hold the title of vice president of a Board was confused by the two local Chinese newspapers, or he was addressed as vice president out of respect. See Michael Godley, op. cit., p. 92; *Ta Ch'ing te-tsung ching-huang-ti shih-lu*, vol. 516, p. 5b.

modernisation of China, emphasising the importance of trade to the nation.[36] Chang's memorial was taken seriously by the Court, which had instructed two high-ranking officials to dwell on it and make suitable recommendations — the result of which was the establishment of a Ministry of Commerce.[37] Chang's emergence as a foremost expert on China economic modernisation pushed his political career to its peak in October 1904, when he was appointed Imperial Commissioner for Investigating Commercial Affairs in Foreign Countries, as well as the Superintendent of Agriculture, Industry, Railways and Mining of Fukien and Kwangtung.[38] It was probably the second time that an Overseas Chinese subject was appointed to such a high position in the imperial bureaucracy and loaded with so many honours.[39]

Throughout most of the year of 1905, the main focus of Chang Pi-shih's official activity was in South China, not in the Overseas Chinese communities. This was perhaps because the coordination of South China's economic activities required more urgent attention and, after all, the region was the homeland that the majority of the Overseas Chinese came from, and any success in the region would automatically attract Overseas Chinese merchants to invest in their home provinces. This was why in early 1905 he set up the Canton headquarters of his Bureau of Agriculture, Industry, Railways and Mining of Fukien and Kwangtung.[40] He was busily occupied with gaining support of local Chinese merchants for the new economic tasks the Court had

36. For a thorough analysis of this memorial and its contents, see Michael Godley, op. cit., pp. 97-114; for indirect reference to this memorial, see *Ta Ch'ing te-tsung ching-huang-ti shih-lu*, vol. 517, pp. 6b, 7a.

37. See *Ta Ch'ing te-tsung ching-huang-ti shih-lu*, p. 7a.

38. Ibid., vol. 535, p. 6b.

39. Another prominent Overseas Chinese from Hong Kong, Wu T'ing-fang, was appointed to a high position in the Ching bureaucracy before Chang. For Wu T'ing-fangs career, see Linda P. Shin, China in Transition: The Role of Wu T'ing-fang, 1842–1922 (unpublished PhD dissertation, University of California, Los Angeles, 1970); for his diplomatic career and protection of the American Chinese, see Yen Ching-hwang, Wu Ting-fang and the Protection of the Overseas Chinese in the United States, 1897–1903, Working Paper no. 12, Centre for Asian Studies, University of Adelaide, 1981.

40. See Michael Godley, op. cit., pp. 115–16.

undertaken. He was also actively involved in organising the merchants in Kwangtung into the proposed Chinese Chamber of Commerce, and in undertaking an ambitious project to build a railway linking Canton with Amoy to facilitate the economic activities of both the Kwangtung and Fukien provinces.[41]

Although Chang Pi-shih's main bureaucratic activity centred in South China throughout most of 1905, he did not lose sight of his responsibility to entice Overseas Chinese merchants to invest in China. When he set up the Canton Bureau in the early part of 1905, he had made clear his intention to protect returned Overseas Chinese merchants in a proclamation which was widely publicised in the Overseas Chinese communities.[42] Having achieved initial success in his work in South China, the time was ripe for him to launch a drive for Overseas Chinese capital. When he set sail for Southeast Asia at the end of 1905, his main objective was to get Southeast Asian Chinese merchants into Chinese chambers of commerce. The chamber as an institution under Ch'ing influence could serve not only as a focal point for tapping Overseas Chinese capital, but also as a stronghold for pro-dynastic influence. Further, his network of contacts in the Overseas Chinese communities must have made him aware of the growing revolutionary and reformist influences in Southeast Asia, especially in Singapore and Malaya.[43] Accompanied by Shih Chu-ching, an officer of the Ministry of Commerce, Chang arrived in Southeast Asia in early December 1905 to carry out the task. He began in Penang, his home base and the town in which his friends and supporters lived and were readily to give him their support. He found the atmosphere in Penang conducive for the founding of a chamber of commerce. Before his arrival in the port the local Chinese merchants had, under the leadership of Lim Kiek Chuan, already organised a commercial organisation similar to the proposed chamber of commerce with the name of Pin-lang-yu shang-wu chu (The Penang Chinese Commercial Association) in September 1903. It was set up

41. Ibid., pp. 116-17, 157.
42. See *Lat Pau*, Singapore, 3 March 1905, and the *Penang Sin Pao*, 11 March 1905.
43. See Yen Ching-hwang, *Overseas Chinese and the 1911 Revolution*, pp. 60–5.

for the promotion of commerce, and it had the solid support of local Chinese merchants of both Fukien and Kwangtung origin.[44] A meeting was arranged for Chang Pi-shih and his aide to speak to the members of the Penang Chinese Commercial Association. Chang praised the leaders of the Association for their foresight, preached unity and solidarity among the Chinese in Penang, and appealed for support by urging them to convert the name of the Association to the Penang Chinese Chamber of Commerce (Pin-lang-yu Chung-hua shang-wu tsung-hui) in line with the rules and regulations set out by the Ministry of Commerce.[45] Even with his new credentials as the Imperial Commissioner, Chang found that it was not an easy task to organise a Chinese chamber of commerce promptly on the island. There was no quick result from the meeting, probably due to the ambivalent political stance of the leadership of the Association.[46] However, Chang's plea to the Penang Chinese merchants probably helped to clear the way for the conversion of the Penang Chinese Commercial Association into the Penang Chinese Chamber of Commerce in January 1907.[47]

44. See *Penang Sin Pao*, 6 December 1905. For the founding of the Penang Chinese Commercial Association, see Cheng Yung-mei, 'Pin-chou Chung-hua tsung-shang-hui chan-ch'ien shih-liao' (Historical records of the Penang Chinese Chamber of Commerce before the Second World War) in Liu Wen-chi et. al. (eds), *Pin-chou Chung-hua tsung-shang-hui tsuan-hsi chi-nien t'e-k'an, 1903–1978* (Souvenir Magazine of Diamond Jubilee Celebration of the Penang Chinese Chamber of Commerce) (Penang, 1978), p. 77.

45. See *Penang Sin Pao*, 6 December 1905.

46. Most leaders of the Association were Straits-born and English-educated. Their political allegiance tended to be directed towards Britain. In addition, some leaders of the Association like Ng Kim Keng were clearly pro-revolutionary. For details, see Cheng Yung-mei, 'Historical records of the Penang Chinese Chamber of Commerce before the Second World War', in Liu Wen-chi et. al. (eds), op. cit., pp. 78–79; Yen Ching-hwang, *The Overseas Chinese and the 1911 Revolution*, pp. 99, 229.

47. The official conversion probably took place in January 1907, and it was officially recognised by the Ch'ing Government in February 1907. See the memorial of the Shang Pu (Ministry of Commerce) to the Court, dated 19th Day of 12th moon of 32nd year of Kuang-hsu (1 February

Chang Pi-shih was undoubtedly disappointed with the result, but this setback did not deter him from executing his overall plan to organise Southeast Asian Chinese merchants into the proposed new institution. A few days after his abortive attempt in Penang, he left for Singapore to organise a chamber of commerce there. He had more success in Singapore than he had expected. A number of factors made the Singapore Chinese merchants more attuned to the Ch'ing government's proposal than their counterparts in Penang. These were the greater need in Singapore for a Chinese commercial organisation, the presence of more Chinese-educated and China-oriented leading merchants, a stronger sense of cultural and traditional Chinese identity, and the quest of some Teochew wealthy merchants for leadership status outside the Teochew community.

The need for a Chinese chamber of commerce to provide a focal point for Chinese merchants in Singapore was obvious. With the growth of entrepot and international trade in Singapore, particularly after the opening of the Suez Canal in 1869,[48] Chinese merchants found themselves handicapped by the lack of a commercial organisation which could safeguard their interests. A serious attempt to found a Chinese chamber of commerce (*Hua-shang kung-so*) was made in February 1896 under the leadership of Seah Liang Seah and Lee Cheng Yan, as a result of debates on the amendments to business bankruptcy legislation which would greatly affect Chinese business community. However the effort failed for unknown reasons,[49] and there had been no further attempts to found a Chinese chamber of commerce for almost a decade until Chang Pi-shih's initiative at the end of 1905.

In contrast with the leadership of the Penang Chinese Commercial Association, most leaders of the Chinese Chamber of

1907) in *Shang-wu kuan-pao* (The Gazettes of Commercial Affairs) original,1906–1910, vol. 1 (Peking, Ministry of Commerce, Ting-wei year [1907]), pp. 9–10.

48.   See Wong Lin Ken, 'Singapore: Its Growth as an Entrepot Port, 1819–1941', in *Journal of Southeast Asian Studies*, vol. 9, no. 1 (March 1978), pp. 56–69.

49.   See C.F. Yong, 'Rivalry between the New and Old Chinese Chambers of Commerce: Contending Elites and Power Struggle within the Chinese Community of Singapore, 1912–1914', in C.F. Yong, *Chinese Leadership and Power in Colonial Singapore* (Singapore, Times Academic Press, 1992), p. 26.

Commerce in Singapore were born in China and had received some form of traditional Chinese education.[50] These factors helped to mould their China orientation. Chinese birth gave them an emotional attachment to their birthplace in China. The scenery and people of the village, district and province from which they came from invariably stirred their imaginations and invoked nostalgia. Traditional Chinese education further strengthened their China orientation. The Confucian values and systems of which they had some experience in Chinese villages helped mould their cultural loyalty towards China rather than to Britain. Further, being discriminated against and sometimes denied leadership status by the British colonial authorities in Singapore naturally led them to look to China for informal political power.[51] Some of these leaders were extremely wealthy and were leading merchants in Singapore. Chua Tse Yung, a Teochew, was a leading merchant in sugar, rice and silk imports, and his business empire spanned from Singapore to coastal China. It was claimed that his annual business turnover reached six million dollars, and his four rice mills in Thailand produced annually more than ten million dollars worth of rice for export, half of which went to Singapore and Hong Kong.[52] Goh Siew-tin, a Hokkien, was another leading merchant in Singapore. He inherited a large fortune and business from his father in 1892, and became a leading trader and shipowner, going on to

50. For a list of early leaders of the Singapore Chinese Chamber of Commerce, see Minutes of Committee Meetings of the Singapore Chinese Chamber of Commerce (manuscript) vol. 1, 1906–1909, pp. 2–3; for an analysis of the leadership of the Chamber, see Yong Ching Fatt, A Preliminary Study of Chinese Leadership in Singapore, 1900–1941, *in Journal of Southeast Asian History*, vol. 9, no. 2 (September 1968), pp. 271–75 (the same article is also published in C.F. Yong, *Chinese Leadership and Power in Colonial Singapore*, pp. 47–81).
51. For British attitudes towards Chinese Community leaders in Singapore, see C.F. Yong, *Chinese Leadership and Power in Colonial Singapore*, pp. 291–92.
52. See A. Wright & H.A. Cartwright (eds), *Twentieth Century Impressions of British Malaya* (London, 1908), p. 715; 'Tsai Tzu-yung hsien-sheng' (Mr Chua Tse Yung) in Pan Hsing-nung (ed), *Ma-lai-ya Ch'ao-ch'iao t'ung-chien* (The Teochews in Malaya) (Singapore, Nan-tao ch'u-pan-she, 1950), p. 195.

become an important leader of the Fukienese community in Singapore.[53]

Singapore emerged at the end of the nineteenth and the beginning of the twentieth centuries as the bastion of Chinese culture. The Lo Shan She Lecture movement, which was intended to reassert traditional Chinese values in the Overseas Chinese communities, was launched in Singapore in 1881. Meanwhile, the Confucian Revival Movement, a larger-scale traditional Chinese cultural movement, was centred in Singapore at the end of the nineteenth and beginning of the twentieth centuries.[54] The convergence of these movements in Singapore placed the island in the spotlight of the Chinese cultural revival in Southeast Asia. The movements revigorated traditional Chinese values and customs, rekindling a strong sense of Chinese identity. This led to a wave of China orientation and moved Chinese merchants closer to the Ch'ing Government.

Chang Pi-shih's initiative to establish a Chinese chamber of commerce in Singapore at the end of 1905 also came at an opportune time. The Teochew community, the second largest dialect group in the Chinese community in Singapore, showed ominous signs of a split at the turn of the twentieth century. Frustrated by the prolonged monopoly of the Teochew community's social power by the Seah family, a group of wealthy and powerful merchants emerged to challenge Seah's hegemony. This group was led by Chua Tse Yung, Tan Hun Chiu and

---

53. For a short biography of Goh Siew-tin, see 'Wu Shou-chen hsien-sheng' (Mr Goh Siew-tin) in Su Hsiao-hsien (ed), *Chang-chou shih-shu lu Hsing tung-hsiang lu* (A Directory of Chang Chou Chinese in Singapore) (Singapore, Ch'iao-kuang chu-pan-she, 1948), p. 59; Yen Ching-hwang, *The Overseas Chinese and the 1911 Revolution*, pp. 273–74; Song Ong Siang, *One Hundred Years History of the Chinese in Singapore* (Singapore, University of Malaya Press, 1967), p. 144.

54. For details about the Lo Shan She Lecture movement, see Yen Ching-hwang, 'Overseas Chinese Nationalism in Singapore and Malaya, 1877–1912', in *Modern Asian Studies*, vol. 16, no. 3 (July 1982), pp. 399–405. For details of the Confucian Revival movement, see Yen Ching-hwang, 'The Confucian Revival Movement in Singapore and Malaya, 1899–1911', in *Journal of Southeast Asian Studies*, vol. 7, no. 1 (March 1976), pp. 33–57.

Liao Cheng-hsing.[55] The entrenched position of the Seah family in the Ngee Ann Kongsi, the key social institution in the Teochew community, blocked the social advancement of the group. This was why members of the group were anxious to seek recognition of leadership status outside the Teochew community.[56] Thus, the proposed founding of a Chinese Chamber of Commerce as a key organisation for the entire Chinese community in Singapore appealed to them. In fact, the key leaders of this Teochew group, Chua Tse Yung, Tan Hun Chiu and Liao Cheng-hsing became founders and important leaders of the Singapore Chinese Chamber of Commerce.[57]

With such favourable conditions for the founding of a chamber of commerce in Singapore, Chang Pi-shih also adopted a successful strategy: recruiting a couple of key merchant leaders in order to produce a chain reaction. Before he left Penang for Singapore, Chang had probably contacted Goh Siew-tin, an old friend and the man who had been close to the Ch'ing bureaucracy, to pave the way.[58] Goh was also

55. For a study of this group, see Yen Ching-hwang, *A Social History of the Chinese in Singapore and Malaya, 1800–1911* (Singapore, Oxford University Press, 1986), pp. 189–90.
56. For a discussion of the power relations in the Teochew community in Singapore at this time, see Yen Ching-hwang, 'Power Structure and Power Relations in the Teochew Community in Singapore, 1819–1930' (A paper presented at the International Conference on Teochew Studies, held at the Chinese University of Hong Kong, 20–22 December 1993, pp. 28–9).
57. See Minutes of Committee Meetings of the Singapore Chinese Chamber of Commerce (manuscript) vol. 1, 1906–1909, pp. 2–3.
58. Goh Siew-tin acquired a Ch'ing brevet title, *Chih-fu*, in 1902. In the same year, he was appointed Acting Chinese Consul-General for the Straits settlements from January to May. See Yen Ching-hwang (transl. Chang Ching-chiang), 'Ch'ing-ch'ao tsu-kuan chih-tu yu Hsin-Ma hua-tsu ling-tao-ch'en, 1877–1912, (Ch'ing Sale of Honours and the Chinese Leadership in Singapore and Malaya 1877–1912), appendix 1, in Ko Mu-lin & Wu Chen-chiang (Ng Chin Keong) (eds), *Hsin-chia-po hua-tsu shih lun-chi* (Papers on the Chinese in Singapore) p. 71. The article also published in Yen Ching-hwang, *Hai-wai hua-jen shih yen-chiu* (Studies in Overseas Chinese History) (Singapore, Singapore Society of Asian Studies, 1992), pp. 3–43. See also *Thien Nan Shin Pao*, 22 January 1902, pp. 1–2; 1 May 1902, p. 2; 2 May 1902, p. 7; 4 June 1902, p. 1.

an acknowledged leader of the local Fukien community. Chang might also have contacted Chua Tse Yung, a wealthy Teochew merchant who commanded considerable influence and respect among Teochew merchants, through whom he also influenced the attitudes of the bulk of Chinese merchants in Singapore. Chang Pi-shih's initiative to found a Chinese chamber of commerce was, therefore, taken by many Chinese merchants in Singapore as an official endorsement by the Ch'ing government. This endorsement was much needed in a society where political power was very highly respected. Many Chinese merchants were enthusiastic and prepared to lend support to Chang's proposal. More than six hundred shop proprietors and individuals signed up to join the proposed institution on the first instance.[59]

In retrospect, Chang Pi-shih's push for the founding of the Singapore Chinese Chamber of Commerce was crucial, and the establishment of the Chamber would have been delayed without Chang's initiative. Being the first Chinese chamber of commerce to be linked officially with the Ch'ing government, the Singapore Chinese Chamber of Commerce had the advantage of consolidating its position and setting an example for other Overseas Chinese chambers of commerce to follow in the Southeast Asian region.

The Role of the Ch'ing Government

The Ch'ing government's initial act of support for the Singapore Chinese Chamber of Commerce was to legitimise it as the leading organisation for the entire Chinese community. This wish was carried out by its Consul-General in Singapore. At the time the Chamber came into existence, the Chinese Consul-General was Sun Shih-ting, a career diplomat. Sun left little mark on the diplomatic history of Ch'ing China. He cannot be compared with his colourful predecessors such as Tso Ping-lung and Huang Tsun-hsien, who proved to be able diplomats as well as Confucian scholars.[60] However, Sun must have been acquainted

---

59. See Minutes of Committee Meetings of the Singapore Chinese Chamber of Commerce (manuscript) vol. 1, 1906–1909, p. 1.
60. See Tan Yeok Seong, 'Tso Tzu-hsing (Tso Ping-lung) ling-shih tui Hsin-chia-po hua-ch'iao te kung-hsien (The Contribution of Consul Tso Ping-lung to

with the work of both these men, who had been trying to arouse national consciousness and to cultivate loyalty among the Overseas Chinese.[61] Part of Sun's task was to continue Huang's and Tso's work to ensure Overseas Chinese loyalty to the dynasty. As a new commercial and social organisation, the Chamber had great potential to be developed into a very powerful body representing the entire Chinese community on the island.

To legitimise the status of the Chamber, Sun was quick to identify issues which could be used to enhance its prestige and authority. Issues which affected the general interests of the Chinese community would give the Chamber credibility as the spokesman for the entire community. Soon after its inception, Consul-General Sun wrote to the Chamber and urged it to participate in negotiations with the British colonial authority in Singapore over a controversial issue concerning the physical inspection of Chinese immigrants at the quarantine station of the port.[62] The Chamber seized this opportunity, and after an intensive discussion it agreed to participate in negotiations with the British authority.[63] The actual role of the Chamber in acquiring a satisfactory settlement on the issue is not fully known, but the Chamber was quick to claim credit by issuing a public notice on 20 June 1906, less than two months after it had fully discussed the issue. The notice drew the attention of the Chinese community to the fact that some members of the Chamber, who were concurrently members of the Po Leung Kuk, had been informed by the government that it

the Overseas Chinese in Singapore) in Tso Ping-lung, *Ch'in-mien-t'ang shih-ch'ao* (The Collection of Poems from the Chin-mien Hall) (Hong Kong, 1959), pp. 3–4; Chen Mong Hock, *The Early Chinese Newspapers of Singapore, 1881–1912* (Singapore, University of Malaya Press, 1967), pp. 115–21; Yen Ching-hwang, *Coolies and Mandarins: China's Protection of Overseas Chinese during the Late Ch'ing Period, 1851–1911*, pp. 253–66; Cheng H'ai-lin, *Huang Tsun-hsien yu chin-tai Chung-kuo* (Huang Tsun-hsien and Modern China) (Beijing, San-lien shu-tien, 1988), pp. 369–76.

61. See Yen Ching-hwang, *A Social History of the Chinese in Singapore and Malaya, 1800–1911*, pp. 288–91.
62. See Minutes of Committee Meetings of the Singapore Chinese Chamber of Commerce (manuscript) vol. 1, 1906–1909, p. 13.
63. Ibid.

had already agreed to reform the process of inspection of Chinese immigrants arriving in Singapore.[64]

The Ch'ing Consul-General consistently buttressed the position of the Chamber in its early stages. For example, the major issue of opium smoking was passed from the Consul-General to the Chamber. An official letter from Sun urged the Chamber to take up responsibility for dealing with the matter on behalf of the entire Chinese community. Although the Chamber decided not to commit itself on the issue, it nevertheless shows the Consul-General's efforts in trying to involve the Chamber in major community issues.[65]

Visits by Ching dignitaries to Singapore provided excellent opportunities for the Consul-General to bolster further the position of the Chamber. In a highly status-conscious Chinese society such as Singapore, these occasions were manipulated for political purposes. Before 1906, the Thong Chai Medical Institution and the residences of some prominent Chinese were selected as temporary offices for visiting dignitaries.[66] Those selected had the honour of being associated with Ch'ing officials, and felt that their status and prestige in the community had been enhanced. In early July 1906, Prince Tsai Tse and Shang Chi-heng stopped over in Singapore on their way home from Europe. Tsai and Shang were members of an important mission sent by the Empress Dowager Tz'u-hsi to investigate Western political systems in preparation for a proposed constitution. The mission left China in December 1905 and visited the United States, Russia, Britain, France, Germany and Italy. Tsai and Shang were in the advance party returning home. The visiting dignitaries arrived in Singapore on a French ship, and were welcomed by the representative of the Governor with an official guard of honour. They were also met by Consul-General Sun together with about

64. See 'Shang-hui pu-kao' (A public notice of the Chinese Chamber of Commerce dated 29th Day of leap 4th moon of 32nd year of Kuang-hsu) in *Lat Pau*, 2 June 1906, p. 1.

65. See Minutes of Committee Meetings of the Singapore Chinese Chamber of Commerce (manuscript) vol. 1, 1906–1909, pp. 19–20.

66. See Chui Kuei-chiang, 'Wan Ch'ing kuan-li fang-wen Hsin-chia-po' (The visits of Ch'ing dignitaries to Singapore during the late Ch'ing period) in Chui Kuei-chiang, *Hsing-Ma shih lun-ts'ung* (Essays on the History of Singapore and Malaysia) (Singapore, South Seas Society, 1977), p. 93.

forty Chinese leaders, and large crowds of Chinese waited at the dock to welcome them.[67] During their stopover in Singapore, the Chinese Chamber of Commerce was chosen by the Consul-General as the temporary office for the visitors. The dragon flag was hoisted and a tea party was arranged at the Chamber.[68] Anticpating the arrival of the two Ch'ing dignitaries, Consul-General Sun had shrewdly decided to use the occasion to boost the image of the Chamber; a letter from Sun suggested using the Chamber as the envoys' temporary office. This proposal was happily accepted by the Chamber.[69] From then onwards, the Chamber replaced the Thong Chai Medical Institution and private residences as the temporary office for visiting Ch'ing dignitaries, including Yang Shih-chi (1907), Prince Tsun (1909) and Chao Chung-fan (1911), until the fall of the dynasty in early 1912.[70]

The strong backing of the Singapore Chinese Chamber of Commerce by the Ching Consul-General was not simply due to personal enthusiasm; it was a part of a well-planned policy of bolstering the Chamber as an all-powerful organisation in the Chinese community. In the battle for political allegiance of the Overseas Chinese in Southeast Asia, the Ch'ing government was shrewd to place Overseas Chinese chambers of commerce under the control of the Ministry of Commerce (after 1907, its name was changed to the Ministry of Agriculture, Industry and Commerce, or *Nung-kung-shang pu*). By linking directly with the Ministry, the status of the overseas chambers had been elevated above the local level. Their leaders were perceived to possess equal status with the Chinese Consul or Consul-General overseas.

In addition to serving as an instrument for the control of the new emerging merchant class in China, the Overseas Chinese

---

67. See *Lat Pau*, 3 and 4 July 1906.
68. See Minutes of Committee Meetings of the Singapore Chinese Chamber of Commerce (manuscript) vol. 1, 1906–1909, p. 25.
69. Ibid., p. 23.
70. See 'Hsing-chia-po Chung-hua tsung-shang-hui shih-chi' (Historical Records of the Singapore Chinese Chamber of Commerce) in *Hsin-chia-po Chung-hua tsung-shang-hui ch'i-shih-wu chou-nien chi-nien t'e-k'an* (Souvenir Magazine of 75th Anniversary Celebration of the Singapore Chinese Chamber of Commerce) (Singapore, 1982), pp. 57–9.

chamber had an additional political role to play: to help the Ch'ing government to control the hearts and minds of ordinary Overseas Chinese. The chamber was not just a modern commercial guild, setting prices and settling business disputes; it had to be all-embracing and even omnipotent. The greater the power of the chamber, the greater influence the Ch'ing government would command in the Overseas Chinese communities. In the contest with the revolutionaries and the reformists for influence in the Chinese community in Singapore, the Singapore Chinese Chamber of Commerce had to be propped up with informal political power from China.

The conferring of an official seal (*kuan-fang*) by the throne met this need. Like other Chinese chambers of commerce in China, the official seal was to be stamped on all official documents of the Chamber, and would carry some weight in dealing with the Chinese authorities in China. The symbolic power of the seal invariably enhanced the power and authority of the Chamber in the eyes of the local Chinese. The arrival of the official seal of the Chamber in Singapore on 14 August 1906 (the twenty-fifth day of the sixth moon of the thirty-second year of the Kuang-hsu reign), about five months after the founding of the Chamber, marked an important event in the history of the Chamber. A solemn ceremony was held on 16 August (the twenty-seventh day of the sixth moon) in the Chamber's building.[71] A participant of this ceremony, Yeoh Chan Boon, recalled that an elegant glass cabinet was erected in the Chambers building facing north, with a big Chinese character *Chueh* (Imperial palace). At 6.30am, all office holders of the Chamber, dressed in full mandarin or traditional Chinese costumes, gathered and performed three kneelings and nine kowtowings to the Emperor for the imperial

---

71. See Minutes of Committee Meetings of the Singapore Chinese Chamber of Commerce (manuscript) vol. 1, 1906–1909, p. 30; 'Hsing-chia-po Chung-hua tsung-shang-hui shih-chi', in *Souvenir of the Opening Ceremony of the Newly Completed Singapore Chinese Chamber of Commerce Building*, p. 150.
72. Yeoh Chan Boon, a junior director of the Chamber, recalled this event fifty years later. Yeoh wrongly put the date of the ceremony as 15 March of 1906, and claimed that this date was therefore taken by the Chamber

grace.[72] The ceremony linked the Chamber with the Ch'ing bureaucracy, the Chamber symbolically became a sub-bureau of the Ministry of Commerce, and the office holders of the Chamber also symbolically became minor officials of the Ch'ing Government. Many leaders of the Chamber must have greatly delighted to have acquired this new social status. Overseas Chinese merchants, like their counterparts in China, had always entertained a strong inferiority complex *vis-à-vis* Chinese mandarins because of their traditionally low social status. Though inflated with new-found wealth and realising the great potential influence of that wealth, Overseas Chinese merchants had a strong desire for Ch'ing official status. Their purchases of Ch'ing brevet titles indicated their enthusiasm for Chinese informal political power and their desire to be close to the Ch'ing bureaucracy.[73]

The Ch'ing government further strengthened the Chamber's authority by granting it the power to issue commercial certificates (*shang-chao*) which was to protect returning Overseas Chinese merchants in China.[74] Probably at the beginning of 1907, the Chamber was empowered to issue the certificate to upright merchant members who would register their certificates with the Chamber's counterparts in the Treaty ports, and through which the returning merchants

---

as its inauguration date. See Yeoh Chan Boon, recorded by Liu Tien-feng, 'Chung-hua tsung-shang-hui ch'ang-shang shih', in *Souvenir of the Opening Ceremony of the Newly Completed Singapore Chinese Chamber of Commerce Building*, pp. 145–46; Minutes of Committee Meetings of the Singapore Chinese Chamber of Commerce, (manuscript) vol. 1, 1906–1909, p. 30.

73. For the Overseas Chinese desire for Ch'ing honours and the impact of the purchase of Ch'ing titles on Overseas Chinese leadership, see Yen Ching-hwang, 'Ch'ing's Sale of Honours and the Chinese Leadership in Singapore and Malaya, 1877–1912', in *Journal of Southeast Asian Studies*, vol. 1, no. 2 (September 1970), pp. 20–32.

74. The granting of this commercial certificate was initiated by the Singapore Chinese Chamber of Commerce. The original idea was to request the right of the Chamber to issue *hu-chao* (visas), but later the name was changed to *shang-chao*. See Minutes of Committee Meetings of the Singapore Chinese Chamber of Commerce (manuscript) vol. 1, 1906–1909, pp. 31, 42.

received protection against extortion or robberies by local bullies or corrupted officials.[75]

The Singapore Chinese Chamber of Commerce did develop close ties with the Ch'ing government in the twilight years of the Manchu rule. It was especially important in the economic arena. The Chamber was instrumental in helping the Ch'ing government to mobilise Overseas Chinese capital in the service of China. It served as an effective channel of communication between the Ch'ing government and the emerging Overseas Chinese merchant class. Overseas Chinese merchants for the first time had direct access to the central government and were able to express their wishes without going through complex diplomatic channels. At the same time, instructions from the Ch'ing government reached the Overseas Chinese merchants in Singapore without unnecessary delays. For instance, the Chamber acted as promoter for the Ch'ing government of the planned industrial and commercial fair to be held in Nanking in 1910. The Chamber actively promoted the scheme in the local daily Chinese newspaper and sent letters to other Chinese chambers of commerce in Southeast Asia for the same purpose.[76]

75. No direct documents relating to the granting of this right to the Singapore Chinese Chamber of Commerce have been found. However, the rules and regulations governing the issue of commercial certificates by the Chinese Chamber of Commerce of Surahbaya, which was based on the Singapore model, can be found in the *Shang-wu kuan-pao*. The request by the Surabaya Chinese Chamber of Commerce was approved by the Ministry of Agriculture, Industry and Commerce on 10 April 1908. See 'Ssu-shui shang-hui fa ke hui Hua shang-chao chang-ch'eng (Rules and Regulations for the issue of Commercial certificate by the Chinese Chamber of Commerce of Surahbaya) in *Shang-wu kuan-pao*, 25th day of 7th moon of 34th year of Kuang-hsu, vol. 19, pp. 37–8, special report section. See also the record of official approval of the Ministry on the 10th day of 3rd moon of 34th year of Kuang-hsu (10 April1908) in *Shang-wu kuan-pao*, 25th day of 3rd moon of 34th year of Kuang-hsu, vol. 7, p. 5.

76. See the advertisement put out by the Chamber dated 1st day of 8th moon of the first year of Hsuan-t'ung (14 September 1909) in *Lat Pau*, 14 September1909, p. 6, and 16 September 1909, p. 13; Minutes of Committee Meetings of the Singapore Chinese Chamber of Commerce (manuscript) vol. 1, 1906-1909, p. 169. For the event and significance of the Nanyang Fair of

The Singapore Chinese Chamber of Commerce also acted frequently as an agent for both private and officially-sponsored companies in China. In August 1906, for instance, the Chamber acted as the agent for the merchant-managed Kiangsu Railway Company, and elected leaders to push for shares among the Chinese in Singapore along dialect lines.[77] In September 1909, the Chamber also acted as an agent to sell stock for the Hupei Rug Company, in an attempt to promote Chinese native produce.[78] But the biggest effort made by the Chamber in the mobilisation of Overseas Chinese capital was to help float shares for the proposed China Commercial Bank (Chung-kuo Hua-shang yin-hang). The idea of founding a commercial bank came from an expectant *taotai* (epistolary designation, Kuan-cha) named Hsu Ching-ming of P'an Yu district, Kwangtung. Hsu, who obviously had close contacts with the Overseas Chinese, came up with the important idea of mobilising Overseas Chinese capital for the founding of a commercial bank, an insurance company and a shipping line. In 1906, Hsu got support from the Ministry of Commerce, which granted him official status to investigate commercial affairs in Southeast Asia for the purpose of promoting industry in China.[79] Hsu visited the major ports in Southeast Asia and gained support from some of the wealthy merchants in the region. He returned to China and further obtained strong support from the Shanghai Chinese Chamber of Commerce for his grand scheme. As the scheme gradually crystallised, Hsu proposed to found the China Commercial Bank first, and drew up rules and regulations for the float of shares

    1910, see Michael Godley, 'China's Worlds Fair of 1910: Lessons from a Forgotten Event', in *Modern Asian Studies*, vol. 12 (1978), pp. 503–22.

77. Twelve leaders were elected from various dialect groups for this purpose. Pushing the sale of shares along dialect lines was the most effective way of doing business at this time. See Minutes of Committee Meetings of the Singapore Chinese Chamber of Commerce (manuscript) vol. 1, 1906–1909, p. 31; Michael Godley, *The Mandarin-capitalists from Nanyang*, p. 127.

78. See Minutes of Committee Meetings of the Singapore Chinese Chamber of Commerce (manuscript) vol. 1, 1906–1909, p. 172.

79. See letter from the Chinese Chamber of Commerce of Shanghai to the Singapore Chinese Chamber of Commerce, published in *Chong Shing Yit Pao* on 2 October 1907, p. 6.

among Overseas Chinese and the Chinese in China. He proposed to float $10 million (in yuan) as capital for the bank, with two million shares of $5 each. The main thrust of his float was the Overseas Chinese from whom he hoped to raise $8 million (1.6 million shares), while the remaining $2 million (0.4 million shares) would come from the merchants in Shanghai.[80] The headquarters of the proposed bank was to be located in Shanghai, and the regional headquarters in Singapore. The bank would also set up branches in Britain, France, Germany, Russia, the United States and Japan and the major ports in Southeast Asia. The foreign branches would be under the control of the Shanghai headquarters, while the Southeast Asian branches would come under the jurisdiction of the Singapore regional headquarters.[81] To initiate the task of raising the capital for the bank, Hsu also nominated some wealthy Overseas Chinese merchants as promotion directors (*ti-chang tung-shih*); and for the British colony of Singapore Goh Siew-tin and Chua Tse Yung, two prominent leaders of the Singapore Chinese Chamber of Commerce, were named.[82]

The Singapore Chinese Chamber of Commerce gave the scheme its strongest support. When Hsu Ching-ming arrived in Singapore in the spring of 1907 from the Philippines, he was met by the leaders of the Chamber and a special meeting was arranged for that purpose. A team for selling shares was elected, and it accompanied Hsu to visit four other major cities in the Malay Peninsula, to which some $2.3 million worth of shares was claimed to have been promised.[83] To further back up the scheme, the Chamber in 1908 elected Dr Lim Boon Keng and Mr Lin Chu-tsai to accompany the two representatives from the Shanghai Chinese Chamber of Commerce

---

80. See Rules and Regulations of the Proposed China Commercial Bank, published in *Chong Shing Yit Pao* on 7 October 1907, p. 6.

81. See Rules and Regulations of the Proposed China Commercial Bank, published in *Chong Shing Yit Pao* on 8 October 1907, p. 6.

82. In addition, Foo Chee Choon of Perak, Loke Yew of Kuala Lumpur and Wong Ah-fook (Huang P'u-t'ien) of Johor Bahru were named to represent British colonies in Southeast Asia. See *Chong Shing Yit Pao*, 5 October 1907, p. 6.

83. See the notice for floating the shares for the proposed bank put out by the Singapore Chinese Chamber of Commerce, in *Chong Shing Yit Pao*, 2 October 1907, p. 6.

to tour other parts of Southeast Asia for the second round of share-selling.[84] At the same time the president of the Chamber, Chua Tse Yung, was elected team leader, to be assisted by other directors of the Chamber, to speed up the selling process in Singapore.[85] By September of 1908, it was claimed that about $4 to 5 million worth of shares was promised from Chinese merchants in Shanghai, Luzon (Philippines), Penang, Kuala Lumpur, Perak and Singapore.[87] The Chamber continued to give the proposed bank strong backing through 1909 and 1910, but for various reasons the proposed bank failed to get off the ground in 1911.[87]

Politically, the Singapore Chinese Chamber of Commerce acted as an ally of the Ch'ing government. It adopted a clear pro-Ch'ing stand and was instrumental in mobilising the support of the community to show political allegiance to the Ch'ing throne. Its political role in supporting the faltering Manchu dynasty was clearly reflected on the occasion of imperial birthdays, visits of Ch'ing dignatories or other extraordinary occasions such as the death of the reigning emperor and the coronation of the new emperor. Handbills were distributed and a public notice calling for the entire Chinese community to observe the occasion was published in local Chinese newspapers. On a significant occasion such as the coronation of the new Emperor Hsuan-tung at the end of 1908, the Chamber instructed all of its members to go to the Chinese Consulate-General building to pay homage to the new monarch. The Chamber also called on Chinese merchants to close shops for trading, and to decorate and hoist dragon flags for the auspicious occasion.[88] On the ninth day of the eleventh

---

84. See Minutes of Committee Meetings of the Chinese Chamber of Commerce (manuscript) vol. 1, 1906–1909, p. 110.
85. Ibid., p. 112.
86. See report on the founding of the proposed Chinese commercial bank, in *Nanyang Tsung-hui Hsin Pao* (*The Union Times*), 24 September 1908, p. 1.
87. See Minutes of Committee Meetings of the Singapore Chinese Chamber of Commerce (manuscript) vol. 1, 1906–1909, pp. 156, 177, vol. 2, 1909–1912, pp. 22, 79.
88. See the public notice of the Singapore Chinese Chamber of Commerce dated 7th day of 11th moon of the 34th year of Kuang-hsu (30 November 1908) in *Lat Pau*, 1 December 1908, p. 8.

moon (2 December 1908), leaders of the Chamber, dressed in mandarin robes or traditional costumes and led by the Ch'ing Consul-General, performed the solemn ceremony of three kneelings and nine kowtowings towards a symbolic throne in the Consul-General's building. Later, various Chinese school students led by their teachers also performed the same homage to the new emperor.[89] On the demise of both Emperor Kuang-hsu and Empress Dowager Tz'u-hsi in November of the same year, the Chamber played a leading role in mobilising the Chinese in Singapore to show sympathy and to mourn the deceased Ch'ing rulers. It had invariably used its influence to mobilise a large number of Chinese to pay their respects and show their loyalty to the Manchu rulers.[90]

In retrospect, the Singapore Chinese Chamber of Commerce did not measure up to the full expectations of the Ch'ing government. It did not become a front organisation of the Ch'ing government, nor did it become actively involved in fighting against the reformists and the revolutionaries. In the growing revolutionary agitation in the Chinese community in Singapore,[91] the Chamber did not seek to curb such agitation or to confront the agitators. At the same time, the fact that the Chamber escaped being a major target for the revolutionary newspapers in Singapore also indicates that it was not considered as a major enemy of the revolutionaries.[92]

What made the Singapore Chinese Chamber of Commerce a pro-Ch'ing institution but not an active anti-revolutionary organisation

89.   See a report of this function in *Lat Pau*, 3 December 1908, p. 3.
90.   See *Lat Pau*, 18 November 1908, p. 8, 20 November 1908, p. 3
91.   See Yen Ching-hwang, *The Overseas Chinese and the 1911 Revolution*, pp. 100–27.
92.   Checking through the *Chong Shing Yit Pao* and *The Sun Pao*, the two main Revolutionary newspapers in Singapore during this period, there were hardly any attacks directly aimed at the Chinese Chamber of Commerce. In fact, the *Chong Shing Yit Pao* on some occasions even published the Chamber's economic involvement in Ch'ing China. For instance, it published the Chamber's public notice for the floating of shares for the proposed China Commercial Bank and its rules and regulations. See *Chong Shing Yit Pao*, 2 October 1907, p. 6, 5 October 1907, p. 6, 7 October 1907, p. 6, 8 October 1907, p. 6.

are perhaps the following factors. Firstly, the death of Goh Siew-tin, a staunch pro-Ch'ing leader in January 1909, deprived the Ch'ing government of a strong supporter within the Chamber.[93] Secondly, although the Chamber was founded by Chang Pi-shih, a high-ranking Ch'ing official, and the Chamber was officially linked with the Ministry of Agriculture, Industry and Commerce, it was essentially an economic and commercial organisation rather than a political organisation. The Chamber was established to promote commerce and industry, and to protect the interests of the Chinese merchant class in Singapore. This perception of the primary role of the Chamber seems to have been shared by the majority of its leaders. Any active participation in the political struggle would have been divisive and destructive for the Chamber. Thirdly, the majority of the leaders of the Chamber probably realised that the long-term interests of the Chamber lay not in China, but in Singapore. Therefore, its activities should be focused on local issues, including economic, social and cultural.[94] Fourthly, most leaders of the Chamber were wealthy merchants, not politicians. Although many of them possessed Ch'ing brevet titles and enjoyed prestige and honour in their relationship with the Ch'ing government, they were not committed politicians, nor did they commit strongly to a political ideology. They were more interested in making money. This led them to take a more ambivalent attitude towards the Ch'ing government politically.

93. Goh Siew-tin died on 25th day of 12th moon of Wu Shen year (16th January 1909), Goh had been the president (*Tsung-li*) of the Chamber since its inception. See Minutes of Committee Meetings of the Chinese Chamber of Commerce (manuscript), vol. 1, 1907–1909, p. 122.
94. Checking through the records of the Chamber during this period, local issues appeared to have dominated the agenda of the Chamber meetings. See Minutes of Committee Meetings of the Chinese Chamber of Commerce (manuscript), vol. 1, 1906–1909, vol. 2, 1909–1912.

CHAPTER 11

Sun Yat-sen and the Chinese in Singapore and Malaya, 1900–1911*

As Dr Sun Yat-sen was a great leader of the Chinese people, so was he a great leader of the Overseas Chinese. He lived in the hearts of millions of the Overseas Chinese. On the other hand, Sun had a deep feeling for them too, and was greatly appreciative of their contributions to the revolution he led. This led to his honouring them with the famous remark, that the Overseas Chinese were the mother of the Revolution of 1911.

Unlike many Chinese in China, Sun was not scornful of his overseas compatriots. Instead, he had profoundly intimate feelings for them. This was because he spent a great deal of time amongst them, communicated with them, and understood their grievances and hopes. The Overseas Chinese reciprocated this feeling with enormous admiration and respect for Dr Sun. They admired his courage, his integrity and dedication to the cause of making China

---

*   This chapter is based on a paper presented at the Centenial Symposium on Su Yat-sen's Founding of the Kuomintang for Revolution, held in Taipei, 19-23 November 1994.

strong and wealthy. They were also impressed by his demeanour, his charming personality and his unfading confidence in the revolution and the future of China.

Sun's Relationship with the Overseas Chinese

Since the founding of the Hsing Chung Hui in 1894 to the founding of the Chinese Republic in early 1912, Sun Yat-sen's political career was closely related to his ability to mobilise Overseas Chinese support. In this sense, the Overseas Chinese were an important part of Sun's political capital. Sun was the only great Chinese leader in modern times who had spent a great deal of time among the Overseas Chinese before the 1911 Revolution. His pre-1911 political activity was almost entirely centred among the Overseas Chinese communities, planning, maneuvering and trying to capture a revolutionary base in the south and southwestern parts of China. In his overall relationship with the Overseas Chinese, his relationship with the Chinese in Singapore and Malaya was especially close. During about sixteen years of wandering overseas between 1894 and 1911, Sun visited Singapore at least eight times, and Malaya six times.[1] Sun also stayed for a considerable period of time in these two places. In Singapore, his residence was the famous Wan Ching Yuan (Bin Chan House), a revolutionary headquarters in Singapore, while in Penang, his secret residence was a two-story villa at 400 Dato Kramat Road.[2]

Sun's close personal relationship with the Chinese in Singapore and Malaya can also be seen from his intimate relations with some local Chinese leaders. He sealed close bonds with Tan Chor-nam and Teo Eng-hock in Singapore, Goh Say-eng and Ng Kim-keng in Penang,

---

1. See Wang Gungwu, 'Sun Yat-sen and Singapore', in Wang Gungwu, *Community and Nation: Essays on Southeast Asia and the Chinese* (Singapore, Heinemann Educational Books, 1981) pp. 128–41. See also Wang Gungwu, 'Chinese Reformists and Revolutionaries in the Straits Settlements 1900–11' (BA Honours thesis, University of Malaya in Singapore, 1953).
2. See Teo Eng-hock, *Nan-yang yu chuang-li Min-kuo* (Nanyang and the Founding of the Chinese Republic) (Shanghai, 1933), pp. 48–9; Tan Kim Hong (ed), *Ping-ch'eng hua-tsu li-shih t'u-p'ien chi* (The Chinese in Penang: A Pictorial Documentation) (Penang, 1987), p. 142.

Tay Lay-seng in Ipoh and Teng Tse-ju in Kuala Pilah. He kept in touch with them constantly through correspondence or a sophisticated ciphering system.[3] During the T'ung Meng Hui period from August 1905 to December 1911, Sun wrote at least ninety-six letters to Overseas Chinese leaders dealing with party affairs or soliciting funds. Sixty-three of these were written to the leaders in Singapore and Malaya, principally to Teo Eng-hock, Tan Chor-nam and Teng Tse-ju.[4]

His personal relationship with Teng Tse-ju was especially cordial. Teng, a successful tin miner and businessman, joined the T'ung Meng Hui in 1906, and became the president of the T'ung Meng Hui branch of Kuala Pilah when it was founded at the end of 1907. Teng soon became Sun's faithful follower and a confidant, partly because he was a Cantonese speaker who could communicate with Sun well. In the period between 1907 and 1910, Teng was the main figure responsible for helping to raise funds from the local Chinese for several planned uprisings in the south and southwest of China.[5] Whenever Sun was in need of money, Teng was one of the first people to be contacted. This was why, out of Sun's sixty-three letters to the Overseas Chinese leaders in Singapore and Malaya during the T'ung Meng Hui period, thirty-eight of them were written to Teng Tse-ju alone.[6] Teng's financial

---

3. See Teo Eng-hock, op. cit., one of the front pages.
4. The other 33 letters were written to Overseas Chinese leaders in the Dutch East Indies, Vietnam, Thailand, the United States, Canada and Hong Kong. See *Sun Chung-shan ch'uan-chi* (The Complete Works of Dr Sun Yat-sen), vol. 1 (Beijing, Chung Hua shu-chi, 1981), pp. 286–586; Chen Hsu-lu, He Sheng-ch'ao (eds), *Sun Chung-san chi wai-chi* (Additional Records to Sun Yat sen's Complete Works) (Shanghai, Shang-hai jen-min ch'u pan she, 1990), pp. 330–37.
5. See Lu Fang-shang, 'Teng Tse-ju yu Hsin-h'ai ko-ming, 1906–1912 (Teng Tse-ju and the 1911 Revolution, 1906–1912) in *Hsin-h'ai ko-ming yu Nan-yang hua-jen yen-t'ao-hui lun-wen chi* (Essays on the Southeast Asian Chinese and the 1911 Revolution) (Taipei, Centre for International Relations, National Cheng Chi University, 1986), pp. 341–59; T'an Hui-ch'uan, Teng Tse-ju shih-lueh, in *Ko-ming hsien-lieh hsien-chin chuan* (Biographies of Revolutionary Martyrs and Leaders) (Taipei, 1965), p. 811.
6. See *Sun Chung-shan ch'uan-chi*, vol.1. pp. 286–586.

contribution to the staging of various uprisings before the 1911 Revolution and his unreserved loyalty to Dr Sun Yat-sen was well recognised by other revolutionary leaders, such as Huang Hsing and Hu Han-min, who spoke highly of him.[7] Thus, Teng became one of Sun's most trusted agents and the main spokesman for the Chinese in the region.

Sun's Perception of the Overseas Chinese Role in the Revolution

In a broad historical perspective, Sun Yat-sen stood out from other revolutionary leaders of modern China such as Hung Hsiu-ch'uan and Mao Tse-t'ung. This was because he had a different revolutionary direction and strategy. Having a different socio-economic background, education and circumstances, Sun differed from Hung and Mao over the aims of the revolution. His ultimate aim was not just to remove the Manchu regime, but to modernise China with the introduction of an advanced political system from the West. Unlike Hung Hsiu-ch'uan who attempted to restore a rather archaic but more equitable feudal system, and unlike Mao Tse-t'ung who emphasised the interests of the Chinese working class and proletarian dictatorship, Sun led a nationalist and democratic revolution.

Sun Yat-sen, to a certain extent, shared the peasant background of Hung Hsiu-ch'uan and Mao Tse-t'ung. But his elder brother's migration to Hawaii and success in business in later years speedily altered the socio-economic status of Sun's family in China. By the time Sun was actively involved in the revolution, Sun's family status would be more appropriately classified as middle class. More importantly, what made Sun different from Hung and Mao was his education. He received most of his education in English outside China, especially in Hawaii and Hong Kong. In 1878, at the age of twelve, Sun arrived in Hawaii to join his brother. His education at the Iolani School, Honolulu, opened up a new world for him, and exposed him

---

7.   See Hu Han-min, 'Kung-chu Tse-ju Teng hsien-sheng wu-shih shou hsu' (A Preface to the 50th Birthday Celebration of Teng Tse-ju) in *Ko-ming hsien-lieh hsien-chin chuan*, p. 812.

to Christian and Western influences.[8] Sun's five years tertiary education at the College of Medicine for Chinese in Hong Kong from 1887 to 1892 further reinforced Western influence on him, and shaped him as a liberal democrat.

Although Sun trained as a medical doctor, he did not confine his reading just to medical science subjects, but also studied a wide range of topics such as economics, politics, geography, history and astronomy, and was especially interested in current affairs.[9] His broad reading and keen observation led him realise how much China was lagging behind the West. He had enormous admiration for Western material civilisation and its democratic systems, and was prepared to borrow these systems to help transform China into a modern state.

Unlike Hung Hsiu-ch'uan and Mao Tse-t'ung, who were brought up in peasant families and spent their formative years in peasant society, Sun was, to a great extent, alienated from the Chinese peasantry. Because of this, he could not use the peasantry in the way Hung and Mao did for his revolution. Thus, his orientation towards the West and his alienation from the peasant masses helped to determine the direction of his future revolution. Instead of roaming the Chinese countryside seeking support, Sun went to the Overseas Chinese communities to find his strength. He mobilised the support of the Chinese in Honolulu and founded the first Hsing Chung Hui there on November 24, 1894.[10] Further, he gained support from local

8.   See *Sun Chung-shan nien-pu* (The Chronology of Dr Sun Yat-sen). (Beijing,Chung-hua shu-chi, 1980), pp. 10–1; Harold Z. Schiffrin, *Sun Yat-sen and the Origins of the Chinese Revolution* (Berkeley, University of California Press, 1968), pp. 12–4.

9.   See Lo Hsiang-lin, *Kuo-fu chih ta-hsueh shih-tai* (University Days of Dr Sun Yat-sen) (Taipei, Shang-wu yin-shu kuan, reprint, 1954) pp. 30–2; Ch'en Hsi-ch'i, 'Kuan-yu Sun Chung-shan te ta hsueh shih-tai' (Concerning the University Days of Dr Sun Yat-sen) in *Sun Chung-shan yen-chiu lun-wen chi, 1949–1984* (Essays on Sun Yat-sen Studies, 1949–1984) (Ch'eng-tu, Shih-ch'uan jen-min chu-pan she, 1986), vol. 1, pp. 66–7.

10. See Feng Tzu-yu, *Ko-ming i-shih* (Reminiscences of the Revolution) (Taipei, Shang-wu yin-shu kuan, 1965), pp. 3–4; Chang Yu-fa, *Ch'ing-chi te ko-ming t'uan-ti* (Revolutionaries of the Late Ch'ing Period: An Analysis of Groups in the Revolutionary Movement, 1894–1911) (Taipei, Institute of

Chinese in Hong Kong to found the Hsing Chung Hui headquarters there on 21 February 1895.[11]

Although Sun Yat-sen gained strong support from Overseas Chinese for his early revolutionary movement, he had no clear perception of the Overseas Chinese role in the revolution before 1900. This was partly because of expediency, and partly because he was trying out a revolutionary strategy: romantic adventurism. His strong-personal contacts with the Overseas Chinese in Honolulu and Hong Kong led him to seek early supporters among them. On the other hand, his strategy of romantic adventurism led him to try to exhaust all avenues of power including the use of Chinese secret society members, Japanese agents and Filipino independence fighters.[12] All these avenues seemed to offer instant success. But the failure of the Waichow (Hui-chou) Revolt in 1900 shattered Sun's hope of an instant revolution. He needed to chart a new course of action.

In retrospect, the failure of the Waichow Revolt in the southern part of Kwangtung was a turning point in Sun Yat-sen's revolutionary career. For the first time, he came to realise his limitations as a revolutionary and a conspirator. He began to realise that a successful revolution required a long-term planning and a massive popular support. In about five years between the Waichow Revolt and the founding of the Tung Meng Hui in August 1905, Sun became more mature as a professional revolutionary. He was no longer hasty and anxious to create a political miracle. He came to gain a long-term view of revolution: it depended very little on luck, but rather on a well-organised and well-executed plan and on broad support. He also came to realise that the revolutionary path was a tortuous one, full of twists and turns. It was this new perspective on revolution

Modern History, Academia Sinica, 1982), pp. 159–62; Chun-tu Hsueh, 'Sun Yat -sen, Yang Chu-yun and the Early Revolutionary Movement in China', in Chun- tu Hsueh (ed), *Revolutionary Leaders of Modern China* (New York, Oxford University Press, 1971), p. 106.

11. See Chang Yu-fa, op. cit., pp. 163–66; Feng Tzu-yu, *Hua-ch'iao ko-ming k'ai-kuo shih* (Overseas Chinese and the Founding of the Chinese Republic) (Taipei, Shang-wu yin-shu kuan, 1953), pp.3–4.

12. See Harold Z. Schiffrin, op. cit., p. 140.

that brought Sun to include the Overseas Chinese into his long-term plans, in particular because of his awareness of their great financial potential.

A post-mortem examination of the Waichow Revolt led Sun to discover that lack of money was a major factor in the defeat of the uprising. Moreover, he was impressed by the reformists' success in raising funds among the Overseas Chinese for their abortive revolt in Hankow in 1900.[13] He was especially impressed by an alleged donation of S$250,000 by a wealthy Singaporean Chinese named Khoo Seok-wan.[14] What made Sun even more aware of the importance of Overseas Chinese money was the reformists' takeover of his old base in Honolulu. To Sun's great surprise and outrage, his letter of introduction for Liang Ch'i-ch'ao in 1900 facilitated this takeover. Sun's friendly gesture to Liang was intended to serve as a bridge to a possible alliance with the reformists, but Liang took advantage of Sun's good faith and converted many local Chinese to the reformist cause, including many of Sun's old supporters.[15] From Honolulu to mainland United States, Liang and other reformist leaders scored further success in recruiting more Overseas Chinese into the Emperor Protection Association (Pao Huang Hui), and succeeded in tapping Overseas Chinese financial resources.[16]

13. See Ting Wen-chiang (ed), *Liang Jen-kung hsien-sheng nien-p'u ch'ang-p'ien ch'u-kao* (Preliminary Draft of Sources for a Chronological Biography of Liang Ch'i-ch'ao) (Taipei, Shih-chieh shu-chi, 1959), p. 134.

14. See Yen Ching-hwang, *The Overseas Chinese and the 1911 Revolution: With Special Reference to Singapore and Malaya* (Kuala Lumpur & New York, Oxford University Press, 1976), p. 56.

15. See Feng Tzu-yu, *Chung-hua min-kuo k'ai-kuo ch'ien ko-ming shih* (A Revolutionary History Prior to the Founding of the Chinese Republic) (Taipei, 1954), vol. 1, p. 44; Chang P'eng-yuan, *Liang Ch'i-ch'ao yu Ch'ing-chi ko-ming* (Liang Ch'i-ch'ao and the Revolution during the Ch'ing Period) (Taipei, Institute of Modern History, Academia Sinica, 1964), pp. 128–33;

16. For Liang and other reformist leaders' activities in Honolulu and mainland United States, see L. Eve Armentrout Ma, *Revolutionaries, Monarchists, and Chinatowns: Chinese Politics in the Americas and the 1911, Revolution* (Honolulu, University of Hawaii Press; 1990), pp. 60–94. For Sun's perception of Liang's success in tapping Overseas Chinese financial resources in San

In envy of the reformists' financial success and realising of importance of Overseas Chinese money, Sun in 1903 and 1904 undertook a trip to Honolulu and the United States mainland in an attempt to recover lost ground in the region. It was in this process of combating reformist influence that Sun gained new insights into the Overseas Chinese and their role in the revolution. We can safely suggest that by 1904 he must have had a clear perception of this: the Overseas Chinese were to be incorporated into his long-term plan, to serve mainly as the benefactors of the revolution.

Sun's perception of the Overseas Chinese role in the revolution was a romantic one. He felt that all Overseas Chinese should share his belief in building a strong and modern China, should fearlessly support the overthrow of the Manchu regime, and should donate generously to fund revolutionary activities. Sun was a nationalist, not a Marxist. Although he was sympathetic with the Marxist theory of fighting for the interests of common people, he rejected the Marxist interpretation of history as being the result of a constant class struggle.[17] He felt that Marxist ideology had no room in his approach to the Overseas Chinese. To his thinking, the Overseas Chinese should think and behave like their compatriots in China. Despite their long sojournment overseas, they should be loyal to China, and should be dedicated to the cause of China's salvation. Thus, despite their class backgrounds, age and sex differences, they should support his revolution wholeheartedly. He further felt that the Overseas Chinese should have even more hatred for the Manchus than their compatriots in China — not only because their ancestors were massacred by the Manchus during the Manchu conquest of China in the mid-seventeenth century,[18] but also because

Francisco, see Letter from Dr Sun Yat-sen to Huang Chung-yang, December 1903, in *Sun Chung-shan ch'uan-chi*, vol. 1, pp. 229–30.

17. See Sun Yat-sen, Min-sheng chu-i (The Principle of People's Livelihood) in Sun Yat-sen, *Sun Chung-shan hsuan-chi* (Selected Works of Dr Sun Yat-sen) (Hong Kong, Ssu Tung ch'u-pan she, 1962), vol. 2, pp. 776-81.

18. Sun's accusation of Han Chinese massacres by the Manchus was repeated again and again to his Overseas Chinese audience: see the public talks delivered by Sun in Penang in 1907 and 1908, in Yang Han-hsiang (ed), *Ping-ch'eng yeh-shu pao-she nien-ssu chou-nien chi-nien t'e-k'an* (Souvenir

they were neglected by the Manchu government, which failed to protect them overseas.[19]

Thus, Sun had arrived a clear perception of role of the Overseas Chinese in the revolution. Because they were generally wealthier than their compatriots in China, the Overseas Chinese were to contribute money and to raise funds for his military programmes. This perception of their role partly stemmed from his strong belief in specific roles for specific groups in the revolution. To Sun, each group in Chinese society, both at home and abroad, had a particular role to play in the revolution. Professional revolutionaries like him were to be the organisers and coordinators of the revolution; the intellectuals and students were to spread revolutionary ideas; the Overseas Chinese were to donate and raise money; and the members of secret societies and the new army were to become the attack forces. The combination of the efforts of these various groups would make a successful revolution. This concept was partly derived from his ideas on the division of labour, and partly from his firm belief that the specific role assigned to each group was most suitable for that particular group. The financial role was given to the Overseas Chinese not only because they were generally wealthier than their compatriots in China, but also because they knew very little about revolution, let alone how to fight a war in a revolutionary uprising in China. Sun had even on one occasion bluntly told Tan Chor-nam, a top leader of the Tung Meng Hui in Singapore, that the Overseas Chinese knew very little about the revolution,[20] and

Magazine of the 24th Anniversary of the Penang Philomatic Society) (Penang, n. d.), pp. 141–43. English translations of these two public talks are found in Yen Ching-hwang, *The Overseas Chinese and the 1911 Revolution*, appendices 2 and 3.

19. See Sun's public talk delivered at the P'ing Chang Kung Kuan (Chinese Town Hall of Penang) in 1907, ibid. pp. 141–42. For an analysis of the Ching Governments failure to protect the Overseas Chinese, see Yen Ching-hwang, *Coolies and Mandarins: China's Protection of Overseas Chinese During the Late Ch'ing Period, 1851–1911* (Singapore, Singapore University Press, 1985), especially Chs. 5 and 7.

20. In my interview with Tan Chor-nam in August 1966, he recalled that Sun had once told him bluntly that the Overseas Chinese knew very little about

repeated this view in a public speech to his supporters in Penang in April 1911.[21]

Sun Yat-sen's perception of the role of the Singaporean and Malayan Chinese in the revolution was that it was no different from the role of the Overseas Chinese in general. Since the founding of the Tung Meng Hui in Japan in August 1905, he felt more confident in the revolutionary movement, and was preparing to launch a series of uprisings in the south and southwest of China. Sun realised that money was the key to the success of his planned revolts. Money was needed to purchase arms and ammunition, to bribe Ch'ing officials and soldiers, and to resettle revolutionary refugees when any revolt failed. He planned to raise $2,000,000 through sales of military bonds, which were to be sold at $250 per bond with a face value of $1,000. The subscribers were to be repaid with the full value of the bonds when the revolution was successful.[22] At that time, Sun had a vague idea that Southeast Asian Chinese communities were full of wealthy merchants, and they could become the main patrons of his proposed military scheme. He claimed that certain sons of these wealthy Chinese merchants in Penang and Java were student members of the Tung Meng Hui, and that they would return soon to Southeast Asia to help persuade their fathers and elder brothers to subscribe.[23] This was why Sun wrote to Tan Chor-nam soon after the founding of the Tung Meng Hui in Tokyo,

politics, and their most effective contribution to the revolution would be to donate money. Interview with Tan Chor-nam on 7 August 1966 at his residence in Singapore.

21. On this occasion, Sun stated that 'Whenever I meet you comrades, my only purpose is to ask for donations ... Overseas Chinese comrades need only to donate money, whereas comrades in China are to sacrifice their lives for the purpose of saving our country.' See Sun Yat-sen, 'Tung-chih kung fu ko-ming chiu-kuo chih chih-jen' (All Comrades must shoulder the Responsibility of Saving the Nation) in Chang Ch'i-yun (ed), *Kuo-fu ch'uan-shu* (Collected Works of Dr Sun Yat-sen) (Taipei, Kuo-fang yen-chiu-yuan, 1966), pp. 482–83.

22. See Feng Tzu-yu, *Ko-ming i-shih*, vol. 1, pp. 254–56; 'Letter from Dr Sun Yat-sen to Tan Chor-nam (Ch'en Ch'u-nan) dated 30 September, 1905', in *Sun Chung-shan ch'uan-chi*, vol. 1, pp. 286–87.

23. 'Letter from Dr Sun Yat-sen to Tan Chor-nam', ibid., p. 287.

to look for rich patrons among the Chinese in Singapore. Sun at this time must also have been fully aware of the numerical strength and economic potential of the Chinese in Southeast Asia, especially in Singapore and Malaya. He must have picked up this information from his early contacts with Dr Lim Boon Keng, Dr Wu Chieh-wu and Huang Nai-shang in Singapore in 1900, when he arrived for the first time on the island in an attempt to rescue his two Japanese supporters from prison.[24] He must also have gained the same information during his visits to Vietnam in 1900 and 1902.[25]

Later, Sun's founding of the Tung Meng Hui branches in Singapore and Kuaia Lumpur in 1906, and his long stay in the region in the following years, led him understand the wealth of the Chinese in Southeast Asia. In November 1909, in order to get a large loan from an American banker, Sun claimed that a group of wealthy Southeast Asian Chinese were willing to be the guarantors, and that their aggregate wealth was estimated to be around US$20,000,000. This group of wealthy Overseas Chinese included one banker, three proprietors of rice mills in Bangkok, several merchants in Singapore and three tin miners in Malaya.[26] Sun seems to have been under the impression that among the Chinese in Southeast Asia, those in Singapore and Malaya were the richest. Because of this perception, Sun rested great hopes on them to contribute to the revolution. This led him to perceive that the Chinese in Singapore and Malaya should play a greater financial role than other Overseas Chinese in the revolution. His rather romantic view that all Overseas Chinese, regardless of their class backgrounds, age and sex should play an equal part in the revolution led him to believe if he could persuade some extremely

24. See Yen Ching-hwang, *The Overseas Chinese and the 1911 Revolution*, p. 40.
25. See Ch'en I-ling, 'Kuo-fu yu Yueh-nan' (Dr Sun Yat-sen and Vietnam) in Chiang Yung-ching (ed), *Hua-ch'iao k'ai-kuo ko-ming shih-liao* (Historical Materials relating to the Overseas Chinese and the Founding of the Chinese Republic) (Taipei, Cheng Chung shu-chi, 1977), p. 385; *Sun Chung-shan nien-p'u*, pp. 47, 55.
26. See 'Letter from Dr Sun Yat-sen to an American Banker, November 1909', in Ch'en Hsu-lu, et. al. (eds), *Sun Chung-shan chi-wai chi*, pp. 331–32.

wealthy merchants to support his cause, all the financial problems for the planned uprisings could be resolved.

One of the merchants singled out by Sun was Loke Yew (romanised in mandarin as Lu Yu; in Sun's correspondences, Lu was referred to as Lu Pi-ch'en, as Pi-ch'en was the courtesy name of Lu Yu). Loke, a native of Ho Shan district of Kwangtung province, made his millions in tin mining in Malaya. He possessed scores of tin mines in Perak, Selangor and Pahang, and other cash crop plantations and commercial enterprises. He was one of the richest Chinese in the late nineteenth and early twentieth centuries in Southeast Asia.[27] Sun had personally approached Loke in Kuala Lumpur in 1906 for a large donation, but was not successful. However, Sun persisted in trying to change Loke's mind, either by correspondence or through his confidant, Teng Tse-ju, who was a close friend of Loke's. Sun persisted in believing that Loke's wealth was the answer to his financial problem, and that his request for a donation of S$100,000 to finance the Hokow uprising in Yunnan in April 1908 was easily affordable to Loke.[28] Although Sun was disappointed with Loke for not patronising his military programmes, his perception of the important financial role of the Chinese in Singapore and Malaya was nevertheless unaltered, and he repeated this message time and again in the period between 1909 and 1911.[29]

27.   See Tsao Yao-fei, 'Lu Yu po-shih (Dr Loke Yew)', in Ma-lai-ya Ku-kang-chou liu-i tsung-hui t'e-k'an (Souvenir Magazine of the Federation of the Associations of the Six Districts of Kukang chou in Malaya), pt. 2 (Penang, Khung Wah Printers, 1964), p. 512.

28.   See 'Letter from Dr Sun Yat-sen to Teng Tse-ju dated 7th March, 1908', 'Letter from Dr Sun Yat-sen to Teng Tse-ju dated 1 April 1908' and 'Letter from Dr Sun Yat-sen to Teng Tse-ju & Huang Hsin-ch'ih dated 20 May 1908 in Teng Tse-ju (ed), *Sun Chung-shan hsien-sheng nien-nien lai shou-cha* (Twenty Years Correspondence of Dr Sun Yat-sen) (double leaves, Canton, 1927), vol. 1; *Kuo-fu ch'uan-shu*, pp. 406-07; *Sun Chung-shan ch'uan-chi*, vol. 1, pp. 360–66.

29.   See 'Ko-ming hsu-yu yung-ch'i yu fang-fa (The making of a revolution requires courage as well as means, a speech given by Dr Sun to the supporters in Penang at the end of 1910); and 'Tung-chih tang kung-fu ko-ming chiu-kuo chih chih-jen' (All comrades must shoulder the responsibility of saving the nation, a speech given by Dr Sun Yat-sen to the supporters in Penang at the end of 1910) in *Kuo-fu ch'uan-shu*, pp. 382–83. English translations of these

The Response of the Chinese in Singapore and Malaya

The popular belief that Sun Yat-sen easily gained the support of Overseas Chinese for his revolution is untenable. In fact, Sun appealed strongly to Overseas Chinese for support, and launched battles against the reformists in the Overseas Chinese communities in the period between 1903 and 1909. His decisive victory over his political opponents came some time in 1909, but the fruit of this victory was hard won. Except for a small number of supporters in Honolulu and Hong Kong, Sun Yat-sen in his early career was known to Overseas Chinese not as a revolutionary leader, but a reckless bandit chief. His daring attempt in the first Canton Revolt in October 1895 earned him condemnation among Overseas Chinese, especially the Chinese in Singapore and Malaya. A leading Chinese newspaper in Singapore, *Sing Po*, published a hostile report about his activities in April 1896, about six months after the revolt. In this report, Sun was described as an unrepentant bandit chief (*fei shou*) who had fled overseas after the failure of his rebellion in Canton, and was again trying to hatch another rebellion in the same city.[30] The editor of the newspaper added a footnote at the end of the report claiming that Sun had planted opium poppies in the district of Nan Hai of Kwangtung province in 1894, and had brought havoc and misery to the Chinese of that province.[31] The report projected a negative image of Sun Yat-sen, fitting him with the traditional image of a bandit chief: red eyebrows and green eyes, crafty and treacherous. The editor's footnote had further portrayed him as a vicious and immoral man who pursued his selfish gains by poisoning his countrymen. *Sing Po* persistently condemned Sun and his revolutionary activities throughout the period between 1896 and 1898, with only slight change of term in referring to Sun Yat-sen as a rebel (*ni tang*) or rebel criminal (*ni fan*) rather than a bandit chief.[32]

---

two speeches are found in Yen Ching-hwang, *The Overseas Chinese and the 1911 Revolution*, appendices 4 and 5.

30. See 'Yu ming fan chih' (To rebel again), in *Sing Po*, 18 April 1896, p. 5.
31. Ibid.
32. See 'Ni -tang pi ch'ang' (The madness of the rebels) in *Sing Po*, 23 September 1897, p. 4; 'Fang lei luan shuo' (On the prevention of internal rebellion) in *Sing Po*, 22 February 1898, pp. 1, 4.

It may be argued that *Sing Po*'s reports only reflected the conservative view of a section of the Chinese in Singapore. But given the fact that *Sing Po* was one of the two major local Chinese newspapers and its influence extended far beyond the island,[33] its negative images of Sun Yat-sen and his revolutionary activities must have impeded an early positive response by the Chinese in the region to the revolution. The conservative view held by *Sing Po* at that time, to a great extent, reflected the cultural and political mood of the local Chinese. The last decade of the nineteenth century saw the rise of a dynamic Confucian revival movement in Singapore, Malaya and the Dutch East Indies,[34] which reasserted Confucian values of loyalty, filial piety and chasity;[35] in particular, the concept of loyalty to one's emperor was obviously incompatible with the revolution preached by Dr Sun Yat-sen. This led the Overseas Chinese to perceive Sun in a negative light, and his activities as great crimes. When Sun made his first visit to Penang in 1907, his arrival on the island appalled local conservative Chinese, who regarded him as a snake or scorpion.[36]

Another factor that inhibited the Singaporean and Malayan Chinese early response to Sun Yat-sen's call was the fear of a Ch'ing government reprisal. Like most Overseas Chinese of the time, the Chinese in Singapore and Malaya were sojourners rather than settlers. Even successful settlers could not cut off family ties with their homeland;

33. See Chen Mong Hock, *The Early Chinese Newspapers of Singapore, 1881–1912* (Singapore, University of Malaya Press, 1967), pp. 54–63.
34. For a study of the movement in Singapore and Malaya, see Yen Ching-hwang, 'The Confucian Revival Movement in Singapore and Malaya, 1899–1911', in *Journal of Southeast Asia Studies* vol. 7, no. 1 (Singapore, March, 1976), pp. 33–57. For the movement in the Dutch East Indies, see Charles A. Coppel, 'The Origins of Confucianism as an Organized Religion in Java, 1900–1923', in *Journal of Southeast Asian Studies*, vol. 12, no. 1 (March, 1981), pp. 179–95; Leo Suryadinata, 'Confucianism in Indonesia: Past and Present', in Leo Suryadinata, *The Chinese Minority in Indonesia: Seven Papers* (Singapore, Chopman Enterprise, 1978), pp. 33–62.
35. Yen Ching-hwang, ibid.
36. See Ch'en Hsin-cheng, 'Hua-ch'iao ko-ming hsiao-shih' (A Concise History of Overseas Chinese Involvement in the Revolution) (manuscript kept in the Kuomintang Archives, Taipei, Taiwan).

they had either aged parents or wives and children in China.[37] At the same time, the establishment of Ch'ing consulates in Singapore (1877) and Penang (1893) enabled Ch'ing diplomats to spy on emigrants political activities.[38] Any serious involvement in activities against the dynasty would be detected and reported to the home government for punishment.[39] This could mean severe punishment for themselves, or for their relatives or kinsmen in China — a deterrent for many Overseas Chinese from responding to the early call of Sun Yat-sen.[40]

However, the main impediment hindering the response of Malayan and Singaporean Chinese to Sun Yat-sen's call was the reformist influence. The abortive Hundred Days' Reform in 1898 forced K'ang Yu-wei and Liang Ch'i-ch'iao to flee China and to seek outside support. They regarded the Overseas Chinese as a most valuable asset for the recovery of their political fortunes in China. Through the propoganda networks, they preached reform and modernisation as the means of regaining China's greatness. Their preaching attracted many Overseas Chinese intellectuals and merchants.[41] Kang's claim of having a close relationship with the deposed monarch, Emperor Kuang-hsu, earned

37. See Yen Ching-hwang, *A Social History of the Chinese in Singapore and Malaya, 1800–1911* (Singapore, Oxford University Press, 1986), p. 10.

38. For the establishment of the Ch'ing consulate in Singapore and vice-consulate in Penang, see Wen Chung-chi, 'The Nineteenth-century Imperial Chinese Consulate in the Straits Settlements' (MA thesis, University of Singapore, 1964); Yen Ching-hwang, *Coolies and Mandarins: China's Protection of Overseas Chinese during the Late Ch'ing Period*, pp. 140–44, 168–76.

39. In 1907, the Ch'ing Consul in Singapore, Sun Shih-ting, reported to the Viceroy of Kwangtung and Kwangsi concerning the activities of Sun Yat-sen and Teng Tzu-yu in Southeast Asia and Hong Kong. See 'Telegram from the Viceroy of Kwangtung and Kwangsi to the Wai Wu Pu (Ministry of Foreign Affairs) dated 24th day of 4th moon of 33rd year of Kuang-hsu (4th June, 1907)', in *Wai Wu Pu shou-fa tien tang* (Telegram Records of the Ministry of Foreign Affairs) 33rd year of Kuang-hsu (1907) (manuscript).

40. It was claimed that many Overseas Chinese in San Francisco were reluctant to join the Hsing Chung Hui in 1903 because they were fearful for the safety of their families and properties in China. See Feng Tzu-yu, *Hua-ch'iao ko-ming kai-ko shih*, p. 62.

41. For the success of the reformist appeal to intellectuals and merchants in the Overseas Chinese communities in North America, see Jung-pang

him considerable sympathy as well as adding to his credentials of appeal to the Overseas Chinese in Southeast Asia.[42] To these Overseas Chinese, the reformists offered a practical alternative to the Ch'ing government in their pursuit of power and fame in China. Further, their support for the reformists was still seen in the context of paying loyalty to the emperor, and was acceptable to many tradition-minded Chinese. In contrast, the revolution preached by Sun Yat-sen was seen as a radical departure from this tradition, one which would incur much personal risk and sacrifice.

Despite all these impediments, support for Sun Yat-sen among the Overseas Chinese grew with the change of mood of the nation. 1900 was a momentous year, dramatically changing the attitude of the Chinese (including the Overseas Chinese) towards the dynasty. The Boxer catastrophe shattered the faith of many Chinese in the dynasty's ability to cope with foreign encroachment, and some far-sighted Chinese started to look for alternatives to save China. More and more Chinese and Overseas Chinese saw Sun and his activities in a different light, and dropped their hostility towards him. As Sun stated in his memoirs, he was no longer looked upon as a snake or

Lo, 'Sequel to Autobiography', in Jung-pang Lo (ed), *Kang Yu-wei: A Biography and a Symposium* (Tucson, University of Arizona Press, 1967) p. 180; L. Eve Armentrout Ma, *Revolutionaries, Monarchists, and Chinatowns: Chinese Politics in the Americas and the 1911 Revolution*, pp. 48–51; Chang Yu-fa, *Ch'ing-chi te li-hsien t'uan-t'i* (Constitutionalists of the Ch'ing Period: An Analysis of Groups in the Constitutional Movement, 1895–1911) (Taipei, Institute of Modern History, Academia Sinica, 1971), pp. 229–30; Edgar Wickberg et. al., *From China to Canada: A History of the Chinese Communities in Canada* (Toronto, McClelland & Stewart Ltd, 1982), p. 74.

42. According to Hu Han-min, a close associate of Dr Sun Yat-sen, K'ang used to boast to the Overseas Chinese that he was a tutor of Emperor Kuang-hsu, and had in his possession a secret edict which he had never shown to anyone. As pointed out by Hu, K'ang was using his relationship with the deposed emperor to hoodwink Overseas Chinese into giving financial support. See Hu Han-min, recorded by Chang Chen-chih, 'Nanyang yu Chung-kuo ko-ming' (Nanyang and the 1911 Revolution) in *Chung-hua min-kuo k'ai-kuo wu-shih-nien wen-hsien* (Historical documents of the Republic of China for the last fifty years), vol. 1, pt. 11, (Taipei, 1963), p. 478.

beast by his compatriots after the Boxer Uprising, and some of them began to sympathise with his cause.[43]

The second decisive year in the Overseas Chinese response to Sun Yat-sen's call was 1905. The period between 1901 and 1904 witnessed the slow but steady growth of revolutionary activities overseas. Through the Hsing Chung Hui and its affiliated organisations such as Chung Ho T'ang, the revolutionaries succeeded in spreading their message in the Overseas Chinese communities. Sun Yat-sen's early visits to Vietnam and Singapore in 1900, and his later activities in Honolulu and continental America in 1903 and 1904, began to establish his credentials among the Overseas Chinese. In the case of Singapore and Malaya, the arrival of Yu Lieh, a leader of Chung Ho T'ang, in Singapore at the beginning of 1901 laid a solid foundation for revolutionary activities in the region. Yu, an experienced organiser, mobilised support among members of the lower class, and succeeded in founding Chung Ho T'ang branches in Singapore, Kuala Lumpur, Penang, Perak, Johor and Seremban.[44] A merge of strength between Yu and a small group of local Chinese revolutionaries, led by Tan Chor-nam and Teo Eng-hock, in Singapore in 1903 further boosted revolutionary activities in the region.[45]

The year 1905 also turned the tide in favour of the revolutionary movement as a whole. With the support of overseas students as well as various revolutionary groups in Japan, Sun founded the famous T'ung Meng Hui (United League) in August 1905 in Tokyo. It signalled the beginning of a more united revolutionary movement with clear political platforms, organisation and propaganda machinery.[46] One

43. See Sun Yat-sen, 'Yu chih ching-ch'eng' (Success for Those who are Determined) (Autobiography) in *Kuo-fu ch'uan-shu*, p. 34.
44. See Hsien Chiang, *Yu Lieh shih-lueh* (A Concise Biography of Yu Lieh) (Hong Kong, 1951) pp. 15–6; Yen Ching-hwang, *The Overseas Chinese and the 1911 Revolution*, pp. 41–5.
45. Yen Ching-hwang, ibid., pp. 60–1.
46. For a discussion of the significance of the founding of T'ung Meng Hui in the revolutionary movement, see Harold Z. Schiffrin, *Sun Yat-sen and the Origins of the Chinese Revolution*, pp. 344–66.

of the main directions of the T'ung Meng Hui was the expansion of its branches in the Overseas Chinese communities. From 1905 to 1911, twenty-four important branches of the T'ung Meng Hui were established outside China, eighteen of which were among the Overseas Chinese.[47] Thus, 1905 can be taken as a landmark year in the expansion of revolutionary activities in the Overseas Chinese communities, and the beginning of an active response of the Overseas Chinese to Sun Yat-sen's call.

With the spread of T'ung Meng Hui branches overseas after 1905, Sun Yat-sen was in a better position than before to mobilise Overseas Chinese support. Through propaganda networks and front organisations, Sun succeeded in indoctrinating tens of thousands of Overseas Chinese with his revolutionary message. However, the entrenched reformist influence in the Overseas Chinese communities proved to be a major stumbling block for Sun Yat-sen, and the struggle with the reformists was crucial for his success or failure in gaining Overseas Chinese support. The fight against the reformists was carried out mainly by Sun's Overseas Chinese supporters; he acted only as supervisor. The struggle took place at two levels: wresting control of schools and social organisations from the reformists, and launching an ideological attack on them.[48]

On the political scene in Singapore and Malaya, the response of the Overseas Chinese to Sun Yat-sen's call was enthusiastic and exuberant. The revolutionary movement in the region was most vigorous among the Chinese in Southeast Asia after 1905. Sun's stopover in Singapore in July 1905 on his way to Tokyo sealed his bond with Tan Chor-nam and Teo Eng-hock, the two most active local revolutionary leaders on the island. Both Tan and Teo were impressed by Sun's charisma and broad knowledge of the West, and were prepared to accept his leadership. Sun's encouragement further strengthened their faith

---

47. Among these 18 overseas branches, 10 of them were in Southeast Asia, 7 in America and 1 in Australia. See Chang Yu-fa, Ch'ing-chi ko-ming t'uan-t'i, pp. 325–37.

48. For the ideological war between the revolutionaries and the reformists, see Ch'i Ping-feng, Ch'ing-mo ko-ming yu chun-hsien te lun-chan (The Polemics between the Revolutionaries and the Reformists during the Late Ch'ing Period) (Taipei, Ching Hua yin-shu-kuan, 1966), pp. 104–234.

in the revolution and stimulated their revolutionary activities.[49] With the groundwork laid by Tan and Teo, the T'ung Meng Hui branch in Singapore was founded on 6 April 1906, witnessed by Dr Sun Yat-sen who arrived on the island from Europe en route to Japan. Fourteen founding members, in the presence of Sun, pledged their commitment to overthow the Manchus and to establish the republic. Both Tan Chor-nam and Teo Eng-hock were elected unanimously as the chairman and deputy chairman of the branch.[50]

The founding of the Singapore T'ung Meng Hui branch, the first of its kind in the Overseas Chinese communities in Southeast Asia, enabled Sun Yat-sen and his close associates to plan for immediate expansion into the Malay Peninsula ,where large number of Chinese were scattered in ports and towns. Sun had to leave for Japan for a short while, and when he returned in July 1906 he immediately undertook the task of setting up new branches in Malaya. Accompanied by some supporters, including Tan Chor-nam and Lim Ngee-soon, Sun's mission succeeded in establishling a T'ung Meng Hui branch in Kuala Lumpur on 7 August 1906, with sixteen founding members. Unfortunately, his mission failed to bear fruit in Seremban and Ipoh,[51] but the unfinished task was completed out by Sun's local supporters, and within two years, T'ung Meng Hui branches were established in Penang, Seremban, Ipoh, Kuala Pilah, Muar and Kuantan.[52]

It is worth noting that the majority of the founding members and the leaders of the T'ung Meng Hui branches in Singapore and Malaya appear to have derived from the merchant class. Ten out of the fourteen

49.   See Tan Chor-nam, 'Wan Ch'ing-yuan yu Chung-kuo ko-ming', in *Chung-hua min-kuo k'ai-ko wu-shih-nien wen-hsien*, vol. 1, pt. 11, p. 535; Teo Eng-hock, *Nan-yang yu ch'uang-li min-kuo*, p. 9.

50.   See Yen Ching-hwang, *The Overseas Chinese and the 1911 Revolution*, pp. 92–3; Feng Tzu-yu, *Hua-ch'iao ko-ming k'ai-kuo shih*, p.79; 'A list of the members of the Early Period of the China's Tung Meng Hui', in Lo Chia-lun (ed), *Ko-ming wen-hsien* (Documentary Records of the Revolution) vol. 2 (Taipei, 1958), pp. 73–4.

51.   See Yen Ching-hwang, *The Overseas Chinese and the 1911 Revolution*, pp. 94–8.

52.   Ibid., pp. 92–100.

founding members in the Singapore branch were rich or well-to-do merchants, while most of the leaders of the T'ung Meng Hui branches in Kuala Lumpur, Penang, Ipoh, Kuala Pilah, Kuantan and Malacca were identified as merchants.[53] However, merchant dominance in the T'ung Meng Hui founding membership, leadership should not mislead us to conclude that only members of this class were enthusiastic in responding to Sun Yat-sen's call. A small minority of the merchant class did support Sun's revolution fervently, but their actions were far from representative of the class to which they belonged. They responded to Sun's call because they were primarily concerned with China's

53. Among the 14 founding members in Singapore branch, Tan Chor-nam, Teo Eng-hock, Li Chu-ch'ih, Hsu Tzu-Iin, Lim Ngee-soon, Lin Ching-ch'iu, Hsiao Pai-ch'uan, Liu Hung-shih, Chiang Yu-t'ien and Wu Yeh-ch'en, were identified as rich or well-to-do merchants. In Kuala Lumpur branch, Loke Chow-thye was a tin miner, Wang Ching was probably a merchant, Yuen Ying-fong, a merchant, and Too Nam, a teacher. In Penang, both the leaders of the T'ung Meng Hui branch, Goh Say-eng and Ng Kim-keng were rich merchants, In Ipoh, the leaders of the branch, Tay Lay-seng and Li Guan-swee, were rich merchants, in Kuala Pilah, the leader of the branch, Teng Tse-ju was another rich merchant. In Malacca, the leader of the branch, Sim Hung-pek, was a rich merchant. In Kuantan, the branch chairman, Loke Chow-lo, was a tin miner. See Feng Tzu-yu, 'Nan-yang ko-ming tang ti-i-jen -Chen Ch'u-nan (Tan Chor nam — The Top Overseas Chinese Revolutionary in Southeast Asia) in Feng Tzu-yu, *Ko-ming i-shih*, vol. 3, pp. 183-89; Anonymous, 'Chang Yung-fu chuan' (A Biography of Teo Eng-hock) in P'an Hsing-nung (ed), *Ma-lai-ya Ch'ao-ch'iao t'ung-chien* (The Teochews in Malaya) (Singapore, Nan-tao ch'u-pan-she, 1950), p. 158; Chan Chan-mooi, 'To Nan hsien-sheng shih-lueh' (A Short Biography of Mr. Too Nam) in Chan Chan-mooi (ed), *To Nan hsien-sheng ai-shu lu* (Obituaries of Mr. Too Nam) (Kuala Lumpur, 1940); 'Interview with Madam T. M. Too (granddaughter of Too Nam) on 7 October 1966 in Kuala Lumpur'; Wu Tee-jen, 'Tao-nien fei-chia shu-nan te Wu Shih-yung lao t'ung-chih' (In Memory of an Old Comrade: Goh Say-eng) (manuscript), p. 3; 'Interview with Mrs. Goh Say-eng on 14 October 1966 in Penang'; Huang Ching-wan, 'Cheng Lo-sheng kuang-yung shih' (A History of Achievements of Tay Lay-seng) in Huang Ching-wan (ed), *Nan-yang P'i-li hua-ch'iao ko-ming shih-chi'* (Historical Records of the Involvement of the Chinese in Perak in the 1911 Revolution) (Shanghai, 1933), p.1; Teng Tse-ju, *Chung-kuo Kuo-min-tang erh-shih nien shih-chi* (Records of China's Kuomintang in the Last Twenty Years) (Taipei, 1948), pp. 1–2.

declining power and its inability to cope with foreign encroachment. They were also concerned with the worsening status of the Overseas Chinese in foreign lands. These patriotic merchants were relatively young in age, and had no political or economic interests in China. Therefore, they were able to respond more freely to the revolution than many other rich Chinese merchants in Singapore and Malaya.[54]

All these branches were integrated into an effective network for carrying out revolutionary activities. The main task for Chinese revolutionaries in the region was to raise large sums of money in support of a series of uprisings in the south and southwest of China. But these funds could not be raised unless more and more local Chinese were converted to the revolutionary cause. For this reason, the revolutionaries mounted aggressive propaganda activities in the bid for financial support. Three major propaganda organisations were formed: newspapers, reading clubs and drama troupes. Newspapers were a powerful medium for transmitting the revolutionary message, as they reached wide sections of the Chinese population. Apart from the *Thoe Lam Yit Poh*, which was founded in 1904, the revolutionaries founded another four papers in the period between 1907 and 1911. The founding of the *Chong Shing Yit Pao* (Restoration Daily) in August 1907 led the way, followed by the *Sun Poo* (The Morning Daily) in August 1909, the *Kwong Wah Yit Poh* (The Glorious Chinese Daily) in December 1910, and the *Nam Kew Poo* (The Straits Chinese Morning Post) in October 1911. Except for the *Kwong Wah Yit Poh* in Penang, all other newspapers were published in Singapore. They made a concerted effort to spread revolutionary message, to attack the Ch'ing government and its policies, and to engage in heated polemics with the reformists.[55]

To reinforce the effect of the revolutionary media, Sun Yat-sen's supporters established a score of reading clubs to help disseminate the revolutionary gospel. A reading club, a kind of cultural and social centre

54. For a detailed discussion of the response of the merchant class to the revolution, see Yen Ching-hwang, *The Overseas Chinese and the 1911 Revolution*, pp. 264–76.

55. See Yen Ching-hwang, 'Chinese Revolutionary Propaganda Organizations in Singapore and Malaya, 1906–1911', in *Journal of the South Seas Society*, vol. 29, pts. 1 and 2 (Singapore, December 1974), pp. 50–2.

where newspapers, magazines and books were made freely available, was deemed by Sun's supporters to be an effective means of reaching out to wider audiences, especially among the poorer section of the Chinese population who could not afford to buy reading materials. At least 58 revolutionary reading clubs were set up in Singapore and Malaya. Prominent among these were the Singapore Reading Club, the T'ung Teh Reading Club, the K'ai Ming Public Speaking and Reading Club in Singapore, and the Penang Reading Club (or known as Penang Philomatic Society) in Penang. All of these reading clubs helped to expose their members to the influence of revolutionary ideas and messages, and enabled many members of the middle and lower classes in the Chinese community to respond to Sun Yat-sen's call.[56]

Revolutionary media and reading clubs had their limitations. They could only reach those who were literate, while the illiterate were beyond the reach of written propaganda. This shortcoming was overcome by the founding of drama troupes. Drama was one of the oldest forms of popular entertainment in rural Chinese villages, and found wide acceptance among the illiterate masses in China. The visit of a revolutionary drama troupe, Chen T'ien Sheng, from Hong Kong at the end of 1908 activated revolutionary drama activities in the region. Its successful performances served as a trigger for starting large-scale revolutionary drama activities in Singapore and Malaya, and at least five local drama troupes were founded.[57] All these troupes performed

56. See Teo Eng-hock, *Nan-yang yu ch'uang-li min-kuo*, pp.91–2; Feng Tzu-yu, *Hua-ch'iao ko-ming k'ai-kuo shih*, p. 85; *Chong Shing Yit Pao*, 7 November 1907, p. 5; Anonymous, 'Min-kuo ch'ien Sing-chou chih ko-ming yun-tung' (Revolutionary movement in Singapore before the founding of the Chinese Republic) (manuscript kept in the Kuomintang Archives, Taipei, Taiwan); Yang Han-hsiang, 'Chung-hua min-kuo k'ai-kuo ch'ien-hou chih pen-she ko-ming shih' (The revolutionary history of the Penang Philomatic Society before and after the creation of the Chinese Republic) in Yang Han-hsiang (ed), *Ping-ch'eng yeh-shu pao-she nien-ssu chou-nien chi-nien t'e-k'an* (Souvenir Magazine of the 24th Anniversary of the Penang Philomatic Society) (Penang, n.d.), p. 8; Chen Hsin-cheng, 'Hua-ch'iao ko-ming hsiao-shih', (manuscript), p. 10.

57. These troupes were Fan Ai Pan (Universal Love Troupe) and Min To She (People's Bell Troupe) in Singapore; The Perak Welfare Troupe in Ipoh; the

popular revolutionary plays which praised martyrdom and dedication to the revolution, exposed the corruption and nepotism of the Manchu government, and effectively brought the revolutionary message to the illiterate masses.[58]

Like other major Overseas Chinese communities throughout the world, the reformist influence proved to be a major obstacle to obtaining Singaporean and Malayan Chinese support for Sun Yat-sen's call. As the reformists had arrived earlier and were well-entrenched in some social and educational institutions in the region, Sun Yat-sen's supporters found it difficult to infiltrate existing urban schools. They were compelled to start night schools and schools in suburban areas, and they took some drastic measures to try to unseat reformist hold on eductional institutions. This led to rivalry and confrontation with K'ang Yu-wei's supporters, and sometimes led to violent clashes.[59]

As an integral part of the global ideological war, Sun's supporters in Singapore and Malaya launched a vehement attack on the reformists. The *Chong Shing Yit Pao*, the main propaganda organ of the revolutionaries in Singapore, took on the *Nanyang Tsung Hui Pao* (The Union Times), the reformist mouthpiece. The *Chong Shing Yit Pao* was under the control of a prominent journalist, T'ien Tung, and was reinforced by the *Min Pao*'s team from Tokyo, including two prominent revolutionary leaders, Wang Ching-wei and Hu Han-min. Sun Yat-sen supervised the ideological war and contributed two articles to the polemic.[60] Meanwhile, reformist literary

---

Chen Wu She (The Anti-Opium Drama Troupe) in Kuala Lumpur, and the Ching Shih Pan (Warning to the Age Troupe) in Penang. See Yen Ching-hwang, 'Chinese Revolutionary Propaganda Organizations in Singapore and Malaya, 1906–1911', in *Journal of South Seas Society*, vol. 29, pts. 1 and 2, pp. 57–9.

58. Ibid., pp. 59–61.
59. See Yen Ching-hwang, *The Overseas Chinese and the 1911 Revolution*, pp. 154–70.
60. Under the pen name of 'Nanyang hsiao hsueh-sheng' (A primary school student), Dr Sun Yat-sen contributed two articles to the *Chong Shing Yit Pao*. The first one was entitled 'Lun chu ko-ming chao kua-fen che nai pu shih shih-wu che yeh' (Those who fear that revolution would lead to partition are ignorant of world affairs) in *Chong Shing Yit Pao*, 12

heavyweights such as Ou Ch'u-chia and Wu Hsien-tzu, two disciples of K'ang Yu-wei who had considerable experience in journalism in North America, came to Singapore to assist the team. The polemic focused on the issues of a racial revolution, a constitutional monarchy, the practicability of a racial revolution and the introduction of a parliament in China.[61] The reformists were placed in a disadvantageous position in this controversy because they constantly had to defend the actions of the Ch'ing government, which were beyond their control. Ch'ing suppression of a reformist-affiliated group in China, the Cheng Wen She (Political Information Society) in July 1908, exposed the government's lack of sincerity in promoting reform; while its proclamation of the outline of a proposed constitution in September 1908 made the proposed constitutional monarchy a mockery.[62] All these fast moving events in China caught the reformists unprepared, and made them defenseless against the revolutionaries. As more and more Chinese in Singapore and Malaya were subject to the intensive influence of revolutionary propaganda, and understood the limitations of the reformists, many of them shifted their position to support Sun Yat-sen.

The loss of ideological war to the revolutionaries worldwide was not the worst problem for the reformists. Their political fortunes took a sharp turn for the worse after 1908. The suppression of the Cheng Wen She crippled their clandestine activities in China; and the proclamation of the outline of the proposed constitution discredited them as power brokers between the Manchus and the Overseas Chinese. More importantly, the untimely death of Emperor Kuang-hsu on 14 November 1908, a day before the death of Empress Dowager

September 1908, p. 2. The second, which appeared three days later in the same newspaper, was entitled 'P'ing Shih shang pu jen-ts'o' (P'ing Shih still does not admit his mistakes).

61.   See Yen Ching-hwang, *The Overseas Chinese and the 1911 Revolution*, pp. 186–201; Chui Kuei-chiang, '*Chong Shing Yit Poh*: Hsin-chia-po T'ung meng-hui te hou-she, 1907–1910' (*Chong Shing Yit Poh*: The Mouthpiece of the Singapore T'ung Meng Hui, 1907–1910) in *Hsin-hai ko-ming yu Nan-yang hua-jen yen-tao hui lun-wen chi*, pp. 139–48.

62.   Yen Ching-hwang, ibid., p. 202.

Tz'u-hsi, deprived them of the main justification for existence, and crushed their hopes of restoring the emperor's power. Many reformist supporters, including those in Singapore and Malaya, felt depressed and switched sides to support Sun Yat-sen. Thus, by 1909, the victory of the revolutionaries over the reformists in the Chinese communities in Singapore and Malaya was almost complete. The removal of this major stumbling block led to a more active response of Singaporean and Malayan Chinese to Sun Yat-sen's call.

Although the revolutionaries had won the battle over the reformists, their strength was weakened by internal strife. T'ung Meng Hui in its original form was not a united and well-integrated political organisation, but a confederation of three major revolutionary groups with distinctive geographical origins. The different educational backgrounds and attitudes towards the West of the leaders further polarised the component groups within the T'ung Meng Hui. This division was clearly reflected in the power structure of the party, where the leaders of the three groups maintained a tenuous balance of power in the executive committee and recruitment of members tended to have a strong provincial bias, wrecking the unity of the party.[63]

As early as 1907, internal discord led to several attempts to unseat Sun Yat-sen's leadership in the T'ung Meng Hui headquarters in Tokyo. These were led by the leaders of the Chekiang-Kiangsu and Hunanese groups.[64] Dissatisfied with Sun's style of leadership and dismayed by the defeats of a series of revolts in south and southwest of China after the end of 1908, leaders of the Chekiang-Kiangsu group, Chang Ping-lin and T'ao Ch'eng-chang, launched an intensive anti-Sun movement. Tao and close associates were particularly active among the Chinese in Southeast Asia attempting to undermine Sun's support. Tao made some headway in the Dutch East Indies and also

---

63. See S. H. Cheng, 'The T'ung Meng Hui: Its Organization, Leadership and finances, 1905–1912' (unpublished PhD thesis, University of Washington, 1962), p. 118; K.S. Liew, *Struggle for Democracy: Sung Chiao-jen and the 1911 Chinese Revolution* (Canberra, Australian National University Press, 1971), pp. 68–72; 'The list of the executive members of the T'ung Meng Hui headquarters in Tokyo', in *Chung-hua min-kuo k'ai-kuo wu-shih nien wen-hsien*, vol. 1, pt. 11, pp. 233–34.

acquired some support from the Chinese in Singapore, headed by Koh Soh-chew and Ch'en Yun-sheng, two Teochew leaders who were deeply involved in the first and second Teochew uprisings in 1907. They began to compete with Sun in the bid for financial support among Southeast Asian Chinese.[65] At the end of 1909, anti-Sun movement went into top gear. A concerted effort by Chang Ping-lin and T'ao Ch'eng-chang to discredit Sun's leadership came to the surface. An open letter, written sometime in November 1909 by T'ao Ch'eng-chang to the T'ung Meng Hui headquarters in Tokyo, accused Sun of ill-treating his comrades and practising favouratism and corruption, and called for Sun's removal from office.[66] At about the same time, Chang Ping-lin in Tokyo also issued a statement vehemently attacking Sun for refusing to help the ailing *Min Pao* (Peoples Tribune) which was under Chang's editorship, accusing Sun of embezzling public funds, and urging the Overseas Chinese not to donate money to Sun and his supporters.[67]

Tao's and Chang's combined attack thwarted Sun Yat-sen's fundraising activities among the Chinese in Southeast Asia, and a large number of the Chinese in the United States also lost faith in Sun's

---

64. S. H. Cheng, ibid., pp. 119-21; K. S. Liew, ibid., pp. 72–84.
65. See Yen Ching-hwang, *The Overseas Chinese and the 1911 Revolution*, p. 215.; Koh Han-hui (ed), *Ko-ming lieh-shih Hsu Hsueh ch'iu chuan* (The Biography of a Revolutionary Martyr: Koh Soh-chew) (Singapore,1962), p. 6; Feng Tzu-yu, *Chung-hua min-kuo k'ai-kuo ch'ien ko-ming shih*, vol. 2, p. 31; Anonymous, 'Tao Ch'eng-chang tsai Nan-yang ts'ou-k'uan chih chang-ch'eng' (Tao Ch'eng-chang's fundraising regulations in Southeast Asia) (original copy kept in the Kuomintang Archives in Taipei, Taiwan).
66. The original letter was lost. Fortunately it was reproduced in the *Nanyang Tsung Hui Pao*, the main reformist organ in Singapore. However, the title of the letter was slightly changed to 'A circular declaring the crimes of Sun Yat-sen by the revolutionaries in Southeast Asia'. See *Nanyang Tsung Hui Pao*, 11 November 1909, p. 2; 27 November 1909, p 2; 29 November 1909, p. 2.
67. Chang's statement was widely circulated in Japan and overseas, and it was also widely reproduced in reformist newspapers in Japan and Southeast Asia, including the *Nanyang Tsung Hui Pao*. See *Nanyang Tsung Hui Pao*, 6 November 1909, p. 2; Young-tsu Wong, *Search for Modern Nationalism: Zhang Binglin and Revolutionary China, 1869–1936* (Hong Kong, Oxford University Press, 1989), p. 76.

leadership. The damage to Sun Yat-sen and the revolutionary movement was so serious that it prompted Sun to write a letter to defend his integrity and reputation.[68] During this crisis of confidence in Sun Yat-sen the majority of the Chinese in Singapore and Malaya stood firmly behind him. A group of Sun's faithful supporters from Seremban, Kuala Pilah, Malacca and Muar, under the leadership of Teng Tse-ju, came out openly to defend him. They issued two public statements in November and December 1909 refuting Tao's and Chang's charges, and attacked Chang and other dissidents. Chang was described as a selfish, partial, narrow-minded, immoral and disgraceful to revolutionary intellectuals.[69] At the same time, the main revolutionary organ in Singapore, *Chong Shing Yit Pao*, showed its support for Sun. Two editorials were published in the paper attacking both Chang and Tao for their vicious slander of Sun, and praised Sun for his dedication and integrity.[70] The editorials were written by Ho Teh-ju, the chief editor of the paper and a founder of the famous K'ai Ming Public Speaking and Reading Club. Ho was one of the few revolutionary leaders in Singapore who came out in strong support of Sun. He also reproduced some articles in the *Chong Shing Yit Pao* from the *Chung Kuo Yit Pao* and *Kung I Pao* in Hong Kong, and the *Jih Hua Hsin Pao* in Japan.

68. Sun's letter was written to Wu Ch'ih-hui (Wu Ching-heng), a revolutionary leader in France, and the principal adherents of the Hsin Shih Chi magazine in Paris. The letter was to defend Sun against accusations of his embezzlement of revolutionary funds. See 'Letter from Dr Sun Yat-sen to Wu Ch'ih-hui of second half of October, 1909', in *Sun Ch'ung-shan ch'uan-chi*, vol. 1 pp, 419–22; Chang Ch'i-yun (ed), *Ko-fu ch'uan-shu*, pp. 418–19.

69. These two published statements appeared in the *Chong Shing Yit Pao* in Singapore. The first statement, entitled 'Tse Yen' (To reprimand), was published in the paper on 22 November 1909, p 1. The second statement, entitled 'Fu Ssu-li wai-yeh tsai chi ni-ming pang-shu tse' (A reply to those slanderers who sent the anonymous letters in Surahbaya), appeared in the *Chong Shing Yit Pao*, 8 December 1909, p. 1.

70. See Teh-ju, 'Tse Chang Ping-lin yu fa ni-ming shu-tse' (Condemn Chang Ping-lin and those who sent anonymous letters) in *Chong Shing Yit Pao*, 6 December 1909, p. 1 and 7 December 1909, p. 1; Teh-ju, 'Wuhu, t'iao-liang chih hsiao-ch'ou' (Alas! The pitiful clown.) in *Chong Shing Yit Pao*, 3 January 1910, p. 1.

These articles were even more critical of the anti-Sun elements, and Chang was accused of betraying the party.[71]

Despite some damage done to the T'ung Meng Hui in Singapore, the majority of Chinese in the region stood firmly on the side of Sun Yat-sen in this internal struggle. They trusted his integrity and continued to give him moral and material support. This was why Sun, after a successful trip to America between 1909 and 1910, decided to use Singapore and Malaya as the first step in reorganising the party. He transferred the T'ung Meng Hui Southeast Asian headquarters from Singapore to Penang in July 1910, and undertook the restructuring of the branch in an attempt to rejuvenate the party.[72]

At the same time, Sun persisted in his plans to stage revolts in south or southwest China, and planned another large-scale uprising in Canton. On 13 November 1910, he convened a crucial meeting in Penang, known in modern Chinese history as the Penang Conference. Most of the participants were either his loyal followers like Hu Han-min and Huang Hsing, or his faithful local supporters such as Goh Say-ying (Penang), Ng Kim-keng (Penang), Teng Tse-ju (Kuala Pilah) and Li Hau-cheong (Ipoh).[73] The choice of the participants, and the manner in which the Penang Conference was called, reflect Sun Yat-sen's determination to organise and stage another major revolt in his own way. The conference was called without the approval of the T'ung Meng Hui headquarters in Tokyo, and the branches in Southeast Asia, which were influenced by his opponents, were not invited to send representatives. Sun was confident and determined that with the support of majority of the Chinese in Singapore and Malaya he would be able to stage another

71.   See *Chong Shing Yit Pao*, 30 November 1909, p. 1, 2 December 1909, p. 1, 18 January 1910, p 7.
72.   See Yang Han-hsiang, 'Chung-hua min-kuo k'ai-kuo ch'ien-hou chih pen-she ko-ming shih', in Yang Han-hsiang (ed), *Ping-ch'eng yeh-shu pao-she nien-ssu chou-nien chi-nien t'e-k'an*, pp. 21–2.
73.   Ibid., pp. 32–3; Tsou Lu, *Kuang-chou san-yeh nien-chiu ko-ming shih* (A History of the Canton March 29th Revolution) (Hong Kong, 1939), p. 3; Yen Ching-hwang, 'Penang Chinese and the 1911 Revolution', in *Journal of South Seas Society*, vol. 41, pts. 1 and 2 (1986), p. 69.

major revolt. The fervent response and generous donations to the Canton 29th March Uprising by the Chinese in the region vindicated Sun's trust in local Chinese support.[74]

Conclusion

Sun Yat-sen had a close personal relationship with the Chinese in Singapore and Malaya, especially with some revolutionary leaders such as Tan Chor-nam, Teo Eng-hock and Teng Tse-ju. His perception of Overseas Chinese role as the main benefactor of the revolution well applied to the Chinese in Singapore and Malaya. Numerical strength and wealth of Singaporean and Malayan Chinese led Sun to expect them to play a greater financial role than other Overseas Chinese. Negative images of Sun, fear of reprisal, conservatism and the influence of the reformists were the factors which thwarted the early response of the Chinese in Singapore and Malaya to Sun Yat-sen's call. However, support for Sun in the region grew with the change of tide from 1900 to 1905. From 1905 to 1911, support for Sun by the Singaporean and Malayan Chinese was substantial and firm. With the establishment of various T'ung Meng Hui branches in Singapore and Malaya, Sun's faithful supporters were able to eliminate the reformist influence and effectively mobilise tens of thousands of local Chinese to support Sun's ongoing revolutionary uprisings staged in the south and southwest of China. During a split within revolutionary ranks, the majority of the revolutionaries in Singapore and Malaya stood on Sun's side, trusted his integrity, and continued to give him moral and financial support. With their solid support, Sun was able to counter the influence of Chang Ping-lin and T'ao Ch'eng-chang, and to stage an important revolt in Canton in April 1911 which indirectly led to the successful Wuchang Revolt in October of the same year.

74. See Yen Ching-hwang, *The Overseas Chinese and the 1911 Revolution*, pp. 234–38.

CHAPTER 12

The Overseas Chinese and the Second Sino-Japanese War, 1937–1945

China's resistance against Japanese aggression during the Second Sino-Japanese War would have been much harder had there been no Overseas Chinese support. China's spirit of resistance would have been weakened if the support of Overseas Chinese had not been forthcoming. The Overseas Chinese were spread widely throughout the world, and their support for resisting Japanese aggression assured China that it was not fighting alone. Its overseas compatriots responded fervently to the war by donating millions of dollars and tons of war materials, and by directly joining the battlefield. Overseas Chinese support sustained China's fighting spirit, toughened its stand against the aggressors and provided it with immense confidence that the final victory would be won. This chapter aims to examine the relationship between China's war of resistance and the Overseas Chinese: the continuous upsurge of Overseas Chinese nationalism, the organisation and techniques of mobilisation of Overseas Chinese support, and the financial and material contributions of the Overseas Chinese to the war.

Overseas Chinese Nationalism and the Japanese Invasion

The Overseas Chinese in Southeast Asia paid a high price for their strong support to China's war of resistance against the Japanese. Tens of thousands of them were massacred by the Japanese invaders who conquered Southeast Asia in the early 1940s and punished the Overseas Chinese for their support of China's resistance. What motivated and sustained their fight against the Japanese aggressors in China was their strong sense of nationalism and their commitment to the well-being of a wretched motherland.

Overseas Chinese nationalism began in the late nineteenth century when China was facing Western and Japanese imperialism, and the commencement of China's courtship of its overseas subjects.[1] The arrival in the Overseas Chinese communities of the reformists, led by K'ang Yu-wei, and the revolutionaries, led by Dr Sun Yat-sen, spurred the growth of Overseas Chinese nationalism, ending large-scale Overseas Chinese participation in the overthrow of the Manchu rule in the 1911 Revolution.[2] The founding of the Republic and the impact of the May Fourth movement in 1919 sustained this burgeoning Overseas Chinese nationalism. At the same time, the pressure and encroachment of Japanese imperialists on China since 1915 gave rise to an upsurge of the Overseas Chinese nationalism. This upsurge went through several stages: outrage against the Japanese Twenty-One Demands in 1915, the anti-Japanese movement in the wake of the May Fourth Incident in 1919, and response to the Tsinan Incident in 1928 and the Manchurian Incident in 1931. All these agitations were targeted at Japan, which emerged after the First World War as the most formidable enemy of the Chinese people.

The weakening of the position of the Western powers in China during and after the First World War stirred the ambitions of the Japanese imperialists and provided them with an excellent opportunity to expand in China. The notorious Twenty-One Demands, which was

---

1. See M.R. Godley, 'The Late Ch'ing Courtship of the Chinese in Southeast Asia', in *Journal of Asian Studies*, vol. 34, no. 2 (1975), pp. 361–85.

2. See Yen Ching-hwang, *The Overseas Chinese and the 1911 Revolution* (Kuala Lumpur and New York, Oxford University Press, 1976), pp. 262–86.

tantamount to effective colonisation of China without firing a shot, was imposed on the Yuan Shih-k'ai Government in February 1915, and it outraged millions of Chinese including the Overseas Chinese. Japan's claim for control of the former German concession in Shantung in 1919 further provoked the Overseas Chinese to respond. Widespread anti-Japanese demonstrations and riots occurred in the Overseas Chinese communities, especially those in Southeast Asia.[3] By the end of the 1920s and early 1930s, the surge of Overseas Chinese nationalism reached new heights. It was brought about by the Tsinan Incident in Shantung in 1928, and the Manchurian Incident in 1931.[4] Both events demonstrated the naked aggression towards China by the Japanese imperialists, who attempted to halt the rising tide of nationalism in China.

This rise of Overseas Chinese nationalism saw the intense politicisation of the Overseas Chinese, who were more conscious than before of the danger that China encountered. Burning with patriotism, they developed a watchful eye on the process of Japanese encroachments on their motherland, and were prepared to take action to help confront the Japanese aggressors. It was in this historical context that the Second Sino-Japanese war occurred.

The timing of the Japanese all-out aggression towards China in July 1937 did not shock all of the Overseas Chinese. Those who had followed closely the events in the 1930s realised that the frustration of the Japanese imperialists would eventually lead to an all-out aggression in China. What astounded and dismayed them most was the speed of China's defeat. In a matter of weeks, China lost most of its territories in the north and the east to Japanese invaders, and the Kuomintang Government was forced to retreat to the deep southwest. The south,

---

3. See Chui Kuei Chiang, 'H'ai-hsia chih-min-ti hua-jen tui wu-shih yun-tung ti fan-hsiang' (The Response of the Straits Chinese to the May Fourth Movement), in *Journal of the South Seas Society*, vol. 20, nos. 1 and 2, pp. 13–8.

4. See Yen Ching-hwang, 'The Response of the Chinese in Singapore and Malaya to the Tsinan Incident, 1928', in *Journal of the South Seas Society*, vol. 43. no. 1 (1988), p. 122; Yen Ching-hwang, *Community and Politics: The Chinese in Colonial Singapore and Malaysia* (Singapore, Times Academic Press, 1995), pp. 306–29.

where the majority of the Overseas Chinese came from, was also under threat. The Japanese had taken ports and key cities and had penetrated into vast rural China. This rather gloomy outlook in the first few months of the opening of the Sino-Japanese war did not demoralise the Overseas Chinese, however. Instead, the war united them and toughened their spirit of resistance to the Japanese aggressors.

Mobilisation of the Overseas Chinese

Dislocated by the war and humiliated by the Japanese invaders, the Nationalist government retreated into the deep southwest of China to bide its time. The Overseas Chinese bureau of the Nationalist government was decimated during the war. Most of its important branches in the south, including those in Canton, Swatow, Amoy, Hai-kou and Shanghai, were closed as result of Japanese occupation.[5] The regrouping of the Nationalist bureaucrats in Chungking enabled the government to formulate an Overseas Chinese policy during the war of resistance. The main thrust of the government's wartime Overseas Chinese policy was the mobilisation of the human and material resources of its overseas subjects in the fight against the invaders. However, what should be noted is that the successful mobilisation of Overseas Chinese resources in support of the war was not so much due to the Nationalist government's ability to execute a well co-ordinated master plan, but more due to the effective response of the Overseas Chinese to the call for assistance. The response fell into three major areas: the anti-Japanese propaganda movement; a boycott and economic sanctions against the Japanese; and financial and material support for the war.

The Anti-Japanese Propaganda Movement

The value of propaganda to China's resistance was beyond doubt. Japan could have got away without international condemnation if its naked aggression had not been so widely publicised to the outside world.

---

5.   See Hsiang Ch'eng (ed), *Ch'iao-wu wu-shih-nien* (Fifty Years of Overseas Chinese Affairs) (Taipei, Ch'iao-wu wei-yuan-hui, 1982), p. 61.

However, Europe in the second half of the 1930s was embroiled with problems of how to cope with the rise of Nazi Germany and Fascist Italy, while the United State's attitude towards the rising tide of world conflicts was ambivalent. In this unfavourable international environment, the support of foreign powers was important to China. A condemnation of Japan for its naked aggression would boost China's morale to fight; and effective propaganda could therefore turn the tide of world public opinion in China's favour.

The Overseas Chinese anti-Japanese propaganda movement operated at two different levels: at an international level, aiming at the shift of the world public opinion in favour of China; and at a local level, in order to mobilise Overseas Chinese popular support. The movement was dominated by the printed media — newspapers, magazines, pamphlets and leaflets. Despite different political viewpoints and sectarian interests, the Overseas Chinese media demonstrated unprecedented unity in fighting against the common enemy. In North America and Europe, the Overseas Chinese propaganda strategy was focused on gaining the support of world public opinion. This support was crucial to China's resistance to Japanese aggression. Since the commencement of the war, the Chinese in European countries, principally those in France, Germany and Britain, organised themselves in a common united front in September 1937. A variety of propaganda measures were adopted, designed to gain public sympathy and support for China's resistance cause. Anti-Japanese leaflets in Western languages were widely distributed; public talks and film shows on China's resistance and the cruelty of Japanese soldiers were organised; and press releases were made to provide accurate information about the war. A small committee to co-ordinate this international propaganda was also established at a French university.[6]

In the United States, the strategy of getting the support of the white communities was given the top priority. Although no national united front was formed, various Chinese organisations in New York, San Francisco, Boston, Chicago and Washington DC concentrated their

---

6. See Jen Kuei-hsiang, *Hua-ch'iao ti-erh ch'ih ai-kuo kao-ch'ao* (The Second High Tide of Overseas Chinese Patriotism) (Beijing, Chung-kuo tang-shih tzu-liao ch'u-pan-she, 1989), pp. 261–62.

propaganda activities on gaining American public support for China's resistance. The Chinese Student Association of Washington, for instance, set up a committee exclusively handling publicity aimed at white communities. It published anti-Japanese weekly in English; liaised with American journalists; corrected inaccurate reports about the Sino-Japanese war; delivered lectures to various church congregations and organised public rallies.[7] Apart from widely publishing China's cause for popular support, the Chinese communities also lobbied American politicians, whose support was crucial, to stop United States' sale of scrap irons and petroleum to Japan. In addition to institutional efforts, individual Chinese in the United States also showed great enthusiasm for propaganda activities in an attempt to gain American support. The story of the devotion of a Chinese woman in Chicago to the propaganda effort is moving. The woman, Madam Ethel S. Kam, was a widow with two daughters running a laundry shop in a suburb of Chicago. After having been informed of China's predicament, she was determined to publicise the brutality of Japanese soldiers in China in an attempt to gain public sympathy for China's cause. She went to the extent of mortgaging her house to finance her lecture tour, which extensively covered major cities and towns, and she delivered at least fifty-one lectures in more than two months.[8]

Unlike in Europe and North America, the propaganda movement in Southeast Asia was focused mainly on gaining financial support from the Overseas Chinese. This was probably due to different needs in relation to those countries. In Europe and North America the Chinese, though constituting an insignificant portion of the entire population, were strategically located, and were thus able to influence public opinion in the West. At the same time, as Europe and North America were the homes of the leading Western powers, any support from these powers would be crucial to bring pressure on Japan. In contrast, western presence in Southeast Asia consisted mainly of European and American colonies, and the Overseas Chinese in the region could not mobilise

7.   See Yang Kuo-piao et. al., *Mei-kuo hua-ch'iao shih* (A History of the Chinese in the United States of America) (Guangzhou, Kuangtung kao-teng chiao-yu ch'u-pan-she, 1989), p. 503.

8.   Ibid., p. 504; Jen Kuei-hsiang, op. cit., pp. 264–65.

any political muscle to bear on Japan by publicising China's cause to the indigenous population. This was why the propaganda movement was mainly targeted at the support of the Overseas Chinese.

Despite political and sectarian differences, the Chinese newspapers in Southeast Asia were able to form into a mighty force. They maintained a constant barrage of reportage on the process of the war, and on the heroic resistance launched by both the Nationalist and Communist forces. Articles and editorials praising the resistance and appealing to the Overseas Chinese for generous donations flooded the pages; names of the donors and the amount of money donated were published in a attempt to solicit more and larger contributions. The patriotic appeals to the Overseas Chinese struck a chord of nationalistic sentiment, and succeeded in keeping the issue of resistance alive in the minds of the Overseas Chinese masses.[9]

Apart from the printed media, other forms of propaganda were also adopted in Southeast Asia and throughout the world. Significant and memorable dates such as 18 September (the day that Japan launched its attack on Manchuria in 1931), the Double Seven (7 July 1937, the day that the Japanese launched a large-scale attack at the Marco Polo Bridge, also known as the Marco Polo Bridge Incident) and the Double Ten (the national day of the Republic of China) were singled out for commemoration. Public gatherings were held to commemorate these occasions: solemn ceremonies were conducted; emotional speeches were made and pledges for fighting the enemy to the end were constantly aired. They were followed by the selling of flowers to raise funds for the resistance cause, as well as staging drama performances which dramatised heroic acts of resistance and the cruelty of the enemies.

Anti-Japanese Boycott and Economic Sanctions

The speedy success of the Japanese invasion of China in the Sino-Japanese war tended to give the impression that Japanese military power

9. See Tseng Jui-yen, *Hua-ch'iao yu k'ang Jih chan-cheng* (Overseas Chinese and the War of Resistance against Japan) (Ch'engtu, Szechwan ta-hsueh ch'u-pan-she, 1988), pp. 74–9.

was unbeatable. But a critical analysis of Japan's strength revealed that this seemingly formidable military power rested on rather shaky ground. Japan was a small country with limited resources, and its ability to continue the war largely depended on the import of war materials from overseas. For instance, more than seventy percent of its iron had to come from China and Southeast Asia before the war, and the war had increased its dependence on supply from these regions.[10] Japan's military power would be weakened if the supply of its pig iron was disrupted. Well-aware of this strategic importance, the Overseas Chinese leaders in Southeast Asia, especially in Malaya where Japanese iron mines were located, were determined to disconnect Japan's supply lines by agitating for the withdrawal of Chinese labour from the mines. At the same time, Overseas Chinese throughout the world launched a widespread movement to boycott Japanese goods. Again, Southeast Asia played a significant role in this movement, partly because the number of Overseas Chinese was large, and partly because they controlled much of the retail trade in the region. Wiping out Japanese goods from Southeast Asian markets would deal a severe blow to the burgeoning Japanese textile industry, which had already established a firm base in the region.[11]

Boycott was a powerful economic weapon designed to crush the enemy and to reap economic and political benefits. Its frequent use by Chinese nationalists both in China and abroad testified to its effectiveness. Overseas Chinese nationalists had mastered this weapon and repeatedly used it against the Americans in 1905, and against the Japanese in 1908, 1915, 1919, 1928 and 1931.[12] By the time the

10. See Hsu Hsiu-ch'ung, 'Hsing-Ma hua-tsu tui Jih Pen te ching-chi chih-ts'ai, 1937–42' (Economic Boycott against Japanese by the Chinese in Singapore and Malaya, 1937–42) in Kwa Bak Lim and Ng Chin Keong (eds), *Hsin-chia-po hua -tsu shih lun-chi* (Essays on the Chinese in Singapore) (Singapore, Nanyang ta-hsueh pi-yueh-sheng hsueh-hui, 1972), p. 139.

11. See Shinya Sugiyama, 'The Expansion of Japan's Cotton Textile Exports into Southeast Asia', in Sugiyama Shinya and Milagros C. Guerrero (eds), *International Commercial Rivalry in Southeast Asia in the Interwar Period* (New Haven, Yale Southeast Asian Studies, 1994), pp. 40–73.

12. See Delber L. McKee, *Chinese Exclusion versus the Opening Door Policy, 1900–1906* (Detriot, Wayne State University Press, 1977), pp. 103–12; Yen Ching-

Japanese all-out invasion occurred in July 1937, Overseas Chinese nationalists did not hesitate to use boycott against their hated enemies. The boycott took various forms: refusing to buy Japanese goods (including manufactured goods and foodstuffs); prohibiting the sale of Japanese goods by Chinese wholesalers and retailers; withdrawing labour from Japanese mining companies; denying services to local Japanese nationals and refusing to obtain services from them.[13] The concentration of Overseas Chinese in Southeast Asia provided the focus for the boycott. As their numerical and economic strength in the region guaranteed the movement its initial success.

At the forefront of the boycott were the Chinese in Singapore and Malaya. In Singapore, the Chinese Cloth Merchants Association imposed a ban on the import of Japanese textiles by members; more than 90 Chinese watch retailers pledged not to import Japanese watches; and Chinese bicycle merchants decided to replace Japanese goods with European products.[14] In Malaya, Selangor Chinese bicycle merchants decided to stop imports from Japan, and 63 grocery-shop proprietors in Taiping ceased to import Japanese foodstuffs; in Penang, the Association of Chinese Doctors and Chinese Medicinal Merchants resolved not to import any goods from Japan; in Ipoh, Chinese trishaw coolies refused to accept Japanese passengers or charged them double fare; and in Seremban, a Chinese

hwang, *Coolies and Mandarins: China's Protection of the Overseas Chinese during the Late Ch'ing Period, 1851–1911* (Singapore, Singapore University Press, 1985), pp. 322–24; Yoji Akashi, 'The Nanyang Chinese anti-Japanese and Boycott Movement, 1908-1928: A Study of Nanyang Chinese Nationalism', in *Journal of the South Seas Society*, vol. 23, nos. 1 & 2 (1968), pp. 70–4; Yen Ching-hwang, 'The Response of the Chinese in Singapore and Malaya to the Tsinan Incident, 1928', in *Journal of the South Seas Society*, vol. 43, no. 1 (1988), pp. 1–22, also in Yen Ching-hwang, *Community and Politics: The Chinese in Colonial Singapore and Malaysia*, pp. 306–29.

13.   See Stephen M.Y. Leong, Sources, Agencies and Manifestations of Overseas Chinese Nationalism in Malaya, 1937–41(PhD thesis, University of California, Los Angeles, 1976), pp. 262–63; *Nanyang Siang Pau*, Singapore, 14 January 1938 and 6 March 1938.

14.   See Hsu Hsiu-ch'ung., 'Hsing-Ma hua-tsu tui Jih Pen te ching-chi chih-ts'ai', op. cit., p. 144.

woman who visited a Japanese dentist was threatened by a crowd with violence.[15] In Burma, Thailand and the Philippines, the boycott of Japanese goods followed the same pattern. In Thailand, Chinese merchants cancelled contracts with Japanese firms for the export of rice and rubber, two of the important raw materials needed by Japan. In Burma, a committee was established to oversee the boycott operation. It organised boycott demonstrations, banned Japanese imports and punished those who dared to violate the impositions.[16] Not all Overseas Chinese were patriots, however. Some Chinese merchants who had established strong trade links with Japan were reluctant to give up their lucrative business, and only paid lip-service to the boycott.

The boycott movement would have failed if the ban on Japanese imports had not been vigorously implemented. Responsibility for enforcement fell on the shoulders of a group of patriotic Chinese, a radical arm of the anti-Japanese mobilisation. With the prohibition of any form of violence imposed by the Western colonial governments in Southeast Asia, these patriotic Chinese went underground and organised themselves into clandestine bodies with extraordinary names such as the Iron Blood Squad (*Tieh Shuai Tuan*) the Red Blood Brigade and the Eliminating Traitors Squad (*Chu Chien Tuan*). They executed the bans by coercive power or violence. Shops selling Japanese goods were tarred black, and Chinese merchants who were suspected of importing Japanese goods or using Japanese materials for their manufactured products were invariably warned with intimidating letters; those who still defied the warning had their ears cut off. It is claimed that in 1938 more than 100 Chinese in Singapore and 14 in Malaya lost their ears because of their unrepentant behaviour.[17]

15. See Stephen M.Y. Leong, op. cit., p. 263; Jen Kuei-hsiang, op. cit.
16. See Tseng Jui-yen, op. cit., pp. 93-4.
17. See Yoji Akashi, *The Nanyang Chinese National Salvation Movement, 1937– 1941* (Kansas, Center for East Asian Studies, The University of Kansas, 1970), p. 18; Yen Ching-hwang, 'Overseas Chinese Nationalism: A Historical Study', in Yen Ching-hwang, *Studies in Modern Overseas Chinese History* (Singapore, Times Academic Press, 1995), p. 146; Jen Kuei-hsiang, op. cit., pp. 281–82.

Withdrawal of labour, a tactic used by modern unionists in the West, was employed by the Chinese in Malaya as another effective weapon to attack Japanese economic power in the region. Japanese economic penetration of Malaya in the pre-war period covered three major areas: rubber planting, iron mining and fishing.[18] The first two were important to the Japanese war economy. Japanese-owned iron ore mines were concentrated in Johor, Trengganu and Kelantan in the southern and northeastern parts of the Malay Peninsula. All of these mines employed large number of Chinese workers. The Bukit Besi mine in Trengganu, for instance, employed some 2,500 Chinese labourers in 1938.[19] The production of rubber and iron ore by Japanese enterprises on the Peninsula became more important to Japan's war machine because of their strategic value in war. Well aware of this fact, the Overseas Chinese nationalists in Singapore and Malaya campaigned for the withdrawal of labour from Japanese-owned enterprises. In December 1937, 800 Chinese quit their jobs at the Ishihara Sangyu Koshi mine in Sri Medan, Batu Pahat in the state of Johor. There were also reports of Chinese labourers abandoning their work in Japanese-owned rubber estates in Mentakab (in the state of Pahang) and Seremban.[20] Foremost among the promoters of this campaign was the Chinese Labour Anti-Japanese Salvation Corps, founded in 1938 and led by the younger members of the Kuomintang branch in Singapore. Its primary aim was to weaken Japanese economic power in Malaya by means of withdrawing labour. It organised a large-scale labour walk-out in the Bukit Besi mine involving more than 2,000 Chinese mining labourers, and arranged their repatriation to Singapore.[21]

Although the boycott and economic sanctions in Southeast Asia did not cripple the Japanese war machine in China, it nevertheless

---

18. See Kee Yeh Siew, 'The Japanese in Malaya before 1942', in *Journal of the South Seas Society*, vol. 20, nos.1 and 2 (1965), pp. 48–88.
19. See *Nanyang Siang Pau*, 6 March 1938.
20. See *The Straits Times*, Singapore, 12 December 1937; *Nanyang Siang Pau*, 14 January 1938.
21. See C. F. Yong and R.B. McKenna, *The Kuomintang Movement in British Malaya* (Singapore, Singapore University Press, 1990), p. 189; *Nanyang Siang Pau*, 12 March 1938.

dealt a severe blow to the Japanese economy, especially with regard to its economic activities in Southeast Asia. This can be seen from the decline of Japanese goods entering the region after the boycott movement began to bite. In 1937, before the boycott movement took effect, total Japanese exports to Southeast Asia were estimated at 386.7 million yen; this slumped sharply to 219.2 million yen in 1938. Although exports to Southeast Asia picked up slightly in 1939 at 235.5 million yen, and 281.1 million yen in 1940, they never recovered to the level of the pre-boycott period.[22] In the countries where the boycott movement was most enthusiastically implemented, the effect was more devastating. In Singapore and Malaya, the import of Japanese goods declined by 67.9 per cent from 71.3 million yen in 1937 to 22.9 million yen in 1938, and by 1941 they had declined to 10 million yen. The effect in the Philippines was equally dramatic. Japanese trade with the Philippines consistently decreased by an annual average of fifty percent from 1938 to 1941, from 60.3 million yen in 1937 to 13.3 million in 1941.[23]

The boycott movement was also carried out by the Chinese in North America and Europe. On 22 August 1938, a public meeting for the boycott of Japanese goods was called in Paris, which was attended by 600 or 700 Chinese, including the Chinese Consul, visiting Chinese dignitaries and the representatives of the Anti-Japanese Alliance from other European countries. The meeting resolved to step up the campaign and widely distributed leaflets for that purpose. A committee of 41 members was established to supervise its operation.[24] In the United States, the thrust of the boycott movement was to thwart American supply of war materials to Japan. The main target was the shipping of scrap iron from the United States to Japan. In December 1938, with the support of the American unions, they succeeded in frustrating the shipping of 2,500

22. See Yoji Akashi, *The Nanyang Chinese National Salvation Movement, 1937– 1941*, p. 143.
23. Ibid., pp. 142–45.
24. See Tseng Jui-yen., *Hua-ch'iao yu kang Jih chan-cheng* (Overseas Chinese and the War of Resistance against Japan), pp. 98–9

tons of scrap iron from San Francisco to Japan.[25] However, the relatively small numbers of Chinese involved, and their weak economic position in North America and Europe, reduced their effectiveness in the boycott.

Financial and Material Support for the War Against the Japanese

The war of resistance against Japan was not just a contest of military might, but also a contest of will, economic power and human resources between China and Japan. China had enormous human resources which could be turned into a fighting force, but China lacked the economic power to arm its troops and sustain protracted warfare. In this sense, the financial and material support of the Overseas Chinese was crucial to sustaining the resistance.

The success of mobilisation of Overseas Chinese financial and material support for the war was predicated on the organisation, techniques and methods on which it was mobilised. The formation of various relief fund organisations was thus vital. Geographical barriers and social divisions in the Overseas Chinese communities thwarted initial efforts, but the intensification of the war crisis in China created a favourable climate for temporary solidarity among them. Being numerically smaller and less complicated socially than their Southeast Asian counterparts, the Chinese communities in Europe had the advantage of being able to take the lead in the formation of a larger organisation for collective efforts. At the time war broke out in July 1937, the Chinese in the whole of Europe were estimated to number 55,364, accounting for only 0.37 percent of total the Overseas Chinese population. They consisted mainly of students and workers who were more receptive to the propaganda of resistance and were easier to be mobilised. Various anti-Japanese and relieve China associations had already sprung up in France, Britain and Germany in the early 1930s in response to Japan's continuous encroachments on China's territories since the Manchurian Incident in 1931.[26] The imminent Japanese

---

25. See Yang Kuo-piao et. al., *Mei-kuo hua-ch'iao shih* (A History of the Chinese in the United States of America), p. 508.
26. See Jen Kuei-hsiang, *Hua-ch'iao ti-erh ch'ih ai-kuo kao-ch'ao* (The second High Tide of Overseas Chinese Patriotism), p. 63.

all-out invasion prompted the Chinese in Europe to form an united body in September 1936. On 13 September, a public meeting was called in Paris, which resulted in the establishment of the Pan Europe Overseas Chinese Anti-Japanese and Relieve China Alliance (Ch'uan Ou hua-ch'iao k'ang Jih chiu-kuo lien-ho-hui). The organisation was formed to co-ordinate all anti-Japanese and support-China activities.[27]

Significant unity was achieved in the Southeast Asian Chinese communities with the founding of the Federation of China Relief Fund Association of Southeast Asia (Nan-yang ch'ou-chen tsu-kuo nan-min tsung-hui) on 10 October 1938.[28] Various anti-Japanese and relieve China associations were established in Southeast Asia soon after the outbreak of the Sino-Japanese war. But these organisations were restricted by their narrow geographical boundaries, which prevented them from more effectively mobilising the support of the Overseas Chinese in the region. At the time war broke out, the Chinese population in Southeast Asia was estimated to number six million, accounting for seventy-nine percent of the total Overseas Chinese population.[29] As the war rolled on, the need for closer co-operation in fundraising and more effectively channelling funds to China prompted the Southeast Asian Chinese to come together under an umbrella organisation. The man who emerged to take the lead was Tan Kah Kee, a prominent leader of the Chinese in Singapore. With the strong support of Chinese leaders in the Philippines and the Dutch East Indies, Tan succeeded in calling a meeting in Singapore on 10 October 1938. It was attended by more than 180 delegates representing major Chinese organisations in Singapore, Malaya, Sarawak, Borneo, Thailand, the Philippines, the Dutch East Indies, Hong Kong, Burma and Vietnam. The week-long convention established the Federation of the China Relief Fund Association of Southeast Asia, with 21 elected office-bearers under Tan's leadership. The founding of this organisation

27. Ibid., pp. 64–9.
28. See Tan Kah Kee, *Nan-ch'iao hui-i lu* (Autobiography) vol.1 (Singapore, Nanyang Printing Press, 1946), p. 48.
29. See Jen Kuei-hsiang, op. cit., pp. 67–8.

highlighted the success of the resistance in gaining the financial and material support of the Chinese in Southeast Asia.[30]

The formation of various similar umbrella organisations throughout Overseas Chinese communities world wide provided an effective focus for the fundraising efforts. These orgnisations worked out strategies and methods suitable to their own conditions. In Southeast Asia, where the Overseas Chinese communities were undermined by dialect conflicts, the strategy was to blur the dialect boundaries in fundraising campaigns; while in North America, where the Cantonese dialect predominated, no such measure was needed. To minimise the impact of dialect difference in the war efforts, the Federation of the China Relief Fund Association of Southeast Asia expanded its dialect base by setting up various sub-committees headed by reputable dialect group leaders. Each sub-committee co-opted influential members from respective dialect groups (*pang*), and worked out strategies and methods for fundraising.[31]

A variety of methods for fundraising were adopted by various Overseas Chinese organisations throughout the world. They fell under three broad categories: straight cash donations; donations of services, food and other materials; and donation of time and effort. The popular Chinese slogan at that time, "Those who have money donate money, those who have physical strength donate manpower" (*Yu-chien chu-chien, yu-li chu-li*), summarised the spirit of co-operation and efforts of the fundraising campaign. Straight cash donations consisted mainly of the monthly donation of wages or cash; donations through personal approaches; donations made on special occasions such as national day or Sun Yat-sen's birthday; donations for special purposes such as the purchase of aeroplanes, tanks or perhaps winter clothes; special contributions saved from expenditure on funerals, weddings and birthday celebrations; and donations collected from donation boxes.

30. See C.F. Yong, *Tan Kah Kee: An Overseas Chinese Legend* (Singapore, Oxford University Press, 1987), pp. 213–16.
31. See Pang Wing Seng, 'The Double-Seventh Incident, 1937: Singapore Chinese Response to the Outbreak of the Sino-Japanese War', in *Journal of Southeast Asia Studies*, vol. 4, no. 2 (1973), pp. 278–79.

Monthly donations of wages or cash were the most important because they were regular and were made on a long-term basis. The idea of monthly donation was first adopted by the China Relief Fund Association of Penang in October 1937, to boost its fundraising activities. It was proven to be very effective and funds were collected regularly. Similar methods were widely adopted in other parts of Southeast Asia.[32]

Special purpose donations were also important because they had a clear target and a single purpose. The purchase of aeroplanes and tanks to strengthen China's military power had a popular appeal to the Overseas Chinese, because these items of military hardware were needed to improve China's ability to fight the enemy. The Chinese in America by the end of 1940 had raised a sum of US$6.3 million for the purchase of aeroplanes, while the Chinese in the Dutch East Indies on one occasion in August 1941 donated $1 million dollars on the spot for the strengthening of China's airforce.[33]

Special contributions saved from expenditure on social occasions was also effective and had wider social implications. The Overseas Chinese spent a great deal of money on special occasions such as funerals, weddings and birthday celebrations to show off their wealth in an attempt to gain social prestige. Channelling this expenditure into the war effort changed the social attitudes of many Overseas Chinese, altered their priorities in the use of money and made their celebrations more meaningful. This appeal seemed to be popular and widespread. For example, the Chinese Consul in the Philippines encouraged collective wedding ceremonies, and the money saved by individual couples was donated to the relief fund; one newly-wedded Chinese couple in the Philippines saved $3,000 in this way. Another Philippine Chinese saved $10,000 from his sixtieth-birthday celebration, and the money was given to help relieve wounded soldiers in China.[34]

The donation of services, food and materials was another form of collecting contributions across all social classes in the Overseas

32. See Tseng Jui-yen, *Hua-ch'iao yu k'ang Jih chan-cheng*, pp. 126–27.
33. Ibid., p. 129.
34. Ibid., p. 132.

Chinese communities. Donation of food was usually made by hawkers and food peddlers who had to earn their living by hawking. They donated their labour and food, and the proceeds went to the relief fund. Donation of services was made by members of the lower class, such as prostitutes and transport coolies (rickshaw pullers). Their services were also transformed into cash for the purpose of helping China to fight against the Japanese. Although the money collected from selling food and services did not constitute a major portion of the funds, it nevertheless reflects the enthusiasm and support from these groups of Chinese, whose lives were a constant struggle to eke out a living. The donation of materials was made by traders and merchants through levies imposed on some import and export items. The donation of manpower was mainly confined to teachers and artists, and their efforts were channelled into collective efforts to organise cultural shows and theatrical performances, the proceeds from which went into the relief funds.

The techniques used by the China Relief Association of Muar, Malaya, epitomises the multifarious methods used by the fundraising movement in the Overseas Chinese communities. These methods included monthly pledges from individuals, shops or groups; donations and fundraising on commemorative days; special donations from individuals and shops through personal approaches; national debt-repayment fundraising; special donations of goods; the sale of national bonds; and fundraising through cultural shows, theatrical performances, concerts and football matches.[35]

The Muar experience shows that the monthly donation constituted the basic income of the movement. The China Relief Fund Association of Muar was very active in the fundraising campaign. A careful plan of how to raise money was worked out.

35. See Tay Lian Soo, 'Ma-po chou-chen mu-huan-ch'i erh-ch'ih ta-chan h'ai-wai hua-jen tui Chung-kuo kung-hsien ke-an yen-chiu (Muar: The Model of Fundraising for China Relief: A Case Study of the Contribution of the Overseas Chinese to China), in Lin Tien-wai (ed), *Ya-Tai ti-fang wen-hsien yen-chiu lun wen-chi* (Collected Essays on Local History of the Asian-Pacific Region: Contribution of Overseas Chinese) (Hong Kong, Centre of Asian Studies, University of Hong Kong, 1991), pp. 338–39.

The Muar district was divided into several zones with name books compiled. Potential donors, either individuals, shops or organisations, were identified and approached personally for monthly donations, and their names and the amount of money were recorded in the books. Money due was paid either at the branch office of the Association or collected by special collectors. Despite some problems, the constant flow of cash from this source became an important part of the total funds. What brought the Association into the spotlight were its dynamic activities in putting on various social and cultural shows. Its aim was to involve the maximum number of local Chinese in its fundraising activities and to broaden the social base of its appeal. This invariably involved local Chinese schools, theatrical troupes, performing art troupes, sports and martial arts associations, Chinese teachers associations, movie companies, and dialect and clan associations. It involved a cross-section of thousands of local Chinese in the shows, regardless of age and sex. Men and women, elderly and young students, all contributed something to make these cultural shows successful. Some were actively involved in organising manpower, some in performances, and many were involved in selling tickets, foods, drinks and flowers. All proceeds went into the coffers of the consolidated relief funds.[36]

The dynamic fundraising movement in the Overseas Chinese communities was undoubtedly a great success. This was reflected in the colossal amount of money collected and remitted to China. Based on government records, the Overseas Chinese Bureau of the Nationalist Government estimated that the financial contributions of the Overseas Chinese to China's war efforts in a period of six years from 1937 to 1942 was C$360,737,997. The breakdown was C$16,696,740 for 1937; C$14,672,136 for 1938; C$65,368,148 for 1939; C$123,804,871 for 1940; C$106,540,574 for 1941 and C$33,653,528 for 1942. (This produces an aggregate figure of C$387,736,046, but by adding all of the figures together, contributions total C$360,737,997.)[37]

36. Ibid.
37. See Ch'iao-wu wei-yuan-hui & Hua-ch'iao chih pien-ch'uan wei-yuan-hui (eds), *Hua-ch'iao chih tsung-chih* (The Historical Records of the Overseas Chinese in the World) (Taipei, Hua-ch'iao chih pien-ch'uan wei-yuan-hui, 1956), p. 489.

This figure of C$360.74 million probably does not represent the entire contributions collected from the Overseas Chinese communities world wide. There were various channels for remitting contributions to the Nationalist government in Chungking, and there were many other forms of contribution as well. At the same time, this figure is not broken down into region, which would give us a more accurate estimate. However, regional estimates have been conducted by modern scholars. Yoji Akashi, a Japanese scholar, estimated that the Chinese in Southeast Asia contributed a total of C$355 million in the period between July 1937 and December 1941.[38] He suggests that the most reliable figure for contributions and bond contributions of the Chinese in Southeast Asia for the period of fifteen months from July 1937 to September 1938 was C$67,134,888, plus SS$219,568 and 1,414,961 guilders. He also suggests that Southeast Asian Chinese contributions in the period from November 1938 to December 1940 were in the vicinity of C$177,748,000. These figures, combined with the contributions of C$106,540,574 for the year 1941, produce a total estimate of C$355 million.[39]

These figures do not make a lot of sense if they are not assessed against the needs and expenditure of the war government in Chungking. To put Overseas Chinese financial contributions in their proper context, a Nationalist government official publication suggests that in the period between July 1937 and January 1940, the Overseas Chinese contributed about C$20,000,000 monthly to government coffers, and that the amount represented almost one-third of the war expenditure of C$70,000,000 per month at that time.[40] This monthly contribution of C$20 million demonstrates the importance of the Overseas Chinese financial contributions to China's war efforts.

Conclusion

The continuing upsurge of the Overseas Chinese nationalism in the 1920s and 1930s ensured a fervent response from the Overseas Chinese

38. See Yoji Akashi, *The Nanyang Chinese National Salvation Movement, 1937– 1941*, p. 125.
39. Ibid., pp. 122-24.
40. See Ch'iao-wu wei-yuan-hui & Hua-ch'iao chih pien-chuan wei-yuan-hui (eds), op. cit., p. 473.

to the Second Sino-Japanese war. The mobilisation of Overseas Chinese support for the war had a high degree of spontaneity, although the Nationalist government also put in a great deal of effort. The fervent response fell into three major areas: anti-Japanese propaganda movement; boycott and economic sanctions against the Japanese; and financial and material support for the Chinese Government. The propaganda movement succeeded in securing a great deal of public sympathy and support from the West, and it also succeeded in paving the way for a large-scale mobilisation of support by all Overseas Chinese for the war effort.

Boycotting and placing sanctions against Japanese goods and services were effective, and the Chinese in Southeast Asia were particularly successful in adopting this strategy. Japan's economic penetration was thwarted, and the supply of war materials from this region to Japan was also disrupted by the Southeast Asian Chinese efforts. In the area of financial and material support for the war against the Japanese, Overseas Chinese money was especially significant. These huge monetary contributions helped the Nationalist government to balance the war budget and to sustain its protracted resistance efforts. Without Overseas Chinese moral, financial and material support, China's spirit of resistance would have been weakened and the war would have been harder for China to win.

Index

Adelaide, 86
Ai Tong School, 197, 204
Alumni association, 29, 268
An Xi International Convention, 47
Analects, 156
Ancestor, 16
Anglo-American companies, 22
Anglo-Chinese College of
    Malacca, 228
Anhwei province, 137
Annam (Vietnam), 149
Anti-Japanese movementss, 257-259
    in 1915, 257
    in 1919, 257
    in Tsinan Incident, 257
    in Manchurian Incident, 257
    boycott of Japanese goods,
        257-259
    denying services to Japanese
        nationals, 259
Anti-Japanese sentiment, 257-258
Apprentice, 59-60, 67-69
Apprentice system, 59-60, 67-69
Apprenticeship, 59-60
ASEAN countries, 171-172
Astra (Indonesian Chinese
    conglomerate), 5n
Au Boon Haw(Hu Wenhu), 194
Australia, 4, 43, 95, 108, 120

Babas, 151, 164, 164n, 238
Babaisation, 238
Baihua (vernacular Chinese
    language), 167
Ban Chye Ho Club, 75
Ban Hin Lee Bank Ltd., 251

Bang (Pang, dialect & geographical
    untity), 52, 62, 77-78
    Hokkien, 209
    Teochew, 210
    See also Pang
Banka, 149
Banking,
    Chinese commercial, 249-252
    British banks in Singapore, 249
    European banks, 249
Baracoons, 83
Barton, Clifton A., 29, 38
Batavia, 149
Batu Kawan, 233
Batu Pahat Bank Ltd., 251
Bei Men village(in Tainan), 32
Beicheng hang, see North City Guild
Benevolence (Ren, Jen), 16, 130
Blacksmith, 54
Bin Chan House (Wan Ching
    Yuan), 340
Book of Change (Yi Jing, or I Ching),
    69, 156
Book of History, 156
Book of Poetry, 156
Book of Rites, 156
Borneo Company, 230
Boustead & Company, 227, 230
Boycotts,
    against Japanese goods &
        services, 257-259
    against the Americans in
        1905, 376
    against Japanese, 376
    forms of boycott against
        Japanese, 377

against Japanese manufactured goods and foodstuffs, 377
against Japanese goods in Malaya, 377
against Japanese goods in Burma, Thailand & the Philippines, 378
withdrawal of labour in Japanese mines and plantations in Malaya, 379
impact on Japanese import into Southeast Asia, 380
against Japanese goods in the United States and Europe, 380-381
British companies in Singapore and Penang, 227
Buddha, 153
Buddhist temples, 153-154
Buhang shangwu ju, see Singapore Piece Goods Traders' Guild
Bukit Ashaham (in Malacca), 248-249
Bukit Tambun, 233
Business ideology, 15-19
Business networks, 23-50
origins of Ethnic Chinese, 23-28
Businessmen's clubs, 75-78
Buttery, (John) and Company in Penang, 227

Cai Yuanpei (Ts'ai Yuan-p'ei), 184
Canada, 43
Canton, 95
Canton Chinese Chamber of Commerce, 313
Canton Revolt, 351
Cantonese, 56, 58, 62
Capitalists, Teochew, 285-286

Carpenters, 54-58
Chaebol (South Korean), 27-28, 28n
Champa, 149
Chan Chan-mooi, 244
Chan, Wellington K.K., 93, 117-118
Chang Chen-hsun, see Zhang Zhenxun, Zhang Bishi and Chang Pi-shih
Chang Pi-shih, 81, 87-88, 140, 289
founding the Singapore Chinese Chamber of Commerce, 315-326
political career, 317-319
holding various Ch'ing titles and offices, 318-319
see also Zhang Bishi
Chang Ping-lin (Zhang Binglin), 363-365, 367
Chang Yu-nan, 88
Chang-kuei (holder of the counter), 93
Ch'ao An (H'ai Yang), 274, 276
Chao Chung-fan's mission, 310, 329
Ch'ao Yang, 276
Cheang Hong Lim, 285
Chee Swee Cheng, 36
Chee Yam Chuan, 236
Chefoo, 132
Chekiang-kiangsu group, 363,
Ch'en Ch'i-hsien, see Tan Chay Yan
Ch'en Chia-keng, see Tan Kah Kee
Ch'en Ch'u-nan, see Tan Chor-nam
Chen Delun, see Tan Teck Lun
Ch'en Hsu-nien, see Tan Hiok Nee
Chen Huanyong (Ch'en Huan-yung), 9
Chen Huichong, 174
Ch'en I-hsi, 88
Chen Jiageng, see Tan Kah Kee
Chen Qixian, see Tan Chay Yan

Ch'en Rener, 199
Ch'en Teh-jun, 300
Chen Tien Sheng, 360
Chen Wu She (Anti-Opium
    Soceity), 246
Ch'en Yun-ch'iu (Tan Hun Chiu),
    see Tan Hun Chiu
Ch'en Yun-sheng, 364
Ch'en Zaifan, 174
Cheng Ch'eng-k'uai, 248
Ch'eng H'ai, 276, 278-279, 293, 297
Cheng Hoon Teng temple, 154n
Cheng Kee Hean Club, 75
Cheng Kuan-ying, 83
Cheng Wen She (Political
    Information Society), 362
Cheong Yeok Choy, 250, 263
Chi Mei, 125, 131, 137, 141
Chia-ying Hakka Association of
    Penang, 223
Chieh Yang, 276
Chien-tu, 104
China, 45-46, 54, 63, 124
China Commercial Bank (Chung-
    kuo Hua-shang yin-hang),
    333-334
China orientation, 323-324
China Relief Association of
    Muar, 385
Chinese biscuit companies, 254
Chinese bourgeoisie, 114n
Chinese businessmen,
 cultivating political influence, 28n
Chinese capital in Malaya, 234
Chinese Chamber of Commerce, 50
    as an institution in China,
        312-314
Chinese Chamber of Commerce of
    Singapore, 183, see also
    Singapore Chinese Chamber
    of Commerce

Chinese class structure, 268-270
Chinese Cloth Merchants'
    Association (Singapore), 377
Chinese commercial agriculture,
    230-234
Chinese commercial banking,
    249-252
    first bank in Singapore, 250
    dialect-based, 251-252
    number of banks in
        Singapore and
        Malaysia, 251
    characteristics of, 251-252
Chinese Commercial Bank Ltd., 35
Chinese communities in Singapore
    and Malaysia,
    changes between two world
        wars, 248-271
    economic change, 248-255
    political change, 255-259
    social and cultural change,
        259-271
Chinese Consul-General in
    Singapore, 309, 326-329
Chinese cultural forms, 150
Chinese cultural identities, 163n,
    238-240
Chinese cultural nationalists,
    163n, 238-240
Chinese customs and tradition,
    150
Chinese dress, 150
Chinese education,
    Republican reform, 183-188
    ordinance, 184
    new textbooks, 184
    new curriculum 184-186
    school system, 185
    educational reform, 185-187
    expansion of secondary
    education, 260-261

Chinese entrepot trade, 226-230
structure of the system, 228
Chinese entrepreneurs, world
conventions, 49-50, 50n
1st convention in Singapore,
49
2nd convention in Hong
Kong, 50n
4th convention in Vancouver,
Canada, 50n
Chinese festivities, 152
Chinese traditional firms, 93-94,
93n
Chinese immigration to Malaysia
and Singapore, 217-219
forces contributing to, 217
patterns of, 218-219
kinship-based, 218
credit-ticket system, 218
ordinances, 265
female immigration, 266
Chinese immigrants, 150-151,153,
218-220
political attitude of, 237-238
various problems of, 238
number in Singapore and
Malaysia (1911-1931), 265
unequal sex ratio, 265-266
female, 266
Chinese industry in Singapore and
Malaysia, 254-255
Chinese Kapitan, 235, 282
Chinese labourers in Southeast
Asia, 150
Chinese literacy, 261-262
Chinese literary societies in
Singapore, 240
Chinese managers, 96n
Chinese merchants,
involvement in social
organizations, 29n

in the Straits Settlements, 234
Chinese migration to Southeast
Asia, 23-25, see also Chinese
immigration
Chinese new year, 152
Chinese pineapple-canning, 253
Chinese political refugees in
Southeast Asia, 148-149
Chinese Reformists, 308, 353-354
in Singapore and Malaysia,
240-242
impact on literacy, 261
Chinese religion, 153-155
Chinese Revolutionaries,
activities in Singapore and
Malaysia, 242-247
propaganda activities,
245-246
newspapers, 245
drama troupes, 245-246
reading clubs, 245
uprisings, 247
anti Sun movement, 247
impact on literacy, 261
Chinese Revolutionary Party, 255
Chinese schools,
traditional, 155-156
modern, 156-157, 259-260
expansion of secondary
schools, 260-261
Chinese secret societies, 59n,
225-226, 291
Chinese settlements in Malaysia
and Singapore, 219-221
patterns of, 220-221
urban port, 220
mining, 220-221
rural agricultural, 221
Chinese Shahbandar, 219
Chinese social structure,
changes in, 266-271

social organisations, 266-269
Chinese temples, 150
Chinese tin-mining industry,
    234-237
    success in industry, 236-237
    mining method, 236-237
    Chinese entrepreneurship,
        237
Chinese tin-smelting, 252
Chinese traders,
    as middlemen in Singapore
        and Malaysia, 227-230
    of Malacca and Hokkien
        origins, 227-228
    early trading companies,
        229-230
Chinese Vice Consul in Penang,
    309, 318
Chinese women
    attitude towards, 262
    changed attitude towards, 263
Ch'ing brevet titles, 289, 331, 337
Ch'ing bureaucracy, 317, 325, 331
Ch'ing Consul (Consul-General) in
    Singapore, 239-240, 329
Ch'ing dignitaries, 240, 328-329
Ch'ing diplomats, 311
Ch'ing dynasty, see Qing dynasty
Ch'ing government, 289, 326,
    and Singapore Chinese
        Chamber of Commerce,
        326-327
    relationship with Singapore
Chinese Chamber of Commerce,
    307-337
    emigration policy after 1893,
        308
    policy dealing with Reformists
        & Revolutionarsies,
        308-311
    close ties with Singapore

Chinese Chmaber of Commerce,
    332-337
    Singapore Chinese Chamber
        of Commerce acted as a
        political ally, 335-336
Ch'ing Ministry of Commerce,
    312-315
Ch'ing missions to Southeast Asia,
    310-311
Ching Shih Pan (drama troupe), 246
Chiu-hsiang yun-tung (Home Province
    Rescue Movement), 267
Chiu Kuo Shih Pa Yu (The
    Eighteen Saviours), 243
Ch'iu Shu-yuan, see Khoo Seok Wan
Chixi district, 43
Chng, David K.Y., 73
Chong Fu Girls' School, 197-198,
    204, 264
Chong Shing Yit Pao, 242, 245-246,
    359, 361, 365
Choon Guan Hock Club, 75
Chu Chien T'uan (Eliminating
    Traitors' Squad), 378
Chua Tse Yung (Ts'ai Tsu-yung),
    297-299, 323-326, 334-335
Chui Huai Lim Club, 75-76, 75n
Chuk Sau Yuan village, 81
Chung, see loyalty
Chung Ho T'ang, 243, 355,
Chung Hwa Biscuit Company, 254
Chung Hwa School (in Seremban),
    260
Chung Kuo Yit Pao, 365
Chung Ling School (in Penang),
    260-261
Cixi (Empress Dowager), see
    Empress Dowager Cixi
Clan organisations, see kinship
    organisations
Class structure, 268-270

Class relationship, 16,
Clubs, 75-78
Cochran, Sherman, 117
Coconut oil, 254
Cold War, 12, 160
Colonialism, 13, 79
Communism, 12
Comprador system, 7
Confucian Classics, 135, 157, 180, 259
Confucian culture, 142
Confucian morality, 157
Confucian Primary School (in Kuala Lumpur), 181
Confucian Revival Movement, 239, 324
Confucain teachings, 69
Confucian values, 15, 16n, 73, 79, 97, 130-131, 135, 162, 239, 323
Confucianism,
  and business ideology, 15-19
  as a modern religion, 165
Confucius, 69
Confucius' birthday, 239
Connaught Road (Hong Kong), 111
Connections(guanxi), see Guanxi
Consumer-driven strategies, 13
Coolie trade, 82n, 83
Coolies, 153n
Courage (Yung), 130
Craftsmen, 54
Credit-rating, 39
Credit sales, 105-106
Credit-Ticket system, 218

Dai Jishan, 42n
Dao Nan School (Daonan School), 181-182, 197-198, 208
  promoting mandarin as teaching medium, 200-201

Tan Kah Kee's involvement, 204
Dejiaohui (Moral Uplifting Society), 155
Deng Zeju, see Teng Tse-ju
Desvoeux Road (Hong Kong), 111
Dialect groups, 32n
Dialect organisations, 223, 266-267
Dialect ties, 31, 68, 283
Doctrine of the True Void, see Zhenkongjiao
Dragon Boat Festival, 152
Drama troupes, 245-246
Duan Meng School (Tuan Mong School), 181, 195
Dutch East Indies, 151, 157n, 273, 352, 363, 382

Eastern Smelting Company Ltd., 252
Ee Hoe Hean Club (Yi He Xuan Club), 75-77
Emperor K'ang-hsi, 239
Emperor Kuang-hsu, 242, 336, 353, 362
Emperor Protection Society (or Association), see Pao Huang Hui
Employer-employee relationship, 17
Empress Dowager Tz'u-hsi, 318, 328, 336, 362-363
Empress Dowager Cixi, 178, see also Empress Dowager Tz'u-hsi
Eng Choon (Yongchun) district, 183, 215
English language, 286-287
Enping, 43
Entrepreneurs, 207
  modern ethnic Chinese, 8-10

perception of employer-
employee relationship,
16-17
Overseas Chinese, 118-121
general concept, 123
Entrepreneurship, 123-124, 123n,
139-144, 237
Ethnic Chinese,
definition, 3-4
number estimated in 1991, 4
in Taiwan, 4
in Hong Kong, 4
in East and Southeast Asia, 4
Gross Domestic Product of, 5
economic strength, 4-5
economic strength in
Southeast Asia, 5,
economic strength in
Indonesia, 5
expand business activities, 13
guilds, 53-71
modern entrepreneurs, 8-10
to Southeast Asia, 23-24
response to China's opening,
45n
Ethnic Chinese business,
conglomerates in Indonesia,
5n
historical roots, 6-11
and Confucianism, 15-19
nature of, 19-22
networking, 20
networks, 23-50
origins of networks, 23-28
organisations, 51-78
different interpretations of the
rise of, 51n-52n
traditional guilds, 60-71
informal organisations, 72-78
Ethnic Chinese culture in
Southeast Asia

formation of, 147-159
stages and forces of change,
159-169
and identity, 169-175
China-centred, 167
Ethnic Chinese education,
traditional, 155-156
modern, 156-159
development in British
Malaya, 188-196
Ethnic Chinese schools,
first school in Southeast Asia,
179-180
early curriculum, 179-180
financial problems, 196
in British Malaya, 189-196
first high school in Singapore,
192-193
Chinese high schools in
Malaya, 193-196
Girls' schools in Singapore,
197-198
first modern Chinese
language girls' school, 197
Hokkien schools in Kuala
Lumpur, 199
Export-oriented Industrialisation
(EOI), 14, 26
Europe, 120

Fa pi, 106-107
Family, 16
Family business, 19
Fan Ai Pan (drama troupe), 246
Federation of China Relief Fund
Association of Southeast Asia
(Nanyang ch'ou-chen tsu-kuo
nan-min tsung-hui), 382-385
Federation of Selangor Chinese
Guilds (Xuelane Hangtuan
zonghui), 66

Fei shou (bandit chief), 351
Fei Xin, 6n, 149n
Female education, see Girls's
    schools, women
Feminist view, 168
Feng Shun, 276
Feuerwerker, Albert., 117
Fiji, 90
Filial piety, 16, 239
Filipinos, 176
First World War, 128, 186, 370
Five Classics, 156
Foo Chee Choon (Hu Zichun,
    Hu Tse-chun), 67, 67n, 157n,
    237, 241
Foochow agricultural settlement in
    Sarawak, 221
Foon Yew School (in Johor Bahru),
    260
Four Books, 156
Four Little Dragons, 79-80, 161
Fu Tsung-li, 110
Fukien community, 326, see also
    Hokkien community
Fukien province, 125
Fuzhou (Foochow), 7

Gambier, 62
    planting in Singapore, 231
    planting and a big success in
        Johor, 231-232
    planters, 274-275
    Teochew planters, 280
Gambling, 283
Gan Clan International
Convention, 47, 47n
Gan Eng Seng, 76
Gao Manhua (Kao Man-hua, Gao
    Chuxiang or Gao Tingkai), 8-
    9, 9n
Ghee Hin (Secret society), 282, 292

Ghee Kiat Huay, see Ghee Kiat
    Society
Ghee Kiat Society, 72
Gift vouchers, 106-107
Girls' schools
    early Singapore, 191, 191n
    in Singapore and Malaysia,
        263-264
Global economic growth, 13
Gockchin, Philip, see Kwok Chin
Gocklock, James, see Kwok Lock
Goddess of Mercy, see Guan Yin
God of War and Prosperity, see
    Guan di
Goh Say-eng, 244, 340, 366
Goh Siew Tin (Wu Shouchen),
    182, 316, 323, 325, 325n,
    334, 337
Golas, Peter J., 59
Goldsmith, 54
Gonghui, 54
Gongshu Ban, 55n
Gongso, 54
Government economic policies and
    strategies in East & Southeast
    Asia, 14
Great Learning, 156
Great Opium Syndicate, 285
Grocers' Guild of Singapore
    (Xingzhou Zahuo hang), 61-62
Guan Di (God of War and
    Prosperity), 154n
Guan Yin (Goddess of Mercy), 154n
Guangdong, 56-58, 60
Guangzhou, 7
Guanxi (Kuan-hsi), 20, 20n, 27,
    31-37, 31n
Gugang Zhou(ancient Gang
    Prefecture), 43
Gugangzhou Six Districts
    Association of Malaya, 43

Guild of Chinese Medicines of
Singapore (Xinjiapo Zhong
Yao Gonghui), 64
Guilds,
traditional Ethnic Chinese,
52-71
craft, 52-60
Guoji Chaoxun(Teochew
International Convention
Bulletins), 47n
Guomindang, see Kuomintang
Guthrie & Company, 227

H'ai Yang (Ch'ao An), 273, 276,
278-279, 293, 297-298, 301
Hakka gold miners in Bau,
Sarawak, 220
Hakka kongsi government, 224-225
Hakka immigrants, 225
Hakka miners, 220
Hakka Studies, 3rd International
Conference of, 48
Hakka world convention, 48, 48n
Hakkas, 48-49, 62-63, 178
Jiaying Hakka community,
158n
being a minority group in
early Malaysia and
Singapore, 223-225
being the late comers in
South China, 224,
in West Borneo gold fields,
224-225
Hakkaology(Hakka Studies), 48
Haiwai huaren(Overseas Chinese),
4, see also Overseas Chinese
Hang, 54
Hanglao, 53
Hangtou, 53
Hankow Revolt, 345
Hao, Yen-ping, 117

Harmony(He), 16, 22
Hawaii, 342
He, see Harmony
Hean Yuen Guild (Xian Yan
Guan), 55
Hee Kee, 219
Heng Pang Kiat (Wang Bangjie),
61, 67
Heshan, 43
Hinghua, 154, 155n
Ho Ho Biscuit Company, 254
Ho Hong Bank Ltd., 35-36, 251
Ho Hong group of companies, 254
Ho Teh-ju, 365
Hokkien Association (Hokkien
Huay Kuan), 198, 267
Hokkien bang, 209
Hokkien community,
participation in rubber, 63n
and modern Chinese
education, 196-215
promoting modern education
in Singapore, 197-198
in Malay Peninsula, 199-201
found Dao Nan School
in 1907, 204
Hokkien Girls' School (in Penang),
264
Hokkien Huay Kuan, see Hokkien
Association
Hokkien kinship organisations in
Penang, 222
Hokkien immigrants, 219
Hokkien scholar, 182-183
Hokkien secret societies, 281
Hokkien shops, 182
Hokkien speakers, 137
Hokkiens, 62-63, 152, 182
Home Province Rescuing
Movement (Chiu-hsiang yun-
tung), 267

Hong Kong, 3, 7, 15, 38, 43, 79, 89-91, 95, 154
Hong Kong Chinese Chamber of Commerce, 110
Hong Kong and Shanghai Banking Corporation, 91
Hong Leong group of companines, 20n
Hong merchants, 8
Hong Qidu, 199
Honolulu, 342, 344, 351
Hoo Ah Kay (Whampoa), 295
Hou Yuli, 32-34
Hsiang Shan district (Chung Shan), 81-82
Hsiang-Shanese, 82-83, 82n, 86, 90, 108-109
Hsiao T'ao Yuan Club, 244, also see Xiao Tao Yaun Club
Hsieh-li (Vice President), 314
Hsien Shih kung-ssu, see Sincere Company
Hsin-yung, see Xinyong
Hsing Chung Hui, 340, 355
Hsu Ching-ming, 333-334
Hsu Yun, 83
Hsueh Fu-ch'eng, 318n
Hu Guolian, see Foo Chee Choon
Hu Han-min, 246, 361, 366
Hu, Richard, 49
Hu Tse-ch'un, see Foo Chee Choon
Hu Wenhu, see Au Boon Haw
Hu Zichun, see Foo Chee Choon
Hua-ch'iao chung-hsueh, see Singapore Chinese High School
Hua Qiao (Hua Ch'iao) Girls' School, 197, 263
Hua Qiao Zhong Xue, see Singapore Chinese High School
Hua-shang kung-so, 322

Huang Chung-han, see Oei Tiong Ham
Huang Dianxian (Huang Tien-hsien), 190, 197, 263
Huang Hsing, 366
Huang Jinqing, see Ng Kim-keng
Huang Nai-shang, 349
Huang Shung-t'ing, 297
Huang Tien-hsien, see Huang Dianxian
Huang Tsun-hsien (Ch'ing Consul-General), 326
Huang Yafu, see Wong Ah Fook
Huang Zhixin, see Oei Tjie Sien
Huang Zhonghan, see Oei Tiong Ham
Huang Zhongji, 199
Huaqiao School, 67
Hui Hsien She, 240
Hui Lai, 276
Huiguan, 32, 54
Hujing Goldsmith Guild, 55
Hujing tajin hang, 55
Hundred Days' Reform, 165, 241, 353
Hung Hsiu-ch'uan, 342-343
H'ung K'ou, 109
Hupei Rug Company, 333

Idea of change and progress, 70
Import Substitution Industrialisation (ISI), 14, 26
Indonesia, 5
Indonesians, 176
Intellectuals, 191
Iron Blood Squad (Tieh Shuai Tuan), 378
I Ching, see Book of Change

Jackman, David., 101
Jacobs, J. Bruce, 20n, 31n

Jao P'ing, 276
Japan, 26, 63
Japanese business groups, 27
Java, 6, 213
Jen, see Benevolence
Jen-li, 94
Jiaoyu jiuguo (Rescuing the nation through education), 205-206
Jiang Zemin (President of China), 172n
Jih Hua Hsin Pao, 365
Jilobu (Club), 75
Jimei High School, 203
Jimei Maritime and Navigation College, 203, 210-211, 214
Jinan Incident, 77, 205, see also Tsinan Incident
Jit Shin Pau, 198, 241
Johor Bahru, 174
Joss-papers, 153n
Joss-sticks, 153n
Ju, 54
Jui-fu-hsiang Company, 93-94, 132, 135

K'ai Ming Public Speaking & Reading Club, 245, 360, 365
Kampar, 194
K'ang-hsi (emperor), see Emperor K'ang-hsi
Kang Yuwei (K'ang Yu-wei), 69, 165-166, 190, 198, 240-243, 246, 298, 308-309, 353, 362, 370
K'ang Yu-wei, see Kang Yuwei
Kangchu (Lord of the River), 221, 232, 292
Kangkar (Foot of the River), 232
Kapitan, 223, 274
Kee Lye Huat, 233
Kee Poh Huat Kongsi, 233

Kepertjajian, 38
Kheh-t'au, 218
Kheng Leong Huay, see Kheng Leong Society
Kheng Leong Society, 72
Kheng Teck Society, 72-73
Kheng Teck Whay, see Kheng Teck Society
Khiam Aik shop, 128, 136
Khoo Kongsi, 222
Khoo Seok Wan (Ch'iu Shu-yuan), 241, 243, 345
Kim Ban Choon Club, 75
Kim Cheng & Company, 229
Kim Seng & Company, 229-230
Kindersley Brothers (European planters), 248
Kinship, 27, 68
Kinship association, 29
Kinship organisations, 221-222, 266
Kinship ties, 283
Koh Seng-li (Xu Shengli, Koh Seng Lee), 193, 261
Koh Soh-chew, 364
Kowtowing ceremony for Ch'ing emperors, 336
Kreta Ayer Incident, 256-257
Kuala Kangsar (in Perak), 248
Kuala Lumpur, 153-154, 181
Kuala Pilah, 341, 366
Kuan-fang (official seal), 330
Kuan-hsi, see Guanxi
Kuang-hsu (emperor), see Emperor Kuang-hsu
Kudat, 221
Kuen Cheng (Kun Cheng) Girls' School, 181, 195, 261, 263
Kung (worker) class, 268-269
Kung I Pao, 365
Kuo Hsien-wen, 95

Kuomintang (Guomindang),
    reorganisation of, 255-257
    branches in Singapore and
        Malaysia, 255-256
    reinvigorated, 256
    pro-Communist elements in, 256
    the Left in, 256-257
    numbers in 1929, 256
    the "Main School" of, 256
    Nanyang branch of, 257
Kwangtung community, 300
Kwok Bew (George), 85, 104
Kwok brothers, 81, 83, 88-90, 97-98,
    102, 104, 118-120, 139
Kwok Chin(Philip Gockchin), 81,
    83-85, 88, 90n, 92, 94-96,
    104, 109-110, 118-120
Kwok Ho Fai, 86
Kwok Lock (Jame Gocklock), 81,
    83-84, 86-87, 92n, 94-96,
    118-119
Kwok Ping Fai, 85
Kwok, Russel (Dr.), 89n
Kwok Yik Fai, 102
Kwong Wah Yit Poh (in Penang),
    245, 359
Kwong Yik Banking Company
    Ltd. (Singapore), 250
Kwong Yik Banking Corporation
    Ltd. (Selangor), 250

Lanfang Gongsi, 163n
Larut, 220, 235
Lau Boon Tit, 248
Lee Cheng Yan, 76, 183, 322
Lee Cheng Yan & Company, 229
Lee Chin Ho, 252
Lee Choon Seng, 35
Lee Hsien Lung, 49
Lee Kong Chian (Li Kuang-ch'ien),
    35-37, 209, 211-212, 214

Lee Kuan Yew, 49
Lee Rubber(Selangor) Sdn. Berhad,
    35
Lee Rubber Company Pte. Ltd., 35,
    214
Lee Seng Png (Li Zhengfeng), 214
Lee Seng Wee, 35
Lee Wah Bank Ltd., 251
Lee Wee Nam, 35
Leung Chong, 86
Levy, Marion, 117
Li(Propriety), see Propriety
Li Chien (gift voucher), 106-107
Li Hung-chang, 318
Li Kuang-ch'ien, see
    Lee Kong Chian
Li Wei-nan, 300, 304-305, see also
    Lee Wee Nam
Li Yen-hsiang, 101
Li Zhengfeng, see Lee Seng Png
Liang Ch'i-ch'ao (Liang Qichao),
    298, 345, 353
Liang Fan-nan, 95
Liang Qichao, 198, 240-242, 263,
    see also Liang Ch'i-ch'ao
Liang Tingfang, 157n
Liao Cheng-hsing, 297, 299, 325
Liem Soe Liong(Lin Jui-liang), 22n
Light, Francis, 230
Lim Boon Keng(Dr. Lin Wen-ch'ing
    or Lin Wenqing), 36, 165-
    166, 190, 199, 241, 248, 251,
    334,
    advocated women education,
        263
    founded Singapore Chinese
        Girls' School, 263
    early contact with Dr. Sun
        Yat-sen, 349
Lim Ho Puah, 76
Lim How Seng, 73

Lim Kiek Chuan, 320
Lim Kongsi(Penang), 222
Lim Mah Hui, 34
Lim Ngee Soon (Lin I-shun, or Lin
    Yishun), 210, 213, 244, 248,
    300-302, 304-305, 357
Lim Peng Siang, 36, 36n, 76, 251,
    254
Lin Chu-tsai, 334
Lin I-shun, see Lim Ngee Soon
Lin Juzhou, 157n
Lin Kequan, 157n
Lin Tse-shen, 101
Lin Wen-ch'ing, see
    Lim Boon Keng
Lin Wenqing, see Lim Boon Keng
Lin Yishun, see Lim Ngee Soon
Lions Club, 29
Lippo (Indonesian Chinese
    conglomerate), 5n
Liu Kunyi, 178
Lo Fang-po, 225
Lo Feng-lu, 309
Lo Shan She Lecture movement,
    239, 324
Loke Chow-thye, 244
Loke Yew (Lu Yu, or Lu Pi-ch'en),
    237, 350
Lorriman, John, 138
Loyalty (Chung, or Zhong), 16-17,
    130-131
Lu Pi-ch'en, see Loke Yew
Lu Yu, see Loke Yew
Lukut, 220, 235

Ma Cho Seng, 86
Ma Huan, 6n, 149n
Ma Yingbiao(Ma Ying Piu), 8, 8n-9n,
    see also Ma Ying Piu
Ma Ying Piu, 85, 89, 101, 118, 139
Ma Zhengxiang, 182

Macao(Macau), 3,7, 15, 82-83, 108
Mahayana Buddhism, 153
Main School in Kuomintang, 256
Malacca, 72-73, 226
Malacca Sultanate, 219-220, 226
Malay chiefs, 235
Malay Peninsula, 6, 129
Malaya, 124, 133
Malayan Chinese Association
    (MCA), 271
Malaysia, 153-154, 172-175
Malaysians, 176
Malaysianisation, 173-174
Management thought, 135
Manchu government, 243-245
Manchurian Incident (1931), 370,
    381
Mandarin(language), 175, 199-200
Mao Tse-tung(Mao Zedong),
    342-343
Marco Polo Bridge Incident, 169, 375
Marketing, 105-107
Marxists, 16
Marxist ideology, 346
May Fourth Movement, 159, 167,
    256-257, 370
Mazu, see Tian Hou
Medan, 153
Melbourne, 85-86
Mencius, 156
Meng Lo-ch'uan, 93-94, 135
Merchant Class (Shang), 268
Merchants, 191
Mestizos, 151, 164
Military bonds, 348
Min Pao (People's Tribune), 361, 364
Min To She (drama troupe), 246
Ming dynasty, 24, 53, 148, 161-162
Ministry of Commerce, see Ch'ing
    Ministry of Commerce
Moon festival, 152

Moral education, 98
Moral Uplifting Society, see
    Dejiaohui
Munshi Abdullah, 280
Mutual-aid societies, 72-74

Nam Kew Poo, 245, 359
Nanhai, 62, 351
Nan Lu Alumni Association
    (Singapore), 268
Nan Qiao Girls's High School
    (Singapore), 211
Nanjing government, 187
Nanyang Ch'ou-chen tsung-hui,
    258
Nanyang Ch'ou-chen tsu-kuo nan-
    min tsung-hui, see Federation
    of China Relief Fund
    Association of Southeast Asia
Nanyang Girls' High School, 194,
    260, 264, 268
Nanyang Khek Community Guild
    of Singapore, 48
Nanyang Siang Pau, 207
Nanyang Tsung Hui Pao (The
    Union Times), 242, 246, 361
Nanyang University, 67, 183, 212
Nationalist government, 158-159,
    372
Nepotism, 137
New Zealand, 4
Ng Kim -keng (Ng Kim Keng,
    Huang Jinqing), 157n, 244,
    340, 366
Ng Shaio Shan, 279
Ngee Ann Kongsi (Yi An Gongsi),
    276-281, 293-296, 300, 303,
    305-306, 325
Ni tang (rebel), 351
Ning Yang Association of Penang,
    56

Ningbo (Ningpo), 7
North City (Beicheng), 55
North City Guild (Beicheng hang),
    55, 57-58, 60
North Nu Guild (Nubei hang), 55
North Vietnam, 12
Nu Ban, 55-56, 58
Nu City Guild (Nucheng hang), 55
Nubei hang, see North Nu Guild
Nucheng hang, see Nu City Guild
Nyonyas, 151, 164, 238

OCBC-Sime Darby clique, 34-35
Oei Tiong Ham (Huang
    Chung-han, or Huang
    Zhonghan), 80, 140,
    213-214
Oei Tjie Sien, 9, 9n-10n, 80
Ong Keng Seng (Wang Jingcheng),
    193, 261
Opium farm, 285
Opium and Gambling farms, 232
Opium-smoking, 77, 283
Opium War, 25, 54, 236
Ou Ch'u-chia, 246, 362
Ou-yang min-ch'ing, 101
Oversea-Chinese Banking
    Corporation (OCBC), 34-37,
    251
Oversea-Chinese Bank Ltd., 35
Overseas Chinese,
    contribution to late Ch'ing
        modernisation, 88n
    protection of, 308
    threat from, 308
    Sun Yat-sen as a great leader
        of, 339
    profound admiration for Sun
        Yat-sen, 339
    close relationship with Sun
        Yat-sen, 340-342

Sun Yat-sen's perception of their role in the 1911 Revolution, 342-350
response to Sun Yat-sen's call, 351-367
and the 2nd Sino-Japanese war, 369-388
response to Japanese invasion in China, 370-372
anti-Japanese propaganda movement, 372-375
anti-Japanese boycotts and economic sanctions, 375-381
financial and material support for China's war of resistance, 381-387
in United States supporting China's war of resistance, 373-374
in Europe supporting China's war of resistance, 373- 374
fund-raising in Singapore and Malaya for China's war of resistance, 383-386
fund-raising techniques in Muar, 385-386
estimated financial contribution to China's war of resistance, 386-387
Overseas Chinese Affairs Commitee, 187
Overseas Chinese Bank Ltd., 251
Overseas Chinese Bureau (Qiaowu weiyuanhui), 158
Overseas Chinese capital, 320
Overseas Chinese Girls' School (Hua Qiao Nu Xiao), 190

Overseas Chinese merchants, 320-322
Overseas Chinese National Salvation movement, 77
Overseas Chinese nationalism, the origins of, 237-240
upsurge of, 255, 257-259
and the Japanese invasion of China, 370-372
Ownership and management, 136

Pacific War, 161
Palembang, 148
Pan Europe Overseas Chinese Anti-Japanese and Relieve China Alliance, 382
Pang (Bang), 316, 383, see also Bang
Pao Huang Hui(Emperor Protection Society), 241, 345
Paternalism, 18, 18n, 29, 97n, 110n, 134
Pawnbroking, 232
Pay Fong School(Malacca), 260-261
Pei Yuan High School (Kampar), 194
Penang, 140, 157, 179, 181
Penang Chinese Chamber of Commerce, 321
Penang Chinese Commercial Association, 320-322
Penang Conference (13 November, 1910), 366
Penang General Merchants' Association, 71
Penang Philomatic Society (Ping Cheng yeshu baoshe), 193, 245, 360
Penang Reading Club, see Penang Philomatic Society
Penghulu (headman of a village), 232

People's Tribune, see Min Pao
Pepper, 62,
    planting in Penang, 230
    planting in Singapore, 231
    planting in Johor, 231-232
    planters, 274-275
    Teochew planters, 280
Perak, 214
Perak Welfare Troupe, 246
Personal trust (xinyong), see
    Xinyong
Perth, 86
Petaling Jaya, 154
Philippines, 6, 151
Pin-lang-yu shang-wu chu, 320
Ping Cheng yeshu baoshe, see
    Penang Philomatic Society
Pontianak (in Borneo), 149, 162
Porcelain, 6
Portuguese, 82
President Enterprise Corporation,
    32, 34n
Prestige, 30
Prince Tsun, 329
Propaganda organisations, 245-246
Propriety (Li), 16, 130
Prostitution, 283
Province Wellesley, 233
P'u Ning, 276

Qing dynasty (Ch'ing dynasty), 24,
    53-54, 148, 158, 178
Qing educational reform, 177-183
Qing government, 156
Qing Ming, 16, 152
Qu Yuan, 152n
Quang-tung, 56
Quanxuepian, 177

Raja Busu, 235
Rawski, Thomas, 117

Reading clubs, 245
Reciprocity, 16, 29
Redding, Gordon, 4
Reformists, see Chinese Reformists
Ren (Jen, Benevolence), see
    Benevolence
Resinification, 171
Respect for age and authority, 16
Restaurateurs' Guild of
    Selangor(Xue Shenzhong
    tang), 61
Restaurateurs' Guild of Singapore
    (Xingzhou Gushu shenjing
    tang), 60
Riau islands, 273-275
Ridley, H.N., 248
Riri xin (to renew everyday), 70
Romantic adventurism, 344
Rotary Club, 29
Rubber,
    Hokkien participation in, 63n
    experimental planting, 248
    first commercial planting in
        Malacca, 248
    promoting in Singapore, 248-
        249
    rising prices of, 249
    processing mills of, 253
    profit from processing of, 253
    manufactured products,
        253-254
Ruifuxiang Company, see Jui-fu-
    hsiang Company
Ryan, Edward, 38

Salim group of companies
    (Indonesian Chinese
    conglomerate), 5n, 22n
San Zijing, see Trimetrical Classic
Sandilands, Buttery & Company
    (Singapore), 227

Sang On Tiy Company, 87
Sanyijiao, see "Three-in-one
    Doctrine"
Scholar-gentry, 8
Second World War, 12, 154, 161, 170
Seah Eng Kun, 304
Seah Eng Tong, 296, 298, 303
Seah Eu Chin (She Youjin, She Yu-
    chin), 275, 284-285, 287-288,
    293-294, 305-306
Seah family, 293-296, 324-325
Seah Liang Seah (She Liancheng,
    or She Lien-ch'eng),
    295-296, 322
Secret societies, see Chinese secret
    societies
See Boon Tiong, 236
See Yap(Siyi, Four districts), 43
Selangor Chinese Medicinal
    Merchants' Guild (Xuelane
    Huaqiao yaoye gonghui), 66
Selangor Grocers' Guild (Xuelane
    Zahuo hang), 61
Selangor Kin Cho Hong, 61
Selangor Wine and Spirit Dealers'
    Association (Xuelane
    Jiushang gonghui), 61
Seng Kee Smelting Works, 252
Seow Poh Leng, 251
Seremban, 195
Shahbandar, 219
Shan Chai Ting, 274
Shang (Merchant) class, 268-269
Shang-chao (commercial
    certificate), 331
Shang Chi-heng, 328
Shang-tung (directors), 314
Shanghai, 7, 95, 99-109, 132, 334
Shanghai Chinese Chamber of
    Commerce, 313, 334
Shanghaiese, 38

She Liancheng, see
    Seah Liang Seah
She Lien-ch'eng, see
    Seah Liang Seah
She Youjin, see Seah Eu Chin
She Yu-chin, see Seah Eu Chin
Sheng Hsuan-huai, 318
Shih(educated elite) class, 268-269
Shih Ch'u-ch'ing, 320
Shih Kuo-heng, 117
Shih-lang hsien (title of a Vice
    President of a Ch'ing
    Ministry), 318
Shulin Yuan Club, 75, 75n
Shunde, 62
Si Food Kee, 236
Sian, 178
Silk, 6
Silin, Robert H., 38
Sime Darby, 34-35, 37
Sinar Mas (Indonesian Chinese
    conglomerate), 5n
Sincere Company (Hsian Shih
    Kung-ssu, or Xianshi gongsi),
    85, 91, 91n, 118, 139
Sing Po (Star Daily), 163n, 351-352
Singapore, 79, 124, 126, 133,
    154, 181
Singapore Chinese Chamber of
    Commerce, 183, 302, 304,
    as a mechanism for controlling
        Overseas Chinese, 312
    founded by Chang Pi-shih,
        315-326
    official record of the founding
        of, 315-316
    founding date of, 316-317
    legitimised by Ch'ing Consul-
        General, 326-327
    position buttressed by Ch'ing
        Consul-General, 328-330

as temporary office for
visiting Ch'ing
dignitaries, 329
conferred an official seal by
Ch'ing government, 330
became a sub-bureau of
Ch'ing Ministry of
Commerce, 331
granted power to issue
commercial certificates,
331
close ties with Ch'ing
government, 332
as an agent for China's
companies, 333-335
political ally of Ch'ing
government, 335-336
reasons for not being anti-
revolutionaries, 337
Singapore Chinese Chamber of
Commerce and Industry,
49, 299
Singapore Chinese High School
(Hua Qiao Zhong Xue, or
Hua-ch'iao chung-hsueh),
192-193, 204-210, 260-261,
268
Singapore Chinese Girls' School, 263
Singapore Grocers' Guild, 70-71
Singapore Hoon Yong Kong See,
277-278
Singapore Maritime and
Navigation School, 210, 212
Singapore Piece Goods Traders'
Guild (Buhang shangwu ju),
60-61, 64
Singapore Reading Club, 245, 360
Singapore Sai Ho Association,
277, 279
Singapore Teochew Kang Hay T'ng,
277, 279
Singapore Teochew Lee Clan
Association, 277-278, 280
Sinagpore Textile Dealers' Friendly
Association, 63
Singaporeans, 176
Sinkheh (new immigrants),
230, 234
Sino-Japanese War, 177
Sishu (Ssu-shu, traditional
Chinese private schools),
155-156
Siyi, see See Yap
Social hierarchy, 18
Social organisations, 29-30
Social prestige, 25n
Song dynasty, 24, 53
Song Ong Siang, 75, 166
Soon An(shop), 127
South Korea, 26, 79
South Korean business groups,
27
Southeast Asia, 6-7, 15, 23-25, 43,
52, 95, 123-124, 149, 153-157,
164-175
Southern Fujianese, 73
Soviet Union, 12
Spring and Autumn Annals, 156
Ssu-shu, see Sishu
Straits Settlements, 151
Sub-Cantonese speakers, 56-58
Sugar, 232-233
European planters in
Province Wellesley, 233
Chinese planters, 233
Teochew planters, 233
Sumatra, 153
Sun Chih-hsing, 101
Sun Chung-shan, see Sun Yat-sen
Sun Poo, 245, 359
Sun Shih-ting (Ch'ing Consul-
General), 326-327

Sun Yat-sen (Dr. or known as Sun Chung-chan or Sun Wen), 165-166, 184, 190-191, 193, 205, 290, 301-302,
first came to Singapore, 242
arrived Singapore and founded T'ung Meng Hui, 244
contribution to debate, 246
anti-Sun movement, 247
kidnapping in London, 311
as a great leader of Chinese people, 339
intimate feeling for Overseas Chinese, 339
close relationship with Overseas Chinese, 340-342
ability to mobilise Overseas Chinese support, 340
visited Singapore eight times, 340
visited Malaya six times, 340
residence in Singapore and Penang, 340
Teng Tse-ju as his main confidant in Malaya, 341
Christian and Western influence, 342-343
received medical training, 343
early revolutionary strategy, 344
envy of Reformist financial success, 346
founding T'ung Meng Hui branches in Singapore and Kuala Lumpur, 349
approached Loke Yew for a big donation, 350
early negative image among Overseas Chinese, 351-352
image as a bandit chief, 351
attack on Sun's leadership, 363-366
anti-Sun movement in Japan and Southeast Asia, 363-366
calling the Penang Conference on 13 November, 1910, 366
spurred the growth of Overseas Chinese nationalism, 370
Sun Wen, see Sun Yat-sen
Sun Yung, see Xinyong
Sungei Bakap, 233
Sungei Ujung, 220
Sydney, 85-86, 90, 92
Sze Hai Tong Banking Company Ltd. (Singapore), 250, 297, 300

Ta P'u, 276
Ta T'ung Hotel (Hong Kong), 116
Tailors, 54
Taiping Rebellion, 236
Tainan business clique (Tainanbang), see Tainanbang
Tainan Spinning Company Ltd., 32-34
Tainanbang, 32-34, 33n
Taishan (Tai Shan), 43, 56, 60, 62
Taishanese, 56
Taiwan, 3-4, 15, 32-33, 79, 154, 173
Takashi Kenjo, 138
Tan Chay Yan (Ch'en Ch'i-hsien or Chen Qixian), 128, 248-249
Tan Cheng Siong, 76
Tan Chin Tuan, 35, 37, 76
Tan Chor-nam (Tan Chor Nam, Ch'en Ch'u-nan), 243-244, 340-341, 347-348, 355-357, 367
Tan Chu Kang (The river settlement of the Tan), 292
Tan Ean Kiam, 36

Tan Hiok Nee (Ch'en Hsu-nien),
285
Tan Hoon Siang, 35
Tan Hun Chiu (Ch'en Yun-ch'iu),
297-299, 316, 324-325
Tan Jiak Kim, 76
Tan Kah Kee (Ch'en Chia-keng,
Chen Jiageng), 37, 76-77,
as an Overseas Chinese
entrepreneur, 123-125
family background, 126-127
as apprentice in business,
127
early business activities in
Singapore, 127-128
building a business empire,
128-129
management ideas, 130-131
structure of business
enterprises, 132-134
management style, 134-139
and Overseas Chinese
entrepreneurship, 139-144
memoirs of, 124n
works on, 124n-125n, 202
self-discipline, 126
life-style, 126
ability to integrate Chinese
values with Western
business practices, 137
leadership in the fund-raising
for China's war of
resistance, 169
early life in China, 202
early career in Singapore, 203
promoting modern Chinese
education in British
Malaya, 201-215
founding Singapore Chinese
High School, 192-193
204-210, 260

motives behind his promotion
of modern Chinese
education, 205-207
impact of his promotion of
modern education in
British Malaya, 211-215
rubber planting, 249
establishing rubber-
processing mills in
Singapore, 253
huge profit from rubber-
processing, 253
as the leader of anti-Japanese
and relieve China
movement, 258
leadership in the Federation
of China Relief Fund
Association of Southeast
Asia, 382
leading Southeast Asian
Chinese resisting
Japanese aggression in
China, 382-383
Tan Kah Kee Company Pty. Ltd.,
129, 133, 141, 215,
254-255
Tan Kee Peck, 127, 203, 253
Tan Keng Hean, 135-136
Tan Kim Seng, 229
Tan Kongsi (Penang), 222
Tan Kye Soon, 282, 292
Tak Lark Sye, 183, 212-213
Tan Say Eng (Dato), 214
Tan Seng Poh, 76n, 284-285
Tan Siak Kew, 35
Tan Teck Lun (Chen Delun), 61
Tan Tock San, 35
Tan Tock Seng, 248
Tang (Hall), 54
T'ang dynasty, 23
T'ao Ch'eng-chang, 363-365, 367

Tao Nan (Dao Nan) School
(Singapore), 268, see also
Dao Nan School
T'aojia huanjia (protracted
bargaining), 71
Taoist, 154
Tapioca, 233-234
Tay Lay-seng, 341
Tea, 6
Teng Tse-ju (Deng Zeju), 188,
341-342, 350, 366-367
Teo Chew (Poit Ip) Huay Kuan, 277
Teo Eng-hock (Chang Yung-fu,
Zhang Yongfu), 243-244, 248,
301, 340-341, 355-357, 367
Teo Sian Keng, 183
Teo Yeonh (Ch'ao Yang)
Association, 277
Teochew, 62
Teochew Bang, 210
Teochew capitalists, 285-286
Teochew clan organisations,
277-280
Teochew clans, 293
Teochew community in Singapore,
299-300,
founded Sze Hai Tong Bank
in 1907, 250
early community, 273-276
structure of , 276-282
power structure of, 282-291
power relations of, 292-305
split and division, 324-325
Teochew Ghee Hin (Triad), 282
Teochew immigrants, 275, 283
Teochew International Convention
(Guoji Chaotuan Lianyi
Nianhui), 46, 47n
Teochew International Convention
Bulletins, 47n
Teochew localised lineage, 278-279

Teochew navigators, 274
Teochew non-localised lineage,
278-280
Teochew occupations, 285
Teochew planters, 273-275
Teochew Poit Ip Association of
Singapore, 267
Teochew secret societies, 280-282
Teochew settlement, 274
Teochew temple, 274
Teochew Triad (T'ien Ti Hui), 280-282
Thailand, 6
The Mean, 156
The United League,
see T'ung Meng Hui
The Union Times, see Nanyang
Tsung Hui Pao
Thien Nan Shin Pao, 198, 241
Thio Thiau Siat, see Zhang Bishi
and Chang Pi-shih
Thoe Lam Jit Poh, 244-245, 359
Thong Chai Medical Institution,
316-317, 328-329
"Three-in-one Doctrine", 154
Tian Hou (Tian Fei or Ma Zu),
154n
Tian Fei, see Tian Hou
T'ien Ti Hui, see Triad
Tientsin flood victim, 268
Tin-mining, see Chinese tin-mining
industry
Tin-smelting, 252
T'ing (pavilion), 75
Ting Juch'ang (Ch'ing Admiral), 75n
Tong An district, 202
Tong Keng Sing, 83
Tongnian, 31
Tongzong (common surname
relations), 33
Trade, 148n, 227
Treaty ports, 7, 7n

Triad, 225-226, 280-282
Trimetrical Classic (San Zijing), 156
Trust (Xinyong), see Xinyong
Tsai Tse (Prince), 328
Tsinan Incident, 141, 257, 370, see
    also Jinan Incident
Tsingtao, 132
Tso Ping-lung (Ch'ing Consul),
    240, 326
Tsung-chien-tu, 96
Tsung-li (president, director), 314
T'u Nan She, 240
Tu Tse-wen, 92, 95
Tuan Mong School, see Duan
    Meng School
T'ung An district, 125, 137, 255
T'ung An people, 126
T'ung Meng Hui (The United
    League), 244-245, 247, 301,
    341, 347-348, 355-358
    branch in Singapore, 244
    branches in Kuala Lumpur,
        Penang, Seremban,
        Ipoh, Kuala Pilah, Muar
        and Kuantan, 244
    founding of, 344
T'ung Teh Reading Club, 245, 360
Tung Wah Hospital (Hong Kong),
    110, 110n
Twenty Four Festivals Drum, 174
Twenty-one Demands(1915), 370

United Chinese Bank Ltd., 251
United States of America, 12, 43, 95
Universal Cements Ltd., 32

Vaughan, J.D., 56, 151
Vernacular Chinese language,
    see Baihua
Vertical integration, 139
Vietnam, 6

Vietnamese, 176

Wai San Knitting factory, 114
Waichow (Hui-chou) revolt, 344-345
Wan Ching Yuan (Bin Chan
    House), 340
Wang Bangjie, see Heng Pang Kiat
Wang Ch'in, 274
Wang Ching-wei, 246, 361
Wang Feng-shun, 274
Wang Gungwu, 51n, 170
Wang Huiyi, 197
Wang Ta-chen mission, 310
Wealth, 25n, 30
Wee Theam Seng, 37
Whampoa Military Academy, 256
Wing On Company, 81-121, 139,
    the origins of, 85-87
    founding of the Hong Kong,
        87-90
    teething problems, 90-92
    structure of, 93-98
    in Shanghai, 99-111
    marketing, 105-107
    credit sales, 105-106
    gift vouchers, 106-107
    diversification, 111-117
    insurance company, 112-113
    banking, 113-114
    manufacturing, 114-116
Wing On Fruits Store, 86
Wing On Insurance Company, 112
Wing On Textile Manufacturing
    Company, 114-116, 119
Wing Sang and Company, 85-87
Wong Ah Fook (Huang Yafu), 1
    90, 250
Wong Siu-lun, 37-38, 143
Wong, S.Q., 35
Workers, see Kung class
Women, 262-264

Women's role in family and
society, 168
World Chinese Entrepreneurs
Convention, 49-50
World Hakka Convention, 48-49
Wu Chieh-wu (Dr.), 349
Wu Hsien-tzu, 246, 362
Wu Hsueh-hua, 263
Wu Kedu, 32-34
Wu Sanlian, 32-33
Wu Shouchen, see Goh Siew Tin
Wuchang Revolt, 367

Xiamen (Amoy), 7
Xiamen University, 131, 137, 141,
183, 203, 212-214
Xian Yan guan, see Hean Yuen Guild
Xianfeng reign, 60
Xianshi gongsi, see
Sincere Company
Xiao Tao Yuan (Hsiao T'ao Yuan)
Club, 75
Xingzhou Gushu shenjing tang,
see Restaurateurs' Guild of
Singapore
Xingzhou Zahuo hang,
see Grocers' Guild of
Singapore
Xinhui, 43, 62
Xinjiapo Zhong Yao gonghui,
see Guild of Chinese
Medicines of Singapore
Xinyong (Hsin-yung), 20, 37-42
Xiong Shangfu, 208
Xiushen (Self-cultivation), 180
Xuan (porch), 75
Xue Shenzhong tang, see
Restaurateur's Guild of
Selangor Xuebu Guanbao
(The Gazette of Qing
Ministry of Education), 157n

Xuelane Hangtuan Zonghui, see
Federation of the Selangor
Chinese Guilds
Xuelane Huaqiao yaoye gonghui,
see Selangor Chinese
Medicinal Merchants' Guild
Xuelane Jianzhao hang, see
Builders' Guild of Selangor
Xuelane Jiushang gonghui, see
Selangor Wine and Spirit
Dealers' Association
Xuelane Zahuo hang, see Selangor
Grocers' Guild
Xuetang, 184

Yang Chin-hua, 101
Yang Hui-t'ing, 102
Yang Jindian, 214
Yang Shih-ch'i mission, 310, 329
Yang Zheng School, 181
Yap Ah Loy (Ye Yalai, Ye Delai),
67, 67n, 80, 81n 237
Yap Kwan Seng, 237
Yau Tuch Seng, 237
Ye Delai, see Yap Ah Loy
Ye Yalai, see Yap Ah Loy
Yeo Hood Ing, 236
Yeoh Chan Boon (Yang Chan-wen),
300-301, 304-305, 330
Yeoh Kongsi (Penang), 222
Yeong Seng What (Coolie agency),
219

Yi An Gongsi, see Ngee Ann Kongsi
Yi He Xuan Club, see Ee Hoe
Hean Club
Yi Jing, see Book of Change
Yin Sin School (Singapore),
158n 180
Yong Ching Fatt (C.F. Yong),
201-202

Yong Pang How, 35
Yu Lieh, 243, 355
Yuan (garden), 75
Yuan dynasty, 24, 148
Yuan Shih-k'ai, 255, 257, 290, 371
Yuanxiao festival, 152
Yueh H'ai Ch'ing temple, 276
Yuk Choy Independent High
    School (Ipoh), 215
Yung Wing, 83

Zaibatsu, 27-28
Zeng Jiangshui, 213
Zhang Binglin, see Chang Ping-lin
Zhang Bishi (Chang Pi-shih), 9, 67,
    67n, 157, 178, see also Chang
    Pi-shih
Zhang Zhenxun, 178, see also
Zhang Bishi and Chang Pi-shih
Zhang Zidong, 177-178
Zhangzhou Hokkien, 36n
Zheng He (Admiral), 149
Zheng-yao zheng-jia, 65
Zhenkongjiao (Doctrine of the True
    Void), 155
Zhengxin lu, 30, 30n
Zhong, see loyalty
Zhong Hua High School (Kuala
    Lumpur), 199, 214
Zhong Hua High School
    (Seremban), 195, 215
Zhong Hua School, 179-180
Zhonghua School(Penang), 157
Zhong Ling High School (Penang),
193
Zhongyuan festival, 152
Zhu Xi, 156